AF750429

Financial Intermediation in the New Europe

Financial Intermediation in the New Europe

Banks, Markets and Regulation in EU Accession Countries

Edited by

Donato Masciandaro

Paolo Baffi Centre, Bocconi University, Italy

Edward Elgar
Cheltenham, UK • Northampton, MA, USA

© Donato Masciandaro 2004

All rights reserved. No part of this publication may be reproduced, stored in a retrieval system or transmitted in any form or by any means, electronic, mechanical or photocopying, recording, or otherwise without the prior permission of the publisher.

Published by
Edward Elgar Publishing Limited
Glensanda House
Montpellier Parade
Cheltenham
Glos GL50 1UA
UK

Edward Elgar Publishing, Inc.
136 West Street
Suite 202
Northampton
Massachusetts 01060
USA

A catalogue record for this book
is available from the British Library

THE UNIVERSITY OF WARWICK
LIBRARY

HG
2974
.F564

ISBN 1 84376 949 2
Printed and bound in Great Britain by MPG Books Ltd, Bodmin, Cornwall

Contents

Contributors

Andrea Beltratti, Bocconi University

Jesús Crespo Cuaresma, University of Vienna

Riccardo D'Antonio, Bocconi University

Giorgio Di Giorgio, LUISS University

Balázs Égert, Oesterreichische Nationalbank

Fabio Farabullini, Banca d'Italia

Giovanni Ferri, University of Bari

Alicia García Herrero, Banco de España

Daniel Gros, CEPS, Bruxelles

Jakob de Haan, University of Groningen

David T. Llewellyn, Loughborough University

Donato Masciandaro, Bocconi University and University of Lecce

Dubravko Mihaljek, Bank for International Settlements

Fabio Mucci, Unicredito Italiano

Daniel Navia Simón, Banco de España

Ilko Naaborg, University of Groningen

Luca Papi, University of Ancona

Viliam Pätoprstý, University of Bratislava

Anna Pilková, Unibanka

Francesca Pissarides, European Bank for Reconstruction and Development

Angelo Porta, Bocconi University and University of Lugano

Thomas Reininger, Oesterreichische Nationalbank

Debora Revoltella, Unicredito Italiano

Martin Summer, Oesterreichische Nationalbank

Michael Würz, Oesterreichische Nationalbank

Foreword

David T. Llewellyn

ECONOMIC AND FINANCIAL REFORM

The period since the early 1990s has witnessed a group of countries in Central and Eastern Europe that, through a series of major economic and financial reform programmes, has embarked on a total transformation of their economic and financial systems in a comparatively short period. Many of these countries have become, or will soon become, members of the European Union (EU) and the euro area. This in turn will have major implications both for the new member states and the EU itself. Apart from two small countries (Cyprus and Malta) the new members had socialist centrally planned economies until the late 1980s. Since then they have undertaken comprehensive reforms of their institutions, policies, economic models and financial institutions and markets. The European landscape has changed radically as a result of these two trends.

The chapters in this volume illustrate various aspects of the reform programmes as a group of countries has embarked on one of the most intensive and extensive economic and financial regime shifts ever experienced. It has involved a shift from, in varying degrees, an essentially centrally planned economy (where real resources and finance were allocated centrally through a bureaucratic procedure based on a national plan) to a market-orientated system where economic and financial resources are allocated through markets and private institutions responding to price signals in liberalised markets for goods, services and finance.

The following chapters analyse the role of financial intermediation and financial markets, the role of foreign banks in the reform process, and the demanding challenges of creating financial regulation and supervisory regimes and the conduct of monetary policy to match the newly-created market-orientated economic and financial systems.

The challenges have been, and remain in an on-going process, formidable. And yet in general, as the following chapters demonstrate, the process has been successful. According to the European Bank for Reconstruction and Development, by 2003 the EU accession states of Central and Eastern Europe had reached advance country levels on small-scale privatisation and liberalisation of prices and trade. The overall leader has been Hungary followed by the Czech Republic, Estonia, Poland, Latvia, Lithuania, Slovakia and Slovenia. The Bank's *Transition Report 2003* stresses that these countries have made substantial progress in becoming "efficient, well-functioning market economies but important gaps remain – for example in the breadth and depth of these countries' financial markets and the restructuring of strategic sectors such as energy, heavy industry and agriculture."

A central issue in any model of an economy is the requirement for consistency between the real and financial sectors. This is equally relevant for centrally planned and market-orientated economies. A major difference between the two alternative models is how this consistency is achieved. Economic liberalisation and financial reform are inseparable twins. Either alone will not be effective and there is an essential complementarity between the two if the overall objectives of reform are to be achieved. Thus, economic reform (the privatisation of industries and the creation and liberalisation of markets and prices of goods and services) without financial reform (implying financial resources flowing in response to price signals and risk-reward criteria) will be ineffective. This is because if real resources are to be allocated on the basis of freely determined market prices, a necessary pre-requisite is that financial resources are also allocated on the basis of price signals. The real and financial sectors of the economy need to respond consistently to the same price signals. Equally, financial reform without economic liberalisation will achieve little because financial resource allocation which responds to price signals cannot work effectively or efficiently in the absence of efficient price signals in the real sector of the economy. The essential feature of a market-orientated economy, therefore, is that prices in the real and financial sectors must be consistent. If this consistency is barred in any way the inevitable result will be a sub-optimal allocation of resources. As put by de Haan and Naaborg in chapter seven, "The development of a financially sound and market-orientated banking system is fundamental to a successful transition from a communist to a market-based economy".

The old system is well described by Mihaljek in his chapter in this volume. The centrally planned model of the economy also had an essentially centralised financial system based on the mono-bank and a number of specialised sectorally-based financial institutions which created closed circuits of finance. There was generally no institutional separation between the central bank and other "banks" in the system. In essence (though the detail is far more complex and with substantial variations between countries) the allocation of finance was part of the centralised budgetary process: it was little more than a book-keeping device to record resource allocation decisions implicit in the central plan for the allocation of real resources. To the extent that there were transfer prices at all, allocations were made at (often fixed and undifferentiated) administered interest rates. Financial firms were not market institutions but agencies of the central planning mechanism. Neither were there any recognisable capital or money markets. As with a market-orientated system (though in fundamentally different ways) the regime was designed to achieve consistency between real resource and financial plans with consistency achieved through the planning process itself as opposed to through markets and responses to price signals. State-owned enterprises could only use funds for the purpose they were allocated and they in turn were allocated on the basis of the central plan for real resources. In particular, there were closed circuits between households and enterprises as lending between the two sectors was barred. In this model there was hardly any role for interest rates, risk premia or the exchange rate in the allocation of finance.

In a market-orientated financial system, risk premia on loans play an important role in the pricing and allocation of credit. In the centrally planned model, on the other hand, the concept of risk premia is largely meaningless. If property rights are limited, there is no concept of enforceable bankruptcy or creditor rights, and all economic enterprises are state-owned, the concept of "risk" as known in finance becomes redundant. If there is no risk as defined in a market economy context, there is no role for financial markets and institutions to allocate financial resources other than through a bureaucratic process based on a central plan for the economy as a whole. It is in this sense that financial reform without economic reform would have no meaning and why the two must go together. This also illustrates the important point that, for a market-orientated system to be effective, a financial infrastructure is needed which includes well-defined property rights, bankruptcy laws and enforcement procedures, efficient accountancy rules and procedures, etc.

As the following chapters illustrate, this all implies that, to be fully effective, economic and financial reform needs to be comprehensive and far-reaching. Making minor adjustments and reforms here and there and in a partial manner will not produce the desired outcomes in terms of an efficient allocation of real and financial resources. This again emphasises the central requirement for consistency.

The problems of transforming a centrally-planned economy to an effective and efficient market-orientated economy and financial system are formidable for two general reasons: 1) the requirement for consistency means that the reform programme necessarily needs to embrace all aspects of the economic and financial system as well as some fundamental issues such as property rights etc, and 2) because of the legacy problem. With respect to the latter, for instance, banks needed to be recapitalised because of the near worthless value of a large proportion of previous loans made under the previous regime. There were also difficult problems and challenges with respect to the requirement for consistency in the dimension of sequencing of the different aspects of the reform package. If economic reform is to proceed and state enterprises are to be privatised and run on the basis of market principles and discipline, there needs to be a well-functioning market financial system with efficient financial institutions and markets. And yet these cannot be created without business to undertake and hence without existing market-orientated enterprises. This sequencing problem posed formidable problems. Partly for this reason, in some countries the privatisation of state enterprises was delayed. The position with respect to banks is outlined by Mihaljek who notes that some countries decided to postpone the privatisation of some large state-owned banks because financial markets and the legal infrastructure were not sufficiently developed to exert effective market discipline.

The Financial System

With respect to finance, sound economic development requires two essential ingredients: an *efficient* financial system, and a *stable and robust* financial system. In many ways, a stable financial system is as important as sound macroeconomic management for the economic development of developing countries. Because of its central role in the reform process in the countries of Central and Eastern Europe, and in order to offer a general context for the chapters to follow, it is instructive to consider the role of a market-orientated financial system and its basic functions in an economy. The financial system plays a pivotal role in an economy by facilitating saving and borrowing, through transferring resources from savers to investors, and through financing real economic activity. The financial system comprises a set of *financial markets*, *financial institutions* and *Exchanges* which, to some extent, are in competition with each other. Financial institutions are intermediaries between ultimate savers and borrowers and operate by issuing their own liabilities as a means of funding their loans to borrowers. They offer savers a choice of instruments through which to save. Financial institutions are categorised as banks and other deposit-taking institutions such as, in the UK, building societies; long-term investment institutions (such as life assurance companies, pension funds and investment or unit trusts) and, in some countries, public sector institutions which are often created in order to finance particular types of investment projects. These different types of institution specialise in different types of assets and liabilities.

Five major roles are performed by the financial system though, as noted below, the way these roles are performed varies from one country to another even with a market-orientated mode:

1) The financial system performs financial intermediation services (channelling funds from one set of agents to another) which means that, by intermediating between different transactors (e.g. savers and borrowers), resources are transferred from those who have excess financial resources to those who wish to borrow.
2) The financial system provides a wide range of other financial services such as payments services, insurance, fund management, etc.

3) It creates for consumers a wide range of assets and liabilities with different characteristics so that their particular portfolio preferences can be satisfied.
4) It engages in asset transformation through financial firms having assets and liabilities with different characteristics which, in the process, enables risks to be shifted to those who are more willing and able to accept them.
5) Through pricing signals (such as interest rates and the prices of assets in primary and secondary markets) it creates incentives for the efficient allocation of resources within the economy.

These are clearly important roles for they impinge on every aspect of the economy and, because of 5), may also have an impact on the overall efficiency of the economy. In its extreme formulation (never in practice attained in any system) the optimal allocation of financial resources in an economy occurs when, at the margin, the risk-adjusted rate of return on all projects is the same. If resources are to be allocated on the basis of such risk-reward criteria, the system must be able to make informed judgements about risk, interest rates must be freely flexible, and accurately assessed risk premia must be incorporated into interest rates on loans. Equally, secondary markets need to generate efficient price signals which accurately reflect the value, and future prospects, of companies. Thus, the efficiency of financial markets and institutions potentially has an important impact on the overall efficiency of the economy.

While the role and functions of financial systems are universal, financial systems in different countries vary considerably in structure and operation. In particular, the relative role of organised markets and financial institutions varies between countries. The universal functions of the financial system are:

- The management of the payments and settlements system.
- The provision of mechanisms for the borrowing and lending of funds so as to remove short-term budget constraints.
- The provision of mechanisms for the pooling of funds and the financing of large-scale projects beyond the capability of individual savers.
- The bridging of different portfolio preferences of ultimate suppliers and borrowers of funds.

- The provision of mechanisms for the transfer of financial (and hence real) resources over time, space, and agents.
- The allocation funds to their most efficient use in an economy as, for instance, indicated by risk-return criteria. This requires markets and institutions to accurately assess risks of borrowers and to reflect these risks in the interest rates charged to borrowers.
- As most financial transactions involve the future, and the future is necessarily uncertain, a central function of the financial system is to enable agents to manage uncertainty by creating risk-sharing facilities.
- To price risk and enable risks to be transferred between different agents according to their ability and willingness to absorb them.
- To offer facilities and markets enabling wealth-holders to change the structure of their portfolios of assets and liabilities.
- To deal with problems of asymmetric information and the resolution of the resultant moral hazard and adverse selection problems. A central problem is that not all transactors have the same information or abilities to assess available information. This creates potential moral hazard whereby those with superior information can use it to the disadvantage of counterparties in a transaction. Financial systems have evolved various techniques to deal with this problem and thereby enable transactions to take place.
- To offer a range of specialist financial services which are demanded in society (insurance, financial advice and fund management, for example).

The financial system performs some of these roles by issuing different types of assets and liabilities. Financial instruments are essentially of three different types: *debt*, *equity*, and *insurance*. Debt contracts (such as a bank loan) require the borrower to repay the loan on specified terms irrespective of the borrower's performance. If an investment project financed by a loan is not successful, the borrower is not absolved from paying interest and repaying the loan. This means that, except in the extreme case of default and bankruptcy, the risk is borne by the borrower. However, it also means that the lender does not share in the upside potential of the project if the project being financed performs better than was initially anticipated. This is because in a debt contract the terms of the loan are fixed in advance. An equity contract, on the other hand, is where the return to the lender is determined by the performance of the borrower: if the project performs well both the lender and borrower share in the gain but equally both share the downside risk that the project performs badly. In this case, and in contrast to debt contracts, the lender and borrower share the risks. A major example of an equity contract is when a company issues shares which are bought by investors.

The simplest form of an insurance contract is where a risk-averse transactor pays a premium in order to shift risk to others. More complex insurance contracts include forward and options transactions. Overall, a market-orientated financial system deals in risks of various types and enables the preferences of transactors with different risk profiles and apetites to be met. An issue arises as to why one transactor is prepared to accept the risks that are being transferred from another: why the counterparty is willing to allow the risk to be shifted to itself? There are three main reasons. Firstly, the counterparty might be a speculator who is willing to take the risk in order to make a speculative profit. This amounts to the two counterparties having different risk appetites. Secondly, the counterparty (e.g. insurance company) might be more able to absorb the risk because it has the advantages of economies of scale and an ability to diversify risks to a greater extent than can the insured agent. A third possibility is that two transactors have equal and opposite risks and both wish to remove the risk.

The Financial System and the Economy

These basic functions (both individually and collectively) impinge on all aspects of the economy and are central to the overall performance of the economy. It follows that the efficiency of the financial system in performing these universal functions is a major ingredient of the efficiency of the economy as a whole. There is substantial empirical evidence (noted by Pilková and Pätoprstý in Chapter 2) that the efficiency and development of the financial system has a positive impact on overall economic performance.

The positive correlation between indicators of financial development and economic growth over the long-term reflects the importance of the financial sector. Financial debt, as measured by the ratio of quasi money to GDP, also displays a strong positive correlation with economic growth. Despite slippages due to unsound practices in the banking sector, financial reforms that have promoted the development of the financial sector and the extension of financial intermediation have been associated with improved economic performance. This is a robust conclusion drawn from case studies of many countries in the developing world. Empirical evidence strongly supports the proposition that a well-developed, efficient and robust financial system contributes positively to a country's economic development.

Financial sector efficiency and the economy

To summarise a complex analysis, the efficiency of the financial system has a significant impact on economic development in several ways:

- Its efficiency determines the cost of financial intermediation and the volume of real resources that are absorbed by the financial system. The more efficient is the financial system in lowering the cost of financial intermediation, the higher is the proportion of savings that is allocated to productive investment.
- It has an impact on the incentive to save and hence on the volume of savings available for investment.
- To the extent that an efficient financial system removes budget constraints to investors, it promotes productive investment.
- As well as determining the volume of investment, the allocation of capital to the most efficient use is a significant determinant of the rate of economic growth. A major role of the financial system, therefore, is to create incentives for the efficient allocation of savings and financial resources. In so doing, the efficient allocation of internal savings (and offering appropriate rewards for savers) may reduce the dependence on foreign capital inflows.
- An efficient financial system also enables risks to be shifted to those agents who are most able and willing to absorb them. In the process, an efficient financial system offers facilities for the management of uncertainty.
- To the extent that the financial system is able to price risk efficiently, this also contributes to an efficient allocation of financial resources on the basis of risk-reward criteria. If this does

not happen, economic development can be impeded in that the allocation of savings is not such as to maximise the risk-adjusted rate of return on capital. This can occur if risk is inaccurately measured or inefficiently priced, or if in any way the optimum allocation of savings is impeded. The last mentioned could occur, for instance, if allocation decisions are distorted by taxes and subsidies, or if some industries or particular borrowers have privileged access to some financing mechanisms.

- An efficient financial system may also contribute to its own stability robustness. An inefficient financial system may induce the most credit-worthy borrowers to borrow overseas which has two potential adverse consequences: it increases the dependence on, and vulnerability to, foreign capital inflows, and the average risk characteristics of domestic lending deteriorates as the loans market becomes more segmented.

Thus an inefficient financial system can impede economic development through low savings and investment, inefficient allocation of financial resources, inefficient and bad pricing of risks with the result that investment funds are allocated inefficiently and in a way that does not maximise economic growth, and by absorbing excessive resources in the financial intermediation process. The last-mentioned means that a smaller proportion of savings actually gets channelled into productive investment.

Robustness of the Financial System

At the outset, two key characteristics of the financial system were established as having a major bearing on its contribution to economic development: its *efficiency,* and its *stability and robustness*. These are two separate, though related, characteristics. The previous section discussed the efficiency dimension in terms of resource and allocative efficiency and the key characteristics of each. In this section the basic characteristics of a robust financial system are outlined. This is an important dimension in that an unstable system is likely to seriously impair economic development. Experience indicates there are substantial economic costs associated with banking instability and financial crises. These may be briefly summarised:

- Confidence in the financial system can be seriously impaired with the effect that users are less inclined to conduct business. As a result, the volume of financial intermediation may decline.
- A financial crisis can disrupt the financial intermediation process with the result that savings and investment are lower, and savings can be badly misallocated in the economy. In particular, banks widen their margins and become more risk-averse. In general, the cost of financial intermediation rises.
- When banks accumulate non-performing loans on a large scale they can become the captive of their weak borrowers with the result that a credit-crunch can emerge, and good projects are not financed because of banks' increased risk aversion and the fact that they face balance sheet constraints due to capital being eroded by previous bad loans.
- The costs of rescues (particularly of banks) can be substantial with the result that the taxpayer is effectively using financial resources to rescue banks which might otherwise be used for more productive investment: rescue operations, in one way or another, utilise investible resources in an unproductive manner.
- Because of the central importance and key role of the financial system, instability in the system, and financial crises in particular, can themselves cause instability in the real economy. The obvious example, as already noted, is the phenomenon of a 'credit crunch' where credit dries up even for viable investment projects. Put another way, instability in the financial system can amplify and exacerbate an existing cyclical instability in the economy. In the process, the two can feed upon each other in an interactive manner: instability in the financial system causes greater fluctuations in the real economy and instability in the economy can itself be a major cause of volatility in the financial system.
- Financial instability and banking crises can also have a significant negative impact on capital flows with voluntary capital inflows drying up and capital flight accentuated.
- In one way or another, a banking crisis requires intervention. Irrespective of the causes of the crisis, the authorities cannot realistically allow major parts of the banking and financial system to cease functioning. The question arises as to how the safety net is to be operated. A central problem is that, dependent on how the rescue is undertaken, a moral hazard for the future can be created.

In particular, if the perception arises that banks will be rescued, the moral hazard is that in the future banks may be inclined to take more risk and depositors and other suppliers of funds to banks may be less concerned about the risk characteristics of banks.
- The failure of any bank causes significant information losses. A bank's major advantage is the information it has about its customers, and borrowing customers in turn have an advantage in sharing information with their bank. Particularly for small companies, whose access to the capital market is limited, the relationship developed with their bankers particularly important. If a bank fails, the embodied information is difficult to transfer to another bank because the information was gained through years of relationship between the bank and the customer.
- A banking crisis can also impose substantial costs on the economy because it may inhibit the government from pursuing correct and appropriate monetary and fiscal policies. For instance, if the banking system is vulnerable, the government might be hesitant to raise interest rates even in the face of inflationary pressure because the rise in interest rates might itself make the banks and other financial firms yet more vulnerable. In its extreme form, this can be another moral hazard as the delay in the government taking corrective stabilisation policy actions may, in the end, mean that the ultimate monetary and fiscal policy adjustment has to be even greater with the risk that the banking crisis might become yet more serious.
- In the worse-case scenario, the payments system can be disrupted.

For all these reasons, the stability and robustness of a financial system is as important as its underlying efficiency. As banking crises frequently occur when there are weak incentives to act prudently, a necessary ingredient of a robust and stable financial system is the creation of appropriate and efficient incentives and disciplining mechanisms for all market participants and most especially bank *owners* and bank *managers*.

Incentives for bank owners
- One route through which to create appropriate incentives is to ensure that banks have appropriate levels of equity capital invested in the institution. Capital serves three main roles as far as incentive

structures are concerned: 1) a commitment of the owners to supply risk resources to the business and which they can lose in the event that the bank makes bad loans, 2) an internal insurance fund, and 3) the avoidance of the bank becoming the captive of its bad debtors. In general, the higher is the equity capital ratio in a bank the more the owners have to lose and hence the greater the incentive for them to monitor the behaviour of managers. Low capital creates a moral hazard in that, given the small amount owners have to lose, they are more likely to condone taking excessive risks in a gamble-for-resurrection strategy. This was evidently the case at times during the savings and loan crisis in the United States, and in some recent crisis-prone countries in Latin America and South East Asia. Regulators must require banks to hold capital commensurate with the risks they take.

- Corporate governance arrangements need to be such that equity holders (i.e. the owners of the bank) actively supervise managers.
- Supervisors and safety net agencies need to ensure that owners (shareholders) lose out in any re-structuring operations in the event of failure. Failure to penalise shareholders in the restructuring of unsuccessful banks was a major shortcoming in rescue operations in Latin America.
- Encouragement needs to be given to ownership structures that foster shareholder monitoring and oversight. This includes private ownership of banks to strengthen the monitoring of management performance and to reduce distortions in incentives for managers.

Incentives for managers

Creating the right incentive structures for the managers of financial institutions is equally as important as those for the owners. In fact, the two are to be seen in combination.

- There need be strong and effective risk analysis, management and control systems in place in all financial institutions. In the final analysis, most bank failures are ultimately due to weaknesses in this area. Regulatory agencies have a powerful role in promoting, and insisting upon, effective systems of internal management and risk control in financial institutions by strict accountability of owners, directors and senior management. This is a central feature of the Basel 2 Capital Accord. This includes prevention of insider abuses and financial crime, control of connected lending and promotion of accurate loan valuation, asset classification, risk assessment, etc.

- Managers should lose through failure. This requires a high degree of professionalism in bank managers and decision-makers and penalties (including dismissal) for incompetence amongst bank managers.
- Subject to prudential standards being maintained, proper incentives can be created by the fostering of competition in the financial sector. This can be achieved, for instance, by removing restrictions on business activity, allowing the entry of foreign banks and other financial institutions, and forcing the abandoning of restrictive practices, cartels and other anti-competitive mechanisms.
- Strict control of concentrated lending, inter-connected lending etc.

Combining appropriate incentives for owners and managers contributes to a robust financial system and, in principle, a free market system would evolve such incentives. However, experience indicates that, in many areas, and most especially when the competitive environment is changing and the regulatory regime is being adjusted, it is hazardous to rely exclusively on the market evolving appropriate incentives.

No Single Model

The following chapters describe the various aspects of reform programmes (both economic and financial) as the countries of Central and Eastern Europe moved from essentially centrally-planned to market-orientated systems. However, while the general characteristics of a market-based system are common, and the basic functions performed by the financial system are universal, there is no single dominant model. There are substantial structural and operational differences between different market-orientated financial systems. The (somewhat artificial) distinction between bank-based and capital market-based models is well established. There are substantial differences between different market-based systems in several areas including, *inter alia*:

- with respect to the relative role of financial markets and institutions,
- the structure of financial institutions and which type of institutions perform which roles,
- the ownership of enterprise equity,
- corporate governance arrangements and the market in corporate control,
- links (including ownership links) between financial firms and industrial and commercial firms,
- the range of assets and liabilities generated in the financial system,
- the efficiency of financial markets and institutions,
- the role, scope and content of financial regulation,
- the portfolio preferences of agents in the system,
- the role of foreign banks in the financial system, and
- the role (if any) of state institutions.

Thus, while the *functions* of market financial systems are universal, the way these functions are performed varies substantially between systems of different countries. There is no universal model of a market-based financial system. In Chapter 3, Pissarides notes that the transitional countries have tended to develop more along the bank-based European model than the capital market-based US model.

It is also pertinent, as noted by Mihaljek, that the reform programmes in Central and Eastern Europe, and the creation of new financial systems, has been occurring, and continues to develop, in the context of fundamental changes in the way financial markets and institutions operate in existing market-based economies. As noted in Llewellyn (1999) the economics of the banking industry in market-based systems is changing radically. One particular dimension to this is the increasing emphasis being given to shareholder-value models (Llewellyn, 2004).

If the long-standing market economies have not converged on a single unique model, there is no reason to expect that the transition economies will do so. In other words, while there are common elements in the reform programmes, there are also substantial differences both with respect to sequencing and final outcome.

Role of Foreign Banks

In many developing countries, and also the transitional economies of Central and Eastern Europe, the role of foreign banks in the evolution of the financial system towards a market-orientated basis has been substantial. If a country (whether it be a developing country or a transition country) seeks to create an efficient market-orientated banking system, three broad strategic options are available: 1) to transform existing state-owned banks into private market-orientated banks, 2) to offer banking licences to newly-created indigenous banks, or 3) to import part of a banking system by allowing foreign banks to conduct business in the country. Part II of this volume is devoted to the third option and contains many valuable insights.

The extent of foreign bank penetration has been substantial. De Haan and Naaborg note in Chapter 7 that "The growing presence of foreign-owned financial institutions during the 1990s is one of the most striking structural changes". Mucci, Papi and Revoltella, in Chapter 6, note that around sixty percent of the New Europe banking sector (as measured by assets) is under foreign control and about eight large international institutions have emerged as leaders in the region. They point out that: "New Europe is now one of the few regional markets in the world where foreign ownership is predominant, and where cross-border strategic players can compete directly in a fairly liberalised framework while exploiting and supporting what has already become their 'second home' market". In some countries, the share of foreign bank business can be as high as 75 percent (see also, Naarborg, et al. 2004). This implies that foreign bank entry into the countries of Central and Eastern Europe has major implications for the evolution of the countries' financial systems, but also for the banks themselves.

There are many positive roles that the presence of foreign banks can perform in a transition economy seeking to develop a market-orientated financial system and many of these are outlined in detail in the chapters in Part II. These may be briefly summarised:

- They bring valuable experience and skills (e.g. credit assessment, risk analysis and management systems, etc) through operating in market-based economies in their own and other advanced countries.

- They have the potential to add substantially to the expertise and the knowledge base of the financial sector (see Mucci, Papi and Revoltella) given that, in the early stages of a transition, skilled personnel are in short supply.
- Through these routes they may significantly enhance the efficiency of the banking system (see Litan et al. 2001).
- They may bring an element of stability to the financial system in that their exposure to the host country is only a small proportion of their overall balance sheet position.
- Foreign institutions tend to be less subject to political pressures in the conduct of their business.
- They may also be less susceptible to local euphoria which, at times, can lead to excessive lending and over-optimistic expectations.
- They can contribute to risk management and risk allocation in the system as a whole because they tend to be more experienced in the use of derivative instruments (see Mathieson and Rolkdos, 2001).
- They can develop the financial system through the force of example and application of "best practice".
- Foreign banks may be able to offer training facilities to indigenous banks and local employees.
- Foreign investment in the banking sector can also be a stimulus for further capital inflows (see Chapter 1).
- They have the potential to accelerate the process of financial development in the economy generally and the financial and banking sectors in particular.
- The injection of capital in itself is valuable and resource-saving for the local economy.
- As noted by Pissarides in Chapter 3, the restructuring process of the banking system can be accelerated through privatisation of banks and sales to strategic foreign partners.
- The presence of foreign banks can have a significant impact on enhancing competition in the financial sector at an early stage in the development of a market-orientated banking sector, and reduce the dominant market power of indigenous banks which, as noted by Papi and Revoltella (1999), often results in the early stages of transition.

- It can also be the case that the presence of foreign banks, with experience of regulatory and supervisory regimes in the their home countries, enhances the quality of official regulation and supervision.

Overall, and as put by De Haan and Naarborg in this volume, "Foreign banks will help improve the quality, pricing, and availability of financial services, both directly as providers of these services and indirectly through increased competition".

Regulation and Supervision

It might, at first sight, appear somewhat paradoxical, or even perverse, that the process of liberalisation and financial reform needs to be accompanied by a new and different regulatory and supervisory regime. However, experience around the world (in industrial countries such as Scandinavia in the early 1990s, countries of South East Asia in the mid-1990s, Latin America in the 1990s, and in some transitional economies) indicates that major regime shifts (especially if this implies a substantial process of economic and financial liberalisation) can create the potential for financial instability. This is not because a liberalised regime is inherently unstable or more prone to instability, but because of the uncertainties created during the stock-adjustment phase of moving from one (constrained) regime to another (unconstrained) regime. It is the behavioural characteristics resulting from the stock-adjustment effect of the movement from one regime to another, rather than the characteristics of the steady-state liberalised regime, that creates the potential for instability.

There are particular problems in transitional economies because the process of liberalisation implies the creation of new institutions which have no experience of market-orientated financial business. As part of the sequencing problem, new institutions were needed urgently and at an early stage of the process of liberalisation. Institutions were needed to finance the newly-created private enterprises. Many of the transitional economies of Central and Eastern Europe turned out to be excessively liberal in granting banking licences in the early stages of reform programmes. In some cases this resulted in substantial financial distress amongst newly-licensed local banks.

It is for these reasons that liberalisation needs to be accompanied by explicit changes in the regulatory and supervisory regimes in the financial sector. In this sense, "re-regulation" rather than "de-regulation" is a more appropriate term to describe how financial regulation evolves in the transition from a centrally planned to a market-orientated financial system. The challenges are substantial as entirely new approaches are needed when financial institutions (including banks) can become insolvent in the market place as opposed to being permanently propped up by the state and the dictates of the central plan. These issues are discussed in Part III of this volume, where the important role of financial regulation and supervision is outlined by Summer and Wurz in Chapter 10, and the important role of deposit insurance is discussed by Di Giorgio in Chapter 12.

These issues relate to the practice and conduct of regulation and supervision. There is also the important issue of the institutional structure of financial regulation and supervision and, in particular, the number of agencies involved, whether or not there is to be a single all-embracing financial regulatory agency, the role of the central bank etc. The trend in the transitional economies (partly motivated by the desire to secure economies of scale and to secure an efficient use of scarce regulatory and supervisory resources) has been to create integrated agencies (see Estonian Ministry of Finance, 2003). This important issue, and the implications for EU enlargement, is discussed by Masciandaro and Porta in Chapter 11. They demonstrate that there is a wide variety of institutional models within the existing EU and that, therefore, as with financial systems generally, there is no universally agreed optimal model for the structure of regulatory and supervisory agencies.

Assessment

As indicated at the outset, the countries of Central and Eastern Europe have embarked upon one of the most dramatic regime shifts ever in both the economy generally and the financial system sector in particular. Many of the countries were in effect creating a banking and financial system from a zero (even negative) base given the substantial legacy overhang in some countries. The financial system inherited from the previous regime could not easily be modified to fit into a market-based economy: as put by Summer and Wurz "there was no possibility to build on the old banking system". There are times when required changes are so great that it is easier, and more efficient, to start from a zero base rather than modify existing institutions.

The challenges in the process have been formidable and inevitably the evolution has not always been smooth or without problems. However, the overwhelming conclusion of the chapters in this volume is that the process has been remarkably successful and that the transition countries have made substantial progress towards creating efficient market-orientated financial systems. Banks in particular have substantially increased their efficiency as shown in the intermediation margins since the late 1990s, although they remain wide in comparison with the European norm. The outcome is summarised by Summer and Wurz: "A little more than ten years after the fall of the old regimes these countries have all built a modern banking system and functioning capital markets that are internationally strongly integrated. Also the legal and supervisory infrastructure that is indispensable for a smoothly working financial system has been developed and implemented at an impressive speed".

The success of the reforms is indicated by the generally improved credit ratings of the transition states, and the narrowing of risk premia on the countries' debt. The financial systems, and most especially the banking sectors, of the transition countries have made significant contributions to general economic reform, and in turn foreign banks have made a particular contribution. In the words of Mihaljek, "Privatisation, foreign bank entry, consolidation, and improvements in institutional framework and financial market infrastructure have resulted in deep structural changes in the banking industry in Central and Eastern Europe".

Even so, the path towards a fully-fledged market economy and market-orientated financial system is an on-going process. The remaining challenges remain formidable if "state-of-the-art" standards are to be attained. This evolution in the transition states will be occurring in the context of radical changes in the economics of the banking industry being experienced in long-standing market-orientated financial systems. This introduces a new dimension to the sequencing issue.

REFERENCES

Litan, E.R., Masson, P. and Pomerleado, M. (2001), "Introduction" in E.R. Litan, P. Mason, M. Pomerleado (eds), *Open Doors: Foreign Participation in Financial Systems in Developing Countries*, Washington, Brookings Institution Press.

Llewellyn, D T (1999), *The New Economics of Banking*, SUERF Study No. 5, SUERF, Vienna.

Llewellyn, D T (2002), *Strategic Implications of the New Economics of retail Financial Services*, Building Societies Association, London.

Llewellyn, D T (2004), "Competition and Profitability in Banking: Are there Lessons from the UK", in S C W Eijffinger, H G van Gemert, G P L van Roij (eds.), *Intermediair tussen Wetenschap en Onderwijs*, Gianotten, Tilburg.

Mathieson and Roldos, (2001), "The Role of Foreign Banks in Emerging Markets", World Bank Discussion Paper.

Ministry of Finance of the Republic of Estonia, 2003, Challenges for the Unified Financial Supervision in the New Millennium, Tallin.

Naarborg, Scholtens, De Haan, Bol and De Haas (2004), "How Important are Foreign Banks in the Financial Development of European Transition Countries?", *Journal of Emerging Markets Finance.*

Pai, L. and Revoltella, D. (1999), "Foreign direct Investment in the Banking Sector: A Transitional Economy Perspective", in Claessens and Jansen (eds), *The Internationalisation of Financial Services*, Kluwer, The Hague.

Introduction

Donato Masciandaro

From entry into the European Union to the Adoption of the Euro: after the 2004 Big Bang, what role will the current evolution of banking systems in the Enlargement countries play in this historic challenge? This volume, a blend of economics and political economy, offers a systematic analysis of the current trends in banking and financial intermediation in the countries of the New Europe, with a particular focus on the directions taken by foreign banks, on the one hand, and by the regulatory and supervisory authorities, on the other. The research work was promoted by the Paolo Baffi Center of Bocconi University.

All the research has led to one substantiated result: in order to enter the Union, the political classes of the countries of the New Europe needed to increase the efficiency of their economic systems rapidly through liberalization and privatization; the entry of foreign banks contributed to this project. Today the efficiency of the banking and financial industry seems improved on average, but the studies proposed in this volume offer new perspectives: will the presence of foreign banks permanently increase financial stability? Will it contribute toward economic growth, especially in relation to fledgling small and medium-sized enterprises? To achieve these objectives, how should the architecture of banking regulation and supervision be designed? We shall examine the how and why of these new perspectives.

It all began when the various countries of East-Central Europe decided to apply for membership in the European Union. This decision meant they had to have economic and financial systems consistent with the principles of market economics; they had to increase the efficiency of their resource allocation.

This need to improve efficiency also applied to the banking industry. The adequacy of the banking and financial system to that task is gauged by its ability to offer households and companies products and services that help them cope with the various forms of risk. To manage their savings, households require at least three things:

security deriving from a form of liquidity (deposits) with zero risk, in terms loss of principal, which enables them to manage various forms of uncertainty; information on the risk-return characteristics of alternative forms of financial investment; a plurality of such forms of investment. Companies, for their part, to manage their investments, require the support of banks that can assess their creditworthiness, as part of a more general ability to propose the financial structures best suited to the characteristics of the companies that utilize their services.

The first part of this volume provides a complete picture of the steps – taken and not taken – in this direction, as well as those yet to be taken, by the banking systems of the New Europe. The study by Dubravko Mihaljek offers a complete picture of the evolution achieved in the banking systems of East-Central Europe. The work of Anna Pilková and Viliam Pätoprstý completes and enhances this picture by proposing, among other things, new indicators for measuring the actual degree of development in banking and financial intermediation, revealing that the results obtained in retail activity – relations with households – are more satisfactory than those achieved in the lending area – i.e. in relations to companies. And it is precisely on the subject of relationships between banking and firms, with particular focus on small and medium-sized enterprises, that Francesca Pissarides has concentrated her study, examining the progress made but also the unknowns yet to be resolved.

In recent years, therefore, the banking and financial systems of the New Europe have generally improved their ability to accompany households and companies in dealing with risk and uncertainty. The result is a positive impact on the judgment of the financial markets regarding systemic risk in those countries: the study by Beltratti and D'Antonio is the first in this direction.

But the task of the Enlargement countries certainly does not end with entry into the European Union. The next step is their ability to adopt the single European currency: it is the challenge of the euro. The challenge of the euro means having market economies that are not only increasingly efficient but also well positioned on a path of stable growth. Thus the banking system will be asked to contribute not only to efficiency but also increasingly to growth and overall stability.

At this point, it becomes important to ask: what role can foreign banks play? Undoubtedly the countries most in need of a rapid increase in the efficiency of their banks, since they are relatively uncompetitive, have thus far derived benefit from the presence of foreign banks. All the studies in the second part of the volume, both theoretical (Daniel Gros) and empirical (Jacob de Haan and Ilko Naaborg, Alicia García Herrero and Daniel Navia Simón), offer consistent messages. The experience of liberalization and privatization of the banking systems in East-Central Europe provides clear indications: efficiency in terms of the quality and quantity of products available to households seems certain, while results in avoiding the risk of credit rationing, especially in the future and particularly to the detriment of small and medium–sized enterprises, seems much less solid thus far. Thus the "foreign effect" in banking seems to have produced gains in efficiency, though its duration and extent still remain to be tested.

Furthermore, we must bear in mind that a market economy does not thrive solely on short-term efficiency. The quest for efficiency alone is a weak strategy in the medium-long term, if one forgets that healthy, steady development in the banking industry is based on the assurance of its stability and systemic integrity.

Here the question of nationality becomes even more interesting: when markets become more volatile and unstable, and banking strategies more probably tend to be zero-sum, from various standpoints, bankers might tend to rally more around their home "flags". In this regard, the work of Farabullini and Ferri shows how tightly the presence of foreign banks has been tied to that of companies of the same nationality.

Thus the national factor – home bias effect – can be significant, in a dynamic overall view of the relationship between efficiency, stability and growth. The point is that the "optimal level" of presence of foreign banks cannot be determined on the basis of simple cost-benefit analysis. We just recall that, on the theoretical level, the presence of foreign banks can generate both costs and expected benefits, and that empirical evidence, recent and scant as it is, provides no definitive answers.

It may be interesting, therefore, to examine the question from a political economy view. A country maintains or alters the level of foreign bank presence in its financial system when its policymakers decide it is advisable to do so. If we do not feel that policymakers are always rational and benevolent, but we also do not wish to exclude that *a priori*, we can consider that these choices are generally determined by structural factors of a financial, economic and institutional nature. The search for these factors is the task of economic analysis.

Policymakers in the Enlargement countries have thus far viewed with favor the entry of foreign banks into their systems, because this benefited the integration and convergence of their economies with those of the Union. This integration–convergence process has been pursued both in the area of monetary policy–subject of the work by Jesús Crespo Cuaresma, Balázs Egert and Thomas Reininger – and in banking regulation – as the study by Martin Summer and Michael Würz demonstrates.

But the attention of policymakers with regard to the euro is certainly not diminished and will increasingly regard not only monetary policy and regulation but also, and especially, banking supervision. In fact, in the area of supervision the degrees of freedom, and therefore the possibility of sustaining "national interest" (and not only on the topic of foreign banks), are greater than in monetary policy and regulation. In monetary policy, acceptance of the euro means renouncing national autonomy in currency and interest rate maneuvering in exchange for greater price stability. In the area of banking regulation, the rules are decided in Brussels. It is true, as the work of Giorgio di Giorgio demonstrates, with particular attention to deposit insurance, that ample space exists for European harmonizing actions, but they will be decided within the collective process of the Union. Supervision, on the other hand, is firmly linked to national territories and will probably remain so for some time in the future.

In fact, unlike what occurred in the 1990s for the design of monetary institutions, Europe has no optimal or dominant model to propose. In the past decade, the principal macroeconomic problem facing the countries of the old Europe was monetary stability. Which institutional structure was best for effectively combating inflation? Economic analysis strongly indicated the creation of an independent central bank. Furthermore, since World War II, the more independent central banks – first and foremost the Bundesbank, Germany's central bank – are those that have turned in the best inflation performance in their respective countries. So a dominant model, in theory as in practice, existed in Europe to respond to the problem of monetary stability. It was therefore natural for the European Union to adopt the independent central bank model, leading to the European System of Central Banks with the European Central Bank (ECB) at its head.

Today the macroeconomic problem the European governments must constantly monitor, because of increasing globalization and integration of financial transactions, is that of financial stability. What is the best institutional structure of supervision for ensuring financial stability? In this case, as the work of Donato Masciandaro and Angelo Porta indicates, economic theory has no widely accepted recipe to offer, and even the institutional models in use are rather heterogeneous.

Schematically, the reforms implemented in recent years, or in the implementation process, show that the surveillance regimes are polarizing toward two models: one dominated by a single authority, the other dominated by the central bank. These two models are equally represented in Europe today. Considering the current members of the Union, eight countries (Austria, Belgium, Denmark, Finland, Germany, Luxembourg, the United Kingdom and Sweden) have structures equivalent to a single authority, while in the other seven (France, Greece, Ireland, Italy, Netherlands, Portugal and Spain) the central bank is relatively stronger. With the prospect of Enlargement, the picture changes little: a single authority prevails in four countries (Estonia, Lithuania, Malta and Hungary) but not in the other six (Cyprus, Czech Republic, Latvia, Poland, Slovakia and Slovenia).

In this case, therefore, no dominant model exists in the European Union, in theory or practice, on which to base a solution. The European choice must therefore be preceded by careful reflection at the national level. Today, in the 15 member states, there are a total of 33 supervisory authorities (and "only" 30 in the Eurozone countries!). Including the Enlargement countries adds another 22. It is evident that the supranational process toward European supervision can hardly be rapid in the presence of 55 centers of surveillance (and bureaucratic power).

But the emergence of stability and confidence problems is certainly not waiting for the European architects of supervision: it is the responsibility of the individual governments and parliaments to define now how best to equip their control networks. And the rationalization of the national supervisory structures will definitely help accelerate the supranational process of selection between a model dominated by the ECB and one managed by a European Financial Authority.

This book presents the results of a research project undertaken by the Paolo Baffi Centre for Monetary and Financial Economics. As editor, I wish to thank, without implicating, Giuseppe Macis for excellent research assistance.

PART I

Intermediation, Firms and Financial Markets

1. Banking Industry in Central and Eastern Europe: The Unexpected Leader in the Transition and Integration with the EU

Dubravko Mihaljek[1]

INTRODUCTION

When the transition started in the early 1990s, commercial banking systems hardly existed in central and eastern Europe. Most "banks" were essentially cash–dispensing offices, channelling credit from the "monobank" to the state-owned enterprises in line with the central plan and the state budget. There was no commercial banking legislation or bank supervision in the sense of market economy. Since credit allocation did not follow strict commercial criteria and the institution of bankruptcy was virtually unknown, much of the inherited stock of bank credit was potentially unrecoverable. Against this background, the banking industry was clearly expected to be a laggard in the transition process, and the financial sector reform one of the most demanding aspects of the transition. How could one have expected the transition economies to rapidly establish functioning commercial banking systems, when socialist economies were not even properly monetized and money failed to perform its basic functions of medium of exchange and store of value (see Box 1.1)?

Yet these pessimistic expectations have turned out to be wrong. By the early 2000s, the restructuring of the banking industry in central and eastern Europe had been essentially completed. Most commercial banks had been privatized, in most cases by reputable banks from the European Union. In the corporate sector, the development of local financial markets has gone hand in hand with the inflow of foreign capital and the ongoing micro-level integration into the EU. Foreign investment in the banking sector has not only helped develop the domestic financial sectors themselves, but has also created a favourable business environment for further foreign capital inflows.

Box 1.1 Money in Socialism

Soon after the October Revolution, in the context of raging hyperinflation, Soviet economists started a debate about the future of their country's monetary system[2]. One group, led by Falkner (1924), argued that, following the financial collapse, socialism would completely reject fiat money and monetary relations and replace them with some form of direct exchange. Another group, led by Katzenellenbaum (1925), argued that despite any possible intentions to demonetise the economy, some form of monetary exchange would survive in the black market. Later developments showed that socialist banking evolved in the direction of complete centralization under the monobank system, in which money became entirely passive, its stability being ensured through strict institutional controls. But the complete control of economic activity was impossible. Market activity and, hence, some scope for the free use of money had to be tolerated by central planners.

At this juncture, a fundamental contradiction between money and socialism emerged[3]. Money is private property par excellence. The fact that money is used even in the most centralized economies (such as Cuba and North Korea today) implies that private property cannot be completely abolished. However narrow the scope for the free use of money, the possession of money gives its owner the opportunity to avoid the authorities' controls. Money in socialism is thus an instrument of economic freedom within a system of economic control. The conflict between the two is unavoidable: socialism cannot forego the conveniences of money nor can it control an economy based on money (Gligorov, 1989, pp. 30–31).

An important insight on the nature of money in socialism comes from the work of Viktor Novozhilov (1924, 1925, 1926), who drew a distinction between money and "coupons." He noticed that coupons, originally issued to provide access to a certain class of commodities (eg, food), were a close substitute for money because they could be traded or sold at a discount for "real" money, and thus used to obtain access to a wide variety of goods and services and smooth consumption over time. A "general coupon", which could be used to purchase any commodity, saved for later use, or sold at discount for "real" money, would thus be similar to real money. However, since the rationale for producing goods in a socialist economy was to achieve a specific allocation of resources envisaged by the plan, holding a general coupon did not guarantee its owner unrestricted access to the goods and services that were produced. In a socialist system money had performed first and foremost a distributive function: it was a coupon that entitled its holder to a certain amount of goods, if he or she queued long enough and/or conformed to other eligibility criteria. So long as the goods and services were not sold at market clearing prices, money could not perform its functions of a medium of exchange and a store of value.

And by expanding the range of investment opportunities to individual and institutional investors, the development of non-bank financial intermediaries and the gradual removal of remaining capital controls have provided an additional stimulus for financial integration with the EU. In terms of convergence and integration of the banking sectors, the banking industry has thus clearly become a leader in the process of transition and integration with the EU.

This chapter traces the remarkable transformation process of the banking industry in central and eastern Europe over the past decade. The first section briefly discusses the difficult initial conditions and the resulting dilemmas of early bank reforms. The second section analyses the far-reaching changes that were taking place in the global banking industry in the 1990s. These changes are essential for understanding the subsequent shift in the course of bank reforms in the transition economies, which is described in the third section. The fourth section analyses the recent performance of the banking industry in central and eastern Europe. The fifth section concludes by addressing some current policy dilemmas related to the state-owned and foreign-owned banks in central and eastern Europe.

INITIAL CONDITIONS

The financial system of a traditional centrally planned economy consisted of a state "monobank", which had a monopoly position in deposit banking and supplying of credit, and a number of specialized financial institutions (agricultural, industrial, construction, foreign trade "banks") that were distributing credit to enterprises in line with the credit and cash plans for the economy. Commercial banking functions were usually limited to the foreign trade bank and the savings banks. A two-tier banking system was in place only in former Yugoslavia and Hungary. But in Hungary, almost all banks were state-owned and the government controlled the credit and money markets, whereas in former Yugoslavia a commercial banking system that began operating in the mid-1960s no longer fulfilled its distinctive intermediary role after retrograde reforms of the 1970s.

This monobank system was further characterized by dichotomized money supply (Garvy, 1977). One financial circuit encompassed households, which received wages and salaries in cash, made payments for consumption in cash, and deposited some of their unspent cash in savings accounts. Another financial circuit served the enterprises, which received credit from the banks and made payments to other enterprises and the budget entities through bank accounts, while paying wages and salaries in cash. The state-owned enterprises could only use their funds for the purposes specified in plan documents. This has led Berliner (1976) to coin the term "documonetary" economy. There was practically no link between the two financial circuits, as lending between the enterprise and household sectors was not allowed.

Monetary policy in this system was conducted through control of the volume of credit to state enterprises and budget entities, and through emission of cash in line with the planned gap between monetary receipts and outlays of the household sector. Given the preponderance of direct credit allocation, interest rates and exchange rates played virtually no role in allocation of resources. The dominant position of state enterprises as borrowers from the banking system further implied that risk considerations were largely absent from the decisions on credit allocation.

Against this background, the transformation of the banking system appeared to raise many difficult questions at the start of the transition. If money was to become freely convertible into commodities, prices in centrally planned economies had to be liberalized and budget constraints had to become binding so as to eliminate shortages. However, it was reasonable to expect – including on the basis of the mid-1960s reform experience of former Yugoslavia – that price liberalization would result in rising inflation. Macroeconomic stability was thus seen as a precondition for successful monetization. However, stabilizing these economies was expected to last long and the final outcome was uncertain, so one could not have anticipated much progress with bank reforms until the later stages of the transition.

As a result, early bank reforms were driven more by pressing macroeconomic concerns than by considerations of optimal timing and sequencing. For instance, it became clear very early that existing banks had to be recapitalized, the stock of inherited bad debt resolved, and that new loans had to be extended on a sound commercial basis in order to harden enterprise budget constraints and eliminate a potential source of inflation. But simple and well-tried solutions were not available – policy makers had to devise new approaches (see Tošovský, 2001). The authorities in several countries thus decided to write off much of inherited bank debt, emphasising the one-off nature of this operation to minimize moral hazard. They also decided to postpone the privatization of the large state-owned commercial banks because financial markets and the legal infrastructure were not sufficiently developed to exert effective market discipline. Furthermore, there was a pressing need to provide banking services to the newly established private firms. Since state-owned banks were not interested in this segment of the market, many countries adopted liberal licensing rules – too liberal as it turned out subsequently – in the hope of speeding up the development of financial markets and putting competitive pressure on the large state-owned banks.

GLOBAL TRANSFORMATION OF THE BANKING INDUSTRY IN THE 1990s

At the time when policy makers in the transition economies began to face the dilemmas of early bank reforms, banking in most industrial countries was still a protected industry, benefiting from the regulated margins between the lending and deposit rates and from restrictions on domestic and foreign competition[4]. But global market and technology developments, macroeconomic pressures and numerous banking crises have forced the authorities to deregulate the industry at the national level and open up financial markets to foreign competition.

Impact of Information Technology

What makes financial intermediaries different from other economic agents is the special functions they perform: processing of information about investment opportunities, spreading of risk through asset diversification, and providing liquidity services through asset transformation. All these activities involve the processing of information, so it is not surprising that the development of new information technology has been of paramount importance for the banking industry. This impact has been evident in particular in the development of new financial products and services, broadening of capital markets, changes in corporate behaviour with an emphasis on shareholder value, and risk management.

Development of new financial products

One of the most significant innovations in the area of financial products over the past two decades has been the development of instruments such as derivatives, which enable risk to be reallocated to the parties most willing and able to bear that risk, thereby inducing more investment in real assets and fostering the development of financial markets (Greenspan, 2000).

The use of derivative instruments has not remained the preserve of industrial countries. With their increasingly sophisticated information technology applications, banks in emerging markets use derivative instruments daily in their transactions. Their banking systems and financial markets are thus in a position to advance much more rapidly from a rudimentary to a fairly advanced stage of development of risk management and other commercial banking functions. Such potential skipping of financial development stages was not possible in the past, when information processing technology was not readily available, and when the development of futures markets and other domestic financial institutions that enable unbundling and shifting of risks on a large scale was much more time consuming and costly.

Information technology has also had a major impact on the development of alternative delivery channels for financial products and services. Automatic teller machines, debit cards, telephone and internet banking have become commonplace. The vast majority of banks in the emerging economies believe that they have to offer such services as an essential marketing tool, although the true demand for them has so far been limited.

New technology has affected the structure and performance of the banking industry in particular through its impact on the costs and the determination of optimal scale. For instance, the average cost of an internet banking transaction is one cent compared with about $1.07 for branch-based transactions (Sato, Hawkins and Berentsen, 2000). This cost advantage would seem to favour smaller institutions, as investments needed to attract deposits or provide banking services via the internet are in principle lower than the costs of setting up a traditional branch network. At the same time, investments needed to develop adequate back office and risk assessment systems are very high, creating major cost advantages for larger institutions.

One source of concern related to new banking technology has been the potential for the emergence of a "digital divide" in the access to banking services. According to this view, better educated and more affluent customers will be able to obtain improved service from banks through the internet, while the services provided to poorer and older customers will deteriorate as branches are closed, particularly in remote areas. These concerns have led some policy makers to seek a continued role for the commercial banks that maintain traditional, nationwide branch networks.

Broadening of capital markets

The impact of information technology on the development of financial markets has been most clearly felt in the case of technology firms. These firms are more or less forced to turn to capital markets because traditional methods used by banks (such as benefit-cost analysis) cannot determine the profitability of projects involving new, untried technologies. As a result, since the mid-1990s technology equity markets (like Nasdaq), venture capital funds, corporate bond markets and initial public offerings have seen remarkable growth. At the same time, the relative share of bank loans in overall sources of financing has become smaller (Table 1.1).

Alternative sources of financing have not been limited to "new economy" firms; the more traditional "old economy" sectors are also beginning to exploit them. Bonds outstanding (in domestic and international markets combined) have risen rapidly in almost all emerging economies over the past few years (Mihaljek, Scatigna and

Villar, 2002) and are now more important than borrowing from domestic banks in some of them. Many large firms can now raise funds by issuing securities more cheaply than they can borrow from banks. Indeed, given their better credit ratings many large companies can borrow more cheaply in the capital markets than the banks themselves.

Table 1.1 Sources of finance, 1999 (in percent)

	Euro area	USA	Japan
Equities	21.0	37.6	31.2
Own deposits in banks	23.0	12.9	22.2
Bank loans	29.7	11.3	21.3
Bonds issued	26.3	38.3	25.2
Enterprises	1.0	6.8	2.9
Financial institutions	9.2	10.6	3.8
Public sector	16.1	21.0	18.5

Source: ECB Monthly Bulletin, January 2000.

Alternative funding sources are not open to all companies, in particular small and medium-sized firms. In addition, deep and liquid markets for non-bank funding are not developed in many countries – only the United States has a large market for high-yield corporate bonds ("junk bonds"). Nonetheless, banks are under increasing pressure to keep their customers. To the extent that more and more creditworthy firms turn to alternative funding sources and the proportion of higher-risk bank customers increases, banks are forced to develop techniques for better pricing and provisioning of credit risk.

Shareholder value

In order to approach the capital market and finance new investments, companies have to assure potential investors about their future profitability. Corporations in English–speaking countries have traditionally placed considerable emphasis on profitability and the capital market. However, in continental Europe and Asia, the interests of shareholders have often been of secondary importance in the past. In Germany, Japan and South Korea, for instance, corporate objectives were often agreed jointly by company management, banks, government and unions. The emphasis was often on the growth of export-oriented industries and employment stability. Banks would finance business investments based on long-term relationships and cross-shareholdings, or even at government request (as once in Korea and Japan).

Since the mid-1990s, however, the principle of shareholder value has started to take hold even in countries with bank-centred financial systems. Greater emphasis on shareholder value has forced banks (as well as other private corporations) to reassess their business mix against the criterion of the rate of return, not the volume of business. Focus has been on core competencies and profitability, with business areas not meeting the target rate of return being abandoned and with outsourcing being used to reduce costs. Banks have been affected by this process on several fronts. With customers becoming more cost sensitive, banks have experienced strong pressures on profit margins in traditional banking services. The reshaping of corporate business has further implied that banks had to respond to the changing needs of their customers by providing new services. Corporations have, in turn, been forced to diversify the sources of their finance and to rely less on bank loans and on services of a particular "house" bank.

Risk management

Greater emphasis on profitability has raised banks' awareness of the scarcity of capital, leading to the development of tools that optimize its use and allocation. The concept of risk-adjusted returns has become central in internal decision-making. With greater emphasis on the risk dimension of business, more sophisticated tools to measure and manage risks have been developed.

Major improvements have been made, for instance, in the area of market risk. The existence of comprehensive data and market prices made it possible to quantify market risk with statistical methods and to mark positions to market. The use of these models has led to the development of a quasi-industry standard for the measurement of market risk. These developments have spilled over to the management of credit risk. The portfolio view of risk – ie, that correlations between the risks of individual assets matter – has led banks to devote considerable resources to the development of credit risk models similar to those used for quantification of market risk.

The focus of financial institutions and corporations on optimization of the trade-off between risks and returns, as well as the progress made in risk measurement techniques, have facilitated the development of markets for the transfer of risks. The development of derivative instruments has played a key role in this area. The availability of risk transfer tools has given more flexibility to risk management and has made markets more complete in the sense that market risk can now be transferred independently from other risks not only within the banking system, but also across sectors and to non-bank financial institutions such as insurance companies.

Deregulation and Opening up to Foreign Competition

A key catalyst for increased domestic competition among financial intermediaries has been the removal of ceilings on deposit rates and the lifting of prohibitions on interest payments on current accounts. These deregulation measures have reduced sources of cheap funding for many banks and put pressure on their profits. Intensified competition has made it harder for banks to cross-subsidize different activities and has forced them to price risks more realistically and to charge explicitly for previously “free” services. This has been unpopular and poses considerable public relations challenges for banks. Banks also increasingly face competition from the non-bank financial industry, especially for lending to large companies. In addition, greater emphasis on capital adequacy has encouraged banks to securitize some assets, generate more fee-based income, and try to improve efficiency. In some emerging economies, higher required capital ratios have been an important spur to mergers (or sales to foreign banks) for poorly performing banks, which would have had trouble raising new capital to meet such standards.

At the international level, the easing of restrictions on foreign entry and the search by global institutions for profit opportunities in the emerging economies have led to a growing presence of foreign-owned financial institutions in domestic banking systems. As a result, most emerging economies now increasingly look to foreign banks to provide the capital, technology and know-how needed in banking. These market developments have been reinforced by various measures to open trade in financial services, such as the WTO process and the creation of the single EU market.

Privatization of State-owned Commercial Banks

The main reason for privatization of the state-owned commercial banks has been their poor performance and frequent costly bailouts, resulting from inadequate systems of governance under state ownership. A second reason has been a widely held perception that the presence of state-owned banks tends to hold back the development of the financial sector. Several empirical studies have indeed established that the presence of state-owned banks generally is associated with a lower level of financial development. In particular, Barth, Caprio and Levine (2000) established a negative, statistically highly significant relationship between state ownership of bank assets and several measures of financial development, including bank credit to the private sector, stock market capitalization, and lending to the private sector by non-bank financial institutions. In addition, the degree of industrial competition was found to be lower and net interest margins higher in countries with a large presence of state-owned banks[5].

Although lending by state-owned banks was subject to numerous controls, bank managers never knew exactly who was the real owner of banks and to whom the management was accountable: the central bank, various ministries, or central or local governments. The state-owned banks found it difficult to evaluate the feasibility of projects they were asked to finance and the value of the collateral their customers had to offer. Many problems of the state-owned banks could be further traced to the obligation to lend to local and central governments and to the poor performance of public enterprises, which were the banks' main customers. These enterprises often received extensive credit privileges, being allowed to roll over bank loans and accumulate arrears.

This state of affairs had left the banking systems weak and vulnerable. Not surprisingly, many state-owned banks succumbed to the crises of the late 1980s and the early 1990s. Barth, Caprio and Levine (2000) showed, for instance, that state ownership of banks increased the probability of a banking crisis in the period from the late 1970s to 1999. In response to the disruptions caused by these crises, many emerging economies introduced reforms, first to improve bank governance systems, and ultimately to privatize the state-owned commercial banks (see Box 1.2). Thus, most state-owned banks gained autonomy in formulating their business plans; their boards of directors were reorganized; and new, professional senior management teams were brought in. Industry surveys in general confirm considerable improvements in bank governance as a result of these reforms (see eg Euromoney, 2000).

Box 1.2 Lessons From Bank Privatizations

Although each country had its own motives for privatizing its state-owned banks, the desire to enhance competition and efficiency in the banking sector and the lack of capital formed a background to virtually all privatization programmes. The following is a summary of experiences to date.[6]

The most successful method for privatization of state-owned commercial banks in recent years has been sale to strategic partners, usually reputable foreign banks. Most successful sales were conducted through open competitive bidding processes to ensure transparency in the divestiture of the government's equity holdings. Some privatizations through the sale of shares on the local stock exchanges were also successful. But this method could not be applied to the majority of state-owned banks in a given country because of the lack of solid bank governance systems and experienced management teams who could run the banks efficiently. In addition, the lack of private domestic savings, especially in the aftermath of a crisis, severely constrained the demand for bank equity.

It pays to clean up the state-owned banks' balance sheets and make their operations transparent before they are privatized. Serious investors are not interested in turning to the government after the privatization, and need to know in advance what assets and liabilities they are buying. Privatization should therefore be contemplated as the last – not the first – transaction in the process of restructuring state-owned commercial banks.

A particularly thorny question is the treatment of hidden liabilities (various off-balance sheet items, unfunded pension obligations, tax arrears) and loans that could turn bad at some future date. Potential buyers usually request some form of guarantee or a mechanism that would allow buyers to sell back assets found to be bad during a specified initial period of ownership.

Virtually all the emerging economies (with the exception of Poland) were forced to offer some form of guarantee to pay the cost of any deterioration in selected existing liabilities, a practice known as "ring fencing". (Hungary did not offer any guarantees but the government spent large sums to clean up the banks' balance sheets before the privatizations.) But even with government guarantees, it may take years to clean the state-owned banks' balance sheets of all their "past sins": during 1994–2000, the government of Brazil spent $15 billion (6% of GDP) in order to privatize seven state-owned commercial banks; so far, it has received $6 billion from the privatization of these banks.

Another difficult issue, which arose in particular after the Asian crisis of 1997–98, is how the banks nationalized during a crisis should be run on commercial lines while sustaining efforts to collect on bad loans. The best approach seems to be the implementation of governance reforms that clearly specify the responsibilities and incentives of the boards of directors and the top management teams. Increasing globalization of financial services and continuing development of new financial products suggest that banks need to cope with an ever more competitive environment: temporarily nationalized banks should therefore be returned to private ownership as soon as possible.

Bank privatizations also raise the issue of mechanisms for the residual influence of the state in these large institutions. Some countries have resolved this issue by reserving a certain percentage of shares for the state (eg, 33% in India). In other countries, the state has kept a "golden share" in some large privatized retail banks, ie the power to veto some strategic decisions. In Israel, the government set up a public committee to nominate managers of two banking groups that were privatized in the late 1980s. Both approaches are potentially attractive as they combine the benefits of private ownership and protection from possible disruptive changes in the banks' business orientation. On the other hand, such arrangements could be potentially disruptive for the shareholders and raise questions about continued non-market influences on the commercial decisions of private institutions.

EFFECTS ON BANK REFORMS IN THE TRANSITION ECONOMIES

Changes in the global banking industry and the mixed experience with half-way reforms of the early 1990s had a major influence on the course of bank reforms in the transition economies in the mid-1990s. In particular, it became clear that it was no longer possible to postpone the privatization of large banks if competition, efficiency and the capital base of the banking sector were to be strengthened. These goals, in turn, could not be realized without foreign participation: there were simply not enough domestic sources of capital, management skills and technical know-how to bring about these changes in a reasonable period of time. One after another, transition economies thus shifted the strategy of bank reform toward the privatization of domestic banks, mainly through foreign strategic partners, while continuing to strengthen the supervisory framework and build the financial market infrastructure.

Polish experience provides an interesting case study. Because of the large size of the domestic market, there was considerable interest among foreign banks to establish operations in Poland. The authorities were thus in a position to extract an "entry fee" from foreign banks – they were of the view that foreign banks would have to make a substantial contribution towards the rehabilitation of Polish banks if they wished to gain a foothold in the local market. Foreign banks thus either had to take over an ailing Polish bank or purchase at special terms government securities issued to recapitalize banks. Foreign banks reluctantly accepted this entry fee because they did not want to forego the opportunities offered by the Polish market. Since the mid-1990s, they have thus set up many subsidiaries or have participated in the privatization of the Polish banks by taking up equity shareholdings as strategic investors, sometimes in stages. Some banks were sold through the Warsaw Stock Exchange without gaining a strategic investor. Such banks were subsequently subject to takeovers, which left the government with a lower budget revenue and no influence on the choice of the final owner. As a result, this method was dropped in recent privatizations.

Hungary privatized most banks through sales to strategic foreign partners in the second half of the 1990s. Having cleaned up the banks' balance sheets, the authorities did not ask foreign investors to pay an "entry fee" as in Poland. A total of ten banks were sold through tenders during 1995–2000. The shares of the largest bank were introduced on the stock exchange and subsequently sold to small foreign financial investors, with the state holding only one "gold share" in the bank, giving it veto power over the appointment by shareholders of some executive and supervisory board members.

Another significant development in bank reforms in central and eastern Europe was a wave of mergers and consolidation that started in the late 1990s. Larger countries in central and eastern Europe still have between 20 and 50 commercial banks each, and individual banks are relatively small. Most countries have no dominant bank in the corporate sector and usually one large retail bank with a market share of 20–25%. As building a new branch network has become very costly, both local and foreign institutions have an incentive to engage in mergers and acquisitions. As in industrial countries, these activities have been aimed at exploiting economies of scale and scope, improving organizational efficiency, and achieving a greater market share – some foreign banks consider a 15% market share as a threshold for profitable operation. Although the authorities sometimes promote mergers to strengthen domestic banks or to restructure ailing banks, especially ahead of privatization, bank consolidation in the region has been by and large market driven. This is a new phenomenon in the emerging economies, where most mergers in the past have resulted from government-led efforts to restructure inefficient banking systems (as in many Latin American countries), or from intervention following banking crises (as in Korea and Southeast Asia).

RECENT PERFORMANCE OF BANKING INDUSTRY

Privatization, foreign bank entry, consolidation, and improvements in institutional framework and financial market infrastructure have resulted in deep structural changes in the banking industry in central and eastern Europe. After the initial boom, the number of banking institutions declined sharply in the second half of the 1990s. Even more significant has been the shift in the shareholder structure from the predominantly domestic and state-owned institutions to almost entirely private and foreign-owned banks. By the end of 2002, the share of foreign bank ownership in banking system assets has risen to 75–90% in most countries (one notable exception is Slovenia). More fundamentally, the strengthening of prudential regulations and bank supervision and better bank governance have improved the efficiency of financial intermediation, asset quality and bank performance.

The most significant change in the commercial bank operations has been a rapid increase in the share of lending to households (Table 1.2). The share of credit to businesses has on average declined since 1999, largely reflecting the contraction of credit to state-owned enterprises. Government continues to absorb a large proportion of bank credit in all countries with the exception of Bulgaria, Croatia, Estonia and Poland. However, lending to governments is generally done on commercial terms. Croatia is the only country in the region where the composition of commercial bank lending has evolved closer to that found in mature market economies: at around 45% of total loans, the share of bank lending to households in Croatia is higher than the share of corporate loans, and by far the highest in the region. In the Czech Republic, Hungary, Poland and Slovenia, there are signs that lending to small and medium-sized enterprises (SMEs) is growing rapidly, often under competitive pressure in the banking industry.

Table 1.2 Composition of commercial bank lending[a]

	Government[b]		Corporate		Household	
	1999	2002[c]	1999	2002[c]	1999	2002[c]
Bulgaria	24.9	1.6	65.2	79.2	9.9	19.2
Croatia	6.1	5.9	58.3	48.9	35.8	45.2
Czech R.	5.4	21.2	83.9	60.1	10.6	18.7
Estonia	2.7	6.3	71.8	56.3	25.6	37.4
Hungary	49.0	34.0	43.7	48.0	7.3	18.1
Latvia	12.4	7.2	74.8	74.6	12.8	18.1
Lithuania	29.4	36.5	62.2	53.1	8.3	10.4
Poland	26.8	26.2	47.1	43.8	26.1	29.9
Romania	64.1	23.7	32.1	58.9	3.8	17.4
Slovakia	29.4	47.5	63.5	41.5	7.1	11.0
Slovenia	19.2	21.6	52.4	54.9	28.4	23.5

Notes: [a] In percent of total credit, excluding interbank credit and credit to non-bank financial institutions. [b] Net claims on government. [c] Data for end-2002 or the latest period available.
Sources: BIS; IMF; national data.

However, loans to SMEs are often extended only against guarantees of their foreign production and trading partners. In general, SMEs remain largely cut off from the bank credit and have to finance their operations with internal funds or rely on special government programmes.

Most central banks in central and eastern Europe, especially in EU candidate countries, are nominally independent, and in recent years there have been no signs of open government pressure on central banks to reduce interest rates so as to, for example, facilitate domestic financing of budget deficits. On the contrary, central banks – notably in Poland, the Czech Republic and Croatia – have publicly voiced concerns about the fiscal deficits and the pressure they are exerting on interest rates and exchange rates. The pressure on central banks to reduce interest rates has more often come from various industry groups (exporters, construction and transportation industry, tourism) that have lobbied the government for preferential access to credit. These industries typically invoke job creation as an argument for lower interest rates, but often their objective is to postpone serious restructuring.

Banks in several central and eastern European economies have significantly improved their efficiency in financial intermediation in recent years. This has been reflected in the decline in bank intermediation margins in virtually all the countries in the region since 1999 (Table 1.3). In the Czech Republic, Hungary, Slovakia, Slovenia and the Baltic states, the spreads between short-term deposit and lending rates, as well as between interbank market and lending rates, are already at (or below) the spreads in Austria, Germany and Italy.

This actually raises concerns that competition among banks has resulted in perhaps excessive contraction of intermediation margins, affecting the financial position of banks. This situation is probably untenable in the medium term give the higher efficiency of banks in western Europe.

In Bulgaria, Croatia and Poland the intermediation margins remain high despite large inroads made by foreign banks. This could reflect attempts by foreign owners to recover the costs of internal restructuring. Even after the state cleaned up the banks' balance sheets, foreign owners had to invest heavily in technology and internal reorganization of banks they acquired. In some countries, high margins could also reflect the marked increase in market concentration. Further increases in market concentration cannot be excluded, as mergers between parent banks in the EU are on the rise.

Table 1.3 Bank intermediation margins

	Lending minus deposit rate		Lending minus interbank rate	
	End 2002[a]	Change since end 1999	End 2002[a]	Change since end 1999
Bulgaria	7.1	–1.4	6.6	–2.6
Croatia	6.9	–1.4	7.9	–0.4
Czech R.	2.5	–1.4	1.1	–1.0
Estonia	4.1	–2.2	4.1	–1.3
Hungary	2.5	–1.0	0.7	–0.2
Latvia	3.5	–4.9	3.4	–6.5
Lithuania	4.2	–0.7	5.0	–3.8
Poland	5.9	–1.0	2.3	–1.3
Slovakia	4.2	–2.3	1.4	–3.4
Slovenia	3.9	–0.7	7.2	–1.5
Austria	3.2	–0.0	2.7	0.4
Germany	3.7	–0.2	3.2	0.0
Italy	4.4	0.4	2.9	0.6

Note:[a] Or the latest period available.
Sources: IMF; national data.

Different stages of banking system reform are reflected in asset quality and other prudential indicators. Compared with industrial countries, non-performing loans (NPLs) are still very high in most central and eastern European economies (Table 1.4). The share of NPLs was reduced in several countries that faced severe banking crises a few years ago (Bulgaria, Croatia, the Czech Republic, Latvia, Slovakia, Romania), but remain unchanged or increased in other countries, often reflecting cyclical developments (as in Poland). The largest share of NPLs in these economies is in the loss category.

Despite large write-offs, the share of this category in total NPLs has been more or less unchanged since 1999, suggesting that new NPLs have moved into loss status.

The high level of NPLs has partly reflected the constraints in legislation – often motivated by tax revenue considerations – that do not allow banks in some countries to write off bad loans quickly. Provisioning for loan losses has nevertheless improved in many countries, but remains low in Hungary, Slovenia and Slovakia.

Table 1.4 Prudential indicators for the banking sector

	Non-perform. loans[a]		Capital adequacy[b]		Loan-loss provisions[c]		Return on assets	
	1999	2003[d]	1999	2003[d]	1999	2003[d]	1999	2003[d]
Bulgaria	29.0	5.5	43.0	25.2	79.3	74.3	2.5	2.1
Croatia	10.3	5.4	20.6	16.9	78.6	64.2	0.8	1.7
Czech R.	21.9	9.4	13.6	14.1	52.3	80.2	-0.3	1.1
Hungary	3.5	2.6	14.2	11.1	52.6	53.8	0.6	2.0
Estonia	4.0	0.9	16.1	14.6	118.3	106.7	1.5	1.5
Latvia	6.2	2.0	16.4	13.1	87.9	95.5	1.0	1.5
Lithuania	12.5	5.3	17.4	14.5	...	...	0.5	1.6
Poland	13.2	17.2	13.2	15.0	104.4	102.0	1.6	0.9
Romania	0.7[e]	2.3	42.7[e]	25.0	...	...	1.5[e]	1.6
Slovakia	23.7	11.0	29.5	21.1	6.4	2.5	-4.0	1.2
Slovenia	5.2	6.5	14.0	11.9	44.6	39.1	0.8	0.4

Notes: [a] As percent of total loans. [b] Risk-weighted capital-asset ratio. [c] As percent of non-performing loans. [d] Data for the first half of 2003 or the latest period available. [e] Data for end 2000.

Sources: Central bank publications and websites; IMF country reports.

Capital adequacy ratios have remained high, especially in countries with more vulnerable banking systems in the recent past (Bulgaria, Romania, Slovakia). In the Baltic states and Hungary, banking supervision has been strengthened even before foreign banks took over ownership of much of the banking system.

As a result, the need to maintain very high capital ratios has diminished, and capital adequacy ratios have declined slightly. Trends in bank profitability were mixed until 2001 and difficult to interpret, as banking systems in some countries that reported high rates of return on assets or very high capital, also had a high share of non-performing loans. But since 2002 there has been a clear improvement in bank profitability in almost all countries in the region. Austrian banks, for instance, derive 30–70% of their pre-tax profits from their activities in central and eastern Europe even though the banks they own in this region represent less than 5% of their total assets.

It should not be forgotten that improvements in the banking sector have came at a very high price for many countries in the region. The total costs of bank restructuring and deposit compensation over 1991–98 in Bulgaria, Croatia and the Czech Republic exceeded 25% of GDP (Table 1.5). Only part of this cost has been recuperated from privatization proceeds.

Table 1.5 Estimated cost of bank restructuring and deposit compensation[a]

	Cost for the government	Cost for the central bank	Total cost
Bulgaria	26.0	11.8	37.8
Croatia[b]	...	...	29.0
Czech R.	20.9	4.8	25.7
Hungary	12.9	0	12.9
Poland	2.4	0.5	2.9
Baltic states[c]	2.3	0.4	2.7

Notes:[a] In percent of GDP, cumulative cost over 1991–98; estimates by Zoli (2001), with the exception of Croatia. [b] Estimates by Babić, Jurković and Šonje (1999) and Vujčić (2001). [c] Average for Estonia, Latvia and Lithuania.

SOME OPEN ISSUES

Despite considerable improvements in banking sector efficiency and stability, there have been lingering concerns about the desirability of bank privatizations and the strong presence of foreign banks in central and eastern Europe. The background of most of these concerns is that governments fear to lose influence over the development of their domestic economy if one of the key sectors is no longer under their control, or to a large extent in the hands of foreign owners. These concerns, however, fail to consider some important aspects of bank governance and performance.

Policy makers in central and eastern Europe and the emerging market economies in general no longer see a useful role for the state-owned commercial banks. Even for development banks, there is a strong preference for institutions pursuing a clear function in an area of market failure. Such banks are increasingly asked to finance themselves by issuing bonds rather than taking deposits. Sometimes, commercial banks are used on a contract basis as distribution channels for state housing and agricultural programmes. Private banks often find this intermediary role profitable, as they assume no credit risk on their own. But there are a few special cases where the state-owned banks are seen as institutions playing a useful role.

In some large countries (eg Russia), only state-owned banks seem to be willing to serve customers in remote areas. Nevertheless, some countries (including Poland and China) see cooperative banks and credit unions as a better alternative to state-owned banks in serving customers in remote areas.

Some countries (eg Thailand, Brazil and Argentina) also see a continued role for the state-owned banks as a conduit for lending to farmers and small and medium-sized enterprises outside large cities. The reason is that the government is often better able to administer specific lending programmes if it owns the banks that provide subsidized loans. In Chile, however, private banks have performed better than the state-owned banks in supplying credit to the small and medium-sized enterprises.

There are some indications that lending by the state-owned commercial banks is less pro-cyclical than lending by the private domestic and foreign banks. During recent recessions in the Asian and some Latin American emerging market economies, state-owned banks expanded credit faster (or cut credit to a smaller extent) than domestic and foreign-owned private banks (see Hawkins and Mihaljek, 2001). This finding could have policy implications for small open economies, where the scope for anti-cyclical policies is generally limited.

In smaller economies domestic capital is limited, so there is a tendency for foreign capital to dominate the privatisation of banks. This may create a backlash against foreign ownership and privatisation in general. There have also been cases (Czech Republic, Hungary, but also Brazil) where the banks' balance sheets had to be cleaned up in order to attract serious foreign investors. Therefore, continued (but temporary) state ownership of banks may in some cases be preferable to quick privatisation.

In some less developed countries the lack of basic market and legal infrastructure may be so severe as to make market failure pervasive and the state-owned commercial banks the only viable alternative. In Russia, for instance, private banks were financially too weak and too small in the aftermath of the 1998 crisis, so only state-owned banks were in a position to provide loans of meaningful size and offer security for household deposits.

While accepting the state ownership of banks as a second best solution, policy makers have nonetheless found it useful to subject the remaining state-owned commercial banks to market discipline and treat them like all other banks from a supervisory perspective, requiring, for example, full monthly disclosure of their operations. In most countries, however, state-owned commercial banks are seen as institutions distorting competition in financial markets. It has been argued in particular that the state-owned commercial banks underprice risk in areas where political leaders want to encourage economic development (or benefit their supporters), and create unfair competition because public shareholders normally do not require the same rate of return on their capital as private investors. Implicit or explicit government guarantees are also seen as a form of unfair competition vis-à-vis the private banks. These factors have induced the European Commission to take action and convince governments in the European Union to reduce implicit or explicit government guarantees. As a result, some EU countries, including Germany, are expected to see a major restructuring of their banking industry in the years to come.

Regarding foreign ownership of banks, the relevant question is what makes a bank a domestic bank. One possible answer is the location of its headquarters. However, most large international banks have more assets, make more profits, and employ more staff in countries outside their home country. Another possible consideration is the nationality of the bank's owners. However, banks whose shares are listed on several stock exchanges have shareholders in a large number of countries; hence, it is often not possible to tell whether the majority of shareholders come from a country where the bank's headquarters is located. Clearly, none of these criteria can be used to distinguish between foreign and domestic banks. It follows that arguments against foreign-owned banks are more emotional than rational. International banks have recognized these concerns and most of them are investing through local vehicles and local brand names, seeking both to exploit customer loyalty and avoid antagonizing local nationalist sentiments. Another reason for this approach is that it enables international banks to focus their "brand name" activities on large financial centres and reduce the number of locations in which they are present.

One concern in this area is that the consolidation of the banking sector and the reengineering of banks' business profiles have led to the emergence of some large complex institutions that act on a global scale. Size and complexity of their business, which often includes banking, securities trading and insurance, is increasingly becoming a concern for central banks, governments and regulators. Moreover, in many emerging economies consolidation and the presence and importance of foreign banks have generated, or may generate over time, a degree of concentration that may raise systemic concerns. There are also concerns about supervision of large branches of foreign-owned banks, which are systemically important in some Baltic countries. Supervisors from the region are therefore increasingly seeking cooperation from their counterparts in EU countries.

NOTES

1. Senior Economist, Bank for International Settlements, Basel, Switzerland. E-mail: Dubravko.Mihaljek@bis.org. The views expressed in this paper are those of the author and do not necessarily represent those of the BIS. An earlier version of this paper appeared in proceedings of the conference *Participation, Stabilisation, Development* (University of Zagreb, Faculty of Economics, September 2002). Helpful comments from Josef Tošovský are gratefully acknowledged.
2. This box draws on Mihaljek (1990).
3. The following insights come from the work of Gligorov (1989).

4. This section draws on the work of Hawkins and Mihaljek (2001), pp. 3–6.
5. The latter relationships were not statistically highly significant, however. The results were obtained after controlling for differences in the level of economic development (measured by real per capita GDP) and the quality of government (measured by a composite index of expropriation risk, the law and order tradition of the country, and the level of corruption).
6. This box is based on Hawkins and Mihaljek (2001), pp. 11–14.

REFERENCES

Babić, Mate, Pero Jurković and Velimir Šonje (1999), 'Banking system development in Croatia', *Zagreb Journal of Economics*, **3**, 75–113.

Barth, James, Gerard Caprio and Ross Levine (2000), 'Banking systems around the globe: do regulation and ownership affect performance and stability?', *World Bank Policy Research Working Paper*, no. 2325.

Berliner, Joseph (1976), *The Innovation Decision in Soviet Industry*, Cambridge: MIT Press.

ECB Monthly Bulletin, January 2000.

Euromoney (2000), 'Banks in Eastern Europe', September.

Falkner, S.A. (1924), *Problemy teorii i praktiki emissionnogo khoziaistva*, Moscow: Ekonomicheskii zhizn.

Garvy, George (1977), *Money, Financial Flows, and Credit in the Soviet Union*, Cambridge: Ballinger.

Gligorov, Vladimir (1989), 'Socijalizam i novac: geneza i priroda sukoba', in Ante Čičin-Šain (ed.), *Financijska Struktura i Monetarni System*, Zagreb: Ekonomski institut, 6–56.

Greenspan, Alan (2000), 'Revolution in information technology and its implications for key government policies', *BIS Review*, **21**, 1–4.

Hawkins, John and Dubravko Mihaljek (2001), 'The banking industry in the emerging market economies: competition, consolidation and systemic stability: an overview', *BIS Papers*, **4**, 1–44.

Katzenellenbaum, S.S. (1925), *Russian Currency and Banking, 1914–1924*, London: King and Son.

Mihaljek, Dubravko (1990), 'On the sequencing of economic reforms in socialist countries: a fiscal view', in Dubravko Mihaljek, *Essays on the Fiscal Aspects of Economic Reforms in Developing and Socialist Countries*, unpublished PhD Dissertation, Pittsburgh: University of Pittsburgh, Department of Economics.

Mihaljek, Dubravko, Michela Scatigna and Agustin Villar (2002), 'Recent trends in bond markets', *BIS Papers*, **11**, 13–41.

Novozhilov, Viktor (1924), 'Politika cen, emissionie potrebnosti i emissionnie vozmozhnosti', *Vestnik finansov*, **11**.

Novozhilov, Viktor (1925), 'Problemi kreditnoy emissii', *Vestnik finansov*, **4**, 29–45.

Novozhilov, Viktor (1926), 'Nedostatok tovarov', *Vestnik finansov*, **2**, 75–96.

Sato, Setsuya, John Hawkins and Aleksander Berentsen (2000), 'E-finance: recent developments and policy implications', Paper presented at the Brookings Institution conference *Tracking a Transformation: E-commerce and the Terms of Competition in Industries*, Washington, 27–27 September.

Tošovský, Josef (2001), 'Banking in central and eastern Europe', speech delivered at *Frankfurt European Banking Congress 2001*, Frankfurt am Main, 23 November.

Vujčić, Boris (2001), 'Managing capital flows in Croatia: experiences, problems and questions', Paper presented at the ICEG/Ford Foundation conference *Managing Capital Flows in Eastern Europe*, Budapest, 19–20 October.

Zoli, Edda (2001), 'Cost and effectiveness of banking sector restructuring in transition economies', IMF Working Paper no. 01/157.

2. Deepening Financial Intermediation in the New Europe: The Role of Banks

Anna Pilková[1] and Viliam Pätoprstý[2]

INTRODUCTION[3]

Banking sectors in the New Europe (NE) countries[4] played a significant role in their process of transition from centrally planned to fully market oriented economies. After more than ten years of transition, however, the financial sectors in NE countries still seem to remain underdeveloped, at least in terms of size. Despite the previous expectations, banks still seem to play a smaller role in their national economies, administering fewer deposits and providing fewer credits than banking systems in traditional market economies (Rother [1999], p. 3).

Although playing a smaller role in general, some authors[5] proved that financial development (regardless of being bank-based or market-based) generally has a positively correlation with economic growth. It is also important that simultaneity bias or reverse causality does not drive these results (Beck et al. [2000], p. 21). However, the question still remains whether different measurement of financial development (or intermediation deepening) can effect the relative positions of banking sectors in individual countries.

From conducted empirical- and literature-based analysis, it is well known that over the first transitional phase of their development, NE banks fulfilled "modified" traditional functions which were connected with taking higher risk than is usual for commercial banks (e.g. participating in the financing of privatization processes, the start-up of SMEs, etc.) mainly due to the non-establishment of other institutions and relevant funds. This approach was subsequently reflected in the banks' results and the worsening of business conditions – particularly for smaller borrowers. As a counterbalance, banks started to finance public debt, which in contrast represented zero risk, but contributed to a crowding-out of bank-dependent borrowers and the enlarging of the gap between NE and developed banking system intermediation functions.

GOAL AND METHODOLOGY OF THE CHAPTER

The financial intermediation level (as subsequently defined) varies from country to country based on its historical development prior to the establishment of a centrally planned economy, as well as economic and social development over recent decades. To define 'financial intermediation level' is a prerequisite for understanding the real role of banks in NE countries, and the term does not fully correspond to the structure of intermediation in EU countries (Dinger [2002]). Due to this fact, an alternative approach was used to measure the effective role of banks in NE that better reflects the local economic conditions.

The main goal of this paper was therefore to prove the hypotheses, that:

- the real effective role of the financial sector[6] in NE, as measured by alternative approaches, varies from its traditionally expressed position in comparison to the level in Eurozone countries,
- the development of effective intermediation, over recent years, has shown significant deepening.

A cross-country analysis has been performed comparing the twelve NE countries and Eurozone countries over the 1995-2002 period.

Financial intermediation is measured differently across various sources – from the mostly used definition of banking assets to GDP (Dinger [2002]); to broad money or credits to GDP (King and Levine [1992]); broad money multiplier and credit to the private sector over monetary base (Rother [1999]); or banks claims to GDP (Riess et al. [2002]), among others. The most common traditional financial intermediation calculation includes banking sector Assets to nominal GDP, Loans to nominal GDP, and Deposits to nominal GDP. Let us define these as Assets intermediation level (AIL) or Total intermediation, Loans intermediation level (LIL) and Deposits intermediation level (DIL).

In line with the goal of this paper, we choose to utilize intermediation measurements, which could better reflect the real economic conditions in the countries in question. To stress the influence of the major factors, which differentiate the developing and developed economies (and to make a comparison), we adopted two approaches – traditional (as described above), and effective. Therefore we have:

- defined indicators of effective intermediation basically aimed at the ability of the banking sector to use the really-available macroeconomic potential to increase the level of banking intermediation, without any reference to P&L development,
- adjusted the overall assets intermediation for the purposes of the explanation of balance sheet structure and total intermediation level was therefore called Effective assets intermediation level (EAIL). In the case of DIL and LIL, the traditional denominators of value added have been replaced by alternative indicators creating Effective loans intermediation level (ELIL), and Effective deposits intermediation level (EDIL). Equations, as well as their economic explanations, are presented below in the corresponding parts of the chapter in order to be more coherent with the explanation of the results,
- used only officially recognized data sources in all calculations, i.e. the International Monetary Fund, Eurostat, and national central banks,
- observed the period 1995-2002 due to the limited availability of coherent data series in the previous periods. 1995 was – in most NE countries – the first year in which summary data for the whole banking sector in a suitable structure (including segments) started to be published. As some of the countries in question only had data for the 1997-2002 period, aggregated NE vs. EU-12 comparisons have only been performed for the 1997-2002 period,
- grouped countries based on geographic location due to better graphic explanation. Baltic countries therefore include Estonia, Latvia and Lithuania. Central European countries are Czech Republic, Hungary, Poland, Slovakia and Slovenia. And the South East European countries of Bulgaria, Croatia, Romania and Turkey.

FINANCIAL INTERMEDIATION AND THE ROLE OF BANKS

The fundamental traditional role of banks is to promote economic growth through the arrangement of effective intermediation of resources between two major players: households and businesses. This core idea that constitutes the raison d'être for the banking sector has also been followed here, when calculations have been made separately for corporate and retail sectors.

As evidenced later, the structure of banking sector balance sheets in NE contrasts with that in developed countries. The NE has different built-in factors, which influenced its basic banking functions, mainly over the period of the banking sector's transition in comparison to developed countries. The significances of these factors are country-variable and mainly depend on a country's stage of development at a particular time.

The main factors that influence these differences result from the macroeconomic environment, own history, historical roles and events such as restructuring, recapitalization, and privatization that affected such countries' respective development over the last ten years. Those factors also have to be reflected in approaches towards financial intermediation measurement. In line with applied methodology, the traditional approach uses generally extended methods of intermediation, while the effective approach is based on quantifying the utilization of economic potential by banking systems in NE. By comparing results from the traditional and effectiveness-based approaches, we expect to obtain outcomes that prove the sensibility of the relative role of banking sectors with respect to the factors, which create major differences between the two systems (developed and developing) from the intermediation point of view.

Traditional Approach

Total intermediation

In terms of the development of intermediation level in NE countries, a moderate increase in financial intermediation occurred in NE countries with AIL growing from 68% in 1997, to 71% in 2002 (Figure 2.1). A relatively sharp increase was recorded in Estonia and Latvia, while stagnation was generally recorded in Central European as well as South Eastern countries (except Croatia). In the same five-year period, banking sectors in the Eurozone recorded a profound increase of intermediation by 33 p.p. to 269%.

Deposits and loans intermediation

As seen in Figure 2.2 (due to better graphic explanation, countries are again grouped based on geographic location), banking sectors in the Czech and Slovak Republics, as well as Croatia, Slovenia and Estonia are the leaders in traditional financial intermediation within NE. Considering the development of intermediation in the period 1995–2002, practically all the banking sectors deepened their intermediation level (despite several restructuring processes and other data distorting elements in many countries). Over the same seven-year period, seven of the twelve countries became stronger in deposit collection compared to loan granting, resulting in a total of ten of the twelve countries being stronger in deposit intermediation. This development is better illustrated by the aggregated NE data (see Figure 2.12) and is basically a reflection of the restructuring processes on credit markets after the period of credit boom in the early 1990s.

From the profit point of view, there was consequently a domination of deposit interest rate spreads in most of the NE countries during this period. This reflected the increased propensity towards banking sector activities on the deposit side, logically accompanied by low deposit interest rates (as most of the emerging economies did not provide alternative investment asset opportunities with comparable risk for households and corporate sector).

The average domination of deposit spreads during the period represents approximately 150% (ratio of weighted deposit spread over weighted lending spread)[7].

Accordingly to the development on the lending side (mainly the bad condition of the corporate sectors and bad experience from the early transition period), the banking sectors started to be more heavily engaged in the financing of public sector needs. While in the Eurozone countries the ratio of claims towards central government to claims towards the private sector hardly reaches the 21% level (even in countries with high public indebtedness it is no more than 52%), NE countries are above the 67% level showing a clearly higher dependence of banks on state refinancing (despite having no difficulties with high public indebtedness on the country level in NE countries)[8]. The average growth of the indicator in the second half of the observed period vis-à-vis the first half represented 37%. Figure 2.3 shows the development of the above stated ratio in the period of 1995-2002 showing the different trends in particular countries. While some countries such as Turkey, Slovakia and the Czech Republic[9] showed a high share of engagement in the refinancing of the state, others – mainly Estonia, Latvia and Croatia – showed an opposite trend.

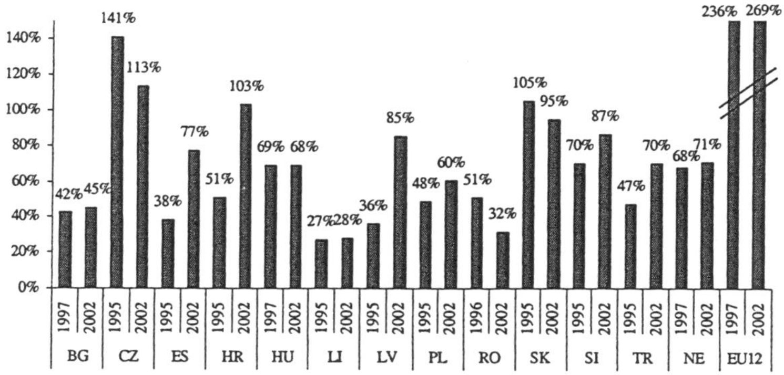

Notes: Bulgaria (BG), Czech Republic (CZ), Estonia (ES), Croatia (HR), Hungary (HU), Lithuania (LI), Latvia (LV), Poland (PL), Romania (RO), Slovakia (SK), Slovenia (SI), Turkey (TR), New Europe (NE), Eurozone (EU-12).
Sources: National central banks, International Monetary Fund (IMF).

Figure 2.1 Financial intermediation development – AIL in NE countries and EU-12

Considering the above stated argument on economic structure, where a significant part of the assets of the financial sectors in central Europe is being allocated in state and central bank liabilities, this has to be regarded in the structural development of financial intermediation.

While the financing of the state is generally fully connected with the refinancing of public debt, sterilization by central banks is also being performed due to the inability of the corporate sector to absorb the liquidity in the banking sectors[10] (i.e. those being in better condition). Both T bonds (or T-bills) as well as transactions with central banks are often crowding out the usually more effective private investments by means of relatively high yield at zero default risk. As credit crunch in several countries led to massive over-liquidity of the sectors, national central banks were acting as “liquidity sterilizers” preventing huge interest rate drops on one hand, whilst – in our opinion – on the other hand contributing towards slower credit activity.

Another feature of NE banking sectors is the stock of non-performing loans in total assets showing the past default rate of banking investments. Although the average NPL ratio recorded a decrease from 5.9% in 1997 to 4.7% in 2002, in NE countries (excluding Hungary) some countries, such as Croatia, Czech Republic, Poland, Slovakia and Turkey, still showed an NPL ratio exceeding the 10% level at the end of 2002.

Effectiveness-based Approach

Considering the effective growth potential of the banking sector, an underdevelopment can be observed in practically all absolute macroeconomic variables in NE countries compared to the EU (or Eurozone) level. As previously mentioned, with regards to the economic environment in which the banking sectors in NE are present, we have approached an alternative measuring of financial intermediation in NE that reflects the economic potential and netting from what we can call the “cost of transition”.

Total intermediation

Methodology Under the cost of transition in the case of assets intermediation, we mainly understand the dependence of banking sectors on central banks and refinancing of the state, as well as the high stock of non-performing assets. These are the direct effects of the high amount of risk being accepted in the previous – early transition periods.

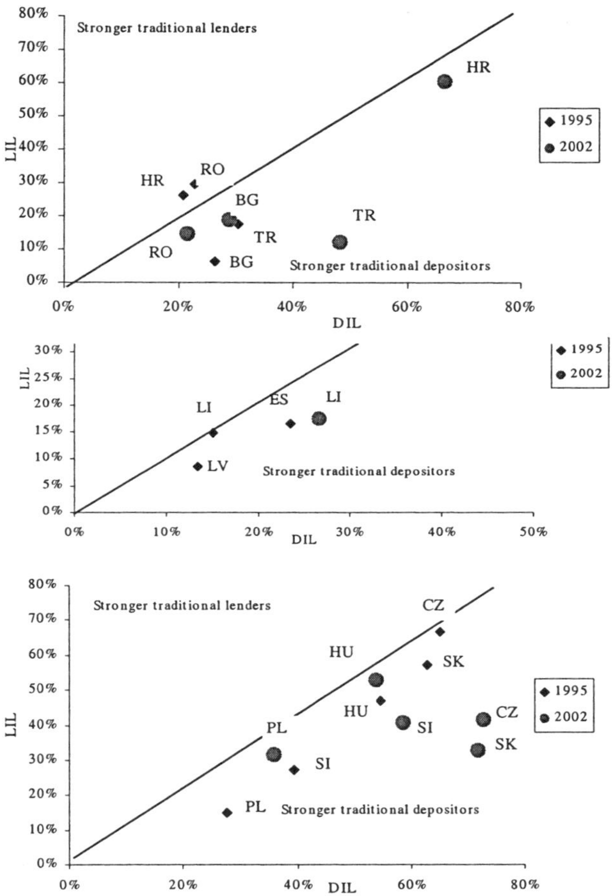

Notes: Countries are grouped based on geographical key. Hungary and Bulgaria data for 1997-2002, Romania 1996-2002. The authors do not mean to express that loan intermediation shall be equal to deposits intermediation.
Sources: National central banks, IMF.

Figure 2.2 Financial intermediation – LIL vs. DIL in NE countries in 1995 and 2002

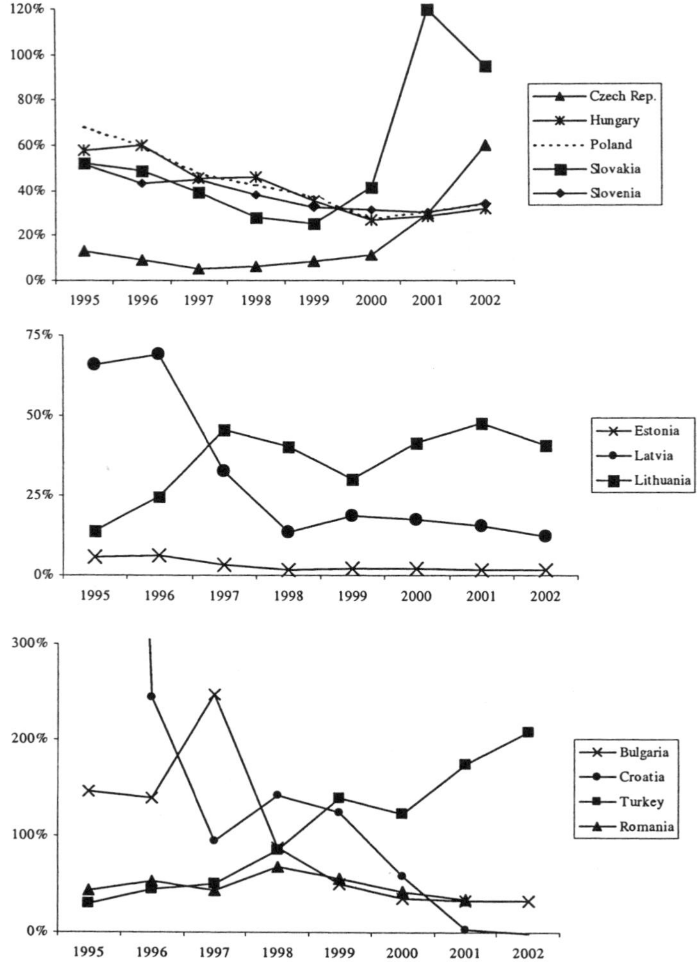

Notes: Countries are grouped based on geographical key.
Source: IMF.

Figure 2.3 Ratio of claims to central government over claims to private sector in NE countries

Let's analyze the real role banks are playing in financial intermediation on their assets side, which is expressed through the adjustment of total assets from claims towards government, central bank and non-performing investments. Effective assets intermediation level (EAIL) would then be as follows:

$$EAIL = (TA - SIS - SCB - NPL)/GDP \qquad (2.1)$$

where TA is Total assets, SIS is Securities issued by state in the assets of local banks, SCB is Sterilization of central banks[11], NPL is Gross non-performing loans, and GDP is Nominal gross domestic product. Focusing on the methodology, 3 points should be mentioned:

- Comparing gross NPL to net assets is certainly not fully precise, however it does enable us to see the actual generation of bad debt and solves the issue of different regulatory practices in terms of provisions creation in different NE countries.
- Possible difference in (national) accounting standards applied in NE countries might cause a certain bias in the results (this issue is also present in traditional approaches). To exclude this problem, a microeconomic approach by calculations would be necessary – summing up all available banks in IAS (Dinger [2002]). This would, however exclude the possibility of comprehensive coverage of whole banking sectors.
- As the effective intermediation ratio is a synthetic value (this is mainly important for loan and deposit intermediation indicators) comparing the absolute value of effective and traditional indicators for each country in the same time period does not make any economic sense. What is, however, important is the change in the multilateral position of countries (e.g. on the scatter graph) when adopting different approaches (as the calculation formula was homogenous for all countries).

From the effective approach, particularly in the case of asset intermediation, we might rather expect a clearer deepening in time compared to EU-12 than a decreasing of the gap between EU and NE over the same time period. This is a logical consequence of netting from transition impact, which tends to be close to zero in EU-12.

Outcomes As also seen in Figure 2.4 that shows traditional and effective financial intermediation in NE countries, the position among countries in assets intermediation has not changed rapidly after adopting the effective approach. However, it is significant that countries leading in intermediation level – the Czech Republic, Slovakia and Croatia – lost much of their intermediation performance outstrip when measured effectively, compared to the rest of the countries (see also Figure 2.6). This is particularly important when considering the future sustainability of high intermediation level in these countries with obvious impacts on the P&L's of stated banking sectors.

With regards to the development in Eurozone, the New Europe banking sectors recorded a significant AIL gap increase (where the gap represents the difference between the intermediation level of Eurozone and NE) of 30 p.p., as in Figure 2.5. At the same time, due to the aforementioned reasons, the gap in EAIL marked a growth of 44 p.p., thereby contradicting the hypothesis on the relatively higher effectiveness of assets intermediation and the mainly positive development of EAIL in NE countries over recent years. There may be several reasons for this relatively unexpected development – to mention a few:

- bad prior experience in investing in higher risk instruments of corporate sector,
- higher prudence of new owners (after the privatization process) when banks were still operating in a relatively high risk environment that led to higher state-financing involvement,
- restructuring process (accompanied by stagnation of lending activity) hand in hand with increased household spending propensity (heavily fueled by imported goods), which was contributing to the significant slow-down of deposits growth in some countries, followed by the slow-down of balance-sheet growth,
- a methodology-based reason may also be the change in the foreign currency structure of assets, where increasing inclination towards EUR (ECU) was negatively influenced by the €/$ exchange rate development. In this case, a 21% appreciation of the USD over this

5-year period contributed to the slow-down of growth, as all calculations were made in USD.

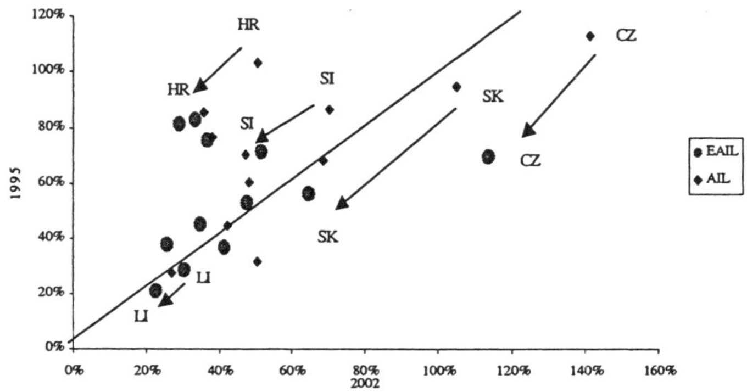

Notes: Hungary and Bulgaria data for 1997 and 2002, Romania 1996 and 2002.
Sources: National central banks, IMF.

Figure 2.4 Effective vs. traditional assets intermediation level in different NE countries

Broken down into the particular NE countries, the in-time shift of the difference between AIL and EAIL (difference in percentage points) was mainly increasing in Turkey and the Czech and Slovak Republics. This means that the banking sectors in these countries were experiencing (due to the above stated reasons) a slow-down of effective intermediation compared to the traditional one.

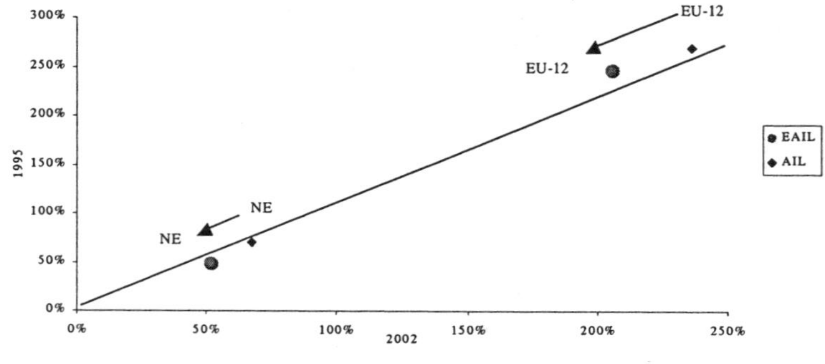

Source: National central banks, IMF.

Figure 2.5 Traditional and effective assets intermediation level in NE and EU-12

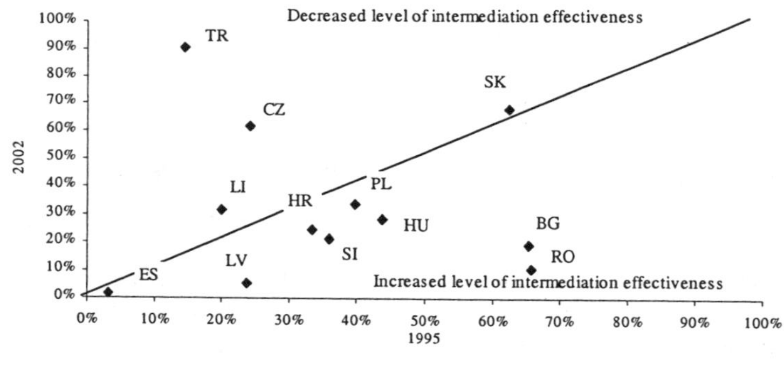

Notes: Hungary and Bulgaria data for 1997 & 2002, Romania 1996 & 2002.
Source: National central banks, IMF.

Figure 2.6 Development of shift in AIL and EAIL difference in NE countries

Loans intermediation

Methodology Considering the benchmarks for the future development of loans and deposits, an alternative macro-oriented approach was also considered, reflecting the potential of banks to grant loans and gather deposits explained by the ability of individuals and corporate entities to repay loans and store their cash-flow in banks.

Based on the 2000 Eurostat data regarding household income distribution among European regions[12] published in 2003, we can clearly observe that considering the NE primary income per capita in PPCS[13], this reached 23%-52% of the EU level. Consequently, the growth potential gap of the banking sector on the retail side contracted (Figure 2.7).

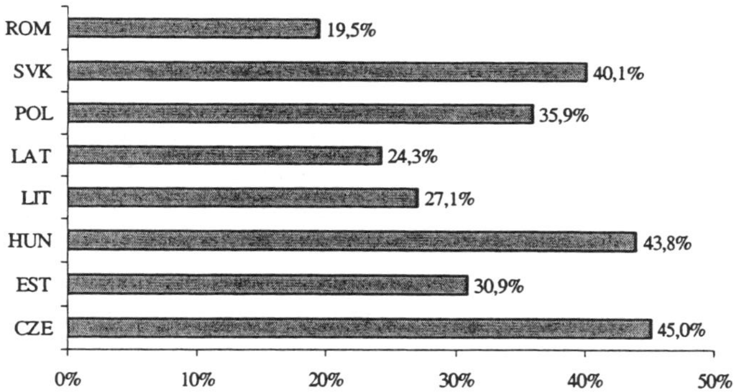

Note: Average of EU 13 (i.e. EU excl. AUT and LUX) is equal to 100.
Source: Eurostat.

Figure 2.7 Primary income per capita in PPCS in selected NE countries (2000)

Whilst assuming the growth potential of the financial sector on the retail side, we have to keep in mind that the transition period accompanied by the transfer of wealth from corporate (or state and common ownership, irrespectively) to private ownership is being characterized by lower labor productivity and generally lower labor intensity of the production. Considering that the average ratio of primary income per capita in PPCS to GDP per capita in PPCS represents 72% in EU countries, excluding Austria and Luxemburg, while reaching from 54% in Lithuania to 66% in Poland (with five out of eight NE countries under 60%), we approximate the average over-estimation of retail potential by using the GDP in traditional intermediation denominator to be at 20% in all NE countries (including those not included in Eurostat data). This leads us to the assumption to use the accumulated income of individuals serving to repay loans in a certain period as a benchmark of measuring the effectiveness of using the loan absorption capacity of retail customers by the banking sector. Therefore we defined the retail[14] part of Effective loans intermediation level (ELIL), as follows:

$$ELIL\ retail = TRL / (AMI * AMRL * NE) \qquad (2.2)$$

where TRL is Total gross retail loans, AMI is Average monthly income, AMRL is Average maturity of retail loan, and NE is Number of employed.

This equation serves as a certain simplification, as it abstracts from the income different than of labor activity origin[15]. It also defines the average maturity of retail loans with rather an expert estimate (in this case it is important that this indicator should be constant for all the countries in order to create a unified benchmark). For the purposes of this calculation, we defined the average retail loan maturity as 60 months.

For the activities of banks on the corporate[16] side, we used an approach of measuring the corporate lending activity with investments in the economy over a certain period, explained by gross capital formation. This abstracts from the bridge and revolving loans potential, serving to refinance financial costs or temporary cash-flow volatility. However, in our opinion, it enables an explanation as to the "growth-driven" need for bank-based refinancing.

The corporate part of Effective loans intermediation level is defined in the following way:

$$ELIL\ corporate = TCL / (GCF * AMCL) \qquad (2.3)$$

where TCL is Total gross corporate loans, AMCL is Average maturity of corporate loan, and GCF is Gross capital formation at current prices[17].

As on the corporate side, the ability to repay the loan is not in correlation with past income, instead it is a mixture of past ability to repay the loans and the rentability of future investments, the logical point of the benchmark (denominator) is different in retail and corporate financing. The AMCL indicator has been estimated at the level of four years, applicable to all the NE countries. Considering the total ELIL, we defined it as the sum of retail and corporate ELIL:

$$ELIL = (CLEU*ELIL\ corporate) + (RLEU*ELIL\ retail) \qquad (2.4)$$

where CLEU is Share of corporate loans in total loans in EU-12, and RLEU is Share of retail loans in total loans in EU-12. Distribution of loans between segments in the Eurozone has been considered as the benchmark NE is likely to be converging to and therefore is used in the calculation.

Outcomes As seen in the results, a different scenario occurred among particular countries during the observed period. While on the retail side, all NE countries achieved significant progress (though still being relatively low in terms of stock), corporate lending activities, being traditionally more spread, recorded stagnation due to contraction in lending activity in the Czech and Slovak Republics, Romania, and Turkey. In the observed period, EU-12 itself recorded a significant increase of intermediation on the retail side. The highest increase in retail loan activity was achieved in Croatia; this was mostly caused by an artificially low official employment rate (representing only half of the Eurozone level). However, the share of retail loans over total loans is also high, almost double that of the rest of NE.

Similarly to asset intermediation, a comparison of the traditional and effective approach was also adopted in lending activity. Figure 2.8 reveals the position of particular NE countries after applying the aforementioned approaches. For the selected countries it is clear that the absolute highest shifts are being achieved by leading traditional intermediation countries. As described above, this is only significant with regard to the change in the positions of countries. The multilateral positions of banking sectors have, however, not changed significantly after applying the effective-based approach.

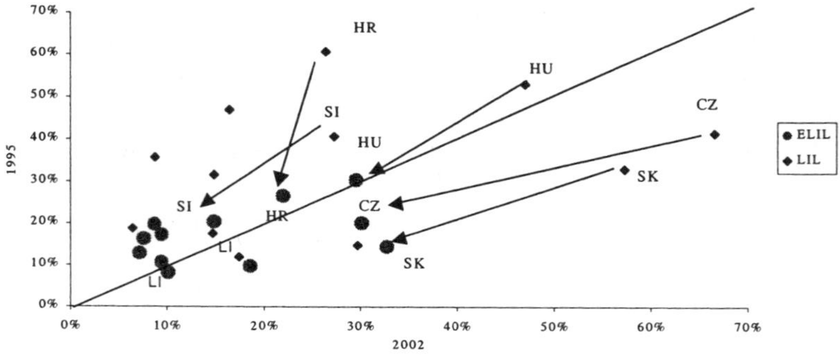

Notes: Hungary and Bulgaria data for 1997 and 2002, Romania 1996 and 2002.
Sources: National central banks, IMF.

Figure 2.8 Effective vs. traditional loans intermediation level in different NE countries

Focusing on the in-time shift of difference between ELIL and LIL, Figure 2.9 reveals that some countries, particularly Czech Republic, Turkey, and Romania lowered their absolute difference between traditional and effective loans intermediation level over the observed period. This means the effective intermediation was growing more quickly than was traditional, i.e. the banking sectors were more effectively gaining their disposable capacity with a dynamic exceeding the traditionally expressed intermediation growth.

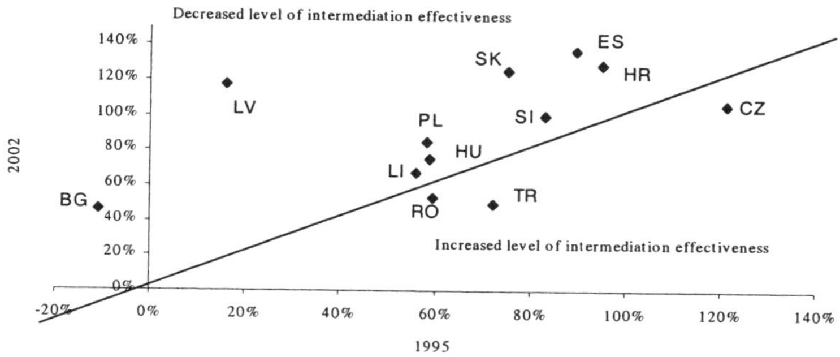

Notes: Hungary and Bulgaria data for 1997 & 2002, Romania 1996 & 2002.
Source: National central banks, IMF.

Figure 2.9 Development of shift in LIL and ELIL difference in NE countries

Deposits intermediation

Methodology Considering the intermediation level of deposits, similar alternative approaches have been used, individually for retail and corporate deposit activities. As for retail deposits, we can consider them to be accumulated mostly from the income of the working population adjusted by current transfers from abroad (cash principle), thereby the Effective deposits intermediation level (EDIL) of retail can be described as follows:

$$EDIL\ retail = TRD / ((AMI * NE * ASP) + NCTA) \qquad (2.5)$$

where TRD is Total retail deposits; AMI is Average monthly income; NE is Number of employed; ASP is Average savings period and NCTA is Net current transfers from abroad. The synthetic indicator of ASP has been considered to be twelve months.

We realize that focusing only on deposits intermediation (particularly in the case of NE) creates certain bias in terms of not covering relatively significant increases of assets managed by banks (usually mutual funds) in some NE countries. These are off-balance items for banks and can be considered both banking as well as capital market intermediation – for this reason we have not included them, although they absorbed relatively significant amounts of former retail deposits (mainly after stronger interest rate drops and legislative standardization of capital market activities).

On the corporate side, a gross value added approach has been used (similar to the traditional expression of intermediation level) with adjustment to the remaining external position of the country not included in the GDP structure (i.e. balance of payments deficit/surplus less net exports of goods and services less net transfers from abroad). The EDIL indicator thus intends to also cover net capital flows in the country, creating a possibility of the banking sector administering not only locally produced but also imported values. The corporate Effective deposits intermediation level can then be defined as follows:

$$EDIL\ corporate = TCD\,/\,(GD - (BP{-}NX{-}NCTA)) \qquad (2.6)$$

Where TCD is Total corporate deposits; BP is Deficit/Surplus in balance of payments; NX is Net exports of goods and services (already included in the calculation of GDP).

Analogically, aggregated EDIL involves EDIL of corporate and retail weighted by the breakdown of segments in EU-12. The aggregated EDIL and EDIL rate indicators are then described by the following equations:

$$EDIL = (CDEU{*}EDIL\ corporate) + (RDEU{*}EDIL\ retail) \qquad (2.7)$$

where CDEU is Share of corporate deposits in total deposits in EU-12; and RDEU is Share of retail deposits in total deposits in EU-12. Distribution of loans between segments in EU has been considered as a benchmark NE is likely to be converging to, and therefore is used in the calculation.

Outcomes With the exception of Romania and Hungary, all NE countries achieved growing dynamics of effective intermediation level in retail deposits and at the same time all NE countries increased their effective intermediation level in corporate depositing in the observed period (see Table 2.1). The 2002 gap (in relative expression) between NE and EU-12 (see also Figure 2.12) in effective intermediation level of deposits (58%) is significantly lower compared to the gap in effective intermediation of loans (193%).

Considering, again, the positions of particular banking sectors in DIL and EDIL indicators (Figure 2.10), most differences occurred in the multilateral positions compared to Assets and Loans measurements, where the labor cost differences among countries represented the main driver of different relative positions of countries after applying two approaches (e.g. Slovakia).

For in-time shift of difference in EDIL versus DIL, Turkey, Estonia and Latvia increased their effectiveness while Romania marked a drop (Figure 2.11). Countries in the negative quadrants still had a negative shift, which means that compared to other NE countries their ratio of effective to traditional intermediation remained higher.

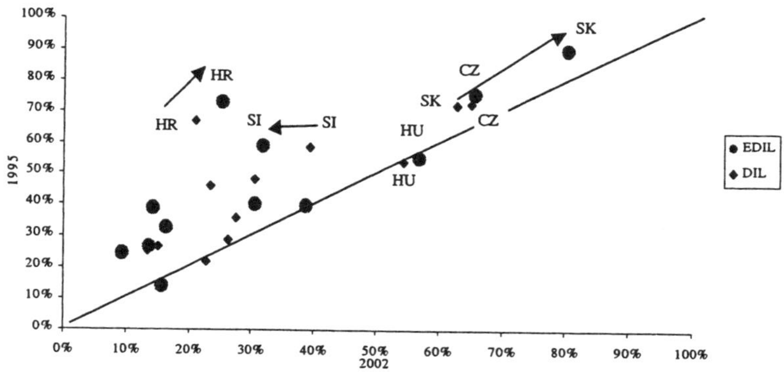

Notes: Hungary and Bulgaria data for 1997 and 2002, Romania 1996 and 2002.

Source: National central banks, IMF.

Figure 2.10 Effective vs. traditional deposits intermediation level in different NE countries

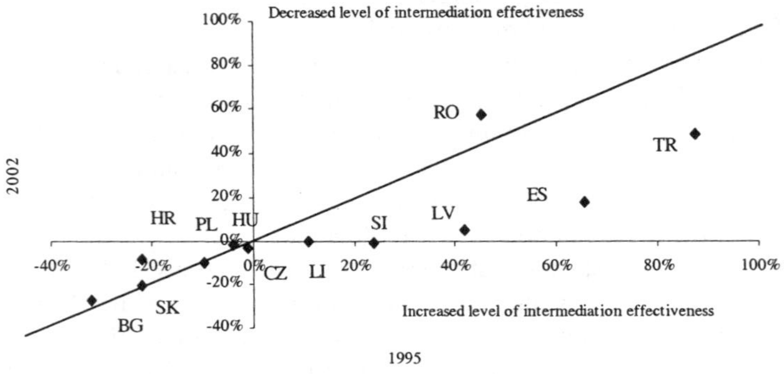

Notes: Hungary and Bulgaria data 1997 and 2002, Romania 1996 and 2002.
Source: National central banks, IMF.

Figure 2.11 Development of shift in DIL and EDIL difference in NE countries

CONCLUSIONS

When generally summing up the results of measuring effective and traditional intermediation in NE countries and Eurozone, 3 the main groups of observations can be stressed thus:

- Measuring total intermediation level (Assets intermediation level), banking sectors in New Europe underwent a surprisingly low increase in the period 1997-2002 growing by only 3 p.p., while even decreasing by 4 p.p. when measured effectively due to the growing engagement of refinancing state debt. In the same period, Eurozone recorded an increase in total intermediation level by 33 p.p. and effectively 40 p.p. This indicates that banking sectors in New Europe were for various reasons not fully able to utilize high economic growth (which was on average three times higher in NE than in EU-12 in this period) to sharply increase their intermediation level. However, there are differences among NE countries in the development of total intermediation. While the Baltic countries, Bulgaria, Croatia, Slovenia, Poland, and Turkey recorded an increase in total traditional intermediation, the remaining countries recorded a drop in intermediation prevailingly due to external reasons (restructuring process, changes in accounting standards, etc.).

- Different results were obtained when measuring the intermediation level on the side of loans. While, similarly to total assets, traditional intermediation level of loans in NE dropped from 32% to 30% over 1997-2002, measured effectively, the level of effective loans intermediation remained unchanged at 16% while in EU-12 it only recorded a 1 p.p. increase to 48%. The absolute gap between EU-12 and NE in traditional intermediation is thus in relative expression higher than in effective intermediation. This can be explained by a relatively better ability of NE banking sectors to effectively utilize the real potential for lending activities in comparison to utilizing the potential of refinancing whole value added in the economy, if EU-12 was set as a benchmark (see Figure 2.12). Increasing engagement in financing retail activities in all NE countries in the observed period mainly backed this enhanced ability. Comparably to total (assets) intermediation, multilateral positions of NE countries have not changed significantly, when approaching traditional or effective measurement.
- The main differences occurred when observing the development of deposit activity in particular NE banking sectors. In the traditional, as well as effective approach, NE countries were experiencing growth of deposit intermediation. The DIL indicator increased by 7 p.p. over 1997-2002 while growing by 2 p.p. in Eurozone. In effective expression, EDIL increased by 11 p.p. while growing by 7 p.p. in Eurozone. At the same time, in stock expression NE was much closer to EU-12 level in deposits collection than it was in lending activities, even consolidating this position over the observed period. Different labor cost levels and an inclination towards bank depositing on the retail side mainly drove shifts of multilateral positions among countries.

The conducted analysis in our opinion proved that the real effective intermediation level in NE is relatively higher if it was measured in the traditional way (compared to EU-12 level). This is particularly valid for lending and depositing activities. This can be explained by the more effective use of the reachable potential of local economic environments in NE than is traditionally considered. Due to the different structure of the assets side with a high presence of elements which could be considered minor in EU-12 banking sectors, the total intermediation level proved to be low in NE when measured by either approach.

Focusing on the change of mutual positions among countries of NE after applying the traditional followed by the effective approach, no radical shifts occurred, with only some exceptions in deposit activities. This can be generally explained by the comparably level effective use of the potential for growth of intermediation among NE countries. However, as evidenced from the in-time shift of the difference between the traditional and effective approaches for particular countries, the shift is generally much more contracted on the deposit side than on the lending side. For a final qualitative distribution of particular NE countries, and a focus on the strengths and weaknesses of the most and least developed banking intermediaries in NE, see Table 2.1.

Considering the deepening of the intermediation level that the analysis was to evidence, with the exception of depositing activities, the intermediation level marked stagnation or even decline over the observed period. Clear evidence of deepening was, however, observed in retail activities.

Any traditional or alternative approach, however, that reveals the level of intermediation on a quantitative basis is certainly far from being suitable to cover the immense qualitative changes that the banking sectors in NE were facing, particularly after the entry of foreign players. Qualitative intermediation deepening mainly involved the increasing number of financial products and the quality of supplied services. Empirically, we therefore have to state that despite the absence of clear signals to suggest the sharp increase of the overall quantitative intermediation level in NE, banking sectors undoubtedly underwent significant improvements in qualitative indicators.

Table 2.1 Final positioning of NE banking sectors in stock and dynamics of intermediation

"Defenders"	"Forwards"	"Restructurers"		"Mid-fielders"
Intermediation NE level	Over NE	Over NE	Under NE	Under
Intermediation Negative dynamics	Positive	Negative	Postitive	
Countries	Croatia Estonia Latvia Slovenia	Czech Rep. Hungary Slovakia	Bulgaria Lithuania Poland	Romania Turkey

Note: Intermediation level compared to New Europe average. For decision on intermediation deepening at least two of EAIL, ELIL, EDIL indicators had to record deepening in the observed period.
Source: Authors' calculations based on national CB and IMF data.

From the above stated conclusions, we assume two basic outcomes might be generally applied when considering the quantitative level of financial intermediation in transition (or post-transition) countries in the future:

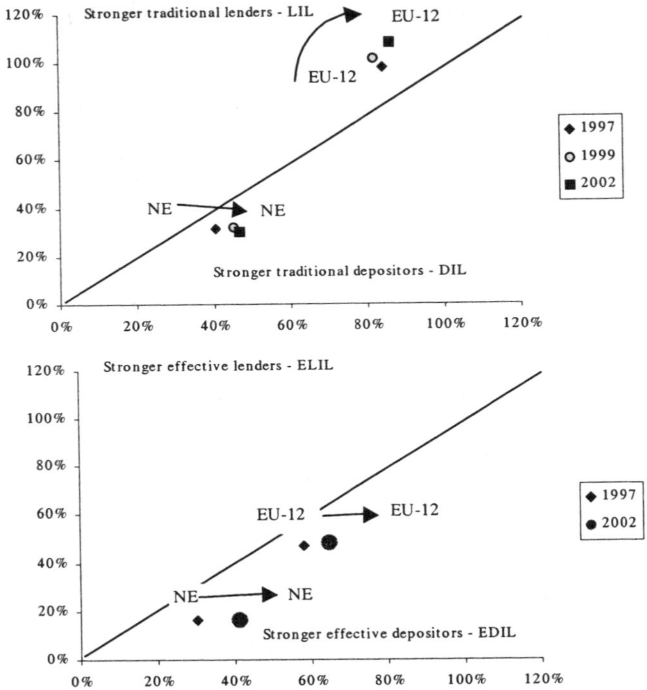

Sources: National central banks, IMF.

Figure 2.12 Comparing position of NE and EU-12 banking sectors in two approaches

- Considerably lower level of accumulated wealth in NE countries, combined with relatively high involvement of foreign capital in value added production[18] and the standardization of credit scoring procedures enables a better expression of the intermediation role of banks when considering the achievable potential rather than the pure value-added based target;

- Due to the process of property possession changes and increasing penetration in the non-banked population, the intermediation level in the transition countries of NE is deepening more significantly in the retail (households) segments than the corporate segments – both in loans as well as deposits.

NOTES

1. Deputy CEO of UniBanka and former associate professor at University of Economics, Bratislava, Slovakia. E-mail: pilkova@unibanka.sk.
2. Chief economist at Economic research of UniBanka, Slovakia. E-mail: patoprsty@unibanka.sk.
3. The opinions expressed herein are those of the authors and do not necessarily reflect the opinion of the institutions which they represent. The authors would like to thank Silvia Ferenecová and Ľubomír Koršňák for their help during writing of the paper. The authors would also like to thank Dubravko Mihaljek for his comments and suggestions. Any errors or inaccuracies are the full responsibility of the authors.
4. Includes Bulgaria, Croatia, Czech Republic, Estonia, Hungary, Lithuania, Latvia, Poland, Romania, Slovakia, Slovenia, and Turkey (the latter included for the purposes of the chapter although it has developped differently past). On the banking sectors in these countries see Haque et al. (1999), Moskow (2001), Thimann. et al. (2002), Ickeset et al. (2003)
5. See e.g. Beck et al. (2000), Levine, Loayza, Beck (2000), Demirgüç-Kunt, Aslı, Huinzinga, Harry (2000), Demirgüç-Kunt, Aslı, Levine Ross (2001) Levine and Ross (2002),
6. For the purposes of this chapter under financial sector we understand aggregated banking sector in the particular country.
7. Authors' calculation based on IMF data.
8. With the exception of Turkey all NE countries have been under the Maastricht criterion of 60% for public debt over GDP ratio (2002).
9. In the Czech Republic and Slovakia due to restructuring process where bad loans to private sector have been replaced by state bonds.
10. Due to different reasons but mainly the inequality of creditworthiness and loan risk premium accepted by the clients.
11. Involves net claims towards CB (excluding required reserves fulfillment)
12. Measured in 13 EU countries, and the Czech Republic, Estonia, Hungary, Lithuania, Latvia, Poland, Slovakia, and Romania.
13. Purchasing power purchasing standard – for detail see Behrens (2003).
14. Retail is equal to all individuals excluding private entrepreneurs.
15. Social contributions are considered to be – to a large extent – covered by the calculi due to the redistribution of tax duties involved in the gross monthly income. Therefore the bias especially applies to financial incomes and rents.

16. Corporate is equal to residual from retail (i.e. Core corporate, Financial sector different from banks and Public Administration). Claims towards banking institutions are excluded – both in loans as well as deposits.
17. Similar approach used by Schardax and Reininger (2001) using δ of corporate loans over gross fixed capital.
18. Foreign owners tend to withdraw (repatriate) capital yields not only via dividend policy but also through internal transfer pricing, managerial and consultancy fees, as well as costs of intra-company lending, thus creating fewer opportunities for domestic banking systems.

REFERENCES

Beck, Thorsten; Demirgüç-Kunt, Aslı; Levine, Ross; Maksimovic, Vojislav (2000), 'Financial Structure and Economic Development: Firm, Industry and Country Evidence', The World Bank.

Behrens, Axel (2003), 'Income of Private Households and Gross Domestic Product in Europe's Regions', *Statistics in Focus*, **7**, Eurostat.

Demirgüç-Kunt, Aslı; Huinzinga, Harry (2000), 'Financial Structure and Bank Profitability', The World Bank.

Demirgüç-Kunt, Aslı; Levine Ross (2001), 'Bank-based and Market-based Financial Systems: Cross-country Comparisons', The World Bank.

Dinger, Valeriya (2002), 'The Banking Sector of the EU Accession Countries from Central and Eastern Europe: Size and Development', ZEI Center for European Integration Studies, University of Bonn.

Haque, Nadeem U.; Hauswald, Robert B.H.; Senbet, Lemma V. (1999), 'Financial Market Development in Emerging Economies: A Functional View', International Monetary Fund.

Ickes, Barry W.; Hagen, Juergen von; Traistaru, Julia (2003), 'Central and Eastern Europe: Economic Developments, Reforms and Geography', *The Global Competitiveness Report 2002-2003*, Oxford University Press.

King, Robert; Levine, Ross (1992), 'Financial Indicators and Economic Growth in a Cross Section of Countries', The World Bank.

Levine, Ross (2002), 'Bank-based or Market-based Financial Systems: Which is Better?', National Bureau of Economic Research.

Levine, Ross; Loayza, Norman; Beck, Thorsten (2000), 'Financial Intermediation and Growth: Causality and Causes', *Journal of Monetary Economics,* **46** (1).

Moskow, Michael H. (2001), 'Financial Infrastructure in Emerging Economies,' *International symposium: Banking in Emerging Markets.*

Riess, A.; Wagenvoort, R.; Zajc, P. (2002), 'Practice Makes Perfect: a Review of Banking in Central and Eastern Europe', *EIB Papers.*

Rother, Philipp C. (1999), 'Explaining the Behavior of Financial Intermediation: Evidence for Transition Economies', International Monetary Fund.

Schardax, F.; Reininger, T. (2001), 'The Financial Sector in Five Central and Eastern European Countries: An Overview', Oesterreichische Nationalbank.

Thimann, Christian et al. (2002), 'Financial Sectors in EU Accession Countries', European Central Bank.

3. Financial Structures and Private Sector Development in the New Europe

Francesca Pissarides[1]

INTRODUCTION

In the wake of the 2004 enlargement of the European Union, increasing attention from both current and future member countries is placed on the ability of the enterprise sector to withstand competition in the single market. As all future member countries now comply with the 'acquis communautaire', the set of rules by which each new member must abide in order to join the union, and, as stated by the European Commission in the last of its regular reports[2], transition to a market economy is now complete, it would be easy to jump to the conclusion that the enterprise sector in new member countries is indeed able to withstand competition in the single market.

To reinforce this impression, data on the allocation of resources in the countries of the New Europe[3], reflecting the advancement of transition, show the private sector as the major driver of the economy. The development of the private sector, however, appears to have been mostly a result of a shift in resource from state to private hands through privatization, rather than of a healthy development of new privately-owned enterprises.

Through the use of both aggregate data on the enterprise sector and results of enterprise surveys, the chapter attempts to shed light on the fragilities and weaknesses characterizing the sector and on the type of investment climate obstacles to its development. It does so analysing the problem from the enterprise sector point of view: enterprise survey data on access to finance used for fixed investment or for working capital are used to assess the extent to which existing enterprises are supported by the financial sector. The question of access to finance and of which sources of finance are available to the enterprises is analysed both in general terms for the sector and in relation to the different size of firms.

The analysis then shifts to the other side of the coin, the financial sector, and investigates the extent to which it responds to the development needs of the local private enterprise sector and in particular to the financial requirements of micro-, small- and medium-sized enterprises (MSMEs) in the New Europe.

The chapter discusses informally various characteristics of the banking sector in the region to gain an understanding of its relation with the enterprise sector.

The chapter is structured as follows. The second section describes the development of the private sector in the new Europe. It compares the state of development of enterprises and MSMEs in the new and the old Europe. The third section uses enterprise survey data to highlight those aspects of the investment climate which mostly hinder the development of the enterprises sector, with particular attention to enterprises at the low end of the enterprise size spectrum. The fourth section analyses the way in which the financial sector addresses the needs of the enterprise sector. It looks at the characteristics of the banking sector in particular and at how these affect the degree of intermediation of savings and the most recent trends in bank lending. The fifth section concludes.

PRIVATE SECTOR DEVELOPMENT

Over the past twelve years countries in the new Europe have experienced impressive growth of their private sector, both thanks to the privatization, restructuring and liquidation of state assets and to the birth and entry and development of new enterprises. The share of private sector in GDP has increased on average from 11 per cent in 1989 to 73.2 per cent in 2002 according to EBRD estimates (Table 3.1). With the progress of transition from command to market economies, the private sector has increasingly become the driver of growth.

The increase in the size of the private sector is not necessarily a sign of a healthy enterprise sector[4]. Most of this increase can in fact be attributed to a shift of production from state-owned enterprises to privatized enterprises, rather than to the creation and growth of new enterprises[5]. Whereas growth of the private sector was very rapid in the first half of the 1990s, it has slowed down considerably in the past few years, with the near completion of privatization in most cases and reflecting difficulties in the further development of the enterprise sector.

A comparative analysis of enterprise data for the New Europe and the EU regions sheds some light on the real weight of the private sector by highlighting the fragilities and rigidities of this relatively new sector of the economy. Data on the enterprise sector in the countries of Central and Eastern Europe are poor and problems of different definitions, collection and aggregation methods make the inter-country comparison difficult.

Table 3.1 Percentage share of private sector in GDP, 1989-2002

	1989	1995	1999	2000	2001	2002
Bulgaria	10	50	70	70	70	75
Croatia	15	40	60	60	60	60
Czech Republic	5	70	80	80	80	80
Estonia	10	65	75	75	75	80
Hungary	5	60	80	80	80	80
Latvia	10	55	65	65	65	70
Lithuania	10	65	70	70	70	75
Poland	30	60	65	70	75	75
Romania	15	45	60	60	65	65
Slovak Republic	5	60	75	80	80	80
Slovenia	10	50	60	65	65	65

Source: EBRD.

Table 3.2 contains the latest available data on the SME sector in the New Europe (as collected by the EBRD through surveys of local statistical offices) and the EU-19 region[6] (European Commission, 2002c).

The data highlight similarities and differences between the two regions. As in the EU-19 area, SMEs dominate to a high degree the enterprise sector in terms of number of units in the New Europe countries. They also account for a similar share of employment in the enterprise sector on average (63 per cent), although some exceptions are noted, with the Hungarian, Slovakian and Slovenian large enterprises being larger employers in relative terms than the large enterprises in the EU and the rest of the New Europe.

Table 3.2 Data on SMEs [a] in the New Europe and EU-19, 2000-2001

	Number[b]	Empl.[b]	Turnv.[b]	Exports/Turnv.[b]	Av. size SMEs	Av. size all enterps.	Date
	In per cent						
Bulgaria	99.7	64.7	62.8	na	4.8	7.3	2000
Croatia	99.1	67.2	na	na	10.6	15.6	2000
Czech Republic	99.8	60.8	na	na	2.2	3.7	2001
Estonia	99.5	74.5	80.2	89.6	9.2	12.3	2000
Hungary	99.6	55.4	39.6	45.3	4.4	7.9	2000
Latvia	99.3	69.8	75.5	na	10.5	15.0	2001
Lithuania	95.6	na	39.0	56.6	na	na	2000
Poland	99.8	65.5	na	na	4.0	6.1	2000
Romania	99.7	71.2	55.9	62.6	8.0	11.2	2001
Slovakia	99.0	54.1	46.0	60.2	2.8	5.1	2000
Slovenia	98.9	54.4	64.5	58.7	9.3	16.8	2001
Europe-19	99.8	66.4	54.5	76.5	4	6	2000

Notes: [a] SMEs are defined as enterprises with fewer than 250 employees except for Lithuania where SMEs are enterprises with fewer than 50 employees. Data for Croatia, the Czech Republic, Poland and the Slovak Republic include sole proprietors and data for the Czech Republic also include farms.

[b] The number of SMEs, the associated employment, turnover and exports in turnover are expressed as a percentage of the same values for the enterprise sector as a whole in each country.

Sources: EBRD and European Commission.

Performance of the SME sector measured in terms of turnover is comparable to the performance of SMEs in the EU-19 except for Hungary, Lithuania and Slovakia for which lower values than the EU benchmark are recorded. In terms of export performance of the SME sector measured by the share of exports in turnover, only Estonia does better than the EU-19 countries, with the worst performing country being Hungary. The consistent underperformance of the SME sector in Hungary can be explained with the unique (in the region) pattern of privatization adopted. Hungary privatized very early on through direct sales to foreign investors while other countries in the region privatized through vouchers and/or internal buy-outs. This generated a mainly foreign-owned large enterprise sector in Hungary which underwent significant and early restructuring and is well performing and responsible for most export capacity, differently from the other New Europe countries. On the other hand, the Hungarian SMEs did not attract significant FDI and thus lagged behind the large enterprises in terms of restructuring and performance.

The largest differences between the New Europe and the EU-19 region, as well as the largest variations across countries, can be observed however in the average size of enterprises and in the average size of SMEs. Only Polish, Hungarian and Bulgarian SMEs approach in size the average size of EU-19 SMEs. All other New Europe countries have relatively larger SMEs than the EU-19 region, with the exception of the Czech Republic where average size of SMEs is low at two employees[7].

As for the average size of enterprises in general, only Poland and the Slovak Republic approach the average size of enterprises in the EU19. The rest of the group shows high variance in the average size of enterprises. Part of this variance might be explained with differences in the definitions used in collecting data (i.e. whether only non-primary enterprises are included, like in the EU-19 region, and whether sole traders are included). Part of this reflects however differences in the creation of enterprises (privatization and spin-offs versus almost completely start-ups in the EU-19 region) and progress with restructuring (at different stages in the New Europe countries).

The European Commission (2002c) attempted a standardization of SME data over time and across countries. It found that during the second half of the 1990s the average enterprise size has been decreasing overall in the New Europe while it has remained constant in the EU. The largest decrease in enterprise size was observed in Hungary, whose overall investment climate is among the best in this group of countries. Other findings include the fact that most enterprises in the service sector are still engaged in trade and retail, rather than in the sophisticated more advanced services common in the EU. Also, enterprises in the manufacturing sector are smaller, younger and less experienced than in the EU's manufacturing sector. Survival rates are relatively low for enterprises in the New Europe.

INVESTMENT CLIMATE

Entrepreneurs in transition countries generally face a number of problems both in their efforts to set up business and in their daily activities. They face a larger number of obstacles in their attempts to expand, in addition to or on a much larger scale than obstacles faced by entrepreneurs in market economies. Entrepreneurs in transition face additional obstacles in areas such as regulation, taxation, finance, corruption, functioning of the judiciary and crime. These obstacles, normally clustered together as different aspects of the investment climate, decrease in number and intensity with the introduction and effective implementation of market reforms and with the development of market institutions.

Despite the advanced stage of reform of the countries in the New Europe area, as compared to countries in the rest of the transition region, the investment climate is not yet sufficiently conducive to enterprise growth. The New Europe investment climate is characterized by remaining market imperfections and still developing market economy structures. In some cases the investment climate impediments are compounded by inappropriate economic policies, targeted at short-term objectives rather than at the maximization of the long-term growth potential of these economies. These factors affect growth mainly by stunting the development of the enterprise sector.

Enterprises in the New Europe area also face a relatively more unstable macroeconomic environment than enterprises in advanced market economies do. Despite the good progress made in terms of economic stabilization, the countries in line for accession to the European Union face some years of increased uncertainty. The increased volume of portfolio flows expected to enter these countries, if on one hand beneficial and necessary to support their growth, is likely to bring in additional volatility. The conflicting objectives of tightening the fiscal position while at the same time increasing the already high investment ratios, and of maintaining competitiveness while at the same time experiencing the real exchange rate appreciation pattern of economies converging towards a richer neighbour, are also likely to cause further instability.

Evidence of the presence of impediments to the growth of the enterprise sector can be gauged by analysing data from targeted enterprise surveys. During the past decade, a large number of enterprise surveys has been carried out in the region with the purpose of reaching a better understanding of the difficulties met by enterprises in their day to day operation and in their growth efforts. For consistency sake, this chapter looks at the results of the EBRD/World Bank-led 1999-2002 Business Environment and Enterprise Performance Survey (BEEPS). The EBRD jointly with the World Bank launched the BEEPS in 1999[8]. The BEEPS asks enterprises to assess the extent to which the business environment creates obstacles to the operation and growth of their businesses. In 2002, a second stage of the BEEPS was undertaken, surveying close to 6,000 firms[9] across 26 countries of the region. As the BEEPS was run simultaneously in all countries surveyed, it is possibly the best comparative tool for assessing the business environment available in the transition region. However, as the business cycle appears to have a strong impact on the perception of the business environment, the comparison of the entrepreneurs' responses over time and across countries was carried out after isolating from the qualitative assessment of the business environment the influence of the business cycle. The statistical adjustments carried out[10] resulted in a data set which allows comparisons over time and across countries of the entrepreneurs' perception of the business environment as if all countries had the same economic performance.

Entrepreneurs were asked to rate those aspects of the business environment which they consider to be obstacles to their day to day activities and to the expansion of their companies (from 1 = no obstacle to 4 = major obstacle). The areas of the business environment which they were asked to rate were the access to finance, the state of infrastructure, taxation (tax rates and tax administration), the regulatory environment, the functioning of the judiciary, crime and corruption.

Table 3.3 Average rating of obstacles to doing business, 1999 and 2002

1999	Fin.	Infrastr.	Tax.	Reg.	Judic.	Crime	Corrup.
Bulgaria	2.9	2.3	3.0	2.2	2.3	2.7	3.1
Croatia	3.1	1.9	3.3	1.4	2.5	2.1	2.8
Czech R.	2.4	2.5	3.3	1.8	2.2	1.9	2.2
Estonia	2.4	1.6	2.7	1.1	1.8	1.6	1.7
Hungary	3.0	1.6	3.1	2.4	2.0	2.1	2.5
Latvia	2.6	2.1	3.2	1.8	2.4	2.1	2.6
Lithuania	2.5	1.8	3.3	1.6	2.3	2.2	2.3
Poland	3.0	1.7	3.2	2.3	2.4	2.5	2.7
Romania	3.0	2.5	3.3	1.4	2.3	2.0	2.2
Slovak R.	3.3	1.9	2.9	1.9	2.2	2.5	2.8
Slovenia	2.9	1.8	2.9	2.2	2.4	1.8	2.2
2002	Fin.	Infrastr.	Tax.	Reg.	Judic.	Crime	Corrup.
Bulgaria	2.9	1.2	2.4	1.7	2.0	2.1	2.2
Croatia	2.5	0.9	2.2	1.7	2.4	1.5	2.0
Czech R.	2.5	1.0	2.4	1.7	1.7	1.7	1.6
Estonia	2.1	1.4	2.0	1.8	1.7	1.7	1.6
Hungary	2.4	0.9	2.4	1.6	1.3	1.3	1.6
Latvia	2.0	1.7	3.0	2.1	2.0	1.8	2.2
Lithuania	1.9	1.6	2.8	1.7	2.3	1.9	2.1
Poland	3.0	0.7	2.9	2.0	1.9	1.9	1.9
Romania	2.7	1.6	3.0	2.0	2.5	1.9	2.7
Slovak R.	2.6	1.0	2.3	1.9	2.2	1.8	2.1
Slovenia	2.1	0.7	1.7	1.4	1.6	1.1	1.3

Source: EBRD.

As can be observed in Table 3.3, the overall perception of the business environment has improved in the region, as individual areas of the business environment are generally rated as less severe obstacles in 2002 than they were in 1999. Estonia, which had the best perceived business environment in 1999, had the second smallest improvement in 2002, after Romania. Hungary, with the fifth best business environment in 1999, made most progress by 2002, when its business environment was second only to Slovenia's.

The area of the business environment in which by far and without exception the largest improvement was perceived by entrepreneurs is the state of infrastructure. This is positively correlated to the progress made in terms of privatization and liberalization of the utilities in the New Europe countries in the 1999-2002 period, as measured by the EBRD "transition indicator for infrastructure" for these countries[11]. Taxation is also perceived uniformly as a lesser problem for business than it was in 1999. In other areas of the business environment exceptions to the overall improvement are recorded. A worsening in the perception of the severity of corruption as a business obstacle in 2002 is recorded in Romania and (minor) worsening of the perception of the effect of crime on business is noted in Estonia. The functioning of the judiciary negatively affects business in Romania and Slovakia more than it did in 1999. The regulatory environment appears to hinder business in five countries (Croatia, Romania and the three Baltic countries) out of eleven in a more severe way in 2002 than it did in 1999. Poor access to finance also appears to constrain Czech and Polish enterprises in their day to day activities and in their efforts to expand more in 2002 than it did in 1999. Correlation of the difference in the perception of the financial constraint with progress in banking reform as captured by the EBRD "transition indicator for banking reform and interest rate liberalization" between 1999 and 2002 is positive but small.

In relative terms finance also went from being on average the second most severe obstacle to business (after taxation) in 1999 to being on average the most binding constraint for enterprises (if size class is taken into consideration then the constraint is more binding for SMEs than for large enterprises) in the Central and Eastern European region. Exceptions are Latvia and Lithuania, where finance comes fourth in 2002 versus third and second respectively in 1999.

The financial constraint affects entry, development and growth of small enterprises all over the world. However, because of the poor level of development of the financial sector in the New Europe as compared to western economies and because of the relatively higher risk aversion of New Europe's banks, the severity of this constraint is much stronger in the New Europe region than in advanced market economies for all enterprises. The 2001 European Network for SME

Research (ENSR)[12] runs a survey of 7,600 SMEs in the EU-19 through computer-assisted telephone interviews. Entrepreneurs were asked to identify from a series of listed potential obstacles the single most important constraint to doing business. Lack of skilled labour appears to be the most frequently (20-30 per cent of sample) quoted "major constraint", affecting relatively more small- and medium-sized companies than micro-sized ones. This is followed by "no obstacle at all" (15-20 per cent of sample) and "other obstacles than those in the list (12-15 per cent). Administrative regulations affect highly between ten and 16 per cent of enterprises in the sample and access to finance between eight and 15 per cent of enterprises with relatively more micro enterprises isolating this as their major obstacle than enterprises of larger size. The results of the two surveys are not directly comparable in that the BEEPS enterprises were not asked to rank the top obstacle to doing business, whereas the ENSR sample was. However the comparison in terms of relative importance of obstacles quoted shows finance as the most highly rated obstacle in the New Europe countries against a mere fifth obstacle in the 19 western European countries.

Table 3.4 Rating of financial constraints in 2002

	Access to Finance	Cost of Capital
Bulgaria	2.8	2.88
Croatia	2.18	2.27
Czech Republic	2.45	2.53
Estonia	1.94	2.01
Hungary	2.22	2.31
Latvia	1.85	2.01
Lithuania	1.62	1.99
Poland	2.65	3.17
Romania	2.55	2.8
Slovak Republic	2.5	2.58
Slovenia	1.82	2.2

Source: EBRD.

In 2002 the BEEPS questionnaire also asked entrepreneurs to differentiate within the finance constraint the role played by (lack of) access to finance and by the (high) cost of capital. Table 3.4 presents the breakdown of responses (on a scale from 1 = no obstacle, to 4 = major obstacle) for the two individual constraints. Entrepreneurs consistently find the cost of capital to be a more binding constraint than generally the poor access to finance. This finding is consistent with findings of previous surveys in the same area (Pissarides et al. 2003) and simply indicates that access to commercially-priced external sources of finance is a marginally more binding constraint than the overall access to financial sources, be they internal or external.

The high rating of access to finance as a constraint is also supported by findings regarding the degree of success of the enterprises in the sample in accessing financial sources in the past. Table 3.5 illustrates the share of firms which managed to access some source of finance (be it internal or external) for making new investments and for satisfying working capital needs.

Overall accessing finance to meet working capital requirements does not appear to have been a problem for the enterprises, regardless of their size, with the exception of large enterprises in Latvia and in the Czech Republic. In these two countries large enterprises faced more difficulty financing their working capital requirements than small-sized enterprises did.

The situation is very different when it comes to financing new investment, for which the financial requirements are usually larger and for a longer duration than working capital requirements. Overall in the region 23 per cent of micro-, small- and medium-sized firms and 18 per cent of large companies do not manage to access the finance they need for their investment requirements. Latvian enterprises in general and Croatian MSMEs appear to suffer the worst from lack of access to this type of finance.

An analysis of sources of finance tapped by enterprises interviewed during the BEEPS reveals a heavy reliance on internal funds. Table 3.6 contains a detailed breakdown for the sources of finance used for new investment by enterprises, disaggregated according to enterprise size. Table 3.7 contains the equivalent information on sources of finance used for working capital requirements. On average between 55 and 70 per cent of finance accessed by enterprises comes from internal sources (i.e. retained earnings, family/friends), depending on the size of the enterprises and the type of financial need, with working capital needs and MSMEs in general depending more on internal funds than large enterprises and new investments.

Table 3.5 Percentage of enterprises which managed to access finance, 2002

	New Investment		Working Capital	
	Large Enterprises	MSMEs	Large Enterprises	MSMEs
Bulgaria	89%	100%	97%	100%
Croatia	81%	65%	92%	91%
Czech Rep.	86%	89%	86%	96%
Estonia	95%	69%	95%	96%
Hungary	83%	84%	95%	99%
Latvia	56%	42%	80%	94%
Lithuania	80%	75%	96%	99%
Poland	85%	76%	95%	98%
Romania	82%	86%	100%	100%
Slovak Rep.	88%	88%	100%	99%
Slovenia	74%	69%	100%	100%

Sources: BEEPS 2002, EBRD.

The banking system accounts on average for 8.6 and 12.1 per cent of finance accessed by MSMEs and for 19.3 and 24.1 per cent of finance accessed by large companies respectively for working capital and new investments. In other words it is easier for all enterprises to access bank loans for investment projects than it is to access funds for working capital needs. This reflects the credit methodologies traditionally used in the New Europe region. These, rather than look at cash flows to evaluate a loan request (more appropriate for working capital loans), evaluate the expected financial returns on investments.

Table 3.6 Sources of funds accessed by enterprises for new investments according to enterprises size class, 2002

	Bulgaria		Croatia		Czech Rep.		Estonia		Hungary	
	MSMEs	LEs	MSMEs	LEs	MSMEs	LEs	MSMEs	LEs	MSMEs	LEs
Internal Funds	72.2	56.5	49.8	28.8	52.1	51.9	60.7	59.1	58.7	48.0
Equity	1.4	0.0	6.3	3.8	6.5	1.4	3.1	0.0	16.6	7.7
Private local banks	4.7	15.3	9.7	15.2	5.9	10.2	8.1	6.5	6.1	22.9
State owned Banks	4.2	2.1	6.3	24.0	4.7	3.8	0.0	0.0	6.8	8.7
Foreign banks	1.5	3.8	5.2	9.3	1.5	11.9	0.0	3.6	0.4	2.9
Family friends	5.5	0.0	2.6	0.5	3.5	1.6	1.1	4.5	3.2	0.0
Moneylanders	1.5	0.0	1.3	0.0	2.4	0.0	0.8	0.0	0.0	0.0
Supplier credit	1.5	1.8	2.6	2.9	2.8	2.9	1.7	1.4	1.0	0.1
Customer credit	0.7	2.9	0.1	1.9	0.6	0.0	0.0	0.5	0.7	2.1
Credit cards	0.0	0.0	0.6	0.0	1.6	0.0	1.0	0.0	0.1	0.0
Leasing	2.7	7.1	5.3	6.9	10.3	12.4	20.9	14.0	3.7	1.6
Government	2.2	10.6	2.7	6.7	3.5	2.2	0.0	0.0	1.4	3.4
Other	2.0	0.0	7.6	0.0	4.6	1.8	2.6	5.9	1.3	2.6

	Latvia		Lithuania		Poland		Romania		Slovakia		Slovenia	
	MSMEs	LEs	MSMEs	LEs	MSMEs	LEs	MSMEs	LEs	MSMEs	LEs	MSMEs	LEs
Internal Funds	46.7	41.8	75.1	53.7	65.4	63.8	72.7	70.6	64.9	59.0	70.3	71.4
Equity	14.7	8.6	.0.	0.0	1.7	3.3	0.8	0.0	9.4	0.5	0.4	0.0
Private local banks	7.5	33.2	4.5	12.2	8.1	9.5	7.0	3.5	5.1	2.5	4.3	10.7
State owned Banks	3.0	3.6	0.8	4.0	5.1	4.7	1.9	8.1	1.7	7.3	12.0	8.9
Foreign banks	0.9	0.0	0.0	2.7	2.0	3.5	1.4	0.6	0.5	6.4	1.8	3.2
Family friends	5.8	0.0	3.2	0.0	3.2	0.0	6.1	0.0	1.3	0.0	1.5	0.0
Moneylanders	1.1	0.0	0.6	0.0	0.5	2.2	0.8	0.0	1.2	0.0	0.3	0.0
Supplier credit	3.5	0.0	1.2	7.3	1.8	3.2	1.4	1.0	1.0	3.6	0.6	0.0
Customer credit	0.4	2.1	0.7	2.5	0.3	0.1	0.1	2.6	0.3	0.0	0.4	0.0
Credit cards	2.5	0.0	0.0	0.0	0.3	0.8	0.6	0.0	0.0	0.0	0.3	0.0
Leasing	4.4	3.6	8.1	14.3	6.3	2.6	3.9	3.9	12.1	11.7	6.3	5.8
Government	3.5	0.0	1.5	0.0	3.0	1.8	2.3	0.0	2.1	4.5	0.6	0.0
Other	6.0	7.1	4.2	3.5	2.3	4.4	1.1	9.7	0.6	4.5	1.2	0.0

Source: EBRD.

Table 3.7 Sources of funds accessed by enterprises for working capital according to enterprises size class, 2002

	Bulgaria		Croatia		Czech Rep.		Estonia		Hungary	
	MSMEs	LEs	MSMEs	LEs	MSMEs	LEs	MSMEs	LEs	MSMEs	LEs
Internal Funds	68.3	54.5	55.3	40.8	55.4	55.0	73.2	66.6	63.5	60.4
Equity	0.1	0.0	10.4	0.0	8.4	1.4	2.0	0.0	15.7	8.3
Private local banks	4.0	9.6	8.3	18.5	5.7	11.2	5.2	6.1	5.7	14.6
State owned Banks	4.5	3.5	3.7	12.1	2.2	7.6	0.9	0.0	3.7	3.0
Foreign banks	1.1	4.1	2.6	7.1	0.7	6.8	0.0	3.6	0.4	2.5
Family friends	7.1	0.0	3.7	0.4	4.9	3.0	2.2	4.5	2.8	0.0
Moneylanders	2.0	0.3	0.7	0.0	2.5	1.4	0.7	1.4	0.1	0.0
Supplier credit	6.3	11.8	4.5	13.4	6.9	6.4	6.7	3.2	3.1	5.9
Customer credit	1.3	2.8	0.4	1.7	1.3	0.5	1.8	0.2	0.5	1.6
Credit cards	0.0	0.0	0.8	0.0	2.2	0.6	0.2	0.0	0.6	0.0
Leasing	0.9	3.6	2.0	1.8	3.3	4.1	4.0	4.1	1.4	0.0
Government	2.8	10.0	0.9	3.5	2.5	0.3	0.0	3.2	1.0	2.6
Other	1.4	0.0	6.8	0.6	4.0	1.9	3.0	2.5	1.3	1.1

	Latvia		Lithuania		Poland		Romania		Slovakia		Slovenia	
	MSMEs	LEs	MSMEs	LEs	MSMEs	LEs	MSMEs	LEs	MSMEs	LEs	MSMEs	LEs
Internal Funds	47.3	35.7	74.4	61.0	69.3	57.6	69.8	68.8	69.8	65.3	82.9	74.3
Equity	17.0	29.9	1.8	0.4	1.7	4.0	2.1	0.0	12.5	2.6	0.3	0.0
Private local banks	3.3	9.7	5.3	13.9	5.4	12.9	7.7	6.3	2.2	6.5	2.6	6.0
State owned Banks	0.9	3.7	0.6	1.7	3.9	6.1	2.5	6.1	1.0	11.5	5.9	9.5
Foreign banks	0.4	0.3	0.0	0.0	1.1	3.3	0.9	0.5	1.3	1.3	0.4	2.4
Family friends	5.3	0.5	1.7	0.0	2.7	0.0	5.6	0.0	2.0	0.0	1.4	0.0
Moneylanders	1.2	0.0	0.8	0.0	0.6	0.0	0.9	0.0	0.7	0.0	0.6	0.0
Supplier credit	10.3	13.1	6.3	8.1	6.9	8.6	3.6	7.2	2.4	6.5	1.7	5.5
Customer credit	4.8	3.7	2.5	7.1	1.1	0.7	1.1	3.1	1.1	0.4	0.9	0.0
Credit cards	0.3	0.3	0.1	0.0	0.7	1.2	0.5	0.7	0.0	0.0	0.2	0.0
Leasing	2.0	2.9	2.3	7.7	2.8	0.3	2.0	0.5	2.5	1.0	1.1	1.3
Government	1.2	0.0	1.3	0.0	2.1	1.3	1.5	0.0	4.3	4.8	0.8	0.0
Other	6.0	0.6	2.9	0.0	1.7	3.9	1.9	6.8	1.0	0.0	1.2	1.1

Source: EBRD.

Also, large enterprises, considered to be less risky than MSMEs by banks, have easier access to bank loans than their smaller counterparts. Enterprises find it easier in general to borrow from private local banks than from state- and foreign-owned banks. Large enterprises have easier access than MSMEs to state-owned bank loans everywhere except for Bulgaria, the Czech Republic, Poland and Slovenia for new investments and for Bulgaria and Hungary for working capital needs. Large enterprises have easier access to foreign bank loans than MSMEs, except in the case of working capital financing in Latvia (by a small margin) and in general in Romania. The findings regarding loans issued by foreign-owned banks are however doubtful. The Estonian entrepreneurs' responses for example indicate that private local banks are far larger providers of finance to enterprises than foreign-owned banks, despite the fact that virtually all Estonian banks are foreign-owned. This response could be explained by the difficulty for borrowers to identify ownership of banks if the banks' names have stayed unchanged after the acquisition by a foreign bank.

Leasing appears to be particularly important in financing new investment, regardless of firm size. Supplier credit plays quite an important role in financing working capital needs in particular for large enterprises. Interestingly equity appears to account for a relatively larger share of finance accessed by MSMEs than of finance accessed by large enterprises, and counter-intuitively it accounts for a higher share of finance accessed for working capital needs than for investment needs, regardless of size of enterprise.

The combined findings on the share of enterprises that managed to procure finance for their needs (regardless of the source used) and on the relative importance of the different type of financial sources used by those that managed to access finance leads to the conclusion that the enterprise sector is poorly served by the financial sector as a whole. With some variation among countries, large enterprises appear to have easier access to finance in general and to external sources of finance in particular. Among the external sources, the most important is by far the banking sector. It accounts for between 9 and 12 per cent of finance accessed by MSMEs and between 20 and 24 per cent of finance accessed by large enterprises.

THE BANKING SECTOR

Most financial sector institutions characterizing a market economy are present in the New Europe countries. In some of these countries these institutions are well capitalized and profitable. However, the relative importance and market share of these institutions in the economy is somehow different from that of financial institutions in advanced market economies.

To begin with, the size of domestic bond and equity markets in the New Europe countries in the financial sector is far smaller than the average for the Euro area (and to each individual country in the Euro area except for Austria, where, for example, stock market capitalization amounts to a mere 12 per cent of GDP in 2001) and insignificant as compared to the US. Stock market capitalization in the New Europe ranges between 27 per cent of GDP in Estonia to three per cent in the Slovak Republic.

Commercial banks account for a far larger share of GDP than equity and bond markets do, although in comparison to the Euro area total assets of commercial banks still account for a small share of the economy. The Czech Republic and Slovakia have the largest banking sectors (in terms of assets) of the whole New Europe area as a consequence of the fact that the banking system of Czechoslovakia during the socialist regime used to be relatively extensively utilised as a tool for corporate financing[13]. Yet, bank assets in these two countries still only account for 52 and 39 per cent respectively of the average of the Euro area. Lithuania and Romania have the smallest banking sectors relatively to the size of their economies (with commercial banks assets accounting respectively for 32 and 28 per cent of GDP). Yet on average commercial banks have a relatively larger role in the New Europe than in the US, where non-bank financial institutions and in particular equity markets play a key role in the financing of the economy. For all countries of the new Europe the distance to cover to reach the level of development of their western counterparts is very large.

The New Europe countries' financial sectors have developed much more along the bank-based European model than the market-based US model. As a consequence of the dominance of the banking sector in the financial sector in the New Europe region, the analysis will focus only on the role played by the banking sector in financing the enterprise sector. Figure 3.1 presents the relation between the banking and non-banking segments of the financial sector through a comparison of stock market capitalization and total assets of commercial banks (in relation to GDP) in the New Europe countries, the Euro area, the UK and the US. Among the New Europe countries the Slovak Republic and Bulgaria have the most heavily bank-based financial sectors. In the Slovak case this is due to a combination of a strong bank system and a non-existent stock market, whereas in the case of Bulgaria this is mainly due to the small size of the equity market.

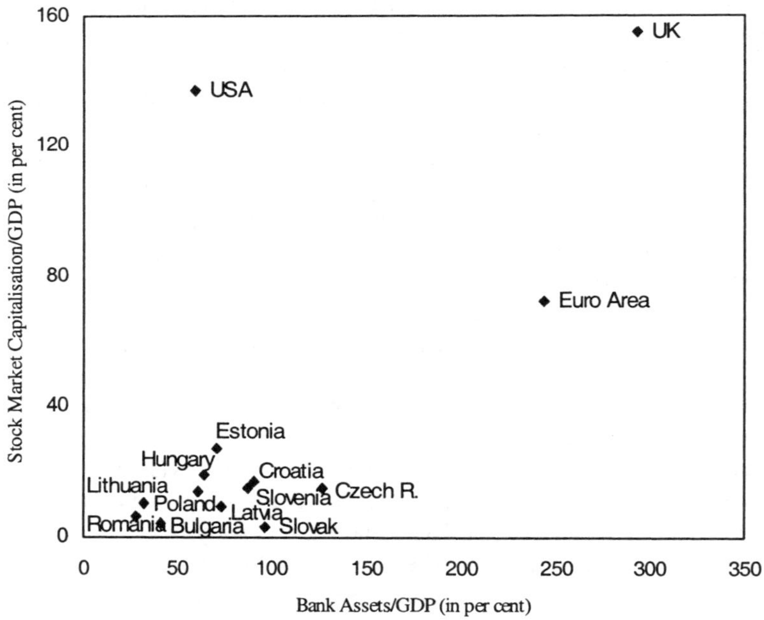

Figure 3.1 Share of total assets of commercial banks and of stock market capitalization in GDP, 2001

Sources: National authorities, EBRD, IMF and S&P.

In most of the New Europe countries reform of the banking sector is significantly advanced both in terms of privatization and restructuring, and in terms of institution building and legal and regulatory framework development. The EBRD transition indicators for banking reform measure this progress against the standards of well functioning industrialized market economies. The measurement scale for these indicators ranges from 1 to 4+, where 1 represents little or no change from a rigidly planned economy and 4+ represents the standard of an industrialized market economy[14]. According to the EBRD analysis, banking sector reform is well advanced in this group of countries, with an average score of 3.4 in 2002, up from 2.8 in 1996, as outlined in Table 3.8. The most advanced banking sector in 2002 is the Hungarian with a score of 4, while the Romanian banking sector lies at the opposite end of the spectrum with a score of 2.7.

Table 3.8 EBRD transition indicators for banking reform and interest rate liberalization, 1996-2002

	1996	1997	1998	1999	2000	2001	2002
Bulgaria	2.0	2.7	2.7	2.7	3.0	3.0	3.3
Croatia	2.7	2.7	2.7	3.0	3.3	3.3	3.7
Czech Rep.	3.0	3.0	3.0	3.3	3.3	3.7	3.7
Estonia	3.0	3.3	3.3	3.7	3.7	3.7	3.7
Hungary	3.0	4.0	4.0	4.0	4.0	4.0	4.0
Latvia	3.0	3.0	2.7	3.0	3.0	3.3	3.7
Lithuania	3.0	3.0	3.0	3.0	3.0	3.0	3.0
Poland	3.0	3.0	3.3	3.3	3.3	3.3	3.3
Romania	3.0	2.7	2.3	2.7	2.7	2.7	2.7
Slovak Rep.	2.7	2.7	2.7	2.7	3.0	3.3	3.3
Slovenia	3.0	3.0	3.0	3.3	3.3	3.3	3.3

Source: EBRD

Privatization of banks (an element not included in the EBRD index of banking sector reform) is almost completed in most countries, as evidenced by Table 3.9, with the one notable exception of Slovenia where the role of the state in the banking sector actually increased between 1994 and 2001, only to drop marginally in 2002 to 48.6 per cent[15], following the privatization of a share of Nova Ljubljanska Banka and of Banka Koper, and Krekova Banka. In the rest of the region the share of banks with majority state capital in total bank assets ranges between zero (Estonia and Lithuania) and 44 per cent (Romania). In some countries the openness to foreign strategic investors early on in transition permitted fast privatization and consequent restructuring of the sector already in the mid-1990s (in 1996 the asset share of banks with majority state ownership amounted to 7 per cent in Estonia and Latvia, 15 per cent in Hungary and 17 per cent in the Czech Republic). A combination of poor loan portfolios, banking crises, vested interests and poor legal and regulatory environment delayed the privatization of banks in some other countries of the New Europe.

The region is characterized by a high degree of foreign ownership in the banking sector (information on the degree of foreign ownership is contained in Table 3.9), with Estonia, Lithuania, Croatia and the Czech and Slovak Republics leading the group and Slovenia having the smallest share of all. In the Euro area, in contrast, foreign ownership is very limited in the sector (only 20 per cent of banks' capital in Euro countries is in foreign hands, and only in four of the Euro area countries foreign ownership accounts for at leasTable 30 per cent[16]). Further integration is however still possible in the future, well beyond the integration measured by ownership. It could for example take place via electronic banking, or cross-border lending, still relatively limited. E-banking in particular could boost regional integration and overcome many of the gaps of the local banking systems by allowing customers to access banking services offered by banks in EU-15 countries. It could also provide a cheaper way for EU-15 banks to enter the new markets by eliminating the need to establish costly branch networks.

The implications of bank consolidation on lending to the MSME sector are not clear cut. Evidence from the United States suggests that large banks lend less to MSMEs than small banks do (Meyer 1998). The reason why this is true is that with traditional lending techniques credit officers in small banks can afford a higher degree of independent judgement than credit officers in large banks, thus being able to rely more on soft information than on quantitative indicators alone. Soft information on MSMEs increases the likelihood of loan extension with respect to quantitative information alone, thus small banks are more likely to lend more to MSMEs than large banks. However, evidence on the outcome of bank mergers and take-overs on small enterprise lending is mixed and inconclusive (Belaisch et al. 2001). Credit scoring techniques adopted by large banks within environment where dissemination of credit information is available, financial deregulation and technology change might increase the likelihood that large banks increase their small loan portfolio.

Table 3.9 Bank ownership

	Assets of banks with majority state ownership		Assets of banks with majority foreign ownership
	1994	2002	2002
	In per cent of total bank assets		
Bulgaria [a]	na	20	73
Croatia	55	4	90
Czech Republic	18	5	86
Estonia	28	0	98
Hungary	62	11	84
Latvia	7	4	43
Lithuania	48	0	96
Poland	80	27	71
Romania	80	44	53
Slovak Republic	67	3	86
Slovenia	40	49	17

Note: [a] Data for Bulgaria refer to 2001.
Source: National authorities.

Both privatization and the entry of foreign strategic shareholders in the New Europe banks stimulated recapitalization and restructuring of the sector. As a pre-requisite of privatization, the state had to recapitalize the banks and clean their balance sheets from the bad loans. These had accumulated mainly as a result of lending to inefficient state-owned enterprises and of lack of lending and risk management skills, but also as a result of economic downturns that affected profitability of the enterprise sector. Restructuring then progressed following privatization of banks, to a relatively higher degree in those cases in which privatization occurred through sale to a strategic foreign investor. Foreign ownership resulted in stronger capitalization, improved banking practices, higher profitability, increased competition (as evidenced by decreasing spreads between lending and deposit rates) but also in increased risk aversion. The timing of this process and its impact on the functioning of the sector varied across the New Europe countries, but the pattern was common to all of them.

The immediate effect of privatization and foreign ownership was that of a clean-up of the banks' portfolios. Typically the bad loans previously extended by public banks to state enterprises were written off and the related losses were shifted to the governments. The clean-up of the banks portfolios was not a linear process in every country. In some countries macroeconomic factors contributed to the increase in non-performing loans. An example is Poland where the economic slowdown in 2001-02 was responsible for a deterioration in the financial performance of enterprises[17], which in turn was reflected in the increase in bad loans to above 20 per cent of total loans. (Yet this is partly a result of rigorous regulatory requirements, including classification of loans by developments in the sector.) Elsewhere, banks' lack of experience in lending practices and risk management, coupled with poor bank supervision, inadequate provisioning and unrealistic collateral valuation resulted in banking sector crises either independently (e.g. Lithuania in 1995, Bulgaria in 1996-97 and the Bancorex episode in Romania in 1999) or as a result of exogenous shocks (e.g. the series of banks failures in Croatia in 1998-99 resulted from the contagion effect on the economy of the Russian crisis of 1998). These episodes were all mirrored by the resurgence of bad loans on the banks' portfolios and were followed by another process of recapitalization and restructuring. Table 3.10 outlines the halving of the share of bad loans in the banks' portfolios on average in the New Europe countries between 1996 and 2002.

Table 3.10 Share of non-performing loans in total bank loans, 1996-2002

	1996	1997	1998	1999	2000	2001	2002
Bulgaria	15.2	13.0	11.8	17.5	10.9	7.9	10.4[a]
Croatia	11.2	8.2	12.6	20.6	19.8	15.0	11.5
Czech Rep	21.8	19.9	20.3	21.5	19.3	13.7	9.4
Estonia	2.0	2.1	4.0	2.9	1.6	1.5	0.8
Hungary	na	6.6	7.9	4.4	3.1	3.1	4.6
Latvia	20.0	10.0	6.8	6.8	5.0	3.1	2.1
Lithuania	32.2	28.3	12.5	11.9	10.8	7.4	5.8
Poland	14.7	11.5	11.8	14.5	16.8	20.1	24.6
Romania	48.0	56.5	58.5	35.4	3.8	3.4	2.3
Slovak Rep	31.8	33.4	44.3	32.9	26.2	24.3	11.2
Slovenia	10.1	10.0	9.5	8.6	8.5	9.2	na

Note: [a] Change in definition of non-performing loans.
Source: National authorities.

Following privatization and entry of foreign players, the sector experienced an increase in concentration. In 2002 the assets of the five largest banks as a share of total bank assets accounted for an average of 70 per cent in the New Europe area, ranging from 55 per cent in Hungary to 99 per cent in Estonia. The ongoing consolidation in the western European banking sector is likely to impact on the New Europe banks given the high degree of foreign ownership which characterizes them. Upon accession to the EU the implementation of the "Single European Passport" will allow EU-15 banks to provide services in the new member countries either directly or via branches (the endowment capital requirement will be lifted). As (with the exception of Slovenia) more than three quarters of New Europe bank assets are foreign owned, it is difficult to assess what effect accession to the EU will have on the structure of the banking sector other than expecting a large number of new foreign entrants through branches.

Privatization resulted in increased efficiency of banks in every country in the New Europe area. Restructuring of banks was associated with a lower number of employees in relation to bank assets. The variance across countries is however large, as shown in Table 3.11, with Bulgaria and Romania saddled with the most inefficient banking sectors and the Czech Republic, Slovenia, Hungary, and Croatia endowed with the most efficient banks in the group. The level of this indicator is yet still lower in the New than in the old Europe, with Germany for example having 0.17 bank employees per million US dollars of bank assets. Profitability of banks, as measured by the average rate of return on assets of all banks (profits before tax divided by total assets of banks), also improved overall in the New Europe area in the 1996-2001, with the exception of Lithuania whose banks registered losses in 2001 and Slovenia where profitability of banks has been dwindling in the same period.

Despite the profound transformation undergone by the banking systems of the New Europe countries, the level of banking intermediation is still low (in 2002 domestic credit averaged about 40 per cent of GDP in the New Europe area, as compared to 135 per cent in the Euro area), and in particular domestic credit to the private sector is even lower at an average of less than 30 per cent of GDP in the region. The low level of domestic credit to private sector in relation to GDP is low not only as compared to the average of the EU countries, but also as compared to that of countries at a similar level of development as proxied by GDP per capita.[19] Once again differences across countries are very marked (see Table 3.12) with the ratio of domestic credit to the private sector as a percentage of GDP ranging from a meagre 8.7 per cent in Romania to 52.3 per cent in Croatia in 2002.

The low levels of bank intermediation are partly a consequence of the severe recession experienced by all New Europe countries in the first years of transition. The economic downturn led to the accumulation of bad loans on the banks portfolio. The subsequent clean-up of banks-portfolios in advance of privatization then led to a significant reduction in the banking sector's assets (the most emblematic case was Bulgaria, where banking sector assets dropped from 350 per cent of GDP in 1991 to 34 per cent in 1997). In some cases the accumulation of bad loans and/or exogenous shocks led to banking crises which further shrank the bank loan portfolios. As a reaction to banking sector crises, more stringent banking regulations and supervisory practices were introduced. This induced a more prudent lending behaviour. Even in the absence of banking crises, a more risk-averse behaviour always followed privatization to foreign owners. The consequence was a drop in domestic credit as percent of GDP.

In the past three years, with the exception of the Czech and Slovak Republics, domestic credit to the private sector as a percentage of GDP started increasing. Improved access to funding for banks should intuitively be a factor driving the increase in domestic credit to the private sector. Both the increase in bank deposits as a percentage of GDP and the increased ability of New Europe banks to attract financing from abroad should in theory be associated with increased bank lending to the private sector.

Table 3.11 Number of bank employees per million US$ of bank assets, 1996-2001

	1996	1997	1998	1999	2000	2001
Bulgaria	na	na	5.5	4.9	4.5	4.0
Croatia	na	1.1	1.1	1.3	1.2	0.9
Czech Republic	0.8	0.8	0.7	0.7	0.6	0.6
Estonia	2.8	1.8	1.2	1.4	1.4	1.0
Hungary	1.1	1.1	1.0	0.9	0.9	0.8
Latvia	na	na	na	na	na	1.4
Lithuania	na	5.0	3.3	3.0	2.4	2.2
Poland	2.1	2.0	1.7	1.7	1.5	1.3
Romania	na	4.3	3.3	4.5	4.3	3.9
Slovak Republi	1.0	1.0	1.1	1.2	1.2	1.1
Slovenia	0.8	0.8	0.7	0.7	0.8	0.7

Source: National authorities.

However a recent study by Cottarelli et al. (2003) finds no clear evidence to this effect. The same study finds a positive correlation between domestic credit to private sector growth and a) the degree of progress on structural reforms, and in particular banking sector reform, b) the level of privatization and/or foreign ownership, c) the degree of retrenchment of the state sector and d) the quality of the legislation to protect creditors' rights.

Table 3.12 Domestic credit to the private sector as a percentage of GDP, 1996-2002

	1996	1997	1998	1999	2000	2001	2002
Bulgaria	35.3	5.6	8.0	10.4	11.9	14.3	18.3
Croatia	29.3	37.3	41.2	37.4	37.4	43.0	52.3
Czech Rep.	74.0	65.4	56.9	52.6	48.6	35.6	33.4
Estonia	19.3	26.5	25.3	26.0	25.5	27.3	29.8
Hungary	22.1	24.3	24.2	26.0	32.3	33.9	37.3
Latvia	7.2	10.5	14.8	15.7	18.5	23.1	29.5
Lithuania	11.1	10.9	11.3	13.0	11.5	11.5	14.2
Poland	22.4	24.1	24.7	27.8	28.7	28.9	29.3
Romania	11.5	8.4	11.6	8.1	7.2	8.0	8.7
Slovak Rep.	30.4	42.1	43.9	37.3	31.0	26.2	29.4
Slovenia	28.8	28.6	32.8	36.0	38.1	40.0	38.8

Source: IMF (2003).

As a result of increased risk aversion, however, the composition of bank assets shifted away from loans to enterprises (with the exception of loans to blue-chip, preferably foreign-owned corporate borrowers) towards government securities and other liquid assets. When foreign entry and increased competition in the banking sector pushed down margins on loans to low-risk corporate clients, and/or with reduced borrowing from governments, banks moved into lending to households, perceived as low-risk clients. (Lending to households was also boosted by rising incomes, the development of mortgage lending instruments and the presence in some cases of subsidized mortgage loans.) Only recently bank lending to local corporates started accelerating, from very low levels, at rates well below those experienced by domestic credit to the private sector and by bank loans to households.

Table 3.13 Cumulative growth rates of bank credit to private sector by final destination, in real terms, 2000-2002

	Private sector	Enterprises	Households
Bulgaria	101.6	111.0	73.4
Croatia	32.0	9.9	75.9
Czech Republic	-11.4	-16.9	33.2
Estonia	62.2	54.3	97.4
Hungary	47.2	27.4	185.8
Latvia	106.5	79.0	278.2
Lithuania	19.1	14.4	54.3
Poland	26.2	14.1	56.0
Romania	7.2	4.5	48.7
Slovak Republic	-27.4	-34.5	56.9
Slovenia	30.9	35.5	20.9

Source: IMF.

As shown in Table 3.13, during 2000-02 bank credit to households increased at a faster pace than both bank credit to enterprises and domestic credit to the private sector for all countries in the New Europe area except Bulgaria and Slovenia[20]. These two countries were also the only countries in which bank credit to the enterprise sector grew in excess of the rate of growth of domestic credit to the private sector. In the Czech and Slovak Republics bank loans to enterprises and to a lesser extent domestic credit to the private sector, decreased on a cumulative basis in the 2000-02 period, while credit to households increased at fast rates.

This shift in the composition of bank credit raises concerns not only as regards the growth of households' indebtedness and the banks' ability to assess the risk of this new group of clients, but mainly as increasingly fewer resources in relative terms are made available to the enterprise sector.

CONCLUSIONS

Privatization appears to account more than new enterprise entry and growth in private sector development in the New Europe. Enterprises in the New Europe are generally smaller, younger and less experienced than in the EU. Their survival rates are relatively lower than those of their European counterparts. The most comprehensive analysis of the past three years' development in the investment climate of the New Europe highlights an overall improvement of the conditions for enterprise development.

However the analysis also points to a shift in the weight assigned by entrepreneurs to different aspects of the business environment characterized as obstacles to growth. Whereas a notable improvement is recorded in the infrastructure and taxation aspects of the investment climate in all the countries, other aspects appear to negatively affect enterprises more in 2002 than they did in 1999. Financial constraints to doing business appear to be the most binding constraints for entrepreneurs among all aspects of the investment climate identified as constraints (although the absolute weight allocated to the financial constraints has decreased). Enterprises in the region are found to be relatively unconstrained in access to finance for working capital needs, but their investment potential is limited by the unavailability of both internal and external sources of finance. Whereas enterprise size matters little in terms of overall access to finance, it makes a big difference in the degree of utilization of different sources of finance available.

The degree of intermediation of savings of which the banking system in the New Europe is capable is far lower than in western economies and also of countries at similar stage of economic development, although generally increasing since the end of the 1990s. An analysis of the breakdown of domestic credit to the private sector by final recipients highlights a worrying trend. The proportion of credit available to the enterprise sector is decreasing fast, as banks recovering from financial crises or simply starting to lend again after restructuring have become more risk-averse and prefer to lend to households rather than enterprises.

Despite its advanced stage of reform, the banking sector is failing to respond adequately to the needs of the local enterprises sector, in particular when it comes to supporting new investments. New investments are critical to the strengthening of the weak local enterprise sector, in particular in view of the inevitable pressures from increased competition after joining the single market. They are critical to the prospects of growth and convergence with the EU for the economies of New Europe as a whole. Under the present conditions the local enterprise sector is ill equipped to withstand the increased competition of the single market.

Whether these trends are simply a reflection of historical developments in the banking sector (a combination of impact of transition recession, financial crises, restructuring, privatization of banks) or a combination of the former with a worse outlook and increased risk associated with the enterprise sector is unclear. What is clear is that the low level of domestic intermediation is not merely a development issue as reflected by a comparative analysis between the countries of New Europe and other countries at similar level of development. Transition to a market economy is clearly not over in as far as the relation between the financial sector and the enterprise sector is concerned. As the institutional reform of the banking sector comes to an end, efforts to guarantee that an efficient intermediation of savings takes place need to gain pace as a second phase of transition.

NOTES

1. The author is grateful to Elisabetta Falcetti, Francois Lecavalier, Peter Sanfey and Imre Tarafas for comments provided on an earlier version. Johanna Leube provided conscientious and prompt research assistance for which the author is also very grateful. This chapter benefited from comments of discussants and participants at the conference on 'Financial Intermediation in the New Europe. Economics, Policies and Institutions' at Bocconi University, Milan, September 2003. All remaining errors are solely the responsibility of the author.
2. See European Commission (2002a).
3. In this chapter the definition 'New Europe' includes the economies of Bulgaria, Croatia, the Czech Republic, Estonia, Hungary, Latvia, Lithuania, Poland, Romania, the Slovak Republic and Slovenia.
4. See European Commission (2002c).
5. See EBRD (1999), chapter 4, p.92.
6. The EU 19 region is composed by all the current (January 2004) member countries of the EU, plus Iceland, Liechtenstein, Norway and Switzerland.

7. As data for the Czech Republic are the most inclusive at the lower end of the enterprise size spectrum (farms and sole proprietors are included thus inflating the role of micro-enterprises) this finding is not surprising.
8. In collaboration with the World Bank, in 1999-2000 the EBRD conducted a large enterprise survey on business environment and enterprise performance. Over 3,000 enterprises in 24 transition countries provided feedback. Samples of firms are stratified to attempt at being fairly representative of the economic structure of each country. Thus industrial and large-size enterprises are a minority of the enterprises surveyed. See EBRD (1999) for a more detailed analysis.
9. The 2002 sample of enterprises does not constitute an expanded panel, as it is unknown whether the enterprises interviewed in 2002 were also interviewed in the 1999 survey.
10. The adjustments consisted in regressing the qualitative assessments of the business environment at firm level on the firm characteristics such as size, ownership and location within a country, reported quantitative measures of the business environment that relate to the qualitative assessments, the country's average growth rate over the past year and country dummy variables to allow for any other country-specific effects. The estimated parameters were then used to construct the answers the entrepreneurs would have given on the business environment, if each country grew at the average growth rate for all countries.
11. The EBRD has assessed progress in structural and institutional reform across the region since 1989 based on its assessment of progress in key aspects of the transition process (i.e. markets and trade, enterprises, infrastructure and financial institutions). See EBRD (2002).
12. See European Commission (2002b).
13. See Ihnat et al. (2002).
14. In particular, 1 indicates little progress beyond the establishment of a two-tier system. 2 denotes significant liberalization of interest rates and credit allocation; limited use of directed credit or interest rate ceilings. 3 indicates for substantial progress in the establishment of bank solvency and of a framework for prudential supervision and regulation; full interest rate liberalization with little preferential access to cheap refinancing; significant lending to private enterprises and significant presence of private banks. 4 stands for significant movement of banking laws and regulations towards BIS standards; well-functioning banking competition and effective prudential supervision; significant term lending to private enterprises; substantial financial deepening. 4+ is associated with standards and performance norms of advanced industrial economies; full convergence of banking laws and regulations with BIS standards; provision of full set of competitive banking services.
15. This indicator is calculated as the share of assets of banks with more than 50 per cent state ownership in relation to total assets of banks.
16. In Ireland, Belgium and Portugal, and in the Nordic countries, the percentage of banks' foreign ownership ranges from around 40 per cent

to some 20 per cent. In France, Italy, Spain and Austria the same ratios range between 15 per cent and 10 per cent.
17. See Bernadski et al. (2002).
18. See Riess et al. (2002).
19. See Cottarelli et al. (2003).
20. See Cottarelli et al. (2003).

REFERENCES

Belaisch A., L. Kodres, J. Levy and A. Ubide (2001), 'Euro-Area Banking at the Cross-Roads', *IMF working papers*, 01/28.

Bernadski, Piotr and Jacek Osinski (2002), 'Financial Sector Issues in Poland', in Christian Thimann (ed.), *Financial Sectors in EU Accession Countries*, Frankfurt am Main, European Central Bank, 171-188.

Cottarelli C., G. Dell'Ariccia and I. Vladkova-Hollar (2003), 'Early Birds, Late Risers and Sleeping Beauties: Bank Credit Growth to the Private Sector in Central and Eastern Europe and in the Balkans', *IMF working papers*, 03/213.

EBRD (1999), 'Transition Report 1999. Ten Years of Transition', London, European Bank for Reconstruction and Development.

EBRD (2002), 'Transition Report 2002. Agriculture and Rural Transition', London, European Bank for Reconstruction and Development.

European Commission (2002a), 'Regular Reports' in http://europa.eu.int/comm/enlargement/report2002/#report202.

European Commission (2002b), 'Observatory of European SMEs, 2002, No.1. Highlights from the 2001 Survey', Luxembourg, Office for Official Publications of the European Communities.

European Commission (2002c), 'Observatory of European SMEs, 2002, No.2. SMEs in Europe, including a first glance at candidate countries', Luxembourg, Office for Official Publications of the European Communities.

Ihnat Pavol and Petr Prochazka (2002), 'The Financial Sector in the Czech Republic: an Assessment of its Current State of Development and Functioning', in Christian Thimann (ed.), *Financial Sectors in EU Accession Countries*, Frankfurt am Main, European Central Bank, 67-84.

IMF (2003), 'International Financial Statistics – June 2003', Washington D.C., International Monetary Fund.

Meyer L. (1998), 'The Present and Future Role of Banks in Small Business Finance', *Journal of Banking and Finance*, **22**, 1109-1116.

Riess A., R. Wagenvoort and P. Zajc (2002), 'Practice Makes Perfect: a Review of Banking in Central and Eastern Europe', *EIB papers*, **7** (1), 31-53.

4. Financial Risk in Accession Countries

Andrea Beltratti
and Riccardo D'Antonio

INTRODUCTION

On the basis of a decision taken at the end of 2002, several countries (from now on accession countries) will join the European Union in 2004. This decision has affected the market prices of financial assets like stocks, bonds and the external value of the currency belonging to these countries. Most importantly from the point of view of the determination of financial risk, the decision has also affected the uncertainty associated with the future values of the same assets. It is plausible to believe that accession is associated with more stable economies and financial markets. If at least part of the risk premia required by markets is due to uncertainty about macroeconomic variables, it follows that accession should decrease uncertainty and risk premia, at least in the long run.

On the other hand, joining the European Union is not equivalent to joining the euro. The difference is relevant for financial markets in that adopting the euro as a currency is associated with truly dramatic changes in the structure of the economy and of the financial markets. Joining the euro automatically deletes extra elements of uncertainties about the uncertainty of asset prices. The interest rate for a country in the euro area is mainly determined by the decision of the European Central Bank and not by the decision of the local central bank. It follows that uncertainty about asset valuations is reduced due to the extra stability associated with the decisions of the European Central Bank. Moreover, entering the euro area amounts to eliminating uncertainty associated with currency volatility. It is true that portions of this risk may simply be transferred elsewhere in the economy. For example an interest rate which is more stable as a consequence of being decided on the basis of a European and not a local inflation target may increase the risk that the productive sector of the economy may suffer from an imprecise response of economic policy to local conditions. The same is true of inflation in that the European interest rate is set at a level which is optimal for the average of the countries involved in the union and may be sub-optimal for each of the same countries.

Overall however the balance seems in favor of a stabilization. For example in Italy and Spain entrance in the euro has meant a massive stabilization of both interest rate and stock return volatility and a reduction in the level of the interest rate. In Italy the short term nominal interest rate has decreased from 11% to 3% in the two years preceding the introduction of the euro. Beltratti and Morana (2002) document the decrease of volatility of the historically unstable European stock markets following the introduction of the euro.

Accession to the EU is therefore a sort of intermediate state which is hopefully preliminary to the significant leap forward represented by the euro. It is interesting to notice that indeed there are informal target dates for adoption of the euro on the part of several accession countries. Until several months ago target dates were around 2006 for most countries, with the exception of the Czech Republic which seemed to target 2007 or 2008. In June 2004 a small accident in Hungary has partially changed the market sentiment. As is well known, Hungary has at first tried to decrease the external value of the currency (by modifying by 2.27% the central parity with respect to the euro) in order to increase its ability to compete in its export markets. But after a few days it has then been forced to raise interest rates twice to prevent an excessive weakening of the currency. This episode has shown that the road to the euro may involve some convergence problems. It has also set up a debate about the rules which should be followed by accession countries in order to enter the euro. Recently the European Commission has suggested that accession countries should enter the European Monetary System and keep the currency within restricted bands of 2.5% for three years before entering the euro. To many this seems an excessive strong requirement which may undermine the process as a whole by imposing countries' rigidity in the nominal exchange rate. According to critics this will cause currency crises and will damage the conversion process of the countries involved (see for example Wyplosz, 2003).

On the other hand, it is noted that speculative attacks in the convergence process can take place anyway, even with enlarged fluctuations bands. It is however reassuring to notice that Poland, Hungary and the Czech Republic seem to be in better shape than "Club Med" countries at the time of their entrance into EMU (see Gros, 2002).

In this chapter we want to analyze three cases of great interest, that is Poland, Hungary and the Czech Republic. We will first present general information on each country, regarding its economic structure and its financial markets. We will then propose an application of Value at Risk to the stock, bond and currency market of each country. We will finally conclude.

A GENERAL DESCRIPTION OF POLAND, HUNGARY AND THE CZECH REPUBLIC

Poland

Macroeconomics

With 40 million people, Poland is the largest economy in Central Europe. Since the mid 1990s the Polish economy has been expanding at a fairly rapid pace, with the GDP growth rate exceeding 4% every year from 1995 to 2000. In 2001, the economy showed a sharp decline in its expansionary path with growth rate declining to 1%. During 2002, the economy began to recover from the weakening of growth, but the recovery is fragile. Private consumption picked up gradually, fueled by rising real fiscal transfers, easing monetary policy and a drop in the savings ratio. Poland's economy grew by 1% in 2000 and by 1.3% in 2002. The decline in the average rate of growth is evident from Chart 4 in the Appendix about Poland.

The slowdown in economic growth has left its mark on the labor market. The unemployment rate was steadily falling from 1993 to 1998. The trend reversed in 1998 and at the end of 2002 the unemployment rate amounted to 18.1%. Chart 7 gives a visual impression of this process of increasing unemployment. A total of 3.2 million people were registered as jobless. This could be attributed to a rise in labour productivity, coupled with a sizeable restructuring process in a number of industries (steel industry, mining, agriculture, railway).

A sustained downward trend is evident in consumer price inflation since 1999, see Chart 5. The inflation rate declined from almost 10% at the end of that year to 0.8% in December 2002. This is even more impressive if compared to inflation levels of more than 100% at the beginning of the 1990s.

In 2002, Polish imports reached a level of USD 55 bn and exports USD 41 billion. In comparison with the previous year export grew by 13.6 per cent and import by 9.6 per cent. Since 2000 exports have been growing at a faster rate than imports. The reason was a slower growth in domestic consumption and improved competitiveness of Polish goods. Chart 8 provides an impression of the improvement in the external balance.

Monetary policy has been substantially relaxed in the past two years. The interest rate easing cycle that began in early 2001 continued, and as of April 2003 the main policy interest rate had fallen by a cumulative 1325 basis points to 5.75% but, with falling inflation, real interest rates dropped more gradually. Public debt jumped to more than 47% of GDP in 2002, compared to less than 42% in 2001. The government deficit also sharply grew from 5.5% in 2001 to 6.7% in 2002.

Overall the situation appears to be not completely stable. The origins of the recent weakness in economic activity are complex and a robust recovery will await corrections on several fronts. At the heart of the slowdown was a long slide in investment growth as the torrid pace of early-transition investment cooled. The fiscal-monetary policy mix remains a problem - even as monetary policy has eased, the risk of a tightening, if the fiscal adjustment is delayed, creates market uncertainty. Privatization and redressing the problems of State enterprises where privatization prospects are remote, largely ground to a halt in 2001-02.The banking system, which is well supervised and largely foreign-owned, was strained by the slowdown. Political uncertainties also cloud the situation. The President and the Prime Minister have called for a general election, originally scheduled for late 2005, in June 2004, and speculation about an earlier date is rife. The need to reconstitute the Monetary Policy Council (MPC) in early 2004 when the terms of all current members expire adds to the uncertainty, see IMF (2003).

Financial markets

The Polish financial system has changed significantly over the past decade. The financial sector has become more diversified as strong foreign players have entered the market acquiring large stakes in banking and insurance. The banking system is still relatively fragmented with the small local banks struggling to survive. The larger part of bank lending is to large corporates. Securities markets are small, although operating on a sound basis. A much awaited privatization program could give a boost to the supply in the equity market.

In 1989, along with political changes, the new non-communist government began creating a capital markets structure. The new legal framework, the Act on Public Trading in Securities and Trust Fund was adopted in March 1991, and the Warsaw Stock Exchange (WSE) joint-stock company was established by the State Treasury in April 1991. At the same time, the Polish Securities Commission, with its chairman appointed by the Prime Minister, was created. As of December 31, 2001, the Exchange's shareholders included the State Treasury and 48 banks and brokerage houses.

The main equity index for the Polish stock exchange is the WIG Index, whose basis is 1000 points on April 16, 1994. The WIG Index is a price index, which excludes dividends and pre-emptive rights, and is composed by 20 shares.

The following securities are traded on the WSE: equities, bonds, subscription rights, allotment certificates and investment certificates, as well as derivative instruments: futures contracts, index participation units and warrants. Equities may be listed on three markets - Main, Parallel, Free - depending on, among other things, the size and verified history of the company, and the value of its shares.

At its first session only five companies were listed, and for the first year the market operated only once a week. At the end of 2002, after 12 years in existence, this has completely changed, 216 companies are listed, average turnover per session value on the public market reached more than 250 million zlotys in 2002, and the capitalization of the listed companies was 110 billion zlotys. The Warsaw Stock Exchange is the largest in Central and Eastern Europe. It has also signed a strategic understanding with Euronext, the pan-European bourse headquartered in Amsterdam.

The growth in the number of Equity securities listed on the Warsaw Stock Exchange stopped in 2002, when the number of listed companies shrunk compared to the previous year. In fact, due to delistings the number of listed companies fell to 216 from 230 the previous year.

The stock index has been relatively flat since 1997, even though with a wide range between 12.500 and 22.500. This by itself would seem to suggest that there exists a large undervaluation, as presumably the state of the economy in 2003 is better than the state of the economy in 1997. However a different picture emerges if we look at other elements. For example, if we study the stock market by means of the Datastream market index we find that the market is in mid 2003 about 30% higher than at mid 1997. Moreover we observe that the price-earnings ratio is today much higher than in 1997, with an average level of 24 for 2003 against about 10 in 1997. The dividend yield on the contrary has risen from 1.37 to 1.99. The numbers are hard to interpret; at face value they describe a market where the price went up moderately (about 5% a year) while earnings were decreasing and dividends increasing.

Bonds have been listed on the Exchange since 1992. At the end of 2002, there were 56 issues of Treasury bonds and five issues of corporate bonds listed, including two issues by a foreign bank and one convertible bond issue by a listed company. Although the number of listed bonds has regularly increased in the past years, the total turnover value shrunk in 2002 by more than 1 bn zlotys.

The spread with respect to German bonds is at historically low levels (see Chart 2) but local inflation is also at historically low levels (see Chart 5). On the other hand the public deficit has recently increased to high levels with respect to GDP (see Chart 10).

The Polish zloty is the official currency of the Republic of Poland. It is an independent, free-floating currency. The currency has been steadily depreciating in the last years, helping the economy to decrease the trade deficit, which is still at high levels with respect to GDP (Chart 8). Foreign debt is relatively constant (Chart 9).

Hungary

Macroeconomics

Since 1997, Hungary has undergone a sustained economic growth, with GDP growth rates exceeding 4% a year most of the times. GDP growth at 5.2% in 2000 was the highest since transition, mainly pushed by strong export growth rates. Despite the world wide economic slowdown, Hungary's economy grew at 3.8% in 2001, and at 3.3% during 2002. Chart 14 shows that the economy is slowing down with respect to the past, but is not losing its strong growth rate.

Unemployment is one of the lowest in accession Countries, at 5.8% at the end of 2002, see Chart 17.

Annual inflation has started to decline since 2001, decreasing from more than 18%, recorded in 1997, to around 4.8%, at the end of 2002, see Chart 15. This followed the adoption of an inflation targeting monetary policy by the National Bank, aimed at achieving price stability in 2005.

Public debt declined to 54% of GDP in 2001, see Chart 19, and the official government deficit stabilized at 2.9% of GDP, except for the strong increase of 2002, see Chart 20.

The external current account deficit widened in 2002 while foreign direct investments fell off sharply. Thus, the deficit was mostly financed by debt and a decrease in official reserves. Buoyed by real appreciation, wage increases, and a fiscally-induced strengthening of domestic demand, import growth was strong. At the same time, tourism receipts fell sharply. This resulted in a current account deficit of 4.1 percent of GDP, compared with 3.4 percent in 2001, see IMF (2003).

Financial markets

The financial sector contains a broad set of institutions, and sound macroeconomic policies have facilitated the development of financial markets and instruments. Financial sector reform has been far-reaching and put strict conditions on bank management and capitalization. Through these well-targeted policies in the recent past, the authorities succeeded in attracting significant foreign strategic investors in all segments of the financial system.

Government ownership in all sectors has been reduced significantly and only remains substantial in the banking sector.

Responsibility for the supervision of the financial system rests with the HFSA, which does not have, though, the right to issue binding rules and regulations.

The Budapest Stock Exchange (BSE), the first of the former socialist Central and Eastern European exchanges to reopen, was formally reestablished in 1990. The 1996 Offering of Securities, Investment Services and the Securities Exchange Act and the 1990 Securities and the Stock Exchange Act govern the public issuance and trading of bonds, shares and other securities. The BSE has 34 members, which are licensed-broker or broker-dealer companies, including several foreign firms. It is a full member of the Federation of International Stock Exchanges and an associate member of the International Securities Market Association. The emergence of the Budapest stock exchange has been associated with the privatization process, since most of the listed companies have gone through privatization.

The main equity index for the Hungarian stock exchange is the Budapest Stock Index (BUX), whose basis is 1000 points on January 2, 1991. It belongs to the group of capital value type indices, i.e. the weight of each stock in the index is tied to the issuer's market capitalization. As of March 2003, the BUX is composed by 14 shares, compared to the limit of 25 set by the Budapest Stock Exchange.

A tendency to uninterrupted growth in the number of Equity securities listed on the BSE came to a halt in 2000, when the number of listed companies shrunk compared to the previous year. Since the introduction of stocks during the period of the privatization, there have been few significant new stock issues on the Budapest bourse. In recent years, this lack of new investment opportunities, the increasing number of delistings and the general negative trend in the stock market caused a sharp decline in the total market cap of Hungarian equities market as a percentage of GDP. On the other side, the increasing value of government debt securities has not negatively influenced the investor appetite for high quality emerging market issues. A major decline in government securities yields began in October 1999. Improving inflation expectations and a bright economic outlook have resulted in a steady increase in bonds price and in the reduction of the spread over German Government bonds. With regards to other listed financial instruments, mortgage backed securities witnessed a sustained growth reaching a market capitalization of almost US$ 700 m.

Looking back at the market in the last five to six years, its activity, as measured by the BUX index trading volume, has gone through waves of sustained growth followed by marked slowdowns. The total trades on the Budapest Exchange can be related to the global stock market movements as well as to specific country reasons. For instance, during the summer and fall of 1999 amid global stock market exuberance (as witnessed also by the performance of the BUX), the trading activity decreased. The reduction of trading volume on the Budapest bourse can be linked to a wave of increases in interest rates globally, an event that pushed down the capital flow into the Hungarian stock market as well as the overall exposure to emerging market shares.

Before the Russian crisis in 1998, Hungarian investors were more active participants in the Budapest bourse, assuring activity even in periods when foreign investors were less enthusiastic market participants. As a result of the Russian crisis, when stock prices fell by as much as 50%, many Hungarian private investors were forced out of the market, and Hungarian retail brokers that once represented a significant part of total turnover, either went bankrupt or decreased their business levels.

Using the Datastream index, the market went up by about 30% in the last six years, even though the price-earnings ratio has dropped from 22 to 14 between 1997 and 2003 and the dividend yield has been steady at about 2%.

Currently Hungary adopts an exchange rate band. The central parity, which is pegged to the euro, is 282.36 forint/euro. The market exchange rate may deviate from the parity within a +/-15% fluctuation band.

The Czech Republic

Macroeconomics

Western observers view the Czech Republic as one of the most politically and economically stable post-Communist states. Its solid image as one of the most stable and prosperous of post-Communist states was only dented by the political and financial crises in 1997-1998. Thanks to a successful campaign to address structural economic weaknesses, the Czech Republic went back on its growth path in 2000. After the deep recession in 1998/99, the Czech economy has again grown since 2000. Despite the global economic downturn, GDP increased by 2.0% in 2002. The main cause of this trend, which can be considered positive compared to other European economies, is high consumer confidence and the continued high level of investment, above all by foreign companies.

Enterprise restructuring and work disincentives arising from the social benefit system have led to rising structural unemployment and large regional disparities in unemployment rates. The unemployment rate in the last five years has steadily grown, increasing from 4.3% in 1997 to more than 10% at the beginning of 2003.

The inflation rate fell from almost 6% mid-2001 to 0.2% in February 2003 and averaged 1.8% in 2002. The upward revaluation of the Czech krone (increased by almost 20% compared to the euro since 2000) led to lower import prices in absolute terms but is a source of growing concern for Czech exporters.

Against the backdrop of the lower inflation rate and the slight drop in growth, the Central Bank lowered the key rate on several occasions in 2002 and early 2003. The lowering of interest rates and intervention on the foreign exchange market have stabilized the exchange rate in recent months to a value of between 31 and 32 krone to the euro. The deficit in the Czech budget is still expected to grow in 2003. The high expected deficit in the foreseeable future will contribute, in the coming years, to an increase in the public debt, which, at its current level of about 25% of GDP, is still well below the 60% threshold set by the Maastricht Treaty.

An important contributing factor to the recent strength of the Czech economy has been significant inflows of foreign direct investments. Gross FDI inflows reached US$4.9 billion in 2001 (8.7% of GDP), the highest in the region, bringing the stock to over $20 billion, some 40% of GDP. Low wages, a well-educated and disciplined work force, a favourable geographic location, political and economic stability, and the prospect of EU accession have made the Czech Republic an attractive destination for FDI. The Czech balance of trade deficit reached approximately EUR 2.5 billion in 2002 and was thus, due to favorable effects on prices, some EUR 1 billion lower than in the previous year. In contrast the current account deficit rose in 2002 to EUR 3.9 billion (5.3% of GDP) due to reduced income from tourism.

In the medium term, potential growth of 3.5-4% seems feasible. Certainly this would require containing cost increases to attract FDI, raise productivity, and sustain rapid export growth. Concerted efforts to improve infrastructure would also be needed. Yet, with the planned restraint on current fiscal expenditure, it should be possible to make room for infrastructure spending and moderate private consumption growth without straining the current account position.

Financial markets

The Czech banking sector still needs to undergo a restructuring process. In fact, the Czech system holds a large stock of non-performing loans which amount to some 25% of the GDP.

After the collapse of the communist regime in 1989, the Preparatory Committee for the Foundation of the Prague Stock Exchange was set up, in May 1991. In August 1992, the new Company, composed of eight banking houses, was transformed into an association. Upon adoption of the Stock Exchange Act, the association was later converted into the Prague Stock Exchange. Within a very short term, the Exchange managed to do all the preparatory work and, as early as 6 April 1993, the first trading session took place on its trading floor. Today, the Prague Stock Exchange enables issuers to trade their issues in four markets: Main, Secondary, New and Free.

The main equity index for the Czech stock exchange is the PX 50 Index, whose basis is 1000 points on April 5, 1994.

Since 1993, the Czech Exchange conditions for admission of a security to trading on the Main, Secondary and Free Markets and the subsequent duty of an issuer to provide information have undergone many changes. These changes were mainly influenced by: an effort to increase the transparency of the market, new segmentation of Exchange markets, amendments to laws applicable to capital markets and an effort to create a standard Exchange environment in harmony with advanced capital markets.

The number of listed securities, as of July 2003, is 151, of which 73 are shares and 78 are bonds.

Bonds have been listed on the Exchange since 1992. At the end of 2002, there were 56 issues of Treasury bonds and five issues of corporate bonds listed, including two issues by a foreign bank and one convertible bond issue by a listed company. Although the number of listed bonds has regularly increased in the past years, the total turnover value shrunk in 2002 by more than 1 bn zlotys. Improving inflation expectations and improving economic outlook have resulted in a steady increase in bonds price and in the reduction of the spread over German Government bonds.

Looking back at the market in the last five to six years, it may very well be said that the Czech market weathered the storm of the world markets in a peculiar way. In fact, in the past two years the CZ50 index has appreciated considerably, about doubling its level.

The Czech Koruna is the official currency of the Czech Republic. It is a managed, floating currency.

VALUE AT RISK

Description

Value at Risk (VaR) (see Jorion (1997) for a general introduction) is a measure of the maximum potential change in value of a portfolio of financial instruments with a given probability over a pre-set horizon. VaR is a methodology for measuring market risk, where, by market risk, we mean the potential for changes in value of a position resulting from changes in market prices.

VaR depends on the horizon over which the portfolio's change in value is measured and the degree of confidence chosen by the risk manager. Suppose one wants to compute the Value-at-Risk of a portfolio composed of a risky assets and a risk-free one, over a 1-day horizon with a 5% chance that the actual loss in the portfolio's value is greater than the VaR estimate. The Value-at-Risk calculation consists of the following steps:

mark-to-market the current portfolio. Denote this value by W_0
define the value of a portfolio W_1, as

$$W_1 = W_0 + (1 + \omega r)$$

where r represents the return on the risky asset and it has been assumed that the risk-free rate is zero for simplicity;

- to carry out the VaR calculation one needs 1-day forecasts of the mean of the 1-day return, $W_0 \omega E_r$. Following the RiskMetrics framework, the mean return over a 1-day horizon period is set equal to zero;
- the variance is computed as:

$$W_0^2 \omega V \omega'$$

VaR corresponds to the value, denoted by W_{VaR}, of the distribution such that there is a 5% chance that the actual return will be less than W_{VaR}. Analytically, the VaR is the results of the following expression:

$$\Pr(\Delta W \leq W_{VaR}) = 0.05$$

Another crucial point in the computation of VaR is the choice of the underlying distribution of returns. One of the most widely applied parametric probability distributions is the normal distribution, which has a number of important properties.

Results for the one-day VaR

In this section we describe the computation of VaR in the three countries we selected, in a broad sense, that is, we present the data and the reasons underlying our many assumptions through the chapter. The detailed results for each country are described in the next section. In our analysis we used daily data ranging from the first day available to the present day.

Our paper calculates Value at Risk for stock returns, foreign exchange against euro and fixed income securities, mainly government bonds yields for two maturities.

The first issue discussed in this section concerns the calculation of the sample mean. It is common practice to set the sample mean to zero. This assumption seems reasonable for 1-day horizons forecasts and we decided to follow it. As a proof for the reasonableness of the assumption, we calculated the 500-day rolling window, that is, every day in the sample period we estimated a mean based on returns over the last 500 days. As can be seen from Table 4.1 below, the assumption of zero mean for returns is justified, at least on a daily basis, for both stocks and bonds:

Table 4.1 Descriptive statistics for mean

	Stock Index	Currency
	Px50	Koruna
Mean	0.000023	-0.00006
St Dev (of mean)	0.00046	0.00014
	WIG	Zloty
Mean	0.000396	0.000093
St Dev (of mean)	0.00069	0.000226
	BUX	Huf
Mean	0.000299	0.00019
St Dev (of mean)	0.00040	0.000236

Yields time series instead showed continually diminishing values, so that their means were significantly different from zero and we thus calculated their VaR using formulae with non-zero means, described in the following sections.

The second step for the computation of Value-at-Risk is to estimate the variance of the normal distribution. Our time series show clear evidence of volatility clustering. It is clear that variance changes with time, thus inducing us to model heteroskedasticity of time series. Moreover, volatility clusters show some evidence of persistence, thus meaning autocorrelation in variances.

As done by J.P. Morgan (1995), in order to forecast variances and covariances we use the exponentially weighted moving average model (EWMA), which can capture the dynamic features of volatility.

In our EWMA model, the last observations carry the highest weight in the volatility estimate, so that after a shock volatility immediately reacts, but then declines exponentially as the weight of the shock observation falls. Analytically:

$$\sigma^{ex} = \sqrt{(1-\lambda)\sum_{t=1}^{T}\lambda^{t-1}(r_t - \bar{r})^2}$$

The exponentially weighted moving average model depends on the parameter λ which is often called decay factor. This parameter determines the relative weights that are applied to the observations and the effective amount of data used in estimating volatility.

The choice of the decay factor can be done by optimization, by minimizing the mean squared error (MSE) over the history of data, as described in the fourth edition of *Risk Metrics Technical* – Morgan. Risk Metrics, however, provides calculations of the optimal decay factor of 0.94 for developed countries, while the measure varies widely in emerging markets, ranging from 0.808 to 0.999. In our empirical work we experimented with different parameter values to evaluate the robustness of the results.

We computed the value at risk for the stock market, the currency and two bonds for each of the three countries under consideration. Computations were performed for a one-day horizon, ten-day horizon and twenty-day horizon. The multi-day VaR was computed assuming the validity of the square root rule.

In every case the computation of the VaR was recursive, that is in order to calculate the risk for day t+1 we estimated the variance by using only data until day t and then we rolled over the sample, by using return data until day t+1 to compute risk for day t+2.

Hungary

In Hungary we calculated the VaR for BUX stock index, Forint against euro, the 6-month T-Bill rate and the five-year government bond. For BUX and Forint, data are available from January 1995, so that our VaR was computed from 19 December. For fixed income securities, the calculations are slightly different, since we possess a shorter sample, spanning October 1997 to July 2003. Furthermore, T-bill and Bond rates are constantly diminishing through the sample, so that their average changes are significantly different from zero and negative, specifically -0.05%. We then modified all the equations to allow for a non-zero mean return.

We initially fix α at level 95% and the decay factor at 0.94. The backtest of the VaR shows positive results both for gains and losses, since only 97 (128) points out of 1930 are outside the band for gains (losses), that is, 5.03% (6.63%). We repeated our calculations fixing α

at 99% and this time the daily forecasts were very poor, since we observed 37 points outside the band for gains and 53% for losses, respectively 1.92% and 2.75% of the times. The model therefore does not work well for extreme risks, since the lower barrier is crossed more than expected.

These contradicting results are due to the violation of the normality hypothesis, as can be seen by the Jarque-Bera test whose value is 12651 and by a kurtosis of 15.39.

With a confidence of 95% and a decay factor of 0.95, we observed 97 points outside the bands for gains and 102 for losses, respectively 5.03% and 5.28% of the times. Results change if we fix α at 99%, with 1.76% of data outside the bands for gains and 2.28% for losses. Therefore a slight change in the decay factor does not change the results.

For the six-month T-bill rate, we initially fixed α at 95% and the decay factor at 0.94 and we observed 62 points outside the band for gains and 43 for losses out of 1174 observations, i.e. respectively 5.28% and 3.66% of the times. We then fixed the confidence level at 99% and again we found that our model underestimates the risks, since we observed 2.64% and 2.30% data outside the bands for gains and losses. For the five-year government bond the results are the same, with a good performance at 95% and a poor one at 99%. Table 4.2 below summarizes our findings for Hungary.

Table 4.2 VaR Hungary

	BUX	Forint	6m T-bill	5y Bond
λ	0.94	0.95	0.94	0.98
95% Losses	5.03%	5.03%	5.28%	5.72%
95% Gains	6.63%	5.28%	3.66%	4.44%
99% Losses	1.92%	1.76%	2.64%	2.13%
99% Gains	2.75%	2.28%	2.30%	1.79%

We calculated the VaR using three different values for λ, the first at 0.98, indicating strong persistence, the second at 0.94, as in developed countries, and the third around 0.90, indicating weak persistence.

The following table summarizes our more general findings with different decay factors. For the sake of simplicity, we reported the results for losses at the 95% confidence level.

Table 4.3 VaR in Hungary for losses at 95% (with different lambdas)

	BUX	Forint	6m T-bill	5y Bond
λ =0.90	5.54%	6.01%	6.81%	7.69%
λ =0.94	5.03%	5.03%	5.28%	6.92%
λ =0.98	4.30%	4.09%	4.17%	5.72%

Table 4.3 shows that the choice of the decay factor is important for the results and should be carefully chosen.

Poland

In Poland we calculated the daily VaR for WIG stock index, Zloty (bilateral rate against the Euro), the two-year and the three-year government bond. For WIG and Zloty, data are available from January 1995, so that our VaR was computed from 19 December. For what concerns fixed income, in Poland, the T-bill rate data were not available. We thus used two-year and three-year government bond yields, spanning from March 1999 to July 2003. The means of the bond series are significantly different from zero and negative, respectively -0.08 for the two-year bond and -0.07 for the three-year maturity. We then modified all the formulae, since all the variances and confidence intervals must be calculated around the new mean.

We initially fixed α at 95% and the decay factor at 0.97 for WIG and 0.92 for Zloty. The results are similar to those obtained in Hungary, with a good performance of our forecasts at 95%, and a poor one at 99%.

In detail, WIG forecasts are outside the bands 5.18% for gains and 5.08% or losses, while Zloty forecasts are outside the bands respectively 5.08% and 6.58% of the times. The same model calculated at 99% seems to underestimate the risks, with violations of the bands occurring almost 2% of the times, as shown in Table 4.4 below.

The computations reflect our findings for Hungary, with overestimation of gains at 95% and a poorer performance, in terms of estimation of risk, at the 99% confidence level. The table below summarizes our findings for Poland.

Table 4.4 VaR Poland

	WIG	Zloty	2y Bond	3y Bond
λ	0.97	0.92	0.965	0.955
95% Losses	5.18%	5.08%	5.15%	5.09%
95% Gains	5.08%	6.58%	4.44%	4.86%
99% Losses	1.87%	1.61%	2.22%	1.97%
99% Gains	1.97%	2.85%	2.11%	2.20%

Also for Poland, we calculated the VaR using three different values for λ, the first at 0.98, indicating strong persistence, the second at 0.94, as in developed countries, and the third around 0.90, indicating weak persistence. Table 4.5 summarizes our more general findings with different decay factors. For the sake of simplicity, we reported the results for losses at the 95% confidence level.

Table 4.5 VaR in Poland for losses at 95% (with different lambdas)

	WIG	Zloty	2y Bond	3y Bond
λ =0.90	6.74%	5.60%	7.02%	6.60%
λ =0.94	6.06%	4.66%	5.85%	5.44%
λ =0.98	5.03%	3.63%	4.68%	4.17%

Czech Republic

In the Czech Republic we calculated the daily VaR for PX50 stock index, Koruna against the Euro, the two-year and the three-year government bond. For PX50 and Koruna, data are available from January 1995, so that our VaR was computed from 19 December. We initially fixed α at 95% and the decay factor at 0.98 for Px50 and 0.955 for Koruna. As to fixed income, in the Czech Republic, the T-bill rate data were not available. We thus used two-year and three-year government bond yields, the former spanning 1997 September 28 to July 2003, the latter from 1997 February 4 to July 2003. The mean of the bond series for the three-year maturity is significantly different from zero and negative, specifically -0.04, while that of the bond series for the two-year maturity is not significantly different from zero. We then modified only the formulae for the three-year maturity. The decay factor chosen is 0.97 for both fixed income securities.

The results are similar to those obtained in Hungary, with a good performance of our forecasts at 95%, and a poor one at 99%. In detail, PX50 forecasts are outside the bands 4.92% for gains and 5.39% or losses, while Koruna forecasts are outside the bands respectively 5.03% and 5.54% of the times. The same model calculated at 99% seems to underestimate the risks, with violations of the bands occurring almost 2% of the times, as shown in Table 4.6 below.

The computations reflect our findings for Hungary, with overestimation of gains at 95% and a poorer performance, in terms of estimation of risk, at the 99% confidence level. For the Czech Republic, however, we observed a very bad performance of VaR also at 95% both for gains and losses for the three-year bond. Table 4.6 below summarizes our findings for Czech Republic.

Table 4.6 VaR Czech Republic

	PX50	Koruna	2y Bond	3y Bond
λ	0.98	0.955	0.97	0.97
95% Losses	4.82%	5.03%	5.00%	6.51%
95% Gains	5.39%	5.54%	4.66%	4.10%
99% Losses	1.71%	1.76%	2.08%	2.49%
99% Gains	2.02%	2.02%	1.83%	1.98%

We calculated the VaR using three different values for λ also in the Czech Republic, fixing the first value at 0.98, the second at 0.94, as in developed countries, and the third around 0.90. Table 4.7 summarizes our more general findings, with different decay factors for losses at the 95% confidence level.

Table 4.7 VaR in the Czech Republic for losses at 95% (with different lambdas)

	PX50	Koruna	2y Bond	3y Bond
λ =0.90	6.22%	6.74%	7.24%	7.75%
λ =0.94	5.44%	5.54%	6.58%	6.95%
λ =0.98	4.82%	3.89%	4.66%	6.44%

The multi-period VaR

Table 4.8 10-day VaR in the various countries

		λ=0.90		λ =0.94		λ =0.98	
		Loss	Gain	Loss	Gain	Loss	Gain
Czech Republic							
PX50	#	9.89%	12.38%	9.37%	10.82%	8.27%	9.37%
	%	190	238	180	208	159	180
Bond3y	#	15.53%	7.21%	13.83%	5.15%	10.82%	4.19%
	%	211	98	188	70	147	57
Bond2y	#	4.66%	4.33%	8.97%	2.01%	6.45%	1.59%
	%	56	52	107	24	77	19
Koruna	#	3.89%	4.66%	2.45%	2.81%	2.13%	2.39%
	%	75	90	47	54	41	46
Hungary							
BUX	#	8.24%	11.52%	7.25%	10.64%	5.58%	8.97%
	%	158	221	139	204	107	172
Bond5y	#	13.33%	9.03%	12.12%	7.57%	9.29%	5.93%
	%	155	105	141	88	108	69
Tbill 6m	#	13.04%	10.46%	11.41%	8.66%	8.92%	7.03%

	%	152	122	133	101	104	82
HUF	#	2.19%	2.45%	1.66%	2.24%	1.40%	1.77%
	%	42	47	32	43	27	34
Poland							
WIG	#	9.73%	9.63%	8.79%	8.12%	7.18%	7.54%
	%	187	185	169	156	138	145
Bond2y	#	7.08%	2.95%	6.73%	1.65%	6.14%	0.24%
	%	60	25	57	14	52	2
Bond3y	#	4.91%	4.21%	4.09%	2.45%	2.69%	1.64%
	%	42	36	35	21	23	14
Zloty	#	2.39%	6.50%	1.93%	5.98%	0.94%	4.58%
	%	46	125	37	115	18	88

Table 4.9 20 day VaR in the various countries

		λ=0.90		λ=0.94		λ=0.98	
		Loss	Gain	Loss	Gain	Loss	Gain
Czech Rep.							
PX50	#	12.34%	14.96%	12.34%	14.96%	10.72%	11.04%
	%	236	286	236	286	205	211
Bond3Y	#	18.16%	6.97%	16.01%	5.78%	12.97%	4.37%
	%	245	94	216	78	175	59
Bond2y	#	7.52%	2.37%	11.33%	3.63%	7.52%	2.37%
	%	89	28	134	43	89	28
Koruna	#	4.18%	2.72%	4.18%	2.72%	3.09%	2.09%
	%	80	52	80	52	59	40
Hungary							
BUX	#	5.49%	11.66%	8.42%	13.55%	5.49%	11.66%
	%	105	223	161	259	105	223
Bond5Y	#	12.58%	9.37%	16.22%	10.58%	12.58%	9.37%
	%	145	108	187	122	145	108
Tbill 6m	#	14.79%	11.07%	14.79%	11.07%	12.28%	8.30%
	%	171	128	171	128	142	96
HUF	#	1.99%	2.77%	1.83%	2.30%	1.88%	1.73%

	%	38	53	35	44	36	33

Poland							
WIG	#	11.61%	10.88%	11.61%	10.88%	8.68%	9.52%
	%	222	208	222	208	166	182
Bond2Y	#	10.16%	2.27%	9.32%	0.36%	10.16%	2.27%
	%	85	19	78	3	85	19
Bond3y	#	5.44%	2.48%	7.33%	4.37%	5.44%	2.48%
	%	46	21	62	37	46	21
Zloty	#	1.83%	8.21%	1.83%	8.21%	0.52%	5.28%
	%	35	157	35	157	10	101

Finally we extended the forecasting period in order to evaluate risk for ten and 20 days, see Table 4.9. This is practically important whenever the VaR is used for portfolio optimization and not simply risk measurement. Portfolio optimization is usually carried out with a time horizon which is longer than one day. It is therefore important to know whether the simple methodology works also for longer horizons.

We present our results (for a 95% level) for the three countries at the same time.

The tables show a massive failure of the simple methodology. The cells should contain numbers not much different from 5%, but actually they report numbers which in general are much larger, especially for the stock market. The bonds are sometimes not far away, while the currencies in general show realized risks which are lower than the theoretical ones. Modifying the decay factor does not help much in general. The results are often very different for the left and the right tails.

CONCLUSIONS

This is a first exploration of risk analysis in three accession countries. The nature of the chapter has somewhat changed from its original goals, which were more of an applied econometrics nature. The original idea was to develop a macroeconomic-based risk model for stock markets, bond markets and currencies. However, the quantity and the quality of the available data have convinced us that it was more realistic to provide a thorough description of the financial markets of these countries rather than attempt the application of difficult models, originally thought for developed markets and requiring long series of data for estimation.

What is especially missing for a complete description of risk is in our opinion time series extending back in time. We have seen that most series are short; even though we have not performed a formal statistical analysis, it is also likely that such series are affected by structural breaks which makes estimation and statistical inference very difficult. A recent interesting attempt at using cointegration analysis for determining the fair value of the currency of the countries involved in this study (see Jamaleh and Ruggerone, 2003) is interesting but in our opinion probably sensitive to the existence of structural breaks in the time series. A long econometric literature has shown that the existence of structural breaks may bias cointegration analysis, especially in short samples.

Even the financial series which are available at high frequency (i.e. daily observations) are subject to elements which are hard to extrapolate. For example, the interest rate has been decreasing since 1997, and this leaves an average increase in bond prices, but this increase is unlikely to be a good estimate of what will happen in the next say 10 years. As another example, there are time series of stock indices. However there are wide differences between different indices. Moreover the market structure has gone through an incredible transformation, described for example by the number of shares traded. Finally, the available data on the price earnings and the dividend yield provide information which is sometimes difficult to interpret.

The only quantitative risk model which has a hope to work in this environment is the standard Value at Risk methodology where the daily variance is estimated by means of a simple adaptive rule. Indeed we have tested this model and showed its efficiency for the short daily horizon and the 5% risk level. However the results become highly unstable whenever risk is forecast for a longer horizon of 10 days or 20 days (horizons which are typical for most portfolio optimization models) and when risk is defined at the 1% level. The severe non-normality of distributions is really damaging to the models in most cases.

REFERENCES

Beltratti, A. and C. Morana (2002), 'The Effects of the Introduction of the Euro on the Volatility of European Stock Markets', *Journal of Banking and Finance,* **26**, 2047-2064.

Gros, D. (2002), 'Central Europe on the Way to EMU', *Rivista di Politica Economica*, January-February, 89-107.

IMF 'Public Information Notice' (PIN) (2003), No. 03/76 – June 19.

Jamaleh, Asmara and Luigi Ruggerone, 'Modelling Eastern Europe Currencies in the Run-Up to Joining the EMU', Collana Ricerche, Banca Intesa, June 2003.

Jorion, P. (1997), *Value at Risk: The New Benchmark for Controlling Marlet Risk*, Irwin-McGraw Hill: Illinois.

Morgan, J.P. (1995), 'Risk Metrics Technical Manual', New York: J.P. Morgan.

Wyplosz, C. (2003), 'Do not Impose a Currency Crisis on Europe', *Financial Times*, June 16.

APPENDIX

Poland

Table 4.10 Summary data

	Type	1995	1996	1997	1998	1999	2000	2001	2002
Stocks	Continous trading	0	21	46	82	99	102	141	152
	Single-price system	65	83	143	198	221	123	89	64
Tot. listed companies		65	83	143	198	221	225	230	216
Tot. stocks market cap (US$ mm)		4,563	8,362	12,469	20,639	29,845	31,479	25,940	29,016
Bonds				44	44	47	48	53	61
Tot number of listed securities		65	83	187	242	268	273	283	277

Chart 4.1 WIG index performance since 1997

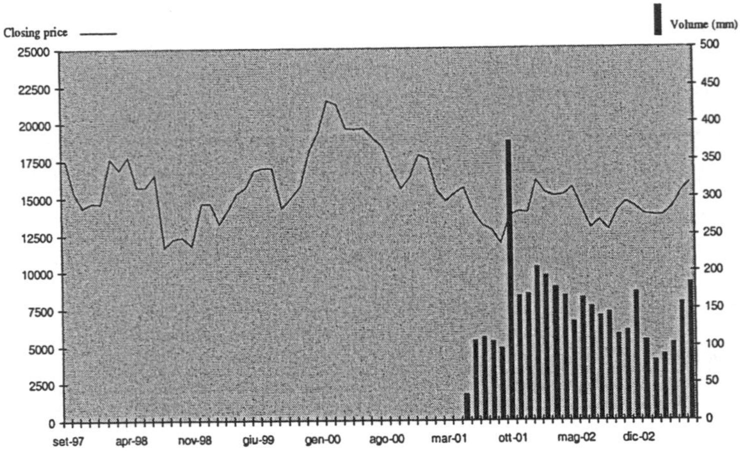

Chart 4.2 Generic 5-year - government bond yield and spread vs. equivalent German rate

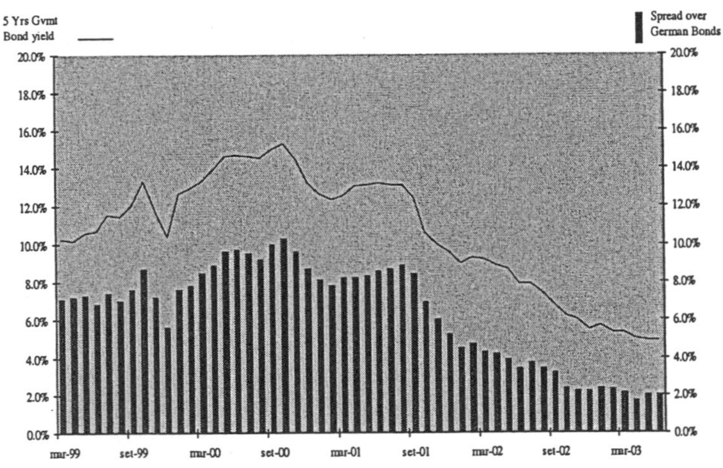

Chart 4.3 Polish market valuation

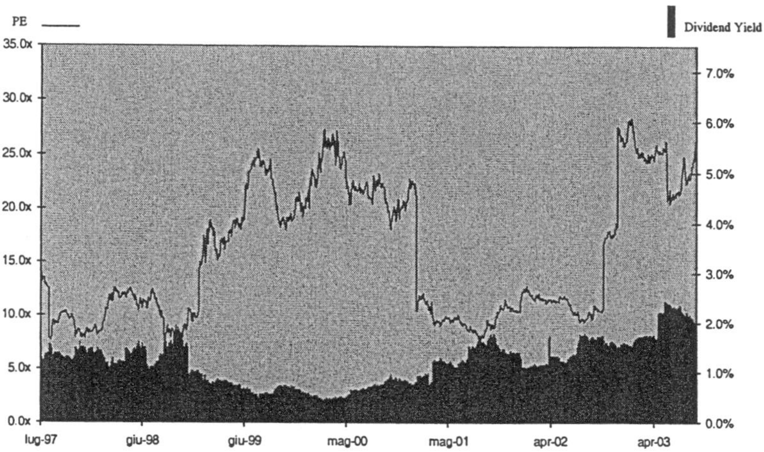

Chart 4.4 GDP at constant prices quarterly growth

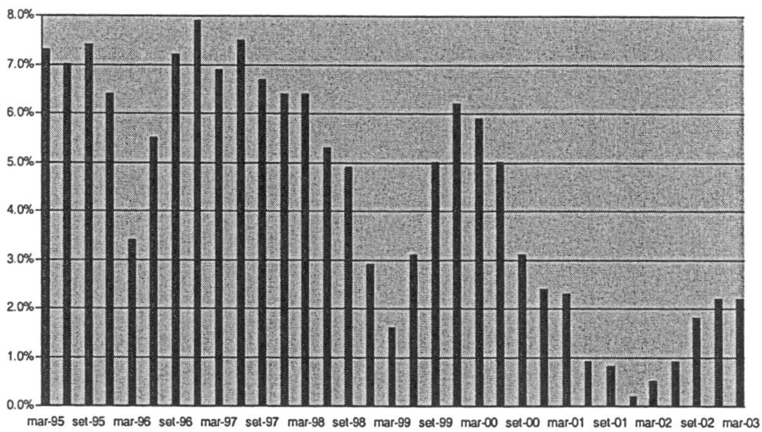

Chart 4.5 Inflation as measured by the CPI

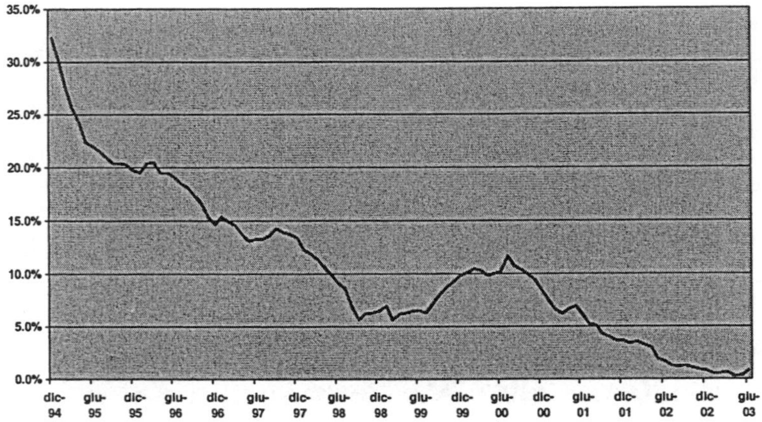

Chart 4.6 Exchange rate PLN vs. euro

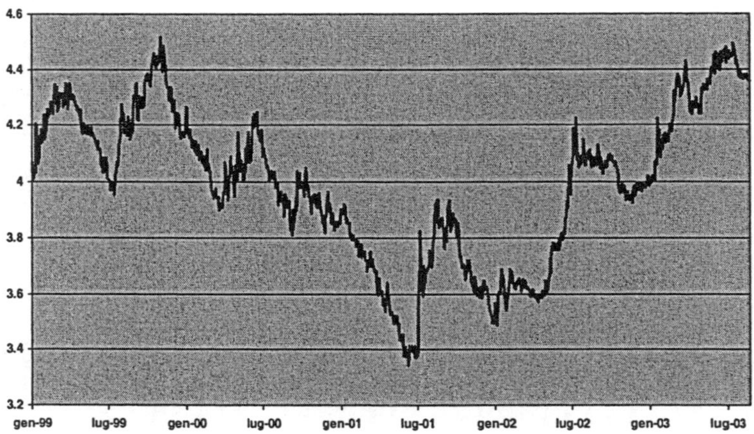

Chart 4.7 Unemployment

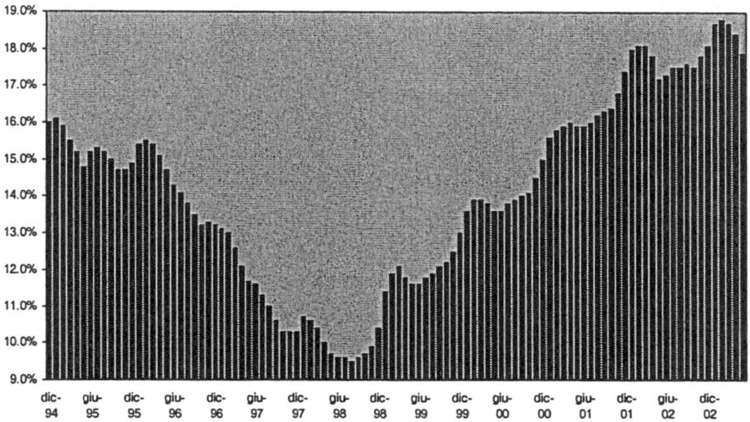

Chart 4.8 Current account and trade balance evolution as % of GDP

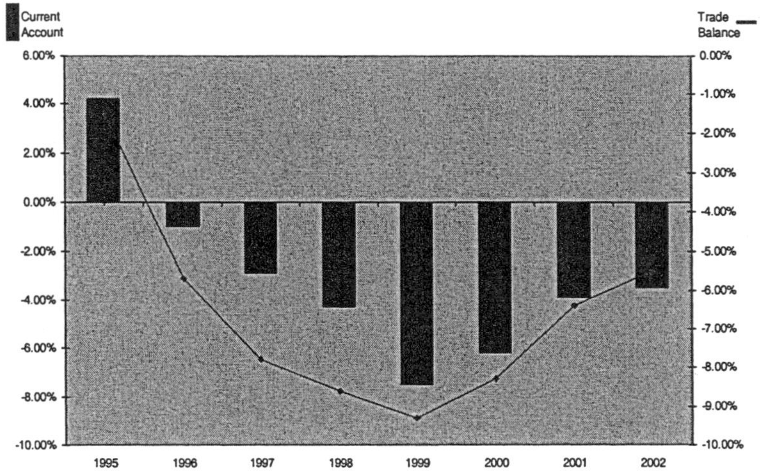

Chart 4.9 Gross foreign debt as % of GDP

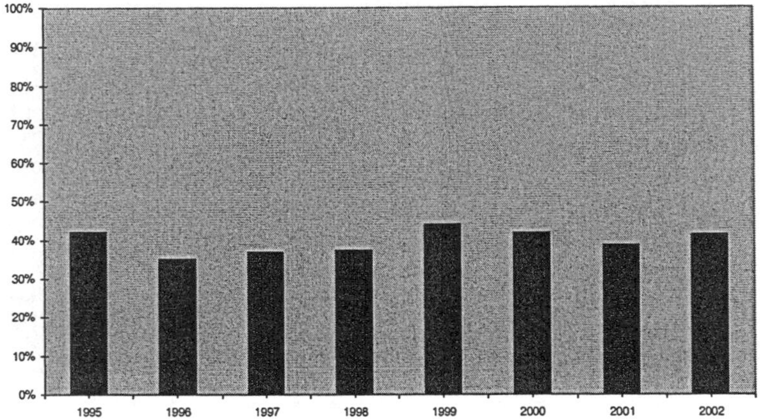

Chart 4.10 Public deficit

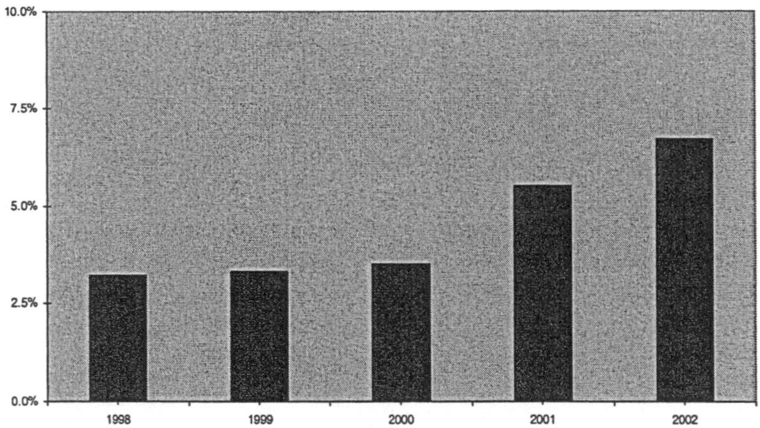

Hungary

Table 4.11 Number of listed securities

Type	1990	1991	1992	1993	1994	1995	1996	1997	1998	1999	2000	2001	2002	2003 YTD
Equities	6	20	23	28	40	42	45	49	55	66	60	56	49	48
Gvmt bonds		1	4	16	25	34	36	28	30	30	29	28	26	26
Corp. bonds		1	1	1	3	3	2	7	8	8	7	7	13	12
Intl. Instit. bonds										2	2	4	2	2
Mtge bonds												3	14	23
T-bills			10	10	31	50	50	44	42	23	10	10	10	10
Investment funds			1	6	20	36	33	20	8	5	3	3	5	5
Compens-ation notes			1	1	1	1	1	1	1	1	1	1	1	1
Tot. number of listed securities	6	22	40	62	120	166	167	149	144	135	112	112	120	123

Table 4.12 BSE market capitalization

Mkt cap (Us$ mm)	1990	1991	1992	1993	1994	1995	1996	1997	1998	1999	2000	2001	2001	2003 YTD
Equities	267	505	562	811	1,64	2,35	5,583	15,029	14,021	16,414	11,92	10,21	13,089	15,076
Gvmt bonds		202	980	2,4	3,55	3,256	4,607	4,677	6,537	8,080	9,159	12,21	18,98	23,81
Corp bonds		1	1	3	16	13	8	182	293	236	198	279	709	827
Intl. Instit. bonds										73	64	116	80	86
Mtge bonds												56	564	1,030
T-bills			648	735	2,165	2,698	4,566	4,464	4,259	3,835	2,800	3,523	5,852	6,882
Investment funds			23	55	174	307	273	166	26	20	16	17	24	44
Compens-ation notes			191	534	440	134	622	618	259	274	236	202	565	763
Tot mkt cap	267	708	2,405	4,538	7,985	8,758	15,659	25,136	25,395	28,932	24,393	26,613	39,863	48,518

Chart 4.11 BUX index performance since 1997

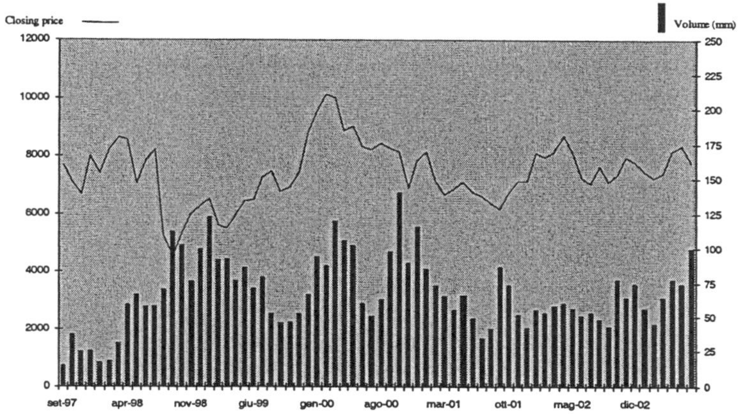

Chart 4.12 Generic 5-year - government bond yield and spread vs. equivalent German rate

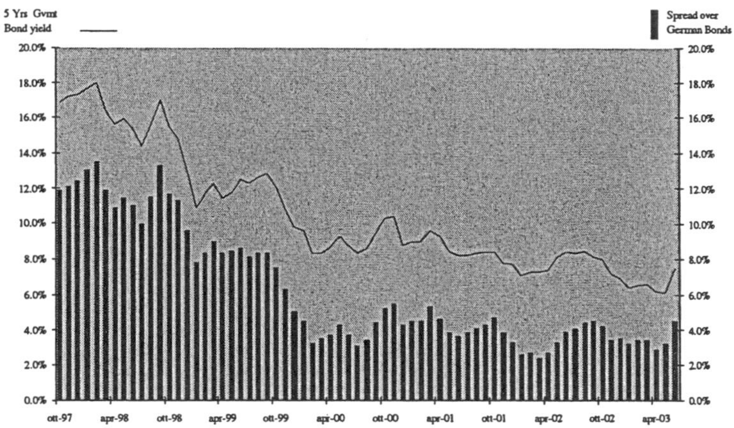

Chart 4.13 Hungarian market valuation

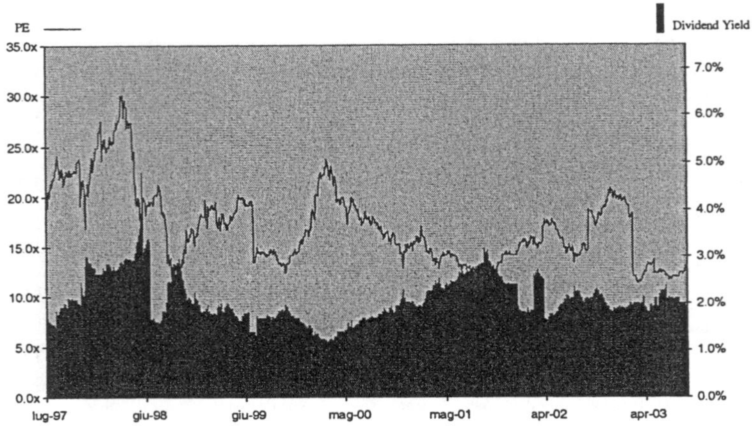

Chart4. 14 GDP at constant prices quarterly growth

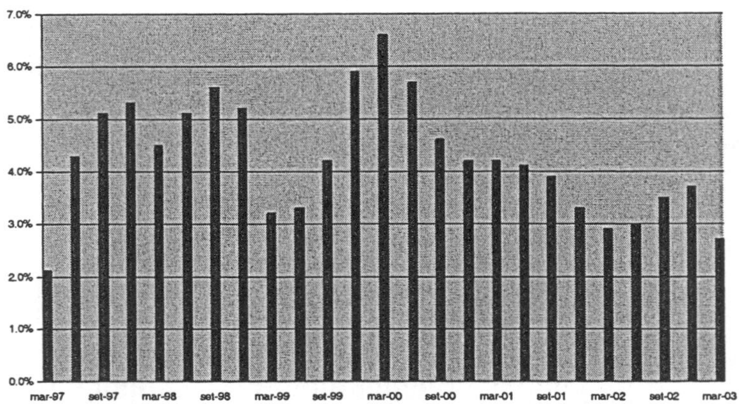

Chart 4.15 Inflation as measured by the CPI

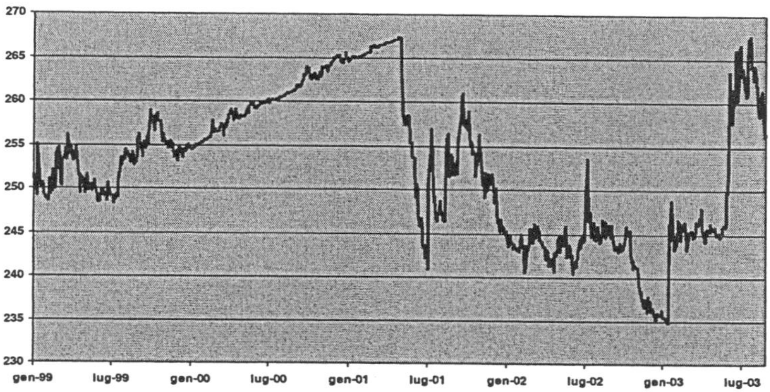

Chart 4.16 Exchange rate HUF vs. euro

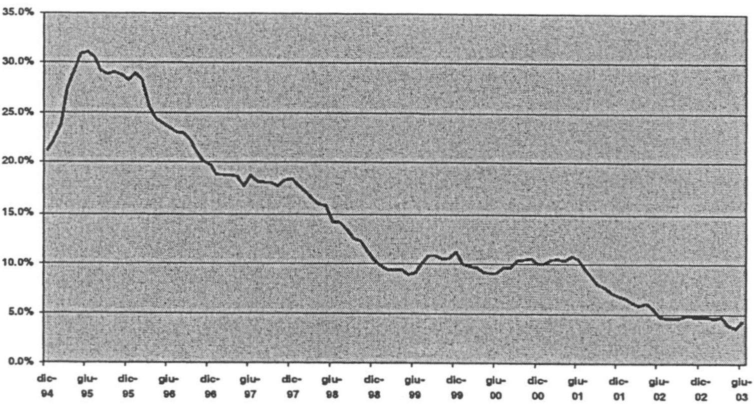

Chart 4.17 Unemployment

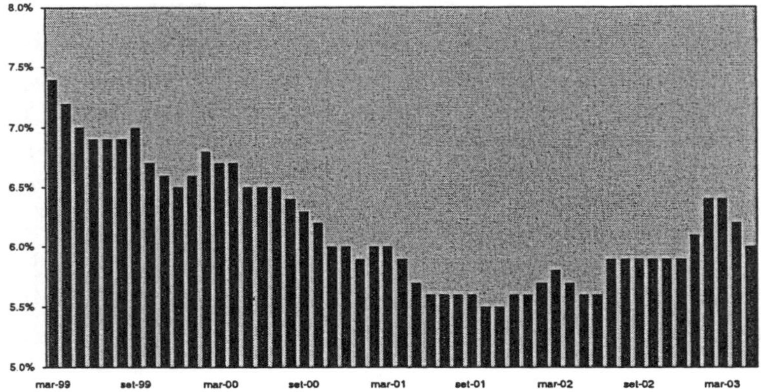

Chart 4.18 Current account and trade balance evolution as % of GDP

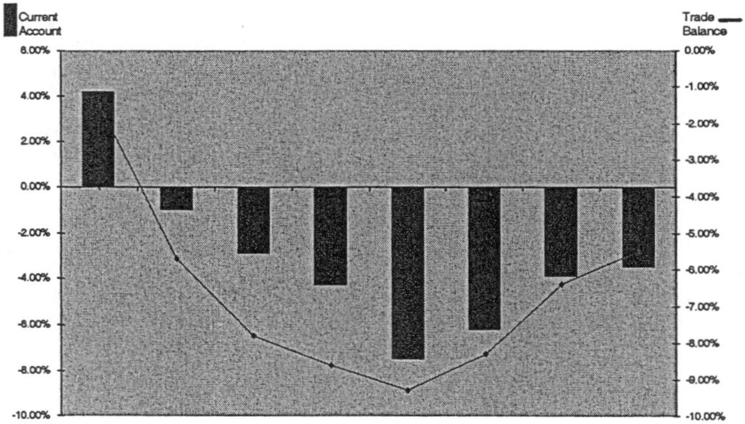

Chart 4.19 Gross foreign debt as % of GDP

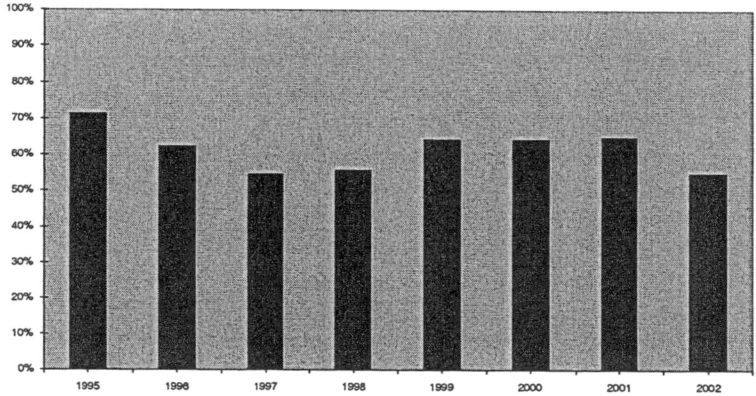

Chart 4.20 Public deficit

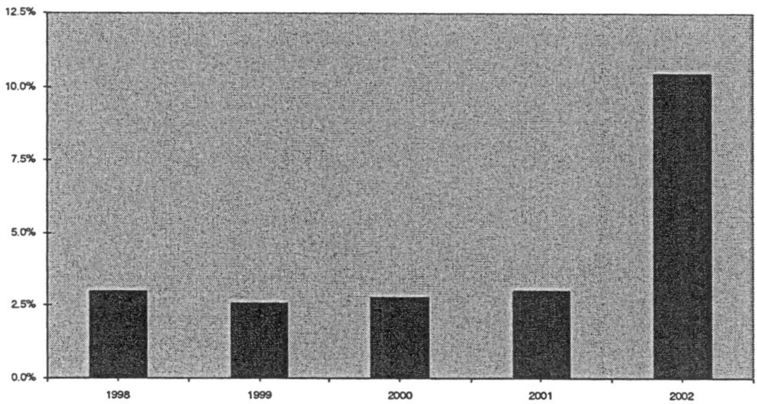

Czech Republic

Table 4.13 Number of listed securities

Market	Type	1995	1996	1997	1998	1999	2000	2001	2002
Main market	Shares	62	44	45	10	8	5	5	5
	Bonds	20	26	33	33	30	30	28	20
Secondary market	Shares	6	52	58	96	81	60	48	41
	Bonds	0	1	2	3	3	11	14	18
Free market	Shares	1,648	1,574	217	198	106	86	49	33
	Bonds	28	53	57	62	62	53	42	36
Tot. number of listed securities		1,764	1,750	412	402	290	245	186	153

Table 4.14 Prague market capitalization

Market	Type	1995	1996	1997	1998	1999	2000	2001	2002
Main Market	Share	10,100	13,659	10,364	6,699	7,436	6,916	6,203	11,266
	Bond	2,181	4,129	12,180	19,876	21,907	19,624	46,203	48,296
Secondary Market	Share	284	1,834	1,383	4,884	4,194	3,185	2,148	3,016
	Bond	0	65	57	73	78	514	2,581	2,182
Free Market	Share	7,624	4,231	2,462	2,246	1,754	1,769	1,224	1,607
	Bond	444	1,045	2,145	2,898	6,592	5,555	3,511	2,559
Tot. capitalization		20,632	24,964	28,592	36,676	41,961	37,563	61,871	68,926

Chart 4.21 CZ50 index performance since 1997

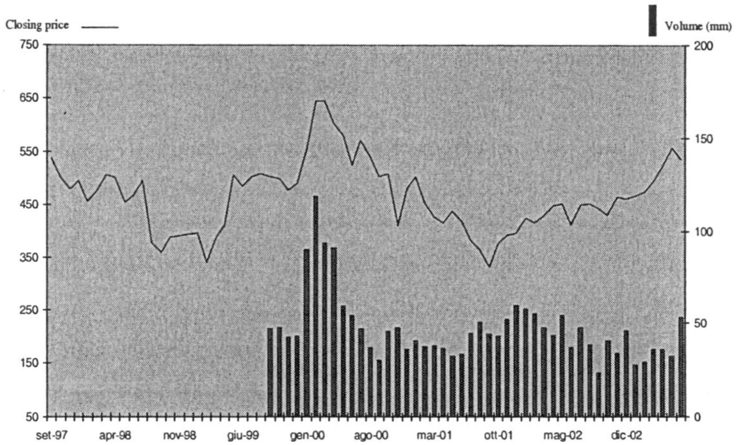

Chart 4.22 Generic 5-year - government bond yield and spread vs. equivalent German rate

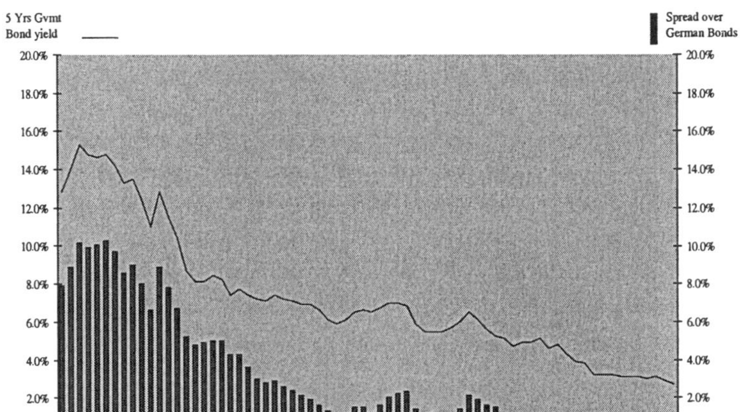

Chart 4.23 Czech market valuation

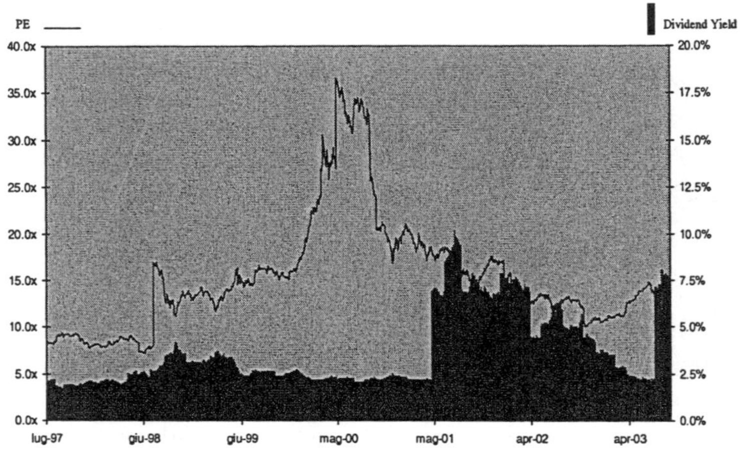

Chart 4.24 GDP at constant prices quarterly growth

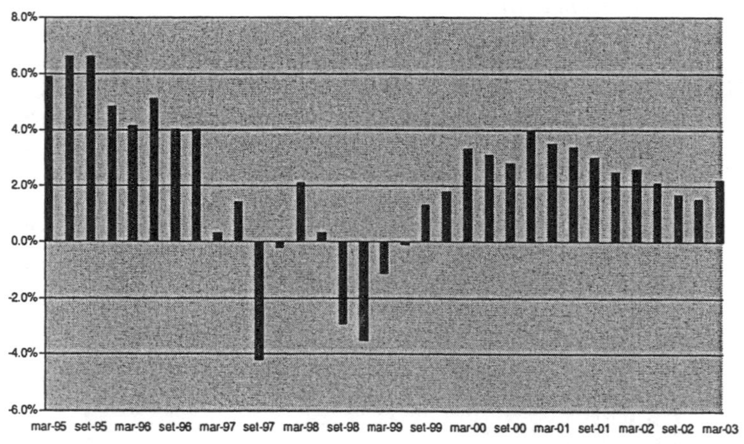

Chart 4.25 Inflation as measured by the CPI

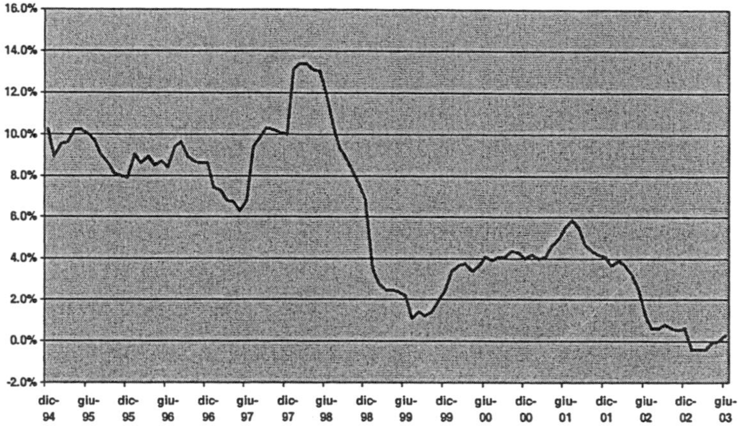

Chart 4.26 Exchange rate CZK vs. euro

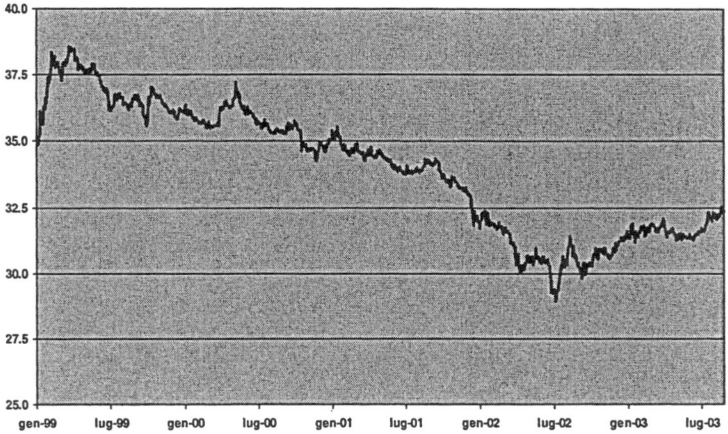

Chart 4.27 Unemployment

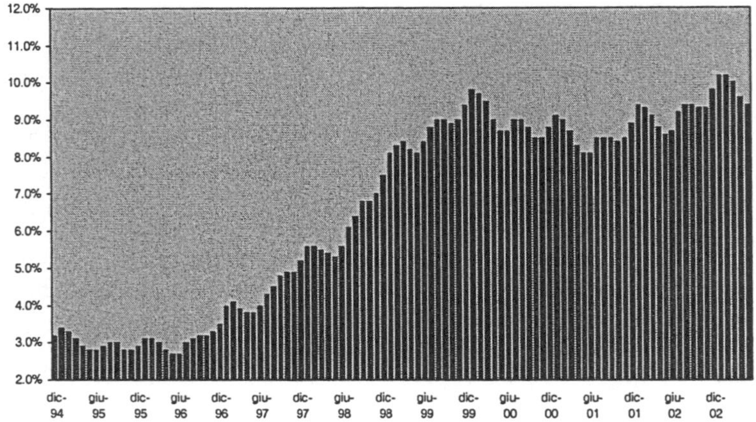

Chart 4.28 Current account and trade balance evolution as % of GDP

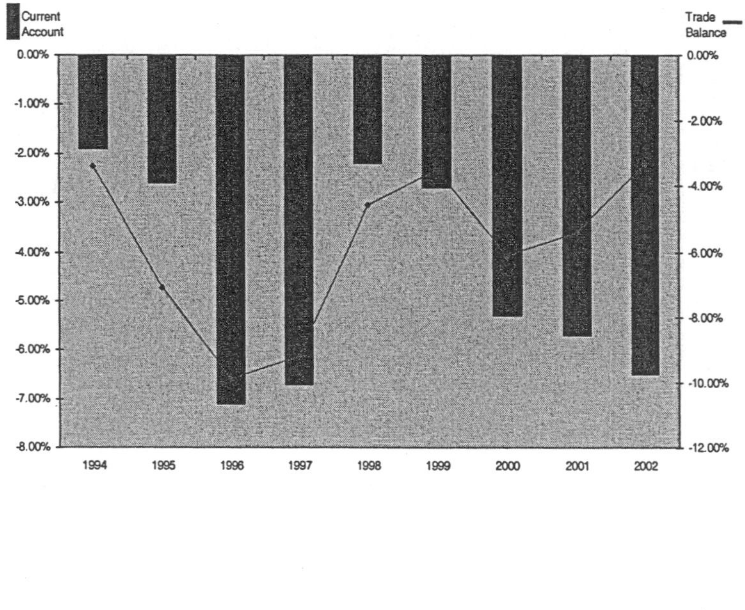

Chart 4. 29 Gross foreign debt as % of GDP

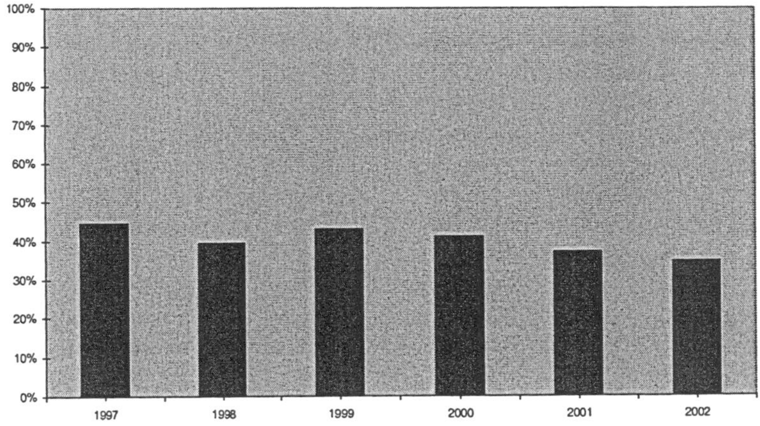

Chart 4.30 Public deficit

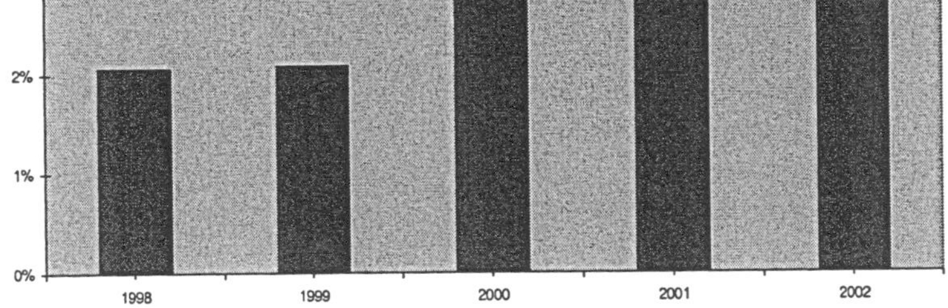

PART II

Foreign Banks

5. Who Needs Foreign Banks?

Daniel Gros[1]

INTRODUCTION

It is well known that highly indebted countries, or countries with weak fiscal institutions, can fall into a low credibility trap. This occurs when a government loses credibility in the eyes of the financial markets and is forced to pay a risk premium in the form of higher interest rates. The higher debt-service burden that results, if inflation is kept low, makes it even more likely that the authorities will abandon efforts to stabilize the situation and attempt to reduce the real value of the debt through a surprise inflation. This further increases the risk premium demanded by financial markets and can lead to a spiral of increasing interest rates until the government caves in and produces the inflation the market expects.

Moreover, countries with weak financial systems tend to accumulate more public debt because the government has to bail out banks, which represent powerful groups (e.g. farming cooperatives, heavy industry). The topic of this chapter is to what extent the presence of foreign banks can mitigate these problems.

One basic prescription of a country with little credibility, and a weak domestic institutional framework, which make it difficult to commit to low inflation, is to use an external anchor. For the Central and Eastern European countries the obvious candidate to be such an anchor would be the euro given that they are joining the EU and given that most of their external trade is with the euro area. Some countries have already de facto joined the euro area by linking their money via a currency board to the DM, or, now, the euro (e.g. Estonia, Bulgaria and Lithuania). But can these commitments be credible? In particular can they withstand the ultimate stress test imposed by financial markets when interest rates go to astronomical levels so that it becomes prohibitively expensive to service the debt at stable prices? This chapter explores whether the presence of foreign banks makes this problem more manageable.

What is a foreign bank? The presence of foreign banks usually takes the form of subsidiaries, rather than branches. It is clear that in most countries there is no legal distinction between a subsidiary, i.e. a bank whose capital is majority foreign owned and other, domestically owned banks. In both cases the bank is incorporated under domestic law and constitutes a separate legal identity. Moreover, in many cases the top management (the lower level management has to remain local for obvious reasons) is also local. In a number of countries the presence of foreigners among the top management is actually limited. Moreover, a foreign owned bank is usually treated, at least on chapter, in exactly the same way as domestically owned banks in terms of banking supervision, reserve requirements, etc. One might thus ask what difference does it make? For the purposes of this chapter it does make a big difference because of something intangible, namely because of the fact that a foreign bank is usually not subject to the same domestic political pressures and, therefore, usually does not accumulate large hidden liabilities on its balance sheet for which the government could in the end become responsible.

Foreign ownership of the banking system is just one facet of a more general phenomenon, namely foreign direct investment (FDI). FDI is usually particularly appreciated because it does not create debt and implies usually also a transfer of know-how. These reasons apply also in banking. Hence, there are many reasons why it might be desirable to have FDI in banking, particularly in transition countries where no banking system existed beforehand so that the skills necessary for running a bank simply did not exist at the local level. While these reasons for welcoming FDI in banking might be very important they will not be discussed in this chapter, which will concentrate on how the presence of foreign banks can improve the efficiency of the macroeconomic framework. For an excellent discussion of the weaknesses of domestic banking systems in transition countries see Berglof and Bolton (2002).

The remainder of this chapter is structured as follows: the next section shows some basic data illustrating the importance of foreign banks in the countries from Central and Eastern Europe which are candidates for EU membership (CEECs). Sections III and IV then present a standard model and its solution if there is no commitment device. This is followed in Section V by a discussion of what difference the presence of foreign banks can make. The model is meant to be illustrative of the effects that are likely to operate in countries with weak fiscal institutions. It does not pretend to be innovative. Section VI then shows how the equilibrium is affected in the standard cases by the presence of foreign banks. Section VII uses the model to discuss how a strong presence of foreign banks can make currency (and public finance) crisis less likely. Section VIII concludes.

FOREIGN BANKS IN CENTRAL AND EASTERN EUROPE

The importance of foreign owned, or foreign dominated, banks is not one of the statistics that central banks or finance ministries publish regularly because in many countries this is not an issue. Moreover, it is not always straightforward to identify what constitutes a foreign owned bank. The threshold of foreign ownership mostly used appears to be 50 %, but it is possible that even with a minority participation management can be dominated from abroad. A recent report from the European Commission, however, gives comparable figures for the ten candidates for EU membership from Central and Eastern Europe (eight of which joined the EU in 2004).

By 2001 foreign banks had more than half of deposits in all of the new member countries, and in some of the larger ones (e.g. Poland, Hungary, the Czech Republic) the share of foreign banks is around two- thirds. It is thus fair to say that foreign banks by now dominate the banking system in the CEECs. It would of course be even more interesting to have data on the capital invested in foreign banks. But the dominance in terms of deposits, which presumably translates into a dominance in terms of loans, implies that foreign banks should also dominate in terms of capital given that the same prudential standards are applied to domestic and foreign owned banks.

The situation in the 'old' EU-15 is quite different. Panel b) of Table 5.1 shows the data collected for 1997 by the ECB. It is apparent that in most member countries foreign banks have only a marginal presence (Luxemburg and the UK constitute exceptions because of their large off -shore banking sectors).

Table 5.1. Share of majority foreign-owned banks in total assets (in %)

Panel a): The CEECs				
	1998	1999	2000	2001
BL	n.a.	n.a.	74.4	75.0
CZ	25.7	28.1	65.5	90.1
EE	5.1	90.0	93.0	97.5
HU	58.9	61.8	62.9	65.5
LA	78.7	78.2	77.2	62.6
LI	51.8	38,3	57.0	83.9
PO	16.6	47.2	69.6	68.4
RO	20.0	47.5	50.9	55.0
SL	n.a.	28.2	42.7	81.0
SI	20.0	47.5	50.9	55.0

Source: European Central Bank, Annual Report (1999).

Panel b): The EU			
Ireland	53.8	Netherlands	7.7
UK	52.1	Finland	7.1
Belgium	36.3	Italy	6.8
Greece	21.9	Germany	4.3
Spain	11.7	Austria	3.3
Portugal	10.5	Sweden	1.6
France	9.8 (1996)	Denmark	n.a.

Source: European Commission (2002).

A STANDARD MODEL

How does the presence of foreign banks contribute to macroeconomic stability? The remainder of the chapter explores this question based on a simple model. The model used here is entirely conventional. The starting point is a standard social loss function, L_t, given by:

$$L_t = [\alpha q_t^2 + p_t^2] \qquad \alpha \geq 0 \tag{5.1}$$

where p_t stands for the inflation rate and q_t stands for tax revenues as a percentage of GDP, which is equivalent to the average tax rate. High taxes and high inflation create distortions and are thus socially costly. The parameter α indicates the relative weight of taxes in the social loss function. A high α could be interpreted to mean that the tax collection system is not efficient, i.e. that it causes high distortion costs for a given revenue. The experience in Central and Eastern Europe has shown that there are indeed great differences in the ability of different countries to raise taxes. In Russia, to take an extreme example, until recently, the government was not even able to raise 15% of GDP, whereas in other countries (e.g. Poland, Estonia) government revenues amount to over 30 % of GDP[2].

To concentrate on the issue at hand it is assumed that the authorities can determine inflation via their control over the money supply (or to be more precise its growth rate), and that this control is perfect. Hence the authorities can set directly the inflation rate.

A second standard element of the model is that the authorities (as usual, no distinction is made between the central bank and the Ministry of Finance) have to satisfy a budget constraint:

$$d(b_t) = g_t + b_t(i_t - p_t) - q_t - p_t\mu + \varepsilon_t \tag{5.2}$$

where b_t is the public debt/GDP ratio and g_t represents (non-interest) expenditure relative to GDP. The last but one term in this budget constraint represents seigniorage revenues under the assumption of a constant velocity money demand function with the cash (or rather monetary base) to GDP ratio constant and denoted by μ. The constant velocity assumption implies that seigniorage increases linearly with the money supply (and hence expected inflation). This is not realistic, but this assumption was chosen in order to show that the results do not depend on a 'Laffer curve' for seigniorage revenues under which the revenues from the inflation tax fall with very high inflation rates as money demand goes towards zero.

The shock ε_t will play an important role later. It arises from the fact that it is not possible to know the exact amount of public debt in countries with opaque financial systems. There are many ways in which banks can finance the government indirectly. Hence it is assumed that ε_t represents a surprise, a real shock with an expected value of zero (meaning its expected component is already incorporated in g_t) and variance σ_ε^2.

How important could these 'shocks' to public debt be? Table 5.2 below shows the data for the so-called stock flow adjustment, i.e. the increase in the debt to GDP ratio that cannot be explained from the deficit and nominal GDP growth. This should be exactly what the disturbance ε is supposed to represent (although not all will come from problems in the banking system. The values are quite high for some countries (above 10% of GDP for Lithuania in 1999, for example). The standard deviation across the ten CEECs was 5.2% of GDP in 1999.

Table 5.2 Stock-flow adjustments to public debt ratios

Panel a) CEECs: Increase in debt/ratio not explained by deficit (% of GDP)	1998	1999	2000	2001
Bulgaria	-6.3	4.6	4.0	-1.9
Czech Republic	6.3	4.2	6.9	14.4
Estonia	0.4	4.8	-0.2	0.0
Hungary	8.1	8.7	4.1	8.7
Lithuania	6.5	12.0	7.7	3.1
Latvia		9.7	5.6	5.0
Poland	1.7	3.8	5.5	8.1
Romania	7.5	8.3	8.6	5.0
Slovenia			6.6	4.1
Slovak Republic	6.2	16.8	23.1	7.4
Standard deviation across CEEC-10	4.9	4.3	6.1	4.6
Average across CEEC-10	3.9	7.7	7.1	5.3

Source: Own elaboration on European Commission data.

Panel b) EU countries (as % of GDP)	1998	1999	2000
Belgium	-1.6	0	0.3
Denmark	-1.7	2.3	-0.1
Germany	-0.5	0.2	1.7
Greece	2.4	3.6	5.3
Spain	-0.4	1.8	1.4
France	0.1	-0.6	0
Ireland	0.6	4.1	0.7
Italy	-1.4	0.1	1.2
Luxembourg	4.1	3.7	6
Netherlands	0.1	0.3	-0.5
Austria	-0.7	0.9	0.1
Portugal	-1.9	1.1	1
Finland	0.2	2.2	7.6
Sweden	2.[illegible]	-0.3	-2.8
UK	0.[illegible]	0.9	3.5
Standard deviation across EU 15	1.[illegible]	1.5	2.8
Average across EU 15	0.[illegible]	1.4	1.7

Sources: European Commission, AMECO.

This is larger than the average deficit of these countries (which was below 3% during this year). The average stock flow adjustment was also consistently positive, increasing from 4% to over 6% of GDP between 1998 and 2000. Unfortunately it is not possible to analyse a longer time series as the data simply does not exist. This fact alone provides a further indication of the uncertainty surrounding the true size of public debts in transition countries.

The average and standard deviation of the stock flow adjustment across the EU countries are much smaller than for the CEECs, see Panel b) of Table 5.2.

Other simplifying assumptions are standard: for the sake of simplicity, real growth is assumed to be zero. Government expenditure could be made endogenous, as in a number of other contributions on the optimal choice of taxes and inflation, but this has not been done here as it would not affect the main results of the chapter, which concentrate on the incentive to use surprise inflation to reduce the real value of the public debt[3]. Another real world qualification could be that it is implicitly assumed that the monetary base consists only of cash. Introducing required reserves on commercial banks (which could be remunerated) would not change the thrust of the analysis. If required reserves were not remunerated (which is usually the case) the value of μ would just be somewhat higher.

The crucial point about the budget constraint (5.2) is that real interest payments, given by $b_t(i_t-p_t)$, are a function of the difference between actual and expected inflation. The simple form of the budget constraint used here assumes implicitly that all government debt has the same maturity, equal to the length of the period of this model. Another interpretation would be that b represents only the government debt that matures in this period. Interest payments on other government debt would then be subsumed under general government expenditure. This is not a serious limitation of the model since most emerging market countries have a relative short average duration of (domestic) debt (and the little long-term debt that exists is indexed on short-term interest rates[4]).

The nominal interest rate, i_t, can be written as the sum of inflation and the real interest rate, required by investors. The latter will be assumed to be constant, denoted by ρ.

$$i_t = \rho + E_t(p_t) \tag{5.3}$$

The budget constraint that the authorities have to observe can thus be rewritten as:

$$d(b_t) = g_t + b_t(\rho + E_t(p_t) - p_t) - q_t - p_t\mu + \varepsilon_t \tag{5.4}$$

... AND A STANDARD EQUILIBRIUM UNDER DISCRETION

The authorities have to take their decisions before the shocks occur. They try to minimize the expected loss during each period while observing their budget constraint. The FOC for a minimum of (5.1), subject to (5.4), are:

$$\frac{\partial L_t}{\partial q_t} = 0 = 2\alpha q_t - \lambda_t \tag{5.5}$$

$$\frac{\partial L_t}{\partial p_t} = 0 = 2p_t - \lambda_t (b_t + \mu_t) \tag{5.6}$$

where λ_t is the shadow price associated with the budget constraint (5.2)'. As usual, it is assumed that the government reflects accurately the preferences of society in setting taxes and inflation.

In order to simplify the notation only the steady state will be considered with a constant debt/GDP ratio, denoted b[5].Conditions (5.5) and (5.6) then yield a simple relationship between inflation and tax revenues (as a percentage of GDP):

$$p_t = (b + \mu)\alpha q_t \tag{5.7}$$

This can be substituted into the budget constraint (5.2)' to obtain an expression for the steady state 'tax rate'. If one assumes that the public anticipates monetary policy and hence inflation correctly the debt-to-GDP ratio remains constant only if:

$$q_t = g_t + b\rho - \mu(b + \mu)\alpha q_t \tag{5.8}$$

If expenditure is constant at g, the optimal tax ratio changes only if the realisation of the interest rate shock is different from zero[6] :

$$q_d = \frac{[g + b(\rho + \mu_t)]}{1 + \mu(b + \mu)\alpha} \tag{5.9}$$

The expected loss under discretion $E(L_{disc})$ would then be given by:

$$E(L_{disc}) = \frac{\{\alpha + [(b + \mu)\alpha]^2\}}{[1 + \mu(b + \mu)\alpha]^2}\left\{[g + b\rho]^2 + \sigma_\varepsilon^2\right\} \tag{5.10}$$

As usual the discretionary equilibrium is not the first best for the country. The social optimum, if there were no constraints on credibility, can be calculated by using the first order conditions (5.5) and (5.6), but without the effect of surprise inflation on debt service in equation (5.6). This means that in the social optimum the relationship between taxes and money supply would be given by:

$$p_{SO} = \mu\alpha q \tag{5.11}$$

which differs from the corresponding relationship (5.7) in that only seigniorage is a valid argument for having inflation. The optimum tax rate is then given by substituting this expression into the budget constraint (and setting the debt-to-GDP ratio constant), which yields:

$$q_{SO} = \frac{[g + b(\rho + \varepsilon_t)]}{[1 + \mu^2\alpha]} \tag{5.12}$$

The expected loss under the social optimum, $E(L_{SO})$, would then be equal to:

$$E(L_{SO}) = \frac{\left[\alpha + (\alpha\mu)^2\right]}{\left[1 + \mu^2\alpha\right]^2}\left\{[g + b\rho]^2 + \sigma_\varepsilon^2\right\} \tag{5.13}$$

which is lower than the loss under discretion. However, in this set-up there is no way the country could easily reach this bliss point. One way would be to fix the exchange rate to an external anchor, which for the CEECs would normally be the euro. This could take several forms: an informal commitment (Latvia), a currency board (Estonia, Bulgaria, Lithuania) or the outright adoption of the euro as the national currency (Montenegro, Kosovo). In whatever form it is done, it implies the loss of inflation as a tax instrument.

THE ROLE OF FOREIGN BANKS

This section describes how the presence of foreign banks can make a difference. There appear to be two ways in which foreign owned banks will affect the working of the economy: foreign banks are more likely to have transparent accounts and foreign banks cannot exert the same pressures for a bail out.

Greater Transparency

A first consequence of the presence of foreign banks is that they in general are less likely to lend indirectly to the government and know their books better than their (unreformed) domestic counterparts. This should limit the potential for nasty surprises on the true size of public debt.

Mitigating Inefficiencies in the Domestic Economic Policy Process

Since this is a macro model it seems natural to assume that the government and the central bank take their decisions in terms of inflation and the overall level of taxation needed to finance a given level of expenditure. If one assumes that the authorities share the preferences of the population it is then natural to assume also that the decisions on the two key macroeconomic variables should reflect the preferences embedded in the social loss function. However, this assumes an efficient domestic policy process and thus is unlikely to be the case in reality, specially in the new democracies of the CEECs (which sometimes are entirely new states).

One particular problem that appears to have been particularly important in the CEECs is the lack of transparency in the financial system and the pressure put by large banks to bail them out when it turned out most of their credits had turned sour. This a particular manifestation of special interest group politics. There are always special interest groups that plead for special treatment. But it appears that large banks which had accumulated a large exposure to (ex-post) loss making enterprises have always been particularly effective in pressuring the central bank (and ultimately the government) into bailing them out. One important reason behind this success of (domestic) banks to obtain large bail outs is that the accumulation of bad debt is not immediately transparent. When it is uncovered it has usually reached already such size that the banks would go bankrupt if there were no help. Since no government can seriously consider letting its own banking system collapse, domestic banks usually are saved and their bad debts are paid by the public exchequer.

Any bail out that is granted to a particular bank (usually representing a particular domestic constituency, e.g. the farmers, large industrial enterprises, etc.) must of course be paid for somehow. In this set-up the only alternative source of revenues is inflationary finance. Using inflation also causes a welfare loss to the special interest group that obtains the bail out. However, as the part of any group in the overall budget will be small, this cost cannot fully offset the direct gain from the bail out (e.g. emergency credit from the central bank). Each special interest group thus faces a shadow price of a bail out which is only a fraction of the economy wide trade-off between inflation and taxes because it takes into account the fact that the overall inflationary impact any bail out has is likely to be proportional to the weight of the special interest group concerned. This fraction should be a function of various elements, for example the share of the interest group in the overall budget, the extent to which benefits have to be shared with other groups (a bail out for one bank alone might not be possible, an exemption for the entire banking system might be acceptable, indeed unavoidable in certain cases)[7].

Foreign owners, with very deep pockets (at least relative to the size of the potential losses in a CEEC) cannot credibly make the same threat as a domestic bank (whose owners, if private, and at any rate managers, are anyway likely to be politically well connected with the ruling elite). Most of the presence of the foreign banks in the CEECs comes from large, internationally oriented EU banks for which the CEEC exposure represents only a small percentage of overall deposits or capital. This is what one would expect given that deposits in the ten CEECs together represent less than 5% of the sum for the euro area. Moreover, it is politically much more difficult to sell to the national public the need to save at great cost a foreign bank. As the likelihood of being bailed out is lower foreign banks have an incentive to be more prudent in their loan policy. This comes on top of the fact that foreign owned banks are more likely to avoid making the bad loans in the first place. In practice this might be the case because they will be less subject to domestic political pressures. This seems to have happened in reality. There have been no large scale bail outs involving foreign banks.

Modelling the Influence of Foreign Banks

It will be clearest to start with the case in which there are no foreign banks. If domestic banks dominate the choices of the central bank and the finance ministry they can determine fiscal and monetary policy (at least at the margin). As the constituencies of the banks share the same preferences they will still like, ceteris paribus, lower inflation and taxes, but with their own special interests in mind as well. In pressuring the finance minister to take over the bad debts of a bank the special interest groups, which accumulated this debt are of course counting on the fact that they get all the benefits (i.e. debt relief) whereas society has to carry all the cost in terms of higher taxes (or rather a combination of taxes and inflation). In a Nash equilibrium with n banks (or the interest groups they represent), all identical in terms of size and influence, the minimization of the loss function (5.1) under the budget constraint[8] (5.4) leads to the following first order condition, for the setting of the overall average tax rate:

$$\frac{\partial L_t}{\partial q_t} = 0 = 2\alpha q_t - \lambda(1/n) \qquad (5.14)$$

where $\lambda(1/n)$ indicates the shadow price perceived by a particular bank or group of banks. This 'private shadow price' is the product of λ, the shadow price of the economy wide budget constraint and *(1/n)*, which indicates the weight of the bank in the economy, or rather the budget. Let-us give a concrete example. Assuming there are four interest groups represented in the domestic banking system and the bank of the farmer's cooperatives is one of them. It asks to be bailed out, representing one fourth of the overall economy and the budget ($1/n = 0.25$). In this case each euro spent on a bail out would be four times as 'valuable' to this bank as one euro given to everybody[9].

It was argued above that foreign banks cannot (and in reality do not) participate in the bail out game. Hence the greater the share of foreign banks the less important this distortion should become. This can be incorporated in the approach followed so far by splitting fiscal policy decisions into two areas: one area is free of special interest groups politics. This area is the one dominated by foreign banks. In the remainder it is 'politics as usual'. Denoting the share of foreign banks in the overall banking system by s, meaning that the 'policy relevant' shadow price becomes:

$$\frac{\partial L_t}{\partial q_t} = 0 = 2\alpha q_t - \lambda[s + (1-s)(1/n)] \, . \qquad (5.15)$$

When foreign banks dominate the banking system (s goes towards one) the particular fiscal inefficiency considered here disappears. To save on notation the fiscal externality in the presence of foreign banks will be denoted by η, which is defined by:

$$\eta \equiv [s + (1-s)(1/n)] \tag{5.16}$$

The parameter η thus shows the inefficiencies that persist in the decision process about domestic fiscal policy. As s goes to one, η also goes to one. Allowing foreign banks to take over the domestic banking system thus eliminates the bail out problem.

It is much easier to model the second consequence of the presence of foreign banks, namely the greater transparency in fiscal accounts. The greater the share of foreign banks the lower and smaller will the shocks be to public debt coming from the banking system. This can be expressed in a slightly modified budget constraint

$$d(b_t) = g_t + b_t(\rho + E_t(p_t) - p_t) - q_t - \mu p_t + (1-s)\varepsilon_t \tag{5.17}$$

The discretionary equilibrium can then be calculated as above, with the only difference being that the first order condition (5.5) is substituted by (5.15) and the budget constraint by (5.17).

EQUILIBRIUM WITH FOREIGN BANKS

The preceding section has provided a way to model the influence of foreign banks in countries with weak fiscal institutions. This makes it possible to consider what difference foreign banks can make to the equilibrium by potentially reducing the social losses associated with excessive inflation. Setting the inflation rate hits all interest groups in the same way; the first order condition (5.6) is thus not affected. However, the inefficiency in the fiscal process implies that the resulting trade-off between taxes and inflation is different:

$$p_t = \frac{(b+\mu)\alpha q_t}{\eta} \tag{5.18}$$

This implies that, ceteris paribus, inflation will be higher as all interest groups push the government to finance their benefits through inflation. As nothing changes in the remainder of the model (i.e. essentially the budget constraint) the resulting tax rate under the discretionary equilibrium is given by an equation that is identical to equation (5.9) above, except that α is substituted by α/η. This implies that the welfare loss under discretion is given by:

$$L_{disc,if} = \frac{\alpha + \left[(b+\mu)\alpha\eta^{-1}\right]^2}{\left[1+\mu(b+\mu)\alpha\eta^{-1}\right]^2}\left\{\left[g+b\rho\right]^2 + (1-s)^2\sigma_\varepsilon^2\right\} \quad (5.19)$$

where the subscript stands for inefficient fiscal policy. For the remaining it will be useful to define a composite parameter Ω, as

$$\Omega \equiv \left\{\left[g+b\rho\right]^2 + (1-s)^2\sigma_\varepsilon^2\right\} \quad (5.20)$$

Ω thus contains the impact of foreign banks on balance sheet transparency.

Inspection of equation (5.19) reveals that the presence of foreign banks is beneficial because it reduces the social loss from having inefficient fiscal institutions in two ways:

- As the share of foreign banks goes to one the surprises from opaque balance sheets disappear (the term $(1\text{-}s)\sigma_\varepsilon$). Moreover, any trend accumulation of debt by domestic banks would disappear, reducing another element of Ω.
- The second effect comes from the rent seeking of special interest groups which is reduced. This has a more complicated effect on the social loss. But if one takes the special case of $\mu=0$ it is clear that any increase in s, which bring η closer to one, leads to a lower welfare loss.

From these results it is also intuitive that when the authorities can commit credibly to a tough monetary policy, the usefulness of foreign banks is reduced as this second effect no longer exist. With a credible low inflation policy special interest groups cannot get any privileges. Bailing out is impossible because the key to the central bank has been thrown away. The welfare loss is given by:

$$L_{credible} = \frac{\alpha + \left[\mu\alpha\right]^2}{\left[1+\mu^2\alpha\right]^2}\Omega \quad (5.21)$$

It follows that the welfare benefit from having more of one's banking system owned by foreigners is lower when the country has a stable and credible monetary framework (for example, a currency board or a central bank with a well-established independence). A country with weak fiscal and monetary institutions would gain more from selling its banking system to foreigners than a country without such problems.

The gain from tying one's hand should be higher if there are too many hands at the tiller. This is indeed the case as become apparent if one takes the difference between the loss for a credible commitment and the loss under discretion. For the special case of μ=0 this yields the simple expression:

$$L_{disc,if} - L_{credible} = \alpha b^2 \eta^{-2} \Omega \qquad (5.22)$$

This expression shows that the lower Ω (i.e. the more important foreign banks become) the smaller the welfare gain from a tight commitment to price stability. If there are no foreign banks the inverse of η is equal to the number of competing special interest groups. In this case the gain from tying one's hand becomes a function of the square of the number of special interest groups (n), see the definition of η (5.16).

FOREIGN BANKS AND THE POTENTIAL FOR SELF-FULFILLING CURRENCY CRISIS

As the focus of this chapter is on the importance of foreign banks there is no attempt to build a new and sophisticated model of exchange rate crises. There exist many different models of currency crises. The basic idea emphasized here is the standard one that a foreign exchange crisis can result if interest rates go so high that it becomes prohibitively expensive to service the public debt at stable prices. This can happen after periods during which the authorities have publicly committed themselves to stabilization, keeping perhaps the price level constant for a while. But if investors stop believing this, interest rates go up and it will become very costly to persevere with stable prices. This implies that there might be a potential for multiple equilibria. This also implies that a self-fulfilling currency crisis become possible. This seems to be the simplest definition one can give of this type of crisis (also called second generation model crisis in a survey of the literature).

Under one equilibrium, the authorities initially enjoy a strong anti-inflationary credibility so that interest rates and the debt-service burden remain low. Under the other equilibrium, credibility is initially weak so that the government, as long as it keeps inflation low, has to pay a very high ex post real interest rate. The high debt burden this implies induces financial markets to doubt the resolve of the government – a state of affairs that leads to even higher interest rates. Depending on the parameter configuration, the risk premium could go so high that the government would find it in the interest of the country to cave in and loosen monetary policy.

In order to keep things as simple as possible here it is assumed that the real exchange rate is constant so that inflation is equivalent to devaluation. The crisis scenario considered here is thus a combined fiscal and exchange rate one. This is not the only way to model foreign exchange crisis, but it seems to be an approach that is used quite frequently.

It is useful at this point to consider the (ex post) alternatives for the authorities under two polar assumptions concerning the ex ante beliefs held by the public:

a. The credibility of the anti-inflationary stance is perfect, and
b. the credibility is zero, i.e. investors expect the government to follow the discretionary equilibrium.

What would be the welfare consequences for the alternatives that are open to the authorities under these circumstances? If credibility is perfect and the government does not exploit the trust of the public and investors the social optimum will result. The resulting welfare losses are calculated in equation (5.20) above. However, as is well known, in this situation the welfare loss can be reduced, at least for one period, if the authorities actually do go for inflation. When the government exploits the public trust, the loss becomes (neglecting all reputation effects for simplicity):

$$L_{surprise} = \frac{\alpha + \left[(b+\mu)\alpha\eta^{-1}\right]^2}{\left[1 + \left[(\mu+b)^2 - \eta\mu b\right]\alpha\eta^{-1}\right]^2}\Omega \tag{5.23}$$

This is usually called ‘temptation’.

The opposite situation arises when the government decides to abstain from inflation finance of debt (and is hence not giving in to interest groups), but the public does not believe its credibility (and believes that interest group politics will in the end dominate), the loss function becomes:

$$L_{tough} = \frac{\alpha + (\mu\alpha)^2}{\left[1 - \left(b^2 + (1-\eta)b\mu - \mu^2\right)\alpha\eta^{-1}\right]^2}\Omega \qquad (5.24)$$

The appearance of a difference in the denominator of this expression implies that the welfare cost of sticking to a tight policy in the face of a market which expects inflation can go to infinity (when $[1-(b^2+(1-\eta)b\mu-\mu^2)\alpha\eta^{-1}]$ goes to zero). This is not surprising if one takes into account the fact that it can become impossible to finance the real ex-post interest burden on a large public. For example, when the debt/GDP ratio is equal to 100% it becomes impossible to stick to zero inflation when the market will re-finance the debt only at interest rates above 100%. This implies that it can become impossible to make a fixed exchange rate regime credible when there is a high combination of public debt (b), an inefficient tax collection system (high value of α) and an inefficient system of expenditure control. As a higher value of η makes it less likely that this happens it follows immediately that selling the domestic banking system to foreigners could be a way to make a fixed exchange rate regime more credible.

The four cases can be tabulated in a compact way for the special case of $\mu = 0$. Table 5.3 table shows the four combinations of *ex post* outcomes and ex ante expectations that are possible in this model (with the simplification that μ=0, i.e. there is no seigniorage).

In this type of model it should be the case that in each row (i.e. given the market expectations), the loss is always smaller (essentially from lower taxes) if the government does inflate. It is apparent that is not necessarily the case in the first row. The last entry could be negative if η is very small. As $1/\eta$ is equal to the number of interest groups if there are no foreign banks this implies that the 'temptation' could actually be negative if n is large, i.e. the fiscal institutions are very fragmented, and if either b (the debt to GDP ratio) or α (the weight of taxes in the loss function) is very low. The last two conditions just say that the main problem of the country is not an excessively high debt or an inefficient tax collection system, but bad interest group politics. Basically this means that if such a country were to leave a straightjacket that kept fiscal policy under control it would no longer be able to control the genie that it has unbottled: interest group politics would run amok. As noted above a stronger presence of foreign banks increases the temptation (because it means that the discretionary equilibrium would not be too bad). This implies that countries with reasonable fiscal institutions might need a stronger political commitment to a fixed exchange rate than countries, which would otherwise be basket cases in terms of inflation.

Table 5.3 Welfare outcames

Ex post / *Ex ante*	Stabilise	Give up (inflate)	Benefit of deviation
credible	$\alpha\Omega$	$\frac{1}{[\eta + \alpha b^2]}\alpha\Omega$	$\frac{[\eta + \alpha b^2 - 1]}{[\eta + \alpha b^2]}\alpha\Omega$
not credible	$\frac{\alpha\Omega}{[1 - \alpha b^2 \eta^{-1}]^2}$	$[1 + \alpha[b\eta^{-1}]^2]\alpha\Omega$	$\frac{[1 + \alpha[b\eta^{-1}]^2][1 - \alpha b^2 \eta^{-1}]^2 - 1}{[1 - \alpha b^2 \eta^{-1}]^2}\alpha\Omega$

Source: Own calculations.

Returning now to the normal case in which a temptation to inflate exists (because interest groups are not too fragmented or because there are enough foreign banks to keep the process within limits, the issue is whether or not the authorities will actually give in to this temptation; which depends on whether there are other costs of inflating and devaluing. These other costs are not captured by the model. Assume now for simplicity that the cost of reneging on the commitment to a stable exchange rate and hence price stability is equal to a constant Γ. The size of Γ should be determined by confidence effects and possibly by the importance a potential member country of the EU attaches to its credibility. For example, a currency board should be harder to break (higher value of Γ) than a commitment within the ERM II. If Γ goes to infinity, the authorities will always keep price stability because the temptation (the one period lower loss from higher inflation) is more than offset by the loss of credibility. The markets will anticipate this as this policy will be credible. And vice-versa, if Γ is very small, the government will always minimize the loss and hence, as the markets know this, the discretionary equilibrium is the only solution.

At first sight, it appears that there must be a critical value for Γ that separates these two situations: if Γ is below this critical value, which is given by the incentive, the commitment to price stability is not credible and high inflation is the only possibility. The problem is that the incentive to renege depends on the interest rate set by the market. If the market sets very high interest rates it might just be too costly to stick to low inflation. The commitment is really credible only if it passes the stress test, i.e. if it is still in the interest of the authorities to stick to the fixed exchange rate even if the markets expect the discretionary equilibrium. This will be the case only if the cost of remaining tough is smaller than the value of Γ.

For values of Γ intermediate between the 'temptation' and the 'stress test', two equilibria are possible: if the market initially believes that the government will stabilize, the loss in terms of higher taxes needed to do so will be low and the government will stabilize. And vice-versa, if the market initially believes the government will not stabilize, the cost of stabilising will be high and the government will indeed not do so.

The region inside which two equilibria are possible is represented graphically below, in Figure 5.1. The question here is whether the presence of foreign banks affects the size of the region for Γ with two equilibria. This seems to be the case on two accounts:

a. Concentrating on the transparency provided by foreign banks and neglecting for the moment the interest group politics by setting $n=1$ (which implies $\eta=1$) it is apparent that the difference between the temptation and cost of remaining tough is proportional to Ω. As this parameter falls with the share of foreign banks, s, this implies that the range for which two equilibria are possible is reduced by the presence of foreign banks if they lead to more transparent balance sheets.
b. But foreign banks can also have a strong impact via their effect on interest group politics, i.e. the value of η. This is apparent when one considers the limiting case of η going to αb^2. In this case the

denominator of the entry in the lower right-hand corner of Table 5.3 goes to zero because the welfare cost of staying tough in the face of a sceptical market goes to infinity. In this case there is no way the authorities can render a fixed exchange rate commitment (or alternatively a commitment to price stability via an independent central bank) credible. The market knows that if the interest rate is fixed at the level corresponding to the discretionary equilibrium it will not make sense for the authorities to resist. As above the key condition refers to the relation of the parameter describing inefficiencies in the fiscal institutions (□) to the debt/GDP ratio (*b*) compounded by the parameter describing the efficiency of the tax system (□). As the upper bound of □ is equal to one (i.e. when the entire banking system has been sold to foreigners) it follows that selling banks to foreigners cannot, on its own, make a fixed exchange rate system resistant to the stress test when the country has a combination of a high public debt and an inefficient tax collection system (like Argentina?).

$$\frac{(\eta + \alpha b^2 - 1)}{(\eta + \alpha b^2)}\alpha\Omega \qquad - \frac{\left[1 + \alpha\left(b\eta^{-1}\right)^2\right]\left(1 - \alpha b^2\eta^{-1}\right)^2 - 1}{\left(1 - \alpha b^2\eta^{-1}\right)^2}\alpha\Omega$$

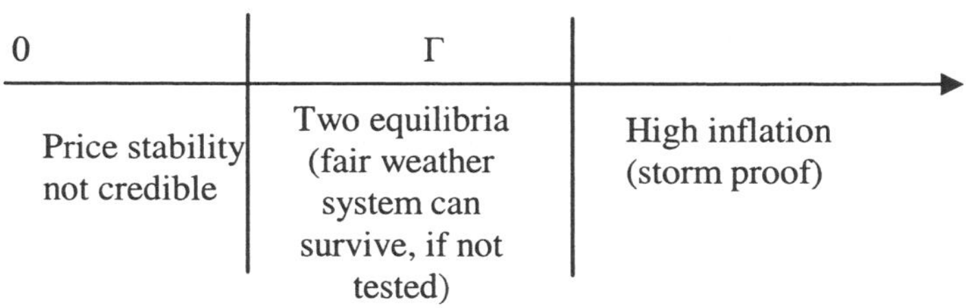

Figure 5.1 Policy outcomes

The conundrum that emerges here is thus that countries with inefficient fiscal institutions and a low presence of foreign banks would gain most from a tight constraint. But this constraint will in general have difficulties passing the stress test of financial markets. A strong presence of foreign banks can mitigate the problem (but not eliminate it).

CONCLUDING REMARKS

This chapter has used a standard model to illustrate the channels through which the presence of foreign banks can mitigate two problems that arise in countries with weak fiscal institutions and opaque financial systems. Most of the CEECs belonged (and some still belong today) to this category because when they emerged from decades of socialist domination they had to create their banking system (including banking supervision) from scratch and their finance ministries had to face completely new tasks. As most of the CEECs also chose to go for financial openness this exposed them to the vagaries of financial markets in which it is sometimes possible that the prior beliefs of markets force governments to do something they would have liked to avoid.

One particular mechanism that has contributed to a number of crisies worldwide is that of a self-reinforcing spiral of higher interest rates on public debt, which makes it more difficult to service this debt at stable prices and thus further increases the doubts of financial markets that the debt can actually be serviced. The long agony of Argentina whose government struggled for years to find the resources to service its large foreign debt at ever increasing rates constitutes just the latest, perhaps also the most tragic example, of this mechanism.

The experience of Argentina also shows that even a massive presence of foreign banks does not constitute a full protection against speculative attacks. One aspect of the recent developments in this country confirms, however, a basic premise of this chapter: the Argentine government has so far refused to bail out the banking system, which was mostly foreign owned. The Argentine authorities have actually gone one step further: they have practically expropriated the foreign owners by the different conversion rates applied to loans and deposits. This step has considerably deepened the crisis while improving only marginally the fiscal position of the government. Such a step would not have been possible in a country that is a candidate for EU membership (or already in the EU).

Among the successful candidates for EU membership a massive presence of foreign banks should be unambiguously beneficial in that it should lead to a greater transparency of the fiscal accounts and mitigate the incentive to bail out banks with links to powerful interest groups. Of course, there are other ways to deal with these problems: strong banking supervision would render balance sheets also transparent and giving the finance minister a veto over bail outs (and an incentive to do so) would also help. But these alternatives either take a long time or are politically just not feasible in the short run. Experience has shown that establishing an effective system of banking supervision takes time because it requires a number of competent staff with the required training and experience, which was (and in some cases still is) simply not available in the transition countries of Central and Eastern Europe. Hence it might be quicker to sell the banking system to foreigners than to build up a system of banking supervision that is strong enough to deal with weak domestic banks.

Similar considerations apply to the other mechanism emphasized in this chapter: in an economy in transition it is more likely than in the settled market economies of the EU that entire sectors run into such difficulties that they have to be closed down and their banks be bailed out. The cases of Crédit Lyonnais and Parmalat show what can happen even in relatively well organized countries, but the scale of the problem must be different in transition countries in which the entire industry mix has to go through a complete overhaul in a decade.

This chapter has not discussed one concern that is sometimes raised in opposition to allowing foreigners to dominate the domestic banking system, namely that foreign banks might the first ones to cut their losses and run in case of macroeconomic difficulties. However, a recent study (de Haas and van Lelyveld (2002)) finds that the opposite has happened so far in the CEECs: when times get tough the lending by foreign banks has tended to hold up better than that of domestic banks. This is actually what one would expect: when the economy is in difficulties all banks might become more prudent in extending loans to domestic enterprises and households. However, foreign owned banks have in general 'deeper' pockets and should thus be more able to take a longer-term view by continuing to lend to solvent enterprises, even if they experience short-term difficulties.

As the CEECs matured, their banking supervision became stronger. EU membership accelerates this change without constituting a discrete step change as the acquis has already largely been taken over beforehand and the screening process that preceded entry concentrated on its effective application. Over time the CEECs might then have less of a need for foreign banks. The newer members might then feel that they are stuck in a situation, which is different from that of the older member countries. But in the meantime it will have helped them to weather the transition.

An interesting topic for future research might then be how to organize the EU system of banking supervision in a situation in which the incentives for bail out and lender of last resort differ. The new member countries might well take a much tougher attitude in this respect than the old EU-15 where the many national central banks still try to jealously defend 'their' banks against the intrusion of foreign capital.

NOTES

1. Centre for European Policy Studies (CEPS) Brussels and CESifo. Many thanks to Alexandr Hobza and Peer Ritter for important research assistance. A first version of this chapter was prepared for the Stockholm conference on 'Managing EU Enlargement', Sverige Riksbank, Stockholm, May 15-17, 2002.
2. An alternative interpretation would be that society and/or the politicians in power dislike high taxes (for example, because their marginal voter is a household with a high marginal tax rate).
3. See, for example, Mankiw (1987).
4. As is well known the time inconsistency problem could also be solved by issuing only foreign currency or inflation indexed debt. In reality this is not done anywhere.
5. In a similar model, Gros (1990) shows that this should not affect the conclusions.
6. Since this chapter's focus is only on steady states, the time subscript will henceforth be suppressed.
7. For a similar approach, regarding fiscal policy decisions see von Hagen and Harden (1994) with an analysis of EU member countries in this respect. Velasco (1998) uses a similar approach with two symmetric interest groups whereas Drazen (2000) presents (in Chapter 10) a model with a large number of competing groups, which try to extract transfers from the government. For reasons unrelated to interest groups, a monetary bail out for the entire banking system is also advocated by Goodfriend and King (1988).
8. It is assumed that the average level of government expenditure remains constant despite the presence of interest groups.
9. As an aside one should note that the model could also be applied to the case of Argentina (and perhaps even Russia) if one substitutes special interest groups with provincial governments. However, if regional governments are the problem the presence of foreign banks should not make a big difference.

REFERENCES

Berglof, Erik and Patrick Bolton (2002), 'The Great Divide and Beyond: Financial Architecture in Transition', mimeo.

De Haas, and I.P.P. van Lelyveld (2002), 'Foreign Bank Penetration and Private Sector Credit in Central and Eastern Europe', *DNB STAFF REPORTS*, No. 91/2002, Amsterdam.

Drazen, Allan (2000), '*Political Economy in Macroeconomics*', Princeton University Press, Princeton, New Jersey.

European Central Bank, Annual Report (1999).

European Commission (2002). 'Report on macroeconomic and financial sector stability developments in candidate countries', *Enlargement Chapters* No.8, DG ECFIN.

Goodfriend, M. and R. King (1988), 'Financial Deregulation, Monetary Policy and Central Banking', *Federal Reserve Bank of Richmond Economic Review*, 74(3).

Mankiw, G.N. (1987), 'The Optimal Collection of Seigniorage, Theory and Evidence', *Journal of Monetary Economics*, 20, pp. 327-341.

Velasco, Andres (1998), 'The Common Property Approach to the Political Economy of Fiscal Policy', Chapter 8 in *The Political Economy of Reform*, Federico Sturwenegger and Mariano Tommasi (eds), MIT, Cambridge, Massachusetts.

Von Hagen, Jürgen and Ian Harden (1994), 'National Budget Processes and Fiscal Performance', *European Economy, Reports and Studies*, 3, Commission of the European Communities, Brussels, pp. 310-418.

Zhu, Haibin (2001), 'Bank Runs without Self-fulfilling Prophecies', BIS Working Chapter No. 106.

6. New Europe Banking: The Role of International Players

Fabio Mucci[1], Luca Papi[2] and Debora Revoltella[3]

INTRODUCTION[4]

In just a decade, New Europe's[5] banking sector has successfully moved from a transition period into a new era of consolidation, strengthening and growth. The privatization process can be regarded as largely completed in practically all countries, and the commitment of the public authorities has been essential in creating a degree of private ownership which even exceeds that of most euro area countries. At present, around 60 per cent of the New Europe banking sector (as measured by assets) is under foreign control, and some seven to eight international players have emerged as clear leaders in the region. These developments have helped create an interesting and distinctive competitive environment. New Europe is now one of the few regional markets in the world where foreign ownership is predominant, and where cross-border strategic players can compete directly in a fairly liberalized framework while exploiting and supporting what has already become their "second home" market. This peculiarity makes New Europe the ideal ground to evaluate both the short- and medium/long-term impact of foreign banking ownership.

The effect of foreign banks' entry into domestic banking markets has been under scrutiny for some time now, and protectionism has traditionally been advocated, in light of the strategic role of the sector as engine of growth, infant industry arguments, fears that foreign banks could drain financial resources from their hosts, etc. On the other hand, economic literature has tended to associate foreign entry with better performances from the acquired institutions, and with improvements in the local financial sector as a whole. More recently, several studies have conducted empirical investigations into the contribution of foreign banks. A first series of studies focused on "first-order"effects; that is the systemic efficiency gains associated with the entry of foreign banks and the resulting increase in competition for domestic banks. Generally speaking, the first-order effects of foreign bank entry have been favourable. The presence of foreign banks has been associated with lower net interest margins for commercial banks (Claessens, Demirgüç-Kunt and Huizinga (2001), Levine (1999 and 2002)), higher cost efficiency (Papi and Revoltella (2000)), improved financial ratings (Crystal, Dages and Goldberg (2001)) and more contestable domestic banking sectors (Claessens, Demirgüç-Kunt and Huizinga (2001)).

Another series of studies looked at second-order effects, analysing the impact of foreign entry on both business cycle variability and system stability, especially in developing countries where financial crises have recently occurred, raising concerns about the stability of the financial sector. However, the empirical implications of increased foreign entry are less clear, although most of the literature seems to suggest that concerns about the increasing volatility and instability of foreign banks are unfounded. For instance, it has been shown that lending by foreign banks during the 1994-95 crises in Mexico and Argentina grew faster than lending by domestic banks (Goldberg, Dages and Kinney (2000)). More recently, Morgan and Strahan (2002) found that integration between foreign banks is either unrelated to the volatility of investment spending or positively related. Unfortunately, these findings are either country-specific or related to short periods of time, and there has been no empirical study of second-order effects on New Europe countries.

This chapter aims to present and evaluate the experience of New Europe countries with respect to foreign banks by looking into both first-order and second-order effects. After a brief descriptive analysis of the market and the role played by international competitors, we investigate the first-order effects of foreign ownership in local banking. First, we compare the performances of foreign and locally-owned institutions with a panel estimate of the determinants of banking profitability and cost efficiency. Second, we use the propensity score method to provide an estimate of the average treatment effect deriving from a change in status from domestic/public to foreign control. The aim here is two-fold: on the one hand, applying this method allows us to identify a causal link between foreign control and the level of profitability, while on the other, it enables us to measure the average effect of a change in ownership status on some summary indicators of bank performance.

To analyse the second-order effects of foreign ownership on stability and the vulnerability of the business cycle, the chapter adopts a microeconomic approach, examining the investment and strategic growth decisions of the top international players in the region. The aim is to provide useful insights into the future development trends of banking systems in New Europe. Given the dominant market role of these international players, an understanding of their current and future strategies and of their commitment to the market is key to forecasting the future competitiveness, concentration and market conditions of New Europe, and may also give some insight into future stability.

THE ROLE OF FOREIGN BANKS IN NEW EUROPE'S FINANCIAL MARKETS: FIRST-ORDER EFFECTS

Foreign banks have now achieved a dominant role in the New Europe banking market, with foreign ownership accounting for 60 per cent of total aggregate banking assets. This share is well above the average in the euro area, where, excluding Benelux and the Nordic countries, which are regional integrated markets, foreign ownership ranges from 5 to 20 per cent of total banking assets. However, despite a shared commitment to restructure and strengthen their financial sectors rapidly, the attitude of large banks towards privatization and the entry of strategic foreign investors has differed greatly between countries and over time.

Hungary and Poland launched the full-scale privatization of their large banks in the second half of the 1990s. In Poland, the biggest national bank, Bank PKO BP, is still in state hands, and the question of whether to sell the controlling share to a strategic foreign investor or to a domestic one is still being debated. In the Czech Republic, the partial privatization of the big banks started at the very beginning of transition through a voucher scheme, but residual state control and corporate governance problems hindered restructuring and transformation. A second round of privatization began at the end of the 1990s, and the entry of strategic foreign investors provided a boost to full restructuring and reform. Since 2000, Slovakia, Bulgaria and Croatia have made great headway in privatizing their banks. In Romania, however, the wider economy has taken time to stabilize, which has delayed privatization, and the country's biggest bank, Banca Commerciala Romana, has yet to be sold off. Domestic state control of the banking sector is still predominant overall in Slovenia, although since 2000 strategic investors have been chosen to take minority shares in the top financial institutions.

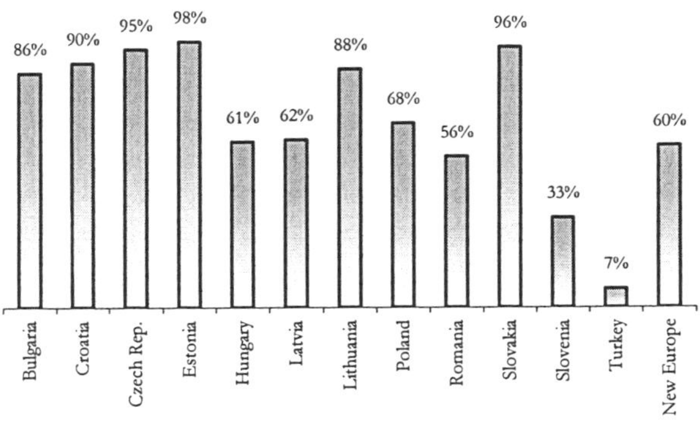

Source: UniCredito Italiano (2003).

Figure 6.1 Foreign ownership of New Europe banks – total assets under foreign control 2003

In Turkey, large public banks still dominate the market, and only 7 per cent of banking assets are under foreign control, following the entry into the market of HSBC and UniCredito in 2002.

Foreign ownership in the region is commonly acknowledged to provide support in restructuring and transforming the competitive framework. At microeconomic level, foreign banks entering as strategic investors into local institutions initially guarantee capital inflows and a commitment to new market behaviour, and subsequently develop new practices and skills (risk management, credit allocation, etc.) and support the creation of new market segments and products.

Similar findings can be found in the empirical literature which evaluates the potential benefits or disadvantages for domestic banks arising from the presence of foreign banks (see Yildirim and Philippatos (2002) for a comprehensive review of the literature).

Several cross-country analyses, beginning with Demirgüç-Kunt and Huizinga (1998), have shown that banks under foreign control generate higher margins and profits than local banks, as a consequence of higher loan quality and lower costs. It is argued that foreign ownership of domestic banks in emerging markets increases the overall strength of financial institutions both quantitatively and qualitatively. Foreign banks are viewed as providing greater access to capital and liquidity and bolstering balance sheet strength. The knowledge, skills and technology transfer that accompany foreign bank entry are expected to help promote an environment of stronger control and risk management. More broadly, foreign banks' presence in emerging markets is said to contribute to improved financial infrastructure by encouraging higher standards of auditing, accounting and disclosure, credit risk underwriting and reserves and supervision.

An Initial Comparison between Foreign-owned and Domestic Banks

Using the above-mentioned approach, and with particular reference to New Europe countries, we have built a profitability and cost model, as tested in Papi and Revoltella (2000). Our panel is based mainly on Bankscope data covering eight New Europe countries[6] during the period 1994-2001, and about 160 individual commercial and savings banks. To account for differences in profitability and cost efficiency, we have used as a proxy the return on average assets and the overheads to total assets ratio respectively.

Our model is as follows:

$$Y_{it} = \alpha + \beta * B_{it} + y * C + \delta * PROP_{it} + \varepsilon_{it} \qquad (6.1)$$

Foreign ownership (*PROP*) has been carefully defined case by case, by considering foreign shareholdings higher than 50 per cent. As bank-specific indicators (B_{it}) we have used the logarithm of total assets (*LOGTA*), which factors in economies of scale; net interest revenues over operating income (*NIROI*), which accounts for a bank's specialization in traditional operations; and net loans over total assets (*NLTA*), to correct for the size of each bank's loan portfolio. Finally, we have used country dummies (*C*) to factor in the influence of different legal, regulatory and macroeconomic environments on banks' performance. The estimation is by Feasible Generalized Least Squares applied to panel data with correction for heteroskedasticity and panel-specific AR(1) autocorrelation. The results are shown in Tables 6.1 and 6.2. Bank variables appear to confirm our a priori conclusions, with the proxy for size significant in both equations, being positively related to profitability and negatively to costs. Specialization in traditional operations has a negative and significant impact on profits, while loan portfolio size is negatively correlated to costs.

Table 6.1 Profitability and foreign ownership (dependent variable – ROAA)

roaa	Coef.	Std.Err.	z	P>|z|	[95% Conf. Interval]	
prop	0.304	0.107	2.85	0.004	0.0953	0.5134
niroi	– 0.005	0.002	– 2.29	0.022	– 0.0086	– 0.0007
nlta	0.003	0.002	1.26	0.209	– 0.0017	0.0079
logta	0.105	0.039	2.71	0.007	0.0290	0.1802
c1	1.471	0.306	4.81	0.000	0.8712	2.0716
c2	– 0.347	0.197	– 1.77	0.077	– 0.7324	0.0382
c3	– 1.225	0.496	– 2.47	0.014	– 2.1982	– 0.2525
c4	– 0.647	0.242	– 2.68	0.007	– 1.1204	– 0.1729
c5	0.198	0.151	1.31	0.189	– 0.0976	0.4943
c6	1.629	0.176	9.26	0.000	1.2843	1.9739
c7	– 0.930	0.180	– 5.18	0.000	– 1.2821	– 0.5780
const	0.430	0.304	1.42	0.157	– 0.1653	1.0245

The coefficient of the *PROP* variable is positive and significant in the profitability equation, meaning that foreign-owned banks tend to outperform their peers on the market. The same variable also presents a negative and significant coefficient in the cost equation, which is an initial indication of a strong focus on efficiency by foreign institutions. These results are consistent with Demirgüç-Kunt and Huizinga (1998)'s findings for developing countries, and is mainly explained by the superior banking techniques and practices of foreign entrants. They also confirm the trend already described by Papi and Revoltella (2000) for the period 1993-1998. The extension of the sample here allows us to consider a period in which restructuring strategies have started to consolidate and lead to the first tangible results. It should be noted, however, that although the above methodology provides evidence of a significant relationship between profitability, costs and foreign ownership, it does not suggest any causal relationship.

Table 6.2 Cost efficiency and foreign ownership (dependent variable – overheads over total assets)

overta	Coef.	Std.Err.	z	P>|z|	[95% Conf. Interval]	
prop	– 0.0081	0.002	– 4.95	0.000	– 0.0113	– 0.0048
niroi	– 0.0000	0.000	1.00	0.319	– 0.0000	0.0000
nlta	– 0.0003	0.000	– 7.88	0.000	– 0.0004	– 0.0002
logta	– 0.0111	0.001	– 14.90	0.000	– 0.0126	– 0.0097
c1	0.0277	0.017	1.64	0.101	– 0.0054	0.0607
c2	0.0020	0.003	0.70	0.484	– 0.0036	0.0077
c3	– 0.0061	0.004	– 1.48	0.139	– 0.0142	0.0020
c4	0.0091	0.004	2.21	0.027	0.0010	0.0172
c5	0.0027	0.003	0.96	0.335	– 0.0028	0.0082
c6	0.0195	0.004	4.96	0.000	0.0118	0.0273
c7	– 0.0057	0.004	– 1.63	0.104	– 0.0125	0.0012
const	0.1259	0.005	23.50	0.000	0.1154	0.1364

Foreign Bank Efficiency: a Causality Analysis

To further investigate the relationship between bank performance and foreign ownership identified in the previous section, we will now formally test the causal relationship between the two using a propensity score model.

To assess causality let us consider our population of banks and suppose that for each of them we can observe a variable T ("treatment", i.e. the potential cause of which we want to estimate the effects) and a variable Y ("outcome", i.e. the effect we want to attribute to the treatment). Let us assume that T is a binary variable such that:

$T_i = 1$ if bank i has been exposed to treatment (from local or public to foreign control);

$T_i = 0$ if bank i has not been exposed to treatment.
The outcome for each bank can be written as:

$$Y_i(T_i) = T_i Y(1) + (1 - T_i) Y_i(0) \tag{6.2}$$

where $Y_i(1)$ is the outcome in case of treatment and $Y_i(0)$ in case of no treatment. Note that each of the aforementioned conditions of treatment are possible ex ante, but only one of them can fulfil itself since bank i cannot be "treated" and "untreated" at the same time. This approach thus requires us to think in terms of counterfactuals. So if bank i is treated ex post, then the counterfactual event is represented by the absence of treatment and vice-versa.

Within this framework we can define the causality link in that the event ($T_i=1$ instead of $T_i=0$) causes the effect $\Delta_i=Y_i(1)-Y_i(0)$. Given that it is impossible to observe for the same individual i the values $T_i=1$ and $T_i=0$ as well as the values $Y_i(1)$ and $Y_i(0)$[7], the statistical solution proposes methods to compute the average causal effect for the entire population or for some interesting sub-groups.

These randomized experiments try to address the fundamental problem of causal inference by simply extracting two random samples from the population and then using one of them (the controls) as counterfactual for the other (the treated) and vice versa.

Since in observational studies randomization does not always represent the best feasible way to solve the problem, other methods have been developed. One of them is matching, which involves pairing treatment and comparison units that are similar in terms of their observable characteristics. When the relevant differences between the two units are captured in the observable (pre-treatment) covariates, matching methods can yield an unbiased estimate of the average treatment impact on treated subjects. The main difficulty with the matching approach is calculating the conditional expectation of the outcome variable when the dimension of personal characteristics is greater than one.

Rosenbaum and Rubin (1983) proposed an equivalent and feasible strategy based on the concept of propensity score and its properties, which reduces the dimensionality problem[8]. They show that under the unconfoundedness assumption it is sufficient to calculate the conditional expectation of the outcome variable on a one-dimensional variable, namely the conditional probability of receiving treatment given a subject's set of personal characteristics.

Our estimates are based on the same sample as the previous section: i.e. a total of 160 banks in eight countries in the period 1994-2001. Treatment *T* corresponds to a change in ownership – from local or public to foreign control, in the observation period. Our treated sample also includes those banks – mainly branches of foreign banking groups – established before 1994, but since their number and size are very limited, we do not expect this to introduce any bias into our estimation results. The outcome of interest is the level of ROAA in 2001.

For model selection we have followed the Becker and Ichino (2003) algorithm, in order to be sure that our pre-treatment variables (covariates) are independent of assignment to treatment, so that, for observations with the same propensity score, the distribution of covariates is the same across the treatment and comparison groups. We have further restricted our test of the balancing property to the common support region to improve the quality of the matches used to estimate the ATT. The resulting specification includes proxies for cost and income structure in 1994 and the Return on Average Assets in 1994 and 1996[9]. The treatment group contains 100 observations and the control group 60, making a total of 160 observations.

The estimate is performed in two steps. First, we have estimated the propensity score using a standard logit model, where the dependent variable is "participation" in the programme of privatization and the independent variables are the factors thought to influence participation and outcome. As an analysis of Table 6.3 shows, most of the coefficient estimates have the expected sign. For example, highly profitable and innovative banks are more likely to be possible targets for foreign acquisition.

In the second step, given the estimated propensity score, we have constructed a comparison group from the non-treatment group to get an estimate of the average treatment on the treated sample (ATT). Various methods are proposed in the literature, but we have focused on three of them: stratification matching, kernel matching and nearest neighbour matching. The results are shown in Table 6.4 to Table 6.6[10]. As can be clearly seen, the results obtained using these three methods are quite similar to each other and, taken together, give evidence of a positive ATT associated with the privatization programmes implemented in our selected sample of New Europe countries. Foreign participation in the capital of local banks is thus found to improve the condition and performance of the acquired institutions, and to make a significant contribution to overall banking and financial stability. More importantly, through the propensity score method we can demonstrate a causal link between the change in ownership status and banks' profitability. Profit-enhancing strategies adopted include revenue generation policies involving the development of new market segments and products, as well as cost and risk control.

Table 6.3 Estimation of the propensity score

t	Coef.	Std.Err.	z	P>|z|	[95% Conf.	Interval]
over	0.085	0.028	3.01	0.003	0.0296	0.1401
over2	– 0.000	0.000	– 2.75	0.006	– 0.0008	– 0.0001
nir	– 0.038	0.020	– 1.89	0.059	– 0.0785	0.0015
nir2	0.000	0.000	1.26	0.209	– 0.0010	0.0005
roaa94	0.240	0.125	1.92	0.055	– 0.0047	0.4847
roaa942	– 0.001	0.018	– 0.05	0.961	– 0.0359	0.0342
roaa96	– 0.090	0.072	– 1.24	0.214	– 0.2314	0.0518
roaa962	0.008	0.006	1.39	0.166	– 0.0035	0.0204
const	– 0.534	0.306	– 1.75	0.081	– 1.1337	0.0649

Table 6.4 Estimation of average treatment effects based on the stratification method

n.treat.	n.contr.	ATT	Std. Err.	t
47	32	0.549	0.328	1.677

Table 6.5 Estimation of average treatment effects based on Kernel Matching method

n.treat.	n.contr.	ATT	Std. Err.	t
100	60	0.487	0.363	1.340

Table 6.6 Estimation of the average treatment effect based on Nearest Neighbour Matching

n.treat.	n.contr.	ATT	Std. Err.	t
100	41	0.563	0.337	1.668

The analysis also allows us to quantify the ATT in the range of 0.487-0.563, which means that banks that changed their status to foreign ownership in the period analysed were able to realize an average 0.5 percentage point increase in ROAA compared with untreated banks. An exact quantification of the ATT should however be considered with caution, as the number can vary according to the specific sample considered.

INTERNATIONAL PLAYERS IN THE NEW EUROPE BANKING SECTOR: A STRATEGIC APPROACH TO ASSESS SECOND-ORDER EFFECTS

To gain a further insight into the impact of foreign banks in the region we have also looked at microeconomic factors. Given the dominant role of a small number of international players, an understanding of their current and future strategies and of their commitment to the market is key to evaluating developments in the market and their potential effects on both the sector's stability and economic volatility.

A wide range of economic literature has shown that the determinants of foreign banks' entry into emerging markets are both macroeconomic and microeconomic (see Papi and Revoltella (2000) and Focarelli and Pozzolo (2003)).

On the macroeconomic side, New Europe is a highly important region which will soon become part of the enlarged EU market. Real and nominal convergence to EU standards will require decades of growth at rates well above EU levels (a 2001 EU Commission report states that growth will exceed the EU average in all candidate countries for the next 13 to 35 years); moreover, the degree of banking penetration is currently low, with the ratio of loans and deposits to GDP standing at 66 per cent compared to the EU figure of 224 per cent, so banking activities in the region are also set to expand in both size and scope. The high growth potential offered by the local market is thus a primary motive for widespread investment in the region, whereas "following the client", i.e. supporting FDI in the real sector, or trade flows, which played a role at the beginning of transition, were soon overtaken as a determinant of bank investment.

At microeconomic level, the first international banks active in the region were medium-sized institutions in search of a "second home" market to expand into. Following the concentration process that also took place within the European Union, some of these institutions (such as HVB-Bank Austria and Banca Intesa) soon became big EU-wide players too. Table 6.7 shows the main features of the seven largest investors in the region, focusing on their absolute size (measured in terms of total assets), market capitalization, market share and ranking in their home markets. It can be seen that investors in New Europe are also among the biggest companies in their home markets. In some cases, constraints on domestic growth have led to their efforts to find new markets elsewhere.

All these determinants of FDI suggest a long-term commitment to the market on the part of major foreign investors. Given the existing link between economic growth and sustainable bank profitability, large regional players are likely to have a strong incentive to support market development and "catching-up" by increasing the range of products and services on offer, generating adequate lending volumes, controlling risk, etc. So far a positive cycle has emerged. For the future, one possible indirect way of gaining an insight into the second-order effects of foreign ownership may be to evaluate the long-term investment strategies of the big players, focusing on their commitment and thus on their incentive to continue supporting sustainable economic growth.

Table 6.8 shows the main figures relating to international banks' presence in New Europe, focusing on total assets controlled, countries of direct operation and number of branches in the region, as well as the importance of regional assets for the bank in percentage terms (as a proxy for its commitment to the strategy), and the share of regional assets under each bank's control. The scenario is very dynamic, with international players like UCI, KBC, HVB and Erste standing out for the combination of total assets controlled, breadth of branch network and returns achieved. Other groups like Intesa, Société Générale, Raiffeisen and Citigroup are experiencing progress, while a few other operators such as ING, OTP, National Bank of Greece, EFG and Volksbank are starting to develop a multi-country presence.

Table 6.7 Largest EU investors in Central and Eastern Europe 2002, EUR m

	Country	Total Assets[a]	Mkt share[b]	MktCap[c]	Rank[d]
HVB/BA	Germany	691 200	10.8%	8 200	2
Soc. Générale	France	501 265	12.0%	24 000	2
Banca Intesa	Italy	280 733	13.6%	16 200	1
Erste Bank	Austria	221 731	21.0%	3 840	3
KBC	Belgium	221 731	21.0%	10 000	3
UCI	Italy	213 349	10.3%	23 400	2
RZB	Austria	46 405	10.8%	-	4

Notes:

[a] Total consolidated figure.

[b] Market shares calculated from total assets of the banking system of home country.

[c] Market capitalization as of end-2002 except for KBC where data refer to October 2002.

[d] Ranking calculated from total assets of the bank.

Sources: UCI table based on Bankscope data and banks' financial statements.

Overall, the top eight investor banks account for 34 per cent of regional banking assets, with individual percentages ranging from 30 per cent in Poland and Hungary to 70 per cent in the Czech Republic and Croatia (while the figure for Turkey and Slovenia is still low).

To gain a full understanding of each company's investment strategy in the region and future developments, different variables need to be considered, including timing of investment and commitment, location choices and specialization strategies.

With respect to timing, we have distinguished between "first" and "fast" investors. The former are banks which approached the New Europe market at the beginning of transition with small investments or greenfield activities, and already have a decade of experience in the region. The latter are players that came into the market only when the privatization of the big banks started, when they had the chance of becoming major competitors in each country. As a proxy for the commitment of investment decisions, we have considered the share of assets held in the region relative to the total assets of each international player.

Table 6.8 Role of international players in New Europe – 2002, EUR m

	Regional tot. assets	Countries of presence	Regional branches	Region as % of bank's tot. assets	Tot. assets of the region under bank's control
KBC	31 826	5	1 221	14.4%	6.62%
UCI	29 808	7	1 333	14.0%	6.20%
Erste Bank	27 041	4	1 021	22.3%	5.63%
HVB/BA	22 124	8	880	3.2%	4.60%
Soc.Générale	17 625	4	614	3.5%	3.67%
CitiGroup	14 123	7	215	1.3%	2.94%
B. Intesa	12 541	3	419	4.5%	2.61%
RZB	11 815	8	524	25.5%	2.46%

Source: UniCredito Italiano (2003).

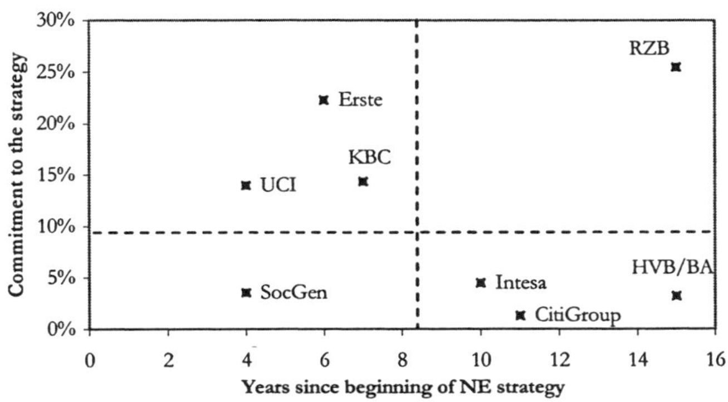

Figure 6.2 Entry strategy: timing and commitment

By matching timing and commitment of the investment decisions, we can classify international players as "positioned players", "stand-by competitors" and "aggressive" and "selective" entrants (Figure 6.2).

RZB is clearly an already positioned player. It is a first investor with a strong commitment to the market. Its positioning since the very beginning of transition, subsequently strengthened, has gained it a strong location advantage. Intesa and Citibank are first movers that did not capitalize on their early presence, but instead adopted a selective approach to markets and segments, and thus saw their overall regional market share gradually eroded by more aggressive international players (despite recording sizable growth in some markets/segments). HVB can be included in the same category, but to understand its positioning it is important to remember that the bank was the result of a merger between HypoVereinsbank and Bank Austria. Both banks were early investors in the region, with the latter also showing a very strong commitment to the region. The New Europe strategy has remained a strong focus, despite accounting for only 3 per cent of the resulting bank's assets.

UniCredito Italiano, KBC and Erste are fast investors with a strong commitment (aggressive entrants). By adopting an active approach to the privatization process, these banks have succeeded in building up a significant network, which already accounts for a large share of their total assets. Société Générale can be considered a selective entrant. It started its expansion strategy in the region relatively late compared with other international players, yet still managed to create a sizable network. The selective approach shows that New Europe still represents only part of a wider international strategy for the bank.

A second strategic approach to consider is market positioning: strategic investors have the choice of building a widespread regional network (i.e. being present in a large number of countries), or focusing on the top institutions in each market (i.e. acquiring a large local market share), or both.

Figure 6.3 shows the strategic positioning of major international players in the region. While KBC, Intesa, Société Générale and Erste have opted for a strong focus on market share, CitiGroup, HVB and RZB appear to be more interested in building a widespread presence, with operations in more than five different countries. UniCredito Italiano has focused on both, and aims to be one of the top institutions (an objective already achieved in three countries), while at the same time creating a widespread network.

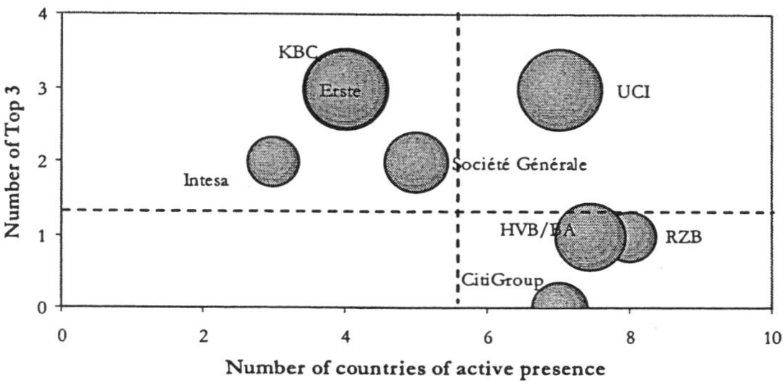

Figure 6.3 Positioning: country of operation and size in each market (size = assets controlled in the region)

Whatever the strategy, it is important to note that achieving a critical mass, either by gaining control of a large number of companies or by a having small number of large shareholdings, already seems to be a necessary condition for operating successfully in the region. Despite big differences between individual countries and markets, potential for economies of scale and scope exists which can only be exploited using a multi-country approach. Some international players, such as ING, CitiGroup and ABN Amro, which entered New Europe without a strong regional presence, are gradually repositioning themselves.

Another important strategic choice in international banks' investment policies is segment specialization. Note that for most banks the segment approach is a dynamic variable which has already changed substantially since the beginning of the investment strategy, depending on different market opportunities and potential, and on the level of each bank's commitment and relative positioning in each country.

In countries like Poland, Hungary and the Czech Republic most first comers began operating in particular market niches, then expanded to other major areas of banking. Citibank, for example, started out by providing retail services to high net worth individuals – a fairly narrow market segment – and is now targeting the wider retail and corporate markets. RZB's services are still primarily tailored to small and mid-size enterprises and their affluent owners. Erste Bank's strategy is aimed mainly at its core business in the retail segment, but with an increased focus on commercial banking for small and medium-sized businesses thanks to a strong positioning advantage gained by acquiring traditional savings banks in the Czech Republic and Slovakia.

Bank Austria Creditanstalt has passed through several stages in developing its approach to business: it began by providing corporate banking services to major local companies, and then enlarged its customer base to include the top segment of private customers and small and medium-sized enterprises. It finally moved on to a "universal bank" approach, by expanding its retail business countrywide. Up to now, and following the merger of the bank into HVB, this last development stage appears to have been implemented only in countries like Poland, Croatia and Bulgaria, where the bank's presence has been built mainly through acquiring local banks with a significant critical mass.

UniCredito, SocGen and Intesa also take a universal approach following their acquisition of the largest banks in the core New Europe countries. KBC is defining its strategy as a universal bancassurance provider by exploiting its strong global commitment to the development of new services.

By matching these strategic approaches we can see several common denominators. It is already recognized that being a regional bank in New Europe requires a well-defined global strategy. Following a first period of "indiscriminate entry", major players need to reposition, strengthen or reshape their behaviour in order to secure long-term success. We can expect several different categories to emerge:

- Aggressive players with a region-wide, strong presence in the market, which can exploit synergies and provide universal services, with special focus on new, highly profitable segments. In the years to come, we expect such players to focus on achieving critical mass at both regional and single country level by taking advantage of residual privatization or internal growth opportunities.

- Specialist players with a widespread market presence, which can leverage on their acquired reputation and positioning and are interested in endogenous growth. Such players will benefit substantially from the development of their target segment.
- Multi-country leaders with strong focus on a limited number of countries, which provide universal services and target the most profitable segments. Some of these players will be involved in M&A activity, and will enter new markets with the aim of moving into the first group. Others will be satisfied with their multi-country leadership, while a third sub-group could decide to leave the region.

The first and second categories, as long-term investors in the region, have a strong incentive to support long-term economic growth as a prerequisite for sustainable market conditions. Their expected dominance is the first indirect evidence of the potential for second-order effects.

Note that a further variable we have not considered, which can have a big impact on regional market dynamics, is that of M&A activity within the European Union. Any big operation between major EU players can change the competitive scenario significantly. New entrants can instantaneously become large competitors in the New Europe market, while banks that are today considered part of a strong regional network can become easy targets.

As a final step, we have looked at the situation at individual country level. We have evaluated the potential for consolidation, transformation and competitive development in each banking sector of the region by focusing on both the current characteristics of each market and the expected development strategies of major international players. Figure 6.4 shows the current competitive scenario in each New Europe market, focusing on the market power of the top banks (measured in terms of total assets of the leading banks) and that of the "competitive followers" (all foreign-owned banks with a market share close to a pre-defined critical mass).

Poland, Hungary and Slovakia are notable for the relatively high power of the "rising" players, which are pushing to increase their market share via M&A activity or endogenous growth, and have already gained some success. Competitive pressures are high and a significant concentration process is already under way. The only opportunities for regional players wishing to enter these countries are the last remaining privatizations (PKO BP[11] and BGZ in Poland and Postabanka in Hungary), or "second-wave acquisitions", i.e. acquiring control of a bank when a former strategic investor decides to leave the market (as happened with ABN Amro, which entered the Hungarian market early without strong commitment and failed to achieve any critical mass).

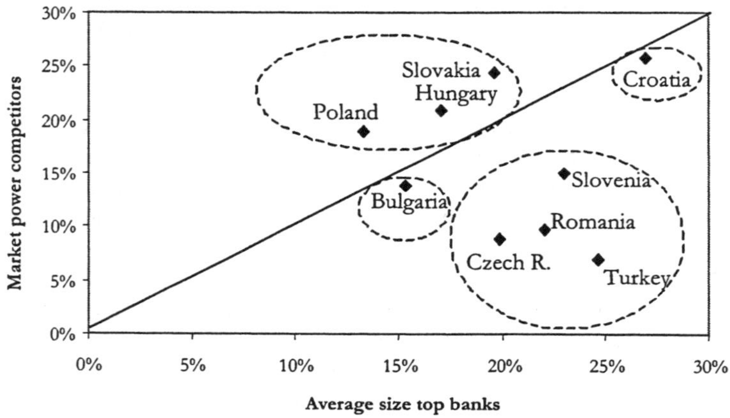

Figure 6.4 The competitive scenario in individual New Europe markets

A second, diverse group of countries comprises the Czech Republic, Slovenia, Turkey and Romania. The top players in all these markets are strongly positioned, with an average market share well above the combined power of potential followers (which also tend to have a small market share). However, whereas Slovenia, Turkey and Romania still offer significant entry opportunities given the large-scale privatization process under way, the Czech Republic appears to be an already closed market. The top players strongly dominate the market, and a large gap exists between them and the smaller operators, despite a sharp focus on endogenous growth by these last.

Bulgaria is similar to these markets but has some distinctive features. While the major operators have a significant average market share at present, the progressive encroachment of aggressive international banks could narrow the gap in the medium to long term. Now that privatization has been largely completed, market entry or a stronger position can only be achieved through second-wave acquisitions or endogenous growth.

In Croatia a small group of foreign banks holds a significant share, while other rising players are well positioned to capture the potential offered by the market. This is a strategic area in which international operators are trying to build a critical mass to enable them to compete with the major players. This trend is confirmed by the recent wave of acquisitions which involved the fourth- and fifth-largest banks, Splitska Banka and Rijecka Banka, bought respectively by HVB and Erste Bank – two groups already present in the country with greenfield investments.

CONCLUSIONS

We have presented and evaluated the New Europe experience with respect to foreign banks. In particular, we tested the impact of foreign ownership on the profitability and efficiency of single banks, by combining a traditional panel analysis with a propensity score methodology, to investigate the existence (or otherwise) of causal relations. The analysis demonstrated that foreign ownership positively influences banking profitability in the region, and also supports cost effectiveness.

As a second step, we analysed international banks' growth strategies in the region using a microeconomic approach, to gain an insight into future market developments. We identified three different kinds of competitors: large aggressive regional players, specialist institutions and focused multi-country leaders. We expect the first group to focus strongly on achieving critical mass at both regional and country level, the second to profit from existing reputations and positioning while leveraging on endogenous growth, and the third to face the decision on whether to grow, remain locally concentrated or even exit the market. The dominant and increasing role of long-term banking investors with a strong focus on regional development suggests that they could potentially have a stabilization effect. As the region is a kind of "second home" market, a strong commitment to global and long-term economic growth is required for the banks to achieve good profitability.

NOTES

1. New Europe Research Team, Foreign Bank Division, UniCredito Italiano. E-mail: fabio.mucci@unicredit.it.
2. Department of Economics, University of Ancona. E-mail: papi@dea.unian.it.
3. Head of New Europe Research, Foreign Bank Division, UniCredito Italiano. E-mail: debora.revoltella@unicredit.it.
4. The opinions expressed in this chapter are those of the authors and do not necessarily reflect the opinion of the institutions to which they belong. The authors would like to thank Bernard Belusic, Andrea Ichino and Matteo Manera for the comments and useful suggestions received during the writing of this chapter. The authors wish also to thank Barbara Alemanni and the other participants to the conference 'Financial Intermediation in the New Europe: Economics, Policies and Institutions' held in Bocconi University in September 2003. Any errors or inaccuracies are of course the responsibility of the authors.
5. "New Europe" includes the central and east European candidates for EU enlargement, plus Croatia and Turkey.
6. Those countries are: Bulgaria, Croatia, the Czech Republic, Hungary, Poland, Romania, Slovakia and Slovenia. Turkey and the Baltic countries have been excluded from the sample.
7. This problem is known as the "fundamental problem of causal inference" following Holland (1986).
8. The propensity score is defined by Rosenbaum and Rubin (1983) as the probability of assignment to treatment, conditional on some pre-intervention characteristics: $p(x)=Pr(T=1|X)=E(D|X)$ where T has the usual meaning and X is the multidimensional vector of pre-treatment characteristics.
9. In Table 6.3, over2 and nir2 denote the square of overheads and net interest revenues while roaa942 and roaa962 denote the square of roaa94 and roaa96 respectively. We also added as an additional control variable a proxy for bank size, without major effects on the results.
10. For details of the estimation procedure see Becker and Ichino (2002).

11. Whether the authorities will allow a foreign strategic investor to take control of the bank is not yet known.

REFERENCES

Becker, S.O. and Ichino, A. (2002), 'Estimation of Average Treatment Effects based on Propensity Scores', *Stata Journal*, 2(4), 358-377.

Claessens, S., Demirgüç-Kunt, A. and Huizinga, H. (2001), 'How Does Foreign Entry Affect the Domestic Banking Markets', *Journal of Banking and Finance,* 25, 891-911.

Crystal J.S., Dages, B.G. and Goldberg, L.S. (2001), 'Does Foreign Ownership Contribute to Sounder Banks in Emerging Markets? The Latin American Experience', Federal Reserve Bank of New York.

Demirgüç-Kunt, A. and Huizinga H. (1998), 'Determinants of Commercial Interest Margins and Profitability: Some International Evidence', working paper.

Focarelli, D. and Pozzolo, F. (2003), 'Where do Banks Expand Abroad? An Empirical Analysis', University of Molise, discussion paper, 9(03).

Goldberg L., Dages G. and Kinney D. (2000), 'Foreign and Domestic Bank Participation in Emerging Markets: Lessons from Mexico and Argentina', *Economic Policy Review* 6(3), Federal Reserve Bank of New York.

Holland, Paul W. (1986), 'Statistics and Causal Inference', *Journal of American Statistical Association,* 81, 945-970.

Levine, R (1999), 'Law Finance and Economic Growth', *Journal of Financial Intermediation.*

Levine, R (2002), 'Denying Foreign Bank Entry: Implications for Bank Interest Margins', University of Minnesota, mimeo.

Morgan, D. and Strahan, P. (2002), 'Foreign Bank Entry and Business Volatility: Evidence from U.S. States and Other Countries', Federal Reserve Bank of New York, mimeo.

Papi, L. and Revoltella, D. (2000), 'Foreign Direct Investment in the Banking Sector: a Transitional Economy Perspective', in Claessens and Jansen (eds), *The Internationalisation of Financial Services*, The Hague, The Netherlands: Kluwer Law International, pp. 437-457.

Rosenbaum, P. and Rubin, D. (1983), 'The Central Role of the Propensity Score in Observational Studies for Causal Effects', *Biometrika*, 70, 41-55.

UniCredito Italiano (2003), 'New Europe Banking Report 2003', mimeo.

Yildirim, H.S. and Philippatos, G.C. (2002), 'Efficiency of Banks: Recent Evidence from the Transition Economies of Europe – 1993/2000', working paper.

7. Financial Intermediation in Accession Countries: The Role of Foreign Banks

Jakob de Haan and Ilko Naaborg

INTRODUCTION

The development of a financially sound and market-oriented banking system is fundamental to a successful transition from a communist to a market-based economy. However, bank intermediation in transition economies remains stunted, particularly in countries where progress in reform is limited (Fries, Neven and Seabright, 2002). Fries and Taci (2002) find that in 1999 most transition countries lay below the market economy benchmark for the ratio of domestic credit to GDP. Between 1994 and 1999 there is no convergence toward the benchmark. According to Fries and Taci (2002), it is primarily the non-governmental sector that suffers from the underdevelopment of the banking sector. Bank credit to enterprises and households rather than credit to the government is undersupplied relative to that in comparable market economies.

The financial systems of most transition countries have changed dramatically over the last decade. The growing presence of foreign-owned financial institutions during the 1990s is one of the most striking structural changes. Currently, more than 60 per cent of the banks in the region are foreign-owned, accounting for about two-thirds of total bank assets. In some countries the share of foreign bank assets relative to total assets of the banking system is even more than 75 per cent (Naaborg, Scholtens, De Haan, Bol and De Haas, 2004).

It is widely believed that allowing foreign bank entry as part of a liberalization process will enhance the efficiency of the banking system (Litan, Masson and Pomerleano, 2001). Foreign banks will help improve the quality, pricing, and availability of financial services, both directly as providers of these services and indirectly through increased competition. The entry of foreign banks may reduce the market power of domestic banks, which was important as at the beginning of transition the creation of a two-tier banking system produced an oligopolistic market structure (Papi and Revoltella, 1999). In addition, foreign banks are often seen as improving the allocation of credit since they have more sophisticated systems for evaluating and pricing of risks. They are also more experienced in the use of derivative products (Mathieson and Roldos, 2001). Also the likely improvement of human capital due to foreign bank presence will be beneficial, because the skills required for the banking business were scarce during the first years of transition. Finally, foreign bank presence may also lead to improvements of bank regulation and supervision, since these banks may demand improved systems of regulation and supervision from the regulatory authorities in the recipient countries. This may contribute to improving the quality of banking operations of domestic banks (Hermes and Lensink, 2004). All these spill-over effects may contribute to more efficient domestic banking practices, which, in turn, may enhance economic growth in transition countries (Koivu, 2002) [1].

However, some worries – notably with respect to the intermediation role of foreign banks – have also been aired. Foreign banks may have troubles in assessing the emerging private sector, notably small and medium-sized enterprises, and therefore direct funds to local subsidiaries of multinational enterprises rather than local firms (Papi and Revoltella, 1999). Indeed, Berger, Klapper and Udell (2001) and Clarke, Cull, Martinez-Peria and Sánchez (2002) find that foreign banks in Argentina, Chile, Colombia and Peru have problems supplying funds to small businesses. Once established abroad, foreign banks focus their activities mainly on large enterprises. Furthermore, foreign bank credit may turn out to be less stable than domestic credit, especially during adverse economic times. Foreign banks may easily withdraw funds in case of a world-wide recession or an economic downturn in the home country (De Haas and Van Lelyveld, 2004). Peek and Rosengren (2000a) find, for instance, that the collapse of the Japanese equity and real estate markets and the subsequent banking crisis in Japan had an impact in the US, as Japanese bank subsidiaries in the US reduced their lending in response to the problems in Japan.

The purpose of this chapter is to analyse the intermediation role of foreign banks in detail in those transition countries that have recently become a member of the European Union, i.e. Bulgaria, the Czech Republic, Estonia, Hungary, Latvia, Lithuania, Poland, Romania, the Slovak Republic and Slovenia. Except for Bulgaria and Romania, who will join at a later stage, these countries have entered the EU in 2004. In our analysis we will also include Croatia as it seems likely that this country will also become an EU member in the near future.

The remainder of this chapter is organized as follows. Section 2 presents figures on bank intermediation in the accession countries. Section 3 shows how the share of foreign banks has evolved over time, both in terms of the number of foreign banks and in terms of their share in total banking assets. Section 4 presents figures on private credit supplied by foreign and domestic banks, while section 5 reviews the scant literature on the stability of credit supply by foreign banks. The final section offers some concluding comments.

BANK INTERMEDIATION IN TRANSITION COUNTRIES

The banking systems in European transition countries typically evolved from the mono-bank model in which a single bank was responsible for both monetary policy and commercial banking. In most countries this structure was abolished in the late 1980s. With the elimination of the mono-bank system, most countries experienced a rapid expansion of the banking sector. Big increases in the amount of non-performing loans led to banking crises in many transition countries during the 1990s[2]. Many of these crises arose out of insolvencies of state-owned or formerly state-owned banks, caused by bad loans inherited from the communist era. Moreover, the transition reduced profitability in certain sectors, thereby reducing the abilities of firms to service their debts (Koivu, 2002).

Despite the rapid developments, the banking sectors in most transition countries are still underdeveloped[3]. Still, they are the most important channel for domestic financing as capital markets in these countries are small, volatile and illiquid. As pointed out by Koivu (2002), stock markets in some transition countries even face a danger of becoming irrelevant, as many companies have been delisted in recent years. Thus, enterprises often have to finance capital investment out of their own cash flows. Berglöf and Bolton (2002) argue that banks in transition countries have not yet begun extending significant long-term finance.

Fries and Taci (2002) have estimated a benchmark model to examine to what extent transition countries deviate from countries with a similar income per capita when it comes to the domestic credit to GDP ratio. The first columns in Table 7.1 are reproduced from this study. The benchmark for each country is calculated using its GNP per capita in international US dollars at purchasing power parity and the estimated equation for a sample of 122 developing and industrialized economies: $y = 34.7 - 20.1\ln(x) + 2.5(\ln(x))^2$, where x is GNP per capita and y is the domestic credit to GDP ratio. It follows from Table 7.1 that in 1994 most accession countries had a much lower credit ratio than the benchmark. In 1999 this situation had worsened. In fact, the gap between the actual credit ratio and the benchmark ratio increased in most countries, Estonia, Romania and Slovenia being the exceptions. Countries that in 1994 had a higher credit ratio than the benchmark (Bulgaria, Hungary and the Slovak Republic), all had a lower ratio than the benchmark in 1999[4]. In 2001, in Croatia, Estonia and Latvia the gap had narrowed substantially while for most countries little had changed. In the Czech Republic and Romania the distance between the credit ratio and the benchmark only widened, in Romania even beyond its 1994 level. The overall picture leads us to conclude that after more than a decade of transition, bank intermediaton in Central and Eastern European countries remains stunted.

Figure 7.1 presents the development of the level of bank claims on the private sector as share of GDP in 11 Central and Eastern European (CEE) countries[5]. This ratio shows the importance of one of the main functions of financial intermediaries, i.e. channeling funds to investors. Private credit captures the loans to the private non-financial sector (Beck, Demirgüç-Kunt, and Levine, 2000). The difference with total deposit money bank assets, which is also shown in the figure, mainly consists of claims on the government and on (semi-)public enterprises. Figure 7.1 shows that credit to the private sector increased in the accession countries but to a lesser extent than total deposit money bank assets.

Table 7.1 Total domestic credit to GDP in transition countries in comparison to benchmark

	1994			1999			2001		
	credit/GDP	benchmark	difference	credit/GDP	benchmark	difference	credit/GDP	benchmark	difference
Bulgaria	103.4	51.1	52.3	18.6	51.5	-32.9	20.4	48.9	-28.5
Croatia	31.6	48.6	-17.0	39.2	57.0	-17.8	53.8	57.3	-3.5
Czech R.	68.3	70.0	-1.7	62.6	76.5	-13.9	49.4	71.7	-22.3
Estonia	12.8	48.7	-36.1	34.8	59.0	-24.2	42.9	61.7	-18.8
Hungary	93.1	60.0	33.1	52.5	68.4	-16.0	50.0	67.7	-17.7
Latvia	22.6	44.5	-21.9	18.9	51.5	-32.6	30.9	55.6	-24.7
Lithuania	19.0	45.7	-26.6	15.3	53.5	-38.1	16.0	54.8	-38.8
Poland	38.5	54.6	-16.1	39.2	65.4	-26.1	36.2	59.7	-23.5
Romania	11.1	48.1	-37.0	19.4	49.7	-30.2	12.2	52.6	-40.4
Slovak R.	79.1	59.7	19.4	68.6	70.0	-1.4	61.6	65.6	-4.0
Slovenia	37.4	73.6	-36.1	48.5	83.4	-34.9	47.7	78.0	-30.3

Sources: Fries and Taci (2002) for 1994 and 1999 and own calculations for 2001.

Two opposing forces may have influenced extending private credit in the transition economies. First, more developed countries generally have more developed financial markets. So, one would expect that economic development in a transition country will lead to more credit to the private sector. Due to relatively underdeveloped equity markets in transition economies, firms in need of external funds depend on bank credit. Second, due to poor conditions in the banking sector credit to the private sector may, however, stagnate. According to De Haas and Van Lelyveld (2004), the reluctance of banks to grant new loans to the private sector partly results from lengthy legal procedures, especially the inadequate enforcement of creditor rights.

When it comes to the intermediation role of banks, major differences exist between the various CEE countries, as Figure 7.2 illustrates. In 2003, Romania, Lithuania, Bulgaria, the Czech Republic and Poland private credit to GDP was less than 30%. In the Slovak Republic, Hungary, Estonia and Slovenia the ratio was between 30 and 40%. Only Latvia and Croatia had ratios above 40% in 2003.

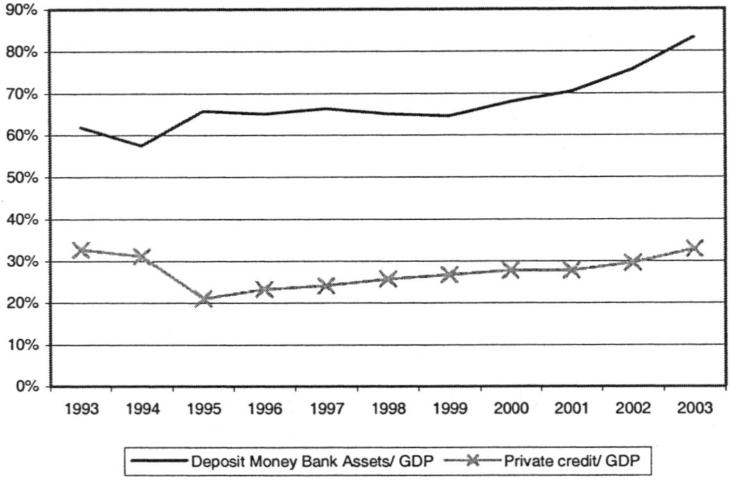

Source: authors' calculations.

Figure 7. 1 Deposit money banks assets and private sector credit in CEE countries (% GDP), 1993-2003

Bratkowski, Grosfeld and Rostowski (2000) find that collateralization is an important determinant for banks in supplying loans to new private firms in the Czech Republic, Hungary, and Poland. Even though the liquidation payoff for the bank is low due to insufficient public contract enforcement and imperfect secondary markets (Hainz, 2002), collateralization may help to reduce moral hazard problems.

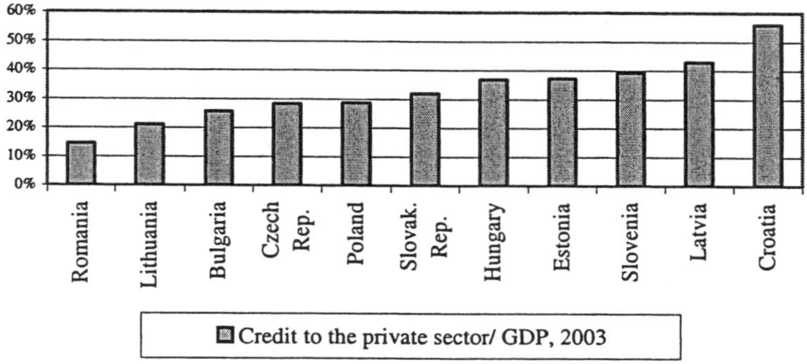

Source: Naaborg, Scholtens, De Haan, Bol and De Haas (2004).

Figure 7.2 Bank claims on the private sector in CEE countries (% GDP), 2003

FOREIGN BANKS IN ACCESSION COUNTRIES

Foreign bank entry is generally defined as a process by which foreign banks set up operations in a host country mainly by either opening a branch or a subsidiary. A bank is considered as foreign if at least 50 percent of its shares are foreign-owned, i.e. when there is foreign control of a bank's operations[6]. Basically, there are two ways how a bank may become a foreign bank: either a foreign bank starts a green-field operation, or a (privatized) domestic bank is being sold to a foreign bank. Of course, a combination of these two is also possible. For instance, the Magyar Hitel Bank (MHB) in Hungary was privatized in 1996 when ABN-Amro bought virtually all of the state's shares, to merge it later with its greenfield operation to create MHB-ABN-Amro.

Reasons for Foreign Bank Entry

Why would a bank go abroad? There is no unambiguous theory to explain foreign bank entry. Nevertheless, several reasons have been suggested in the literature (see, for instance, Williams, 1997, Buch, 2000 and Focarelli and Pozzolo, 2000). As pointed out by Clarke, Cull, Martinez-Peria and Sánchez (2003), empirical research on the factors that compel banks to enter another country indicate that the degree of economic integration between the home and the host country, the market opportunities available, and entry restrictions and other regulations (including tax treatment) affect foreign bank entry.

An important reason for foreign bank entry is to 'follow the customer', otherwise called the defensive expansion hypothesis (Williams, 2002). According to this view, a bank follows its customers abroad to support its already existing relationship in the new country. Indeed, various studies have found a positive and significant correlation between foreign bank entry and the extent of *integration between the home and the host country*. For instance, Konopielko (1999) reports a significant correlation between the presence of a foreign bank in some transition countries on the one hand, and trade between the host and home country and Foreign Direct Investment (FDI) from the home country on the other. However, it is unclear to what extent there is also a causal relationship, as causation may run from FDI of banks to FDI in the non-financial sectors. It is also possible that some omitted factor(s) is (are) driving FDI in both sectors.

A second reason why a bank might go abroad is *the attractiveness of the host market*. The market of the host country may offer new opportunities to make money, depending on the characteristics of the market (like size, stability of the country, features of the local banking sector). A number of recent studies offer support for the view that profitable opportunities in host countries drive foreign bank entry. For example, Claessens, Demirgüç-Kunt, and Huizinga (2000) model foreign bank presence in 80 countries, including some transition countries, from 1988-95 and find that foreign banks are attracted to markets with low taxes and high per capita income. In addition to controls for the degree of economic integration between countries (non-financial FDI, bilateral trade, and geographical distance) and regulatory restrictions, they include variables that measure the prospects for economic growth and the competitiveness of the banking sector of the host countries. Likewise, Papi and Revoltella (1999) find in their study on nine transition countries that various variables that proxy the attractiveness of the new market are positively and significantly correlated with FDI initiatives by foreign banks. Similar results are reported by Mathieson and Roldos (2001) in their study on 15 emerging countries, including the Czech Republic, Hungary, and

Poland. Variables that are significant in this study include the rate of return on equity, non-performing loans and banking crises. Again, for some of these variables causality may go in both directions. For instance, a foreign bank may be attracted to a country with an efficient banking system, but the entry of foreign banks may enhance the overall efficiency of the banking sector.

Based on a survey among banks, Kraft (2004) concludes that high interest margins were the strongest reason for foreign bank entry in Croatia at the moment of entry. Following high interest margins, with almost equal scores, were the search for new clients and the unused credit potential of Croatian households and businesses. Following clients from the home country was rated much lower. Interestingly, foreign banks indicated that high interest margins are not very important in keeping them in Croatia. Most important are other pull factors: the search for new clients, and the unused potential of households and businesses, in this order.

A third consideration for foreign bank entry is *host country regulation*, which generally limits competition and protects inefficient domestic banks (Clarke, Cull, Martinez-Peria and Sánchez, 2003). Focarelli and Pozzolo (2000) find that foreign banks prefer to invest in countries with fewer regulatory restrictions. However, this study does not deal with transition countries. Lensink and De Haan (2004) provide strong evidence that foreign bank entry in transition countries positively responds to economic reform measures. Moreover, they find that reforms significantly affect foreign bank entry via the efficiency of the financial sector and by stimulating domestic investment. Papi and Revoltella (1999) find that the attitude of the authorities in the host country concerning entry of foreign banks is a significant determinant of FDI initiatives of banks in contrast to bank taxes.

Foreign Banks in Accession Countries

One way to measure the presence of foreign banks is simply to calculate the share of the number of banks that are foreign majority owned. Alternatively, the proportion of total bank assets held by foreign investors is often employed. The relative number of foreign banks is an appropriate measure if the number of domestic and foreign banks determines competitive conditions. This might be the case if domestic banks adjust their activities as soon as foreign entry occurs to prevent the new entrants from capturing a significant market share. The asset share measure can be appropriate if foreign banks have an impact on domestic banks only after gaining market share (Claessens, Demirgüç-Kunt, and Huizinga, 2001).

The increasing foreign bank presence since the 1990s is one of the most striking developments in the banking system in the transition economies. On average, foreign-owned banks account for more than half of the total number of banks in 2000 and hold more than two-thirds of total bank assets in most transition economies (Naaborg, Scholtens, De Haan, Bol and De Haas, 2004). Data presented below show that this trend has continued in recent years. However, the importance of foreign banks varies a lot among countries[7].

Table 7.2 shows the share of foreign banks in the total number of banks for the period 1995-2003. In 1995, 123 foreign banks were present in the countries in our sample, accounting for 30 per cent of total banks. In 2000, their number had risen to 220, accounting for almost 65 per cent of all banks. In particular in Bulgaria, Croatia, Hungary, Lithuania, Poland, and Romania the number of foreign banks grew very strongly. In the Czech Republic, Estonia, Latvia, the Slovak Republic, and Slovenia the number of foreign banks is in 2002 about the same as in the first year of observation. Only since 2000 foreign banks really began to dominate domestic banks.

Table 7.2 Share of foreign bank in total number of banks, 1995-2003

	1995	1996	1997	1998	1999	2000	2001	2002	2003
Bulgaria	17%	30%	41%	50%	56%	66%	66%	66%*	
Croatia	2%	9%	12%	17%	25%	47%	56%	50%	49%
Czech R.	43%	44%	49%	58%	66%	68%	70%	72%	76%
Estonia	5%	7%	8%	50%	43%	57%	57%	57%*	
Hungary	54%	63%	78%	73%	78%	86%	83%	79%	
Latvia	28%	42%	48%	42%	54%	59%	43%	43%*	
Lithuania	0%	25%	42%	58%	54%	69%	67%	60%	
Poland	22%	31%	35%	49%	51%	65%	68%	76%	77%
Romania	48%	48%	53%	56%	63%	71%	78%	82%	
Slovak R.	55%	48%	45%	38%	40%	57%	71%	85%	
Slovenia	19%	14%	14%	13%	20%	24%	24%	30%	
Average	27%	33%	39%	46%	50%	61%	62%	64%	

Sources: Based on data provided in Naaborg, Scholtens, De Haan, Bol and De Haas (2004). * Estimations based on most recent available data.

Table 7.3 shows foreign banks assets as a percentage of total banks assets for the period 1995-2003. It appears that foreign bank participation increased considerably during the second half of the 1990s. In 2002, the share of banking assets under foreign control had reached almost 80 per cent. After several banking crises hit most transition countries in the mid-1990s (see Caprio and Klingebiel (2003) for an overview of the different crises), bank privatization furthered foreign participation. Initially, most sales involved medium-sized banks. Later on, the larger state-owned saving banks were sold too. For example, in Estonia, the first foreign-owned bank was already established in 1992. But only in 1998 the share of foreign bank assets rose to 90 per cent. In the same year, the number of foreign banks as share of the total number of banks in Estonia increased from 8 to 50 per cent, reflecting that the two largest banks (Hansa Bank and Eesti Uhispank) were sold to foreign banks (EBRD, 2001).

Table 7.3 Foreign banks assets as share of deposit money bank assets, 1995-2003

	1995	1996	1997	1998	1999	2000	2001	2002	2003
Bulgaria	1%	2%	18%	25%	42%	73%	72%	81%	
Croatia	0%	1%	4%	8%	41%	87%	89%	90%	91%
Czech R.	17%	20%	24%	27%	40%	66%	94%	93%	
Estonia	2%	2%	2%	90%	90%	97%	98%	97%	
Hungary	19%	46%	62%	62%	68%	70%	70%	91%	
Latvia	36%	53%	72%	81%	76%	78%	77%		
Lithuania	0%	28%	41%	52%	38%	57%	81%[b]	88%[b]	89%
Poland	4%	14%	15%	17%	47%	70%	69%	67%	67%
Romania				30%	48%	50%	55%	56%	58%
Slovak R.	19%	23%	30%	33%	33%	44%	90%	96%[a]	
Slovenia	5%	5%	5%	5%	5%	12%	16%	33%	33%
Average	10%	20%	27%	39%	48%	64%	74%	80%	

Notes: [a]Data from Mero and Valentinyi (2003).[b] Capital, in %.
Sources: Naaborg, Scholtens, de Haan, Bol and De Haas (2004), National Central Banks and Bank Austria Creditanstalt (Banking in CEE, April 2004).

Consequences of Foreign Bank Entry

As outlined in the Introduction, foreign bank entry is often argued to have beneficial effects, like improved soundness and efficiency of the financial system.

Das, Quintyn and Chenard (2003) have analyzed the soundness of financial systems for a sample of 43 countries, including various transition countries. As expected, financial system soundness tends to be associated with low government budget deficits, low real interest rates and low inflation. In addition, the structure of the banking system matters: the presence of foreign-owned banks is positively and significantly related to financial stability.

The most comprehensive study on the efficiency and competition effects of foreign bank presence is provided by Claessens, Demirgüç-Kunt, and Huizinga (2001). Using a large data set containing individual bank accounting information of domestic banks in 80 countries, including Russia and six transition countries in Central and

Eastern Europe, for the period 1988-1995, they show that increased presence of foreign banks is associated with lower profitability, non-interest income and overall expenses of domestic banks. Apparently, the competitive pressure of foreign banks leads to positive efficiency effects at domestic banks. Moreover, these authors find that these efficiency effects occur as soon as foreign banks enter the market; they do not seem to depend on the market share of foreign banks.

Lensink and Hermes (2004) focus on the short-term effects of foreign bank presence on domestic bank performance, using data of 990 banks for the period 1990-1996 in 48 countries, including the Czech Republic, Hungary, Poland, and Romania. These authors investigate the short-term effects of foreign bank entry on the behavior of the domestic banking sector, arguing that these effects are dependent on the level of economic development of the host country. They show that at lower levels of economic development foreign bank entry is generally associated with higher costs and margins for domestic banks. At higher levels of economic development the effects appear to be less clear: foreign bank entry is either associated with a fall of costs, profits and margins of domestic banks, or is not associated with changes in these domestic bank variables. Similar results are reported in Hermes and Lensink (2004). These authors interpret their results as follows. At lower levels of financial development foreign bank presence has a strong effect on domestic banks in terms of spill-overs of modern bank techniques and practices, since there is a large gap between the development of domestic and foreign banking. Yet, domestic banks need to make investments to implement these techniques and practices. Therefore, costs rise. At the same time, since domestic banks still have a relatively strong market power in domestic financial markets due to the fact that these markets are rather segmented in less developed banking markets, they are able to raise interest rate margins and non-interest income to pay for the investments made. This may lead to an increase of income of banks. Although foreign bank presence may put competitive pressure on domestic banks, this effect is cancelled out. At higher levels of financial development spill-overs are less important since the gap between domestic and foreign banks is smaller and banking markets are more competitive. Domestic banks are mainly confronted with the need to reduce costs and become more efficient in an effort to keep their market shares.

The papers referred to so far do not exclusively deal with transition countries. Recently, quite a few studies have been published that focus on transition countries only. Grigorian and Manole (2002) have analyzed 17 transition economies over the 1995-1998 period and find that foreign ownership enhances commercial bank efficiency. For future research they suggest to examine whether the efficiency gains are due to better managerial control or to transfer of technology from the banks' foreign owners.

Havrylchyk (2003) has investigated the efficiency of the Polish banking industry between 1998-2000, using Data Envelopment Analysis (DEA), which allows to distinguish between cost, allocative, technical, and scale efficiency. This author concludes that bank efficiency has not improved during the analyzed years. Foreign banks were found to be more efficient than their domestically owned counterparts. Loan portfolio quality, higher productivity of labor and market power have the largest impact on efficiency.

Weill (2003) has studied banks in the Czech Republic and Poland using the stochastic frontier approach to compute cost efficiency scores. Also this study reports evidence that foreign banks are more efficient than domestic banks. Weill (2003) also concludes that the advantage of foreign banks does not result from differences in the scale of operations or the structure of activities.

Yildirim and Philippatos (2002) study twelve transition economies of Central and Eastern Europe over the period 1993-2000 and find that foreign banks are more cost efficient but less profit efficient relative to domestically-owned private banks and state-owned banks.

Bonin, Hasan, and Wachtel (2003) have used data from 1996 to 2000 for eleven transition countries to investigate the effect of foreign ownership on the banking sectors in general and bank efficiency in particular. Using stochastic frontier estimation procedures, they compute profit and cost efficiency scores. Their results indicate that banking sectors in these countries became more efficient and more competitive toward the end of the 1990s. They also find that government banks are less efficient than their private counterparts and that majority foreign ownership generates higher efficiency scores. Moreover, they report that banks with a participation by international institutional investors, about 10 per cent of their observations, earn higher returns on assets and are more efficient by the profit measure; however, these banks are not significantly more cost efficient.

A recent paper by Green, Murinde and Nikilov (2004) focuses on economies of scale and scope in transition countries, distinguishing between domestic and foreign banks. Their conclusion is somewhat out of line with those of most previous studies on foreign bank entry. Using a panel of 273 foreign and domestic banks located in nine European transition economies (Bulgaria, Croatia, the Czech Republic, Estonia, Hungary, Latvia, Lithuania, Poland, and Romania) during 1995-1999, they reject the hypothesis that foreign banks are more efficient than domestic banks in these economies. They also find that foreign ownership is hardly an important factor in reducing the banks' total costs. However, as pointed out in note 6, this finding may be the result of the uncommon definition of foreign banks used in this study.

INTERMEDIATION BY FOREIGN BANKS

This section analyses the role of foreign-owned banks in intermediation, focusing on lending to the private sector. As foreign banks have gradually increased their presence in the financial sector, one has to correct for this development when comparing total private credit extended by foreign and domestic-owned banks. Averaging the figures in Tables 7.2 and 7.3 we came up with a relative foreign bank presence indicator for each country, for each year. Next, we calculated the relative share of *foreign* bank private credit extension relative to the private credit extended by *domestic* banks.

Figure 7.3 shows that in 1995 and 1996 foreign banks extended less private credit than one would expect based on their presence in the region. From 1997 up to 1999 private sector intermediation by foreign banks improved but it was only after 1999 that foreign banks lend relatively more to the private sector than domestic banks; in previous years domestic banks were more important in serving the private sector.

As can be observed from Figure 7.4, there are still substantial differences among the countries with respect to the relative importance of private lending by foreign banks. The most extreme case is Estonia, where foreign banks dominate the provision of credit to the private sector while based on their presence one would expect that the role of domestic banks could be of significance as well. In the two other countries of the Baltic area, Latvia and Lithuania, as well as in Slovenia a similar pattern is present. In the Czech Republic, Hungary, and Poland foreign banks' presence is in line with their operations in extending credit. Only in Croatia domestic banks seem to dominate private credit extension[8].

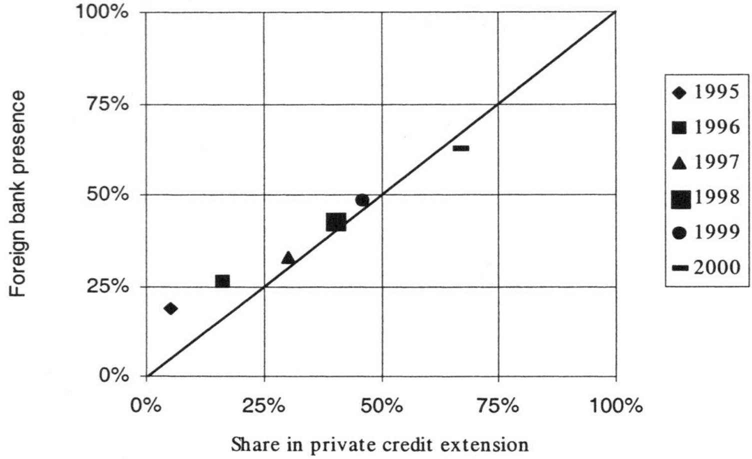

Source: authors' calculations.

Figure 7.3 Foreign banks: relative presence and relative share in private credit extension, CEE region, 1995-2000

Fries and Taci (2002) have estimated a reduced form model that relates the real growth of bank loans to observable demand and supply factors. Their data covers 515 banks from transition countries over the years 1994-99. They differentiate between high and low reform countries and years. The accession countries generally belong to the high reform countries and years. Table 7.4 is reproduced from this study. The results of Fries and Taci (2002) show that loan growth is significantly associated with lagged real GDP growth.

However, the estimated coefficients are in the range of 0.9-1.0, which implies that lending is expanding at about the same rate as output. This result is in line with Figure 7.1. The estimates also show that budget deficits crowd out real growth in customer lending. From the point of view of this chapter it is interesting that foreign ownership does not influence loan growth. Foreign banks on average expand at the same rate as privatized or ab initio banks. Still, the share of foreign banks in the total assets of the banking sector has a positive effect on the expansion of customer loans. According to Fries and Taci (2002), this may reflect the positive effect of the presence of foreign banks in the loan market by increasing the competitive pressure in the sector as well as spillover effects from the introduction of better banking technologies, skills and lending products[9].

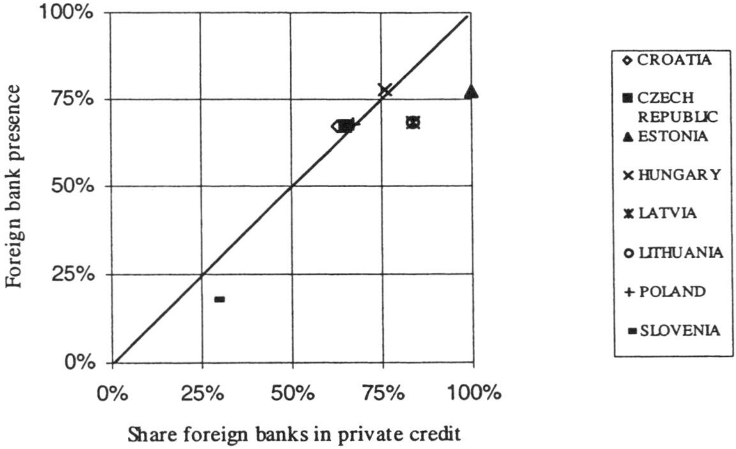

Source: authors' calculations.

Figure 7.4 Foreign banks: relative presence and relative share in private credit extension, per country, 2000

Foreign banks are expected to have comparative disadvantages in areas requiring detailed knowledge of local conditions. Lending to small enterprises is a classic example of such an activity (Berger, Klapper and Udell, 2001 and Berger and Udell, 2002). This may imply that the lending to the private sector is mainly directed toward larger firms. Unfortunately, there is not much evidence on this issue.

However, it is clear that SME lending in Central and Eastern Europe is yet in an early stage. As the substantially lower risks associated to large firm lending and retail business as well as the opportunities to expand on these markets made banks unwilling to expand SME lending in earlier years, increased competition in the banking sector will probably force banks, both foreign and domestic ones, to focus more on SME lending in the coming years.

Table 7.4 Real growth in bank loans to customers

	Model 1	Model 2
Lagged real GDP growth	0.87 (2.57)***	1.02 (3.10)***
Lagged real loan growth	0.23 (1.93)**	0.27 (2.06)**
General government balance (% GDP)	0.69 (2.06)**	0.84 (2.50)**
Inflation (%)	-0.21 (-2.81)***	-0.21 (-2.98)***
Asset share of foreign banks (%)	0.12 (1.66)*	0.12 (1.66)*
Total real assets	0.09 (0.61)	
Deposits market share (%)		-0.05 (-0.95)
State-owned banks (dummy)	-1.56 (-0.97)	-2.26 (-1.51)
Ab initio private banks (dummy)	-2.11 (-1.03)	-2.77 (-1.34)
Foreign-owned banks (dummy)	1.00 (0.54)	0.53 (0.27)
Lagged equity/Total assets (%)	0.32 (4.31)***	0.23 (2.90)***
Constant	-1.75 (-0.50)	-0.23 (-0.07)
Nr. Obs.	672	661
R^2	0.23	0.22

Source: Fries and Taci (2002).
Notes: *, **, *** Indicate statistical significance confidence levels at 10, 5 and 1 percent respectively.

According to the survey data presented by Kraft (2003), the arrival of foreign banks in Croatia has contributed to improved assortment and quality of products and services. In addition, the foreign banks indicated a keen interest in broad market segments both on the retail side (car loans and housing loans in particular), and on the wholesale side (including long-term loans for investment). Importantly, foreign banks profess keen interest in lending to small and medium enterprises.

STABILITY OF CREDIT BY FOREIGN BANKS

As pointed out in the introduction, it is sometimes argued that credit supplied by foreign banks may be less stable than loans provided by domestic institutions. According to the IMF (2000), it is still unclear whether a greater foreign bank presence contributes to a less volatile supply of credit in emerging economies. However, Buch, Kleinert, and Zajc (2003) argue that one might expect that FDI in banking has stabilizing features for two reasons. First, FDI flows are typically less volatile than other forms of capital flows such as international portfolio investments and international bank lending. Second, because FDI provides banks with superior information on host markets and because it requires a stronger commitment to servicing the foreign market, it may be less destabilizing than other forms of entry. Furthermore, Buch, Kleinert, and Zajc (2003) argue that FDI of banks has an additional stabilizing feature since it allows banks in transition countries to draw on the liquidity buffer of their headquarters abroad. This can be done at lower variable costs than borrowing on the inter-bank market. Hence, local liquidity shocks originating in these countries would have smaller effects on local banking markets than in a system with local banks only.

Much empirical evidence on this issue refers to Latin America. Dages, Goldberg, and Kinney (2000) and Crystal, Dages, and Goldberg (2002), for instance, show that foreign banks that have been present in Latin America for a relatively long time exhibit stronger and less volatile loan growth than domestic banks. Likewise, Peek and Rosengren (2000b) and Soledad Martinez Peria, Powell, and Vladkova Hollar (2002) find that foreign bank subsidiaries did not reduce their credit supply during adverse economic times in the host country. However, Peek and Rosengren (2000b) also show that cross-border lending did in some cases retrench during economic slowdowns in Latin America. Soledad Martinez Peria, Powell, and Vladkova Hollar (2002) find evidence of foreign banks transmitting home country shocks to Latin America.

There is less empirical evidence for transition countries. Kraft (2004) shows that foreign banks expanded their credit supply after the

Croatian banking crisis of 1998-99. The most extensive study on this issue is De Haas and Van Lelyveld (2004), who analyse whether aggregate foreign bank credit declined during periods of economic and/or financial downturn, and if so, whether such declines were steeper than those of domestic banks. They explicitly pay attention to both cross-border credit flows and activities of foreign subsidiaries within the region itself. To that end, they constructed a dataset on the quantitative importance of foreign banks which combines data from the Bank for International Settlements (BIS) with data on more than 100 banks in the Czech Republic, Estonia, Hungary, Poland, and Slovenia. Table 7.5, which is reproduced from this study, shows the changes in foreign subsidiaries' credit as well as cross-border credit during each period in which domestic banks on aggregate contracted their credit (in absolute terms and denominated in US dollars). It is striking that in all but one period during which domestic banks contracted their credit, foreign bank subsidiaries increased theirs (cross-border credit shows less unambiguous behavior during these periods). The strongest negative effect of the Russian crisis was felt in Estonia, where economic growth turned negative in 1999 and a banking crisis reduced the number of banks. Additionally, stock prices declined heavily between end-1997 and mid-1999.

Although initially there was a temporary drop in total credit from BIS reporting banks during the first half of 1999, the crisis ultimately proved to be an opportunity for foreign banks to expand. The lower stock prices made Estonian banks an attractive take-over target and the two largest banks were bought by Swedish strategic investors. The Czech Republic experienced a recession in 1997-99, following the currency crisis of May 1997. During the following years, credit by domestic banks contracted and in 1998 and 2000 cross-border foreign credit declined as well. However, the bad financial health of the domestic banks proved to be an expansion opportunity for foreign bank subsidiaries, which increased their market share at both the deposit and the credit side.

GDP-growth in Poland showed a declining trend since 1995. At the same time, growth rates of domestic credit declined as well, even turning negative in 2000. Cross-border credit did not show much growth either, as opposed to credit by foreign subsidiaries, which has been increasing rapidly. Only in the case of Slovenia in 1999, domestic bank credit and foreign subsidiary credit declined simultaneously. However, the relatively large increase in cross-border credit led to a situation in which the broad loan penetration measure did increase in 1999 all the same. In sum, the results of De Haas and Van Lelyveld (2004) show no evidence of "cut and run" behavior by foreign banks. Temporary reductions in cross-border credit into Estonia, Hungary, and the Czech Republic were met by increases in local subsidiaries' credit, which noticed an opportunity to expand. Foreign banks local affiliates have been rather stable credit sources, even when domestic banks reduced their credit supply.

Table 7.5 Behavior of foreign banks during periods of domestic credit contraction

	Period	Credit by foreign subsidiaries	Cross-border credit
Estonia	1999-2000	+	-
Hungary	1996-2000	+	+
Poland	2000	+	-
Slovenia	1999	-	+
Czech R. (I)	1997	+	+
Czech R. (II)	1999-2000	+	-

Source: De Haas and Van Lelyveld (2004).

CONCLUDING COMMENTS

The growing presence of foreign-owned financial institutions during the 1990s is one of the most striking structural changes in accession countries. In 2000 domestic banks became minority players in the financial sector and in 2002 two-thirds of total banks were foreign-owned as well as almost 80 per cent of total banking assets. This chapter has analyzed intermediation by foreign banks. It is concluded that – in comparison to countries with similar incomes per capita – bank intermediation in transition economies in 2001 remains stunted, Croatia, and the Slovak Republic being the exceptions.

Since 2000 foreign banks generally lend more to the private sector than domestic banks, especially in the Baltic States and Slovenia. Previously domestic banks were in general more involved in private credit extension. There is not much support that foreign banks only lend to large borrowers. Finally, available empirical evidence suggests that the credit supply of foreign banks is quite stable.

NOTES

1. Koivu (2002) finds in his unbalanced panel data set from 25 transition countries that the margin between lending and deposit rates is significantly and negatively related to economic growth. In contrast, the amount of outstanding credit allocated to the private sector is not related to economic growth. Koivu argues that this could reflect the numerous banking crises that the transition countries have experienced and the soft budget constraints that are still prevalent in many transition countries.
2. Three types of strategies were used to deal with the crises. The Central and Eastern European (CEE) countries generally pursued extensive restructuring and recapitalizing of banks; most CIS countries pursued large-scale liquidation; and the Baltic states generally pursued a combination of liquidation and restructuring. See Zoli, Tang, and Klytchnikova (2000) for further details.
3. At the same time, transition countries may be over-banked. Jaffee and Levonian (2001) calculated a benchmark value for the number of banks in transition countries, using data on the number of banks in OECD countries. They find that the number of banks is lower than the benchmark value in the Czech Republic, Hungary, and Poland; in all the other countries it is higher.
4. As argued by Koivu (2002), in transition countries the size of the financial sector does not tell much about the quality of the sector, as soft budget constraints are still prevalent in various countries. According to Mitchell (2001), banks may make the situation worse by keeping counterproductive loans on their balance sheet.
5. The CEE-area here comprises Bulgaria, Croatia, the Czech Republic, Estonia, Hungary, Latvia, Lithuania, Poland, Romania, the Slovak Republic, and Slovenia.
6. However, some authors use a broader definition. For example, Green, Murinde, and Nikolov (2004) include all banks with at least one foreign shareholder. In addition, Green et al. classify a bank as foreign for the entire sample period based on the information referring to the most recent year of their sample. The authors acknowledge that this is a simplification,

since banks in CEE countries are subject to ownership changes, but consider it justified due to lack of better data in BankScope.

7. For a more detailed analysis of foreign ownership in transition economies see Naaborg, Lensink, and Schôltens (2003). These authors have analyzed 22 CEE countries and former Soviet states using BankScope data for 2001. Data on foreign ownership of that study are consistent with figures presented here. Lang and So (2002) have investigated the relation between bank ownership structure and performance in 1997 for 78 countries including seven accession countries. These authors do not rely on BankScope's classification of a bank's nationality based on its direct owners; instead, they search for banks' ultimate owners.
8. In addition to the weighted average of the number of foreign banks and foreign-owned banking assets, we took an alternative measure of foreign bank presence based on the data shown in Table 7.3, the foreign-owned banking assets. The results showed that the Baltic States fitted the 45 degrees-line better while for the other countries there was no significant change. The reason for this is that in an economy like Estonia with relatively few banks, some large foreign-owned banks that dominate the rest of the small domestic banks makes the foreign bank indicator based on number of banks less relevant.
9. The estimation results for the sub-sample of low-reform countries and years stand in sharp contrast to those reported in Table 7.4, as none of the estimated coefficients is significantly different from zero, with the exception of the inflation variable.

REFERENCES

Bank Austria Creditanstalt, Economics department, ExtraReport 'Banking in CEE', April 2004.

Beck, T., A. Demirgüç-Kunt, and R. Levine (2000), 'A New Database on the Structure and Development of the Financial Sector', *World Bank Economic Review*, **14**, 597-605.

Berger, A.N., L.F. Klapper, and G.F. Udell (2001), 'The Ability of Banks to Lend to Informationally Opaque Small Businesses', *Journal of Banking and Finance*, **25**, 2127-2167.

Berger, A.N. and G. Udell (2002), 'Small Business Credit Availability and Relationship Lending: The Importance of Bank Organisational Structure', *The Economic Journal,* **112**, 32-53.

Berglöf, E. and P. Bolton (2002), 'The Great Divide and Beyond. Financial Architecture in Transition', *Journal of Economic Perspectives*, **16**, 77-100.

Bonin, J.P., I. Hasan, and P. Wachtel (2003), 'Bank Performance, Efficiency and Ownership in Transition Countries', mimeo.

Bratkowski, A., I. Grosfeld, and J. Rostowski (2000), 'Investment and Finance in De Novo Private Firms: Empirial Results from the Czech. Republic, Hungary and Poland', *Economics of Transition*, **8** (1), 101-116.

Buch, C.M. (2000), 'Why do Banks go Abroad? - Evidence from German Data', *Financial Markets Institutions & Instruments*, **9** (1), 33-67.

Buch, C.M., J. Kleinert, and P. Zajc (2003), 'Foreign Bank Ownership: A Bonus or Threat for Financial Stability?', mimeo.

Caprio, G. and D. Klingebiel (2003), *Episodes of Systemic and Borderline Financial Crises,* Washington: World Bank.

Claessens, S, A. Demirgüç-Kunt, and H. Huizinga (2000), 'The Role of Foreign Banks in Domestic Banking Systems', in S. Claessens and M. Jansen (eds), *The Internationalization of Financial Services: Issues and Lessons for Developing Countries*, Boston: Kluwer Academic Press.

Claessens, S., A. Demirgüç-Kunt, and H. Huizinga (2001), 'How Does Foreign Entry Affect Domestic Banking Markets?,' *Journal of Banking and Finance*, **25**, 891-911.

Clarke, G., R. Cull, M.S. Martinez-Peria, and S.M. Sánchez (2002), 'Bank Lending to Small Businesses in Latin America: Does Bank Origin Matter?', World Bank, January.

Clarke, G., R. Cull, M.S. Martinez-Peria, and S.M. Sánchez (2003), 'Foreign Bank Entry: Experience, Implications for Developing Economies, and Agenda for Further Research', *World Bank Research Observer*, **18** (1), 25-59.

Crystal, J., B. Dages, and L. Goldberg (2002), 'Has Foreign Bank Entry Led to Sounder Banks in Latin America?', *Current Issues in Economics and Finance*, Federal Reserve Bank of New York, **8**, 1-6.

Dages, B., L. Goldberg, and D. Kinney (2000), 'Foreign and Domestic Bank Participation in Emerging Markets: Lessons from Mexico and Argentina', *Federal Reserve Bank of New York Economic Policy Review*, 17-36.

Das, U.S., M. Quintyn, and K. Chenard (2003), 'Does regulatory governance matters for financial stability? An empirical analysis', paper prepared for the Bank of Canada Conference 'The evolving financial system and public policy', 4-5 December, 2003.

De Haas, R.T.A. and I.P.P van Lelyveld (2004), 'Foreign Bank Penetration and Private Sector Credit in Central and Eastern Europe', *Journal of Emerging Markets Finance*, forthcoming.

European Bank for Reconstruction and Development (EBRD) (2001), *Transition Report*.

Focarelli, D. and A.F. Pozzolo (2000), 'The Determinants of Cross-Border Shareholdings: an Analysis with Bank-Level Data from OECD Countries', Banca D'Italia, Temi di discussione del Servizio Studi, No. 381.

Fries, S., D. Neven, and P. Seabright (2002), 'Bank performance in transition countries', EBRD Working Paper, No. 76, November 2002.

Fries, S. and A. Taci (2002), 'Banking Reform and Development in Transition Economies', EBRD Working Paper, No. 71, June 2002.

Green, C.J., V. Murinde, and I. Nikilov (2004), 'Are Foreign Banks in Central and Eastern Europe more Efficient than Domestic Banks?', *Journal of Emerging Markets Finance*, forthcoming.

Grigorian, D.A. and V. Manole (2002), 'Determinants of Commercial Bank Performance in Transition: An Application of Data Envelopment Analysis', IMF Working Papers, No. 02/146.

Hainz, C. (2002), 'Are Transition Countries Overbanked? An Answer from Industrial Organization', mimeo, University of Munich.

Havrylchyk, O. (2003), 'Efficiency of the Polish Banking Industry: Foreign vs. National Banks', paper presented at the 24th SUERF Colloquium on Stability and Efficiency of Financial Markets in Central and Eastern Europe, June 12-14, Tallinn.

Hermes, N. and R. Lensink (2004), 'Foreign Bank Presence, Domestic Bank Performance and Financial Development', *Journal of Emerging Markets Finance*, forthcoming.

International Monetary Fund (2000), *International Capital Markets: Developments, Prospects and Key Policy Issues*, Washington DC: IMF.

Jaffee, D. and M. Levonian (2001), 'Structure of Banking Systems in Developed and Transition Economies', *European Financial Management*, **7** (2), 161-181.

Kraft, E. (2004), 'Foreign Banks in Croatia: Reasons for Entry, Performance, and Impacts', *Journal of Emerging Markets Finance*, forthcoming.

Koivu, T. (2002), 'Do Efficient Banking Sectors Accelerate Economic Growth in Transition Countries?', Bank of Finland, BOFIT Discussion Papers, No. 14.

Konopielko L. (1999), 'Foreign Banks Entry into Central and East European Markets: Motives and Activities', *Post-Communist Economies,* **11** (4), 463-485.

Lang, L.H.P. and R.W. So (2002), 'Bank Ownership Structure and Economic Performance', preliminary draft, Hong Kong.

Lensink, R. and J. de Haan (2004), 'Do Reforms in Transition Countries Affect Foreign Bank Entry?', *International Review of Finance*, forthcoming.

Lensink, R. and N. Hermes (2004), 'The Short-term Effects of Foreign Bank Entry on Domestic Bank Behaviour: Does Economic Development Matter?,' *Journal of Banking and Finance*, forthcoming.

Litan, E.R., P. Masson, and M. Pomerleano (2001), 'Introduction', in E.R. Litan, P. Masson and M. Pomerleano (eds), *Open Doors: Foreign Participation in Financial Systems in Developing Countries*, Washington, DC: Brookings Institution Press.

Mathieson, D.J. and J. Roldos (2001), 'Foreign Banks in Emerging Markets', in E.R. Litan, P. Masson and M. Pomerleano (eds), *Open Doors: Foreign Participation in Financial Systems in Developing Countries*, Washington, DC: Brookings Institution Press.

Mero, K. and M.E. Valentinyi (2003), 'The Role of Foreign Banks in Five Central and Eastern European Countries', Magyar Nemzeti Bank Working Paper, No. 2003/10.

Mitchell, J. (2001), 'Banks' Bad Debts: Policies, Creditor Passivity, and Soft Budget Constraints', in A. Meyendorff and A.V. Thakor (eds), *Designing Financial Systems in Transition Economies*, Cambridge (Ma): MIT Press.

Naaborg, I., B. Scholtens, J. de Haan, H. Bol and R. de Haas (2004), 'How Important are Foreign Banks in the Financial Development of European Transition Countries?', *Journal of Emerging Markets Finance*, forthcoming.

Naaborg, I., R. Lensink, and B. Scholtens (2003), 'Banking in Transition Economies: A Study into Foreign Ownership and Performance', mimeo.

Papi, L. and D. Revoltella (1999), 'Foreign Direct Investment in the Banking Sector: A Transitional Economy Perspective', Bocconi University, Development Studies Working Papers, Nr. 133, November 1999.

Peek, J. and E.S. Rosengren (2000a), 'Collateral Damage: Effects of the Japanese Bank Crisis on Real Activity in the United States', *American Economic Review*, **90** (1), 30-45.

Peek, J. and E.S. Rosengren (2000b), 'Implications of the Globalization of the Banking Sector: The Latin American Experience', *New England Economic Review*, September/October, 45-63.

Soledad Martinez Peria, M., A. Powell, and I. Vladkova Hollar (2002), 'Banking on Foreigners: The Behavior of International Bank Lending to Latin America, 1985-2000', World Bank Working Papers, No. 2893.

Weill, L. (2003), 'Banking Efficiency in Transition Economies: the Role of Foreign Ownership', *The Economics of Transition*, **11** (3), 569-592.

Williams, B. (1997), 'Banking: Eclectic Theory versus Internalisation Theory', *Journal of Economic Surveys*, **11** (1), 71-100.

Williams, B. (2002), 'The Defensive Expansion Approach to Multinational Banking: Evidence to Date', *Financial Markets, Institutions & Instruments*, **11** (2), 127-203.

Yildirim, H.S. and G.C. Philippatos (2002), 'Efficiency of Banks: Recent Evidence from the Transition Economies of Europe 1993-2000', Department of Economics, University of Tennessee, Knoxville, working paper.

Zoli, E., H. Tang, and I. Klytchnikova (2000), 'Banking Crises in Transition Economies: Fiscal Costs and Related Issues', World Bank Working Paper, No. 2484.

8. Foreign Banks and Financial Stability in the New Europe

Alicia García Herrero and Daniel Navia Simón[1]

INTRODUCTION

The last decade has witnessed an unprecedented increase in the activities of international banks in emerging markets; a trend that has been nowhere more apparent than in accession countries. At the present time, no other emerging region has a higher level of foreign participation in banking and financial markets. Foreign institutions act as market leaders in most accession countries, with two-thirds of the assets of the domestic banking systems owned by their branches and subsidiaries. These figures are even more remarkable if we consider the fact that only ten years ago these countries financial systems' were practically closed to foreign participation[2].

The fast penetration of foreign banks has been welcomed by accession countries. The contribution of foreign banks was instrumental for the smooth transition of their financial systems. The capital injected by foreign banks was crucial in the success of privatizations programs and the restructuring of banking systems after the crises experienced in some of the transition economies. Although harder to quantify, the impact of the management skills introduced by foreign banks on the efficiency and scope of financial intermediation is also widely recognized. While there is plenty of room for further improvement, size and efficiency were probably the most important objectives of liberalization programs in these countries. As a result, a general consensus that foreign banks have been beneficial for accession countries has emerged in the last years.

Now that privatization processes are mostly concluded in the majority of these countries, the attention of bankers and policy makers alike has partially shifted from size and efficiency to stability. Do foreign banks contribute to greater financial stability? Since foreign banks constitute a fundamental part of accession countries' banking systems, the answer to this question is probably more relevant for them than for any other region of the world. Several theoretical arguments have been advanced for a positive, but also for a negative, role of foreign banks as regards financial stability. Some of them are not entirely contradictory but rather refer to different aspects of financial stability or different forms of foreign bank activities. The existing empirical evidence tends to support the hypothesis that foreign banks have a neutral or even positive effect on financial stability. Nonetheless, more applied research in this area is still needed. It seems that the debate will remain open for some time to come.

The objective of this chapter is to summarize the actual state of the debate and suggest some venues for further research that have not been fully considered in previous contributions. The structure is as follows. Section 2 analyzes the recent evolution of foreign bank activities in accession countries, including a brief comparison with other areas of the world. Section 3 reviews the literature on the role of foreign banks in financial stability. Given the scarcity of results for accession countries, inference is sometimes drawn from the findings in other groups of countries. Section 4 concludes and suggests possible directions for future research.

THE EVOLVING ROLE OF FOREIGN BANKS: SIZE AND COMPOSITION OF FOREIGN BANKS' LENDING TO ACCESSION COUNTRIES

Two features stand out in the evolution of international bank lending to accession countries. First, the impressive growth of total lending, which exceeded 200,000 million dollars by end-2002, from less than 30,000 in 1993[3]. Second, the rapidly increasing trend towards local operations by foreign banks through subsidiaries and branches, as opposed to cross-border lending[4]. Figures 8.1 and 8.2 clearly show these two features.

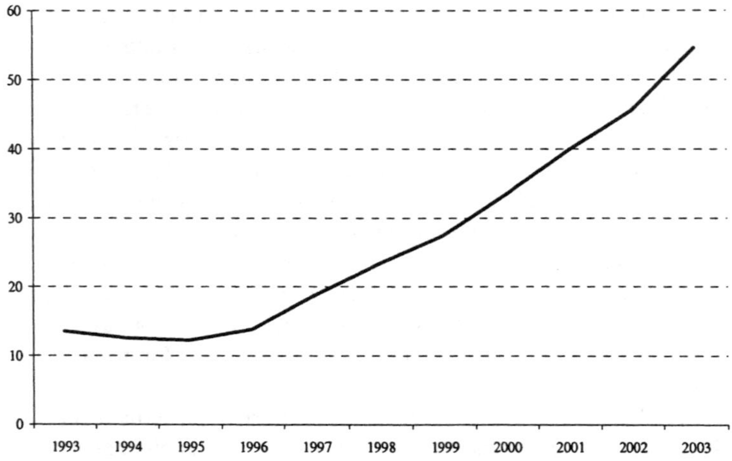

Figure 8.1 Foreign claims to accession countries (as a % of GDP) 1991-2003

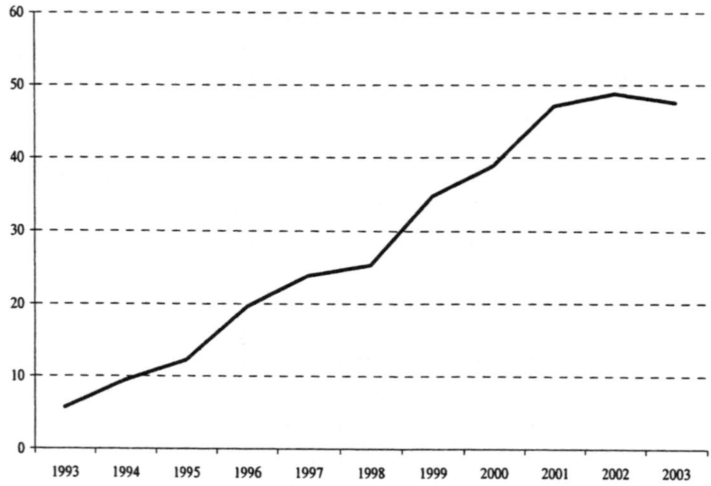

Figure 8.2 Local claims in local currency (as a % of Foreign Claims) 1993-2003

Total claims on accession countries by foreign banks have increased from 14% of GDP in 1993 to 54% in 2003. This figure is much larger than in other regions of the world where foreign bank lending is perceived to be very important, such as Latin America, where it reached 29% of their combined GDP in 2003[5]. Moreover, the expansion of foreign bank lending has been faster in accession countries than in Latin America. It grew 40 points of GDP in accession countries during the last decade, as opposed to 8 points of GDP in the second group. When we look at the composition of foreign claims, the trend is more similar. Local activity represents 48% of total foreign bank claims in accession countries today, from less than 5% in 1993. The corresponding figures in Latin America are 54% of total foreign claims today and 10% in 1993[6].

Table 8.1 Foreign claims in accession countries (1994-2002)

	Foreign Claims (% of GDP)		Local Claims in Local Currency (% of Foreign Claims)	
	2002	1994	2002	1994
Cyprus	81	50	1	0
Czech R.	61	14	67	27
Estonia	85	1	2	0
Hungary	55	23	35	8
Latvia	32	0	29	0
Lithuania	23	1	13	0
Malta	228	54	31	0
Poland	40	8	57	7
Slovakia	58	3	62	0
Slovenia	31	5	18	0

Sources: BIS, IFS and authors' calculations.

While these two trends are common to all accession countries, the aggregate picture hides important differences between them. As Table 8.1 shows, some countries already had an important exposure to foreign lending in 1993, mainly through cross-border operations. This is the case of Cyprus, Hungary, Malta and, to a lesser extent, Poland and the Czech Republic. On the contrary, foreign lending was almost insignificant in Estonia, Latvia, Lithuania, Slovenia and Slovakia. In 2002, however, foreign lending represented more than 20% of GDP in every accession country, and more than 40% in seven of them. Local activity, although growing as a percentage of total foreign lending in every country except Cyprus, remains relatively small in Slovenia and Estonia. In contrast, it is the main source of foreign financing in the Czech Republic, Poland and Slovakia, and represents about one third of total lending in the rest of the countries.

FOREIGN BANKS AND FINANCIAL STABILITY

Some of the apparent contradictions in the debate on the effect of foreign banks in financial stability can, in our view, be traced back to two potential sources of confusion. First of all, assertions are sometimes made without being explicit about the specific measure of financial stability being considered. Very frequently, "stability" is identified as a situation of low volatility of asset prices. This identification is too simplistic, since it is not hard to think of situations where complete stability of asset prices was the result of the poor functioning of the financial system, generally because of over-regulation.

It is important to recognize that financial stability is a complex concept with many dimensions. Among the very many definitions, Padoa-Schioppa (2002) offers a relatively general one, namely "a condition where the financial system is able to withstand shocks without giving way to cumulative processes which impair the allocation of savings to investment opportunities and the processing of payments in the economy". While conceptually satisfactory, this definition is too vague for the purposes of the present chapter.

We shall, therefore, focus on the three aspects of financial stability that seem to be more closely related to the debate about the effect of foreign banks in financial stability: the volatility of credit supply, the probability of banking crises and the potential for contagion. Although the distinction between these three facets of financial stability is not always clear-cut, we find this separation useful for analytical purposes. We shall, thus, structure our analysis along these three dimensions.

The second source of confusion is due to the different nature of international banks' activities in any host country. At a minimum, a distinction between cross-border lending and local activity is warranted. Cross-border lending tends to be more wholesale oriented than local activity, particularly if the latter is conducted by large foreign-owned banks. The decision making process of granting a cross-border loan or expanding local activity by a foreign affiliate is also different, taken at the home country in the first case and being more decentralized in the second. This has a bearing for financial stability since the home country conditions are, in principle, more likely to affect cross-border lending than the local activity of foreign affiliates and the opposite is true for host country conditions. Table 8.2 summarizes the most important differences between cross-border lending and local activity from a financial stability perspective.

Table 8.2. Differences between cross-border and local operations of foreign banks

MARKET	Wholesale	Retail
Operative center	Home country	Host country
Supervision	Home market regulator	Host regulator for the affiliate and home regulator for the conglomerate
Regulatory constraint	Low	Domestic and home regulation applies
Capital requirements	For the parent	For the affiliate and/or the conglomerate

The Impact of Foreign Banks on the Volatility of Credit Supply

Substantial attention has been devoted to the effects of foreign banks lending on the stability of credit supply. However, as previously mentioned, volatility of credit supply *per se* is not always a bad thing. As long as changes in the supply of funds are related to variations in fundamentals, increased volatility could be the result of sounder lending policies and could conceivably be a positive indicator of financial stability. Nevertheless, microeconomic models of banking have shown that, if no regulatory constraints are put in place, informational asymmetries and misaligned incentives make it likely that banks take excessive risks during expansionary periods and cut their credit lines too drastically during slowdowns. In this setting, excessive credit volatility results in the emergence of a pattern of booms and busts that is very damaging for long-term economic growth. A stable financial system should be able to smooth fluctuations in credit supply, without impairing the efficient allocation of resources among economic agents.

There are theoretical arguments to think that the participation of foreign banks in a financial system – as long as they are better managed and capitalized than domestic banks – could mitigate the underlying problems that contribute to the emergence of credit cycles. First, they should tend to reduce informational asymmetries and incentive problems. Foreign banks introduce better management practices, such as more sophisticated risk control procedures and more transparent decision processes. Under normal conditions, competitive pressure on domestic banks will result in the diffusion of these practices to the rest of the financial system. Moreover, surveillance of lending practices is reinforced by the control of the parent bank over its affiliate. Finally, the need to preserve the value of their international franchises makes foreign banks less prone to suffer from some of the problems that traditionally have affected domestic banks in emerging economies: connected lending, corruption or fraud.

Another reason to suspect that foreign participation in the banking system may help reduce the volatility of credit lies in the higher capitalization of international banks compared to that of their domestic rivals. In a typical boom and bust credit cycle, when economic activity slows down, loan loss provisions increase and solvency ratios worsen. In response, banks cut their credit lines, in an attempt to restore the health of their balance sheets. The fact that international banks tend to be better capitalized than their domestic counterparts makes them more able to withstand losses on their assets (either cross-border or local) before resorting to credit cuts. This is specially the case of accession countries, where the relatively high capitalization[7] of their banking systems can be traced back to the privatization processes and the acquisition of domestic banks by foreigners. The same line of argument goes for another important phenomenon which has mitigated financial instability in emerging countries; this is "flight to quality". In several banking crisis episodes in this decade, foreign banks have attracted large amounts of deposits which have fled from other domestic banks perceived as unsafe. Although it may induce the collapse of some institutions, such process is more beneficial than outright capital flight from depositors, as would usually happen in the absence of well capitalized banks that are perceived as such[8].

On the other hand, some hypotheses suggest that foreign banks could increase the volatility of credit. These are usually based on the conception that geographic diversification by international banks may result in higher local volatility for individual countries. It is generally accepted that international banks have a wider scope for geographic diversification than their domestic competitors. Although this higher diversification will result in lower aggregate risk for the international bank, the reallocation of capital among individual countries may result in a more volatile credit supply at a local level. If international banks' portfolio allocation is more sensitive to economic fluctuations than domestic banks', a high presence of foreign banks will result in a more procyclical credit supply.

Before analyzing the empirical evidence, it is interesting to note that the arguments above may have a different weight when applied to cross-border lending or to local activity. As regards the reduction in information and incentive distortions, it seems natural to consider that gains derived from foreign participation in the banking system will mostly accrue when it involves subsidiaries and branches. On the contrary, the cross-border operations of international banks are typically centralized under the parent and remain relatively isolated from the domestic banking system. This makes them more dependent on home country developments and, thus, potentially more volatile.

As regards the effects of diversification, cross-border operations need to be backed directly by the parent's capital. If the parent chooses to cut its exposure in a country, it will be easier to do it on a specific cross-border loan than on a claim related to a foreign direct investment. Given this higher flexibility, cross-border lending is sometimes used as a way of testing the waters of new markets. This is so because fixed investments in the country can only be liquidated quickly at a substantial loss. Moreover, other countries will show comprehensible reticence to accept banks that have a reputation of abandoning their investments at the first sight of problems. Finally, cross-border lending is subject to less strict regulatory constraints. Branches and, to a larger extent, subsidiaries of foreign banks face more strict regulatory limitations. As such, it is not clear why foreign affiliates' assets should be more geographically diversified than domestic banks'.

The empirical evidence available tends to support the view that foreign banks do not increase the volatility of credit[9]. For selected countries in Latin America, Crystal et al. (2000) show that subsidiaries and branches of foreign banks with a long-term presence in the host country showed stronger credit growth than domestic rivals even in periods of local economic downturns. Martinez Peria et al. (2002) find that cross-border plus local lending in foreign currency by foreign banks was less volatile than aggregate domestic credit, despite having higher average growth. Moreover, credit by foreign banks did not retrench in periods of crisis at the host markets. Finally, Peek and Rosengren (2000), for Latin America, and De Haas and Lelyveld (2002), for the three largest accession countries, find that cross-border lending did decrease during economic downturns in the host country, but its reduction was compensated by the expansion in the credit supply of subsidiaries of foreign banks[10].

In sum, there seems to be a growing consensus that foreign banks can help reduce the volatility of credit. More precisely, this beneficial effect is due to the activities of subsidiaries and branches of foreign banks, whereas the impact of cross-border lending is not so clear-cut.

Foreign Banks and the Probability of Banking Crises

As for financial stability, the literature offers several definitions of banking crises. Early definitions concentrated on bank panics, while more recent definitions have adopted a wider scope[11]. An example of the latter is Gupta (1996), who characterizes a banking crisis as a situation where liabilities exceed the market value of banks' assets, leading to portfolio shifts or to deposit runs and/or the collapse of financial institutions and/or government intervention. While being useful for descriptive purposes, such broad definitions generally make no attempt to investigate into the causes of crises. Broadly speaking, banking crises come in two different flavours, according to the underlying fragility that causes them.

The first is related to the lack of liquidity. Starting from Dymond and Dybvig (1983), the focus is on liquidity shocks and the fractional nature of banking systems. Banking crises are the result of liquidity shocks, where ex-ante solvent institutions are forced to liquidate their assets by excess liquidity demand on the part of their depositors. There are several ways to relate banking crises stemming from liquidity problems to foreign banking. For example, Buch et al. (2003) extend the model by Allen and Gale (2000) and show that increased financial integration can help reduce the probability of liquidity crises. In addition, to the extent that liquidity needs are not perfectly correlated among regions[12], cross-border interbank lending allows for a better diversification of shocks. Moreover, financial integration stemming from the direct operation of foreign banks in a country's financial sector can reduce the dependence on domestic liquidity as far as foreign banks have access to financing from the parent (see Stein, 1997). This is certainly the case of branches and, to a much lesser extent, of subsidiaries. Note also that these advantages are likely to be substantial for accession countries, since their small relative size should allow for the hedging of their liquidity risks by drawing on the pool of liquidity available in EU financial markets.

The other source of bank fragility and banking crises is related to solvency, and not so much liquidity. In this vein, solvent financial systems should be able to withstand aggregate risks, such as macroeconomic shocks, more easily. As for the impact of foreign ownership of the probability of such type of crises, several issues are worth mentioning. On the one hand, subsidiaries of foreign banks are typically better capitalized and managed than their domestic competitors. This would, in itself, increase the solvency of the whole banking system. On the other hand, it is widely accepted that the entry of foreign banks tends to increase competition and reduce the profitability of the banking system as a whole. If profitability becomes too low because of over-competition, this could be a problem for solvency in the future. The empirical evidence up to date suggests that the first effect is likely to be dominant. Demigürç-Kunt, Levine and Min (1998) and Levine (1999) find that a high presence of foreign banks reduces the probability of banking crises[13]. This is probably because emerging countries are still far away from over-competition and profitability – albeit lower – is still high for international standards. These findings are in line with recent results in the empirical literature that challenge the notion of a trade-off between competition and stability, thereby weakening the case for a negative impact of foreign entry over financial stability. In the case of accession countries, this case may be even weaker, since in many of them foreign banks substituted fragile and/or state-owned banks, whose negative effect over financial stability has been empirically documented on many occasions.

Foreign Banks and Financial Contagion

Vulnerability of the banking systems to external shocks is a cause of financial fragility. The transmission of external economic fluctuations or external crises results in the loss of autonomy of domestic economic policies and can have substantial effects on welfare. As such, contagion phenomena are a source of concern for policy makers. Foreign ownership of the banking system or a high dependence on cross-border credits might result in increased vulnerability to external shocks. This issue has received substantial attention in the recent literature. A natural classification for contagion phenomena related to the presence of foreign banks distinguishes according to the source of the shock being transmitted.

A first source of concern is the possibility that economic fluctuations (or even financial crises) in the home country of an international bank could translate into the credit supply of its foreign affiliates and its cross-border financing. It is generally argued that capital regulations at home may force international banks to reduce their credit supply to accession countries in response to adverse economic conditions in their home markets, which can be considered a wealth effect. However, since home investment projects will be less profitable during home market slowdowns, parents could choose to dedicate a higher share of their resources to accession countries, in an attempt to improve their overall profitability, implying a substitution effect.

The empirical literature confirms the existence of a link between the home country's cycle and the amount of credit foreign banks offer. Whether wealth or substitution effects are prevalent, however, remains a subject of debate. Peek and Rosengren (1997) show that the collapse of the Japanese stock market reduced the supply of credit by Japanese branches in the US. Therefore, their results provide evidence of the prevalence of the wealth effect. On the contrary, De Haas and Lelyveld (2003) show that local subsidiaries of foreign banks expanded their credit in Eastern and Central European countries during economic slowdowns in their parents' home markets, pointing to important substitution effects. Martinez Peria et al. (2002) do not find a clear pattern for Latin American economies. While Japanese and Canadian banks' lending seemed to be more influenced by wealth considerations, for French, German, Spanish, British and US banks the substitution effect seemed more important. These apparently contradictory results could be interpreted as evidence that the relationship between the home market's economic cycle and foreign lending is influenced by national and bank-specific characteristics[14].

A second source of financial contagion is related to the transmission of shocks between countries sharing a similar distribution of international lenders. In these circumstances, the occurrence of a crisis in a country could potentially force international banks to reduce their exposure in other areas. In this vein, the existence of a common lender could generate the transmission of crisis. Note, however, that for this possibility to become a reality, common lenders should satisfy two conditions. First, their exposure in the country where the crisis originates should be high. Otherwise, the reallocation of funds due to the crisis is likely to be of little significance. Second, financing in the receiving host country should be highly concentrated in those creditors.

Although some empirical evidence supports the risk of a common lender channel for financial contagion[15], these two conditions seem too stringent to be met in practice. In the case of accession countries, the high concentration of borrowing and foreign ownership of banks in some countries (Germany, Belgium and Italy mainly) has given rise to some alerts about the possibility that a shock to any accession country could easily translate to the whole region. However, the size of German and Belgian exposures to these countries is small when compared to their total international lending (around 3% and 6%), which reduces this potential risk.

CONCLUSIONS

All in all, the above arguments and empirical evidence seem to be supportive of a neutral or positive role of foreign banks in the financial stability of emerging countries. First of all, foreign banks seem to increase the stability of credit supply. Second, there is no evidence that foreign ownership increases the probability of a banking crisis, but rather the opposite. Finally, as regards contagion, there are arguments to think that foreign banks could potentially increase the vulnerability of the host economy to external shocks but the conditions for this risk to materialize are fairly stringent. Moreover, given the typically high current account deficits in developing economies, it is not clear whether alternative forms of foreign finance (namely, portfolio flows) would be less prone to spread contagion.

Several arguments suggest that this beneficial role could be further enhanced in the case of accession countries. Most of them are related to their special position as future EU members and the likely consequences of their convergence processes. In many cases, the opening of banking systems in other emerging areas has been accompanied by incomplete or unsatisfactory reform of financial institutions. On the contrary, EU accession will act as a catalyser for the harmonization of banking regulations. The high involvement of foreign banks in accession economies will greatly facilitate this harmonization and reduce the risks associated with it. In this sense, the degree in which foreign banks can be expected to import best practices from their home market is higher than in other emerging areas. Beyond that, as real integration with the EU advances the risk of asymmetric shocks between investor and host countries will be lower. This will reduce the scope for the occurrence of situations where the interests of international banks and the needs of host economies collide.

Nevertheless, several areas of debate still remain open and more research into this area is still needed. Further empirical efforts in the distinction between cross-border and local activity is an area where more research is likely to yield interesting results. Another potentially rewarding subject, especially for accession countries, would be the link between economic cycles in the home market and foreign banks' lending. Beyond establishing the factors that influence the sign of this relationship, theoretical analyses of its potential implications in the synchronization of economic fluctuations between the EU and accession countries would be very valuable.

NOTES

1. Alicia García Herrero is affiliated with Banco de España and Johns Hopkins University (alicia.garcia-herrero@bde.es). Daniel Navia Simón is affiliated with Banco de España (dnavia@bde.es). The views expressed in this chapter are the authors' and do not necessarily reflect those of Banco de España.
2. It should be noted that the article focuses on Eastern and Central Europe countries so several of the conclusions are of limited value in the cases of Cyprus and Malta.
3. The source of this data is the BIS consolidated statistics, namely foreign claims from BIS reporting countries.
4. Due to limitations in the BIS International Banking Statistics, we use the term "cross-border lending" to refer to BIS reporting banks' "international claims", which include pure cross-border lending plus the local claims of their foreign affiliates in foreign currency. On the other hand, the measure of local activity that can be drawn from the BIS statistics only includes local claims of their foreign affiliates in local currency. As a result, the amount of local activity by foreign banks is biased downward, the more so the more dollarized/euroized a country is.
5. Average of the seven largest countries, Brazil, Mexico, Argentina, Chile, Colombia, Venezuela and Peru.
6. This is so notwithstanding the underestimation of the local activity of foreign banks (and over estimation of their cross-border operations) inherent in the available data (See Footnote 4 above).
7. As of 2001, no accession country showed a capital to assets ratio lower than 12.5%.
8. It should be acknowledged that sometimes state-owned banks attract deposits because they are perceived to have a full implicit guarantee from the government.
9. For an exception, see Morgan and Strahan (2002).
10. In a more recent paper, the authors qualify the previous result and circumscribe the expansion of credit to greenfield subsidiaries. Privatized banks, on the contrary, showed a pattern similar to that of their domestic competitors.

11. For a brief review of alternative definitions of banking crisis, see García Herrero and Del Rio (2003).
12. Their calculations show that the correlation of deposits between accession and EU countries is substantially smaller than between individual EU members.
13. Nevertheless, recent studies by Barth et al. (2002) and Beck et al. (2003) find no direct relation between foreign ownership and the probability of crises. What these authors do find, however, is a direct relationship between restrictions to the entry of foreign banks and banking crises.
14. Martinez Peria et al. (2002) present evidence that the relationship between home market cycle and foreign lending gets weaker as international banks gain more experience in the host country. De Haas and Van Lelyveld (2003) find that this link exists only for greenfield banks.
15. See Kaminsky and Reinhart (2000) on the role of Japanese banks during the Asian crisis.

REFERENCES

Allen, F. and D. Gale, (2000), 'Financial Contagion', *Journal of Political Economy*, 108, pp. 1-33.

Barth, J., G. Caprio and R. Levine (2002), 'Bank Regulation and Supervision: What Works Best?', NBER Working Paper 9323, November 2002.

Beck T., A. Demigürç-Kunt and R. Levine (2003), 'Bank Concentration and Crises', NBER Working Paper 9921, August 2003.

Buch, C.M., J. Kleinert and P. Zajc (2003), 'Foreign Bank Ownership: A Bonus or Threat for Financial Stability', in 'Securing Financial Stability: Problems and Prospects for New EU Members', SUERF Studies 2003/4.

Crystal, J., G. Dages and L.S. Goldberg, (2002), 'Has Foreign Bank Entry Led to Sounder Banks in Latin America?', Current Issues in Economics and Finance Volume 8 Number 1, Federal Reserve Bank of New York.

De Haas, R. and I. Van Lelyveld (2002), 'Foreign Bank Penetration and Private Sector Credit In Central and Eastern Europe', DNB Staff Reports No. 91/2002, De Nederlandsche Bank, Amsterdam.

De Haas, R. and I. Van Lelyveld (2003), 'Foreign Banks and Credit Stability in Central and Eastern Europe: Friends or Foes? A Panel

Data Analysis', MEB Series no. 2003-04/Research Series Supervision no. 58, De Nederlandsche Bank, Amsterdam.
Demigürç-Kunt, A., R. Levine and H.G. Min (1998), 'Opening to Foreign Banks: Issues of Stability, Efficiency and Growth' In Proceedings of the Bank of Korea Conference on the Implications of Globalization of World Economic Financial Markets, December 1998.
Diamond, D.W., and P.H. Dybvig (1983), 'Bank Runs, Deposit Insurance and Liquidity', *Journal of Political Economy*, 105, pp. 928-956.
García Herrero A. and P. Del Rio (2003), 'Financial Stability and the Design of Monetary Policy', Bank of Spain Working Paper 0315.
Gupta, P. (1996), 'Currency Crises, Banking Crises and Twin Crises: a Comprehensive Review of the Literature', mimeo, International Monetary Fund.
Kaminsky, G. and C. Reinhart (2000), 'On Crisis, Contagion and Confusion', Journal of International Economics, 51, 145-168.
Levine, R. (1999), 'Foreign Bank Entry and Capital Control Liberalization: Effects on Growth and Stability', University of Minnesota, mimeo.
Martinez Peria, M. S., A. Powell, and I. Vladkova (2002), 'Banking on Foreigners: The Behaviour of International Bank Lending to Latin America, 1985-2000', World Bank Working Paper 2893.
Morgan, D.P. and P.E. Strahan (2002), 'Foreign Bank Entry and Business Volatility: Evidence from U.S. States and Other Countries', Central Bank of Chile Working Paper 229, October 2003.
Padoa-Schioppa, T. (2002), 'Central Banks and Financial Stability: Exploring a Land in Between', paper presented at the Second ECB Central Banking Conference 'The transformation of the European financial system', Frankfurt am Main, October 2002.
Peek, J. and S. E. Rosengren (1997), 'Collateral Damage: Effects of the Japanese Bank Crisis on Real Activity in the United States', *American Economic Review*, 87:4, pp. 495-505.
Peek, J. and S.E. Rosengren (2000), 'Implications of the Globalization of the Banking Sector: the Latin American Experience' New England Economic Review, September/October, pp. 45-63.

Stein, J. (1997), 'Internal Capital Markets and the Competition for Corporate Resources', Journal of Finance, 52, pgs. 111-134.

9. Eastern Passages for Italy's Banks and Industrial Districts: Are the Two Related or Independent?[1]

Fabio Farabullini and Giovanni Ferri

INTRODUCTION

During the early phases of the transition to a market economy, Eastern European countries experienced widespread corporate collapse giving rise to deep banking crises. The urgency to address the meltdown of their banking sectors and to remedy the great damage caused by a dysfunctional system of intermediation (sooner or later) convinced otherwise hesitant Eastern European governments to open up to foreign bank entry. Foreign banks took the opportunity offered to them. By 2000, on average, they served almost one third of domestic banking markets in Eastern Europe. In some of these countries the share of foreign banks reached 62% (Hungary) or even 85% (Estonia).

Although various authors have already studied this massive entry of foreign banks in Eastern Europe, many questions remain to be addressed. Specifically, in this chapter we aim to concentrate on whether Italian banks' entry is motivated by the need to follow their national customers, which may have already entered the Eastern European markets, or whether it depends on different reasons. Specifically, we notice that, in recent years, otherwise little internationalized Italian banks have made considerable investment to acquire a retail banking network in Eastern Europe. In addition, we notice that, over the last decade, many Italian industrial districts specializing in traditional goods responded to growing competition from emerging economies walking their own Eastern Passage. Specifically, these industrial districts found a new way to safeguard their competitive hedge by largely moving (heavy unskilled labour phases of) production to low-labour-cost Eastern Europe. Our main aim is to shed light on whether the two Eastern Passages – that of Italian banks and that of Italy's industrial districts – are related or independent.

To address this question, we use detailed data for Italy. In particular, the Italian case presents two main features: (i) intense productive outsourcing to Eastern Europe by Italian firms, especially the small and medium-sized enterprises (SMEs) clustered in industrial districts, attracted there by low labour cost, since the mid-1990s; (ii) more recent acquisitions of a retail network in Eastern Europe by some large Italian banking groups. In this respect, we wish to ascertain whether business interaction has intensified between the group of Italian banks entering the Eastern European markets and those industrial districts that have more forcefully outsourced their production to this area. Since we lack information to assess business interactions in Eastern Europe between Italian banks and Italian industrial districts' firms, we analyze whether the market share of these banking groups in Italy has grown exactly in those industrial districts which have more intensely outsourced their production towards Eastern Europe.

Our main finding is that Italian banks that have acquired a retail network in Eastern Europe have also had a significantly better market share performance in Italy precisely in those industrial districts that have more forcefully outsourced production to Eastern Europe. In all, even though possibly motivated by other factors as well, the move by Italian banks to Eastern Europe may also be interpreted as a strategy catering for the home market. Hence, the two Eastern Passages seem to be related to some extent.

The remaining of the chapter is structured as follows. Section 2 starts with a brief summary of the literature on the links between bank and firm internationalization. Next, in Section 3, we outline our methodology to draw the map of Italian industrial districts' outsourcing to Eastern Europe, as well as the map of the retail presence in Eastern Europe of Italian banks. Finally, we analyse econometrically whether those banks with a retail base on Eastern Europe are gaining market share in their business in Italy exactly in those industrial districts that have more forcefully outsourced their production to Eastern Europe. The last section summarizes our main findings and sketches possible avenues for future research.

WHO'S LEADING IN THE MOVE OF EU BANKS AND FIRMS TO EASTERN EUROPE?

Since the early 1990s, Foreign Direct Investment (FDI) from the EU-15 to Eastern Europe has played a primary role in shaping the economic reintegration of the Eastern European countries within an enlarged Europe. Such FDI flows were mostly motivated by the need to reduce production costs in response to increasing competition from emerging economies: indeed, EU-15 manufacturing firms have fragmented their production process relocating high unskilled labour-intensive phases to low-labour-cost transition economies (Arndt and Kierzkowski, 2001; Baldone et al. 2001). Eastern Europe was the favoured destination for such outsourcing given its proximity and flexibility.

An important question at this juncture is whether there was any sequencing between manufacturing FDI and productive outsourcing from West to Eastern Europe, on the one hand, and bank FDI from West to Eastern Europe, on the other. We may contemplate two alternative hypotheses. On one hand, FDI from EU banks to Eastern Europe might lead FDI in the area by their national manufacturing clients. This could happen if two features attain: (i) opportunities for bank FDI in Eastern Europe materialized early on, and (ii) EU-15 firms wishing to enter Eastern Europe faced intense information asymmetries that could be reduced thanks to the previous entry by their lending banks. On the other hand, the opposite view holds that EU banks follow their customers to Eastern Europe. According to this hypothesis, EU-15 manufacturing firms move first to Eastern Europe, either with their FDI or with their productive outsourcing. Their lending banks move to Eastern Europe only later to: (i) improve their services (following their customers to avoid losing them), and (ii) keep track of the overall risk profile of their borrowers, which tend to become more opaque after shifting their activities to Eastern Europe.

While it is well known that total FDI flows from the EU-15 to Eastern Europe were massive, little attention is often devoted to the bank component within such flows. Indeed, all transition economies suffered pervasive banking distress and closure in the years after 1989. Following that, the penetration of foreign banks in transition economies has become increasingly widespread: by the mid-1990s almost half of domestic bank assets were already in the hands of foreign (mostly EU-15) banks, twice as much as in Asia or Latin America (Claessens, et al., 1998).

To be sure, a large retail presence of foreign banks may be desirable from the perspective of transition economies for two main reasons: (i) it may improve the efficiency of the domestic banking system (Claessens, et al., 1998; Focarelli and Pozzolo, 2000) and better management makes national banks more resilient to external negative shocks, and (ii) it may also perform a stabilizing role vis-à-vis such shocks via a different channel stemming from the fact that the local assets make a small share over the total assets of the foreign bank to which the local unit belongs (Dages et al. 2000)[2], thus foreign banks may cushion the shock to the local economy providing more liquidity and possibly even preventing the occurrence of twin crises jointly hitting the exchange rate and the banking system (Kaminsky and Reinhart, 1999; Reynoso, 2002).

As far as the countries of origin of bank FDI to Eastern Europe – something that will be important later on in the chapter – these were largely from Austria and Germany at the beginning of the 1990s, while only later they took off from other EU-15 countries, like France, Italy and the Netherlands (Papi and Revoltella, 1999).

Furthermore, regarding the internationalization of Italian manufacturing firms in Eastern Europe, some specific considerations pertain to the Italian experience. In fact, their small size can hinder the internationalization of Italian firms. On one hand, the few large Italian firms have undergone a downsizing process. On the other hand, Italy has witnessed the vitality of its many local productive systems centred on small and medium-sized enterprises (SMEs) clustered within industrial districts. Hence, according to the latter case, the internationalization of Italian firms mainly materializes alongside the internationalization of their production process which, given the small size of the firms involved, is likely channelled through outsourcing modes (e.g. subcontracting) not involving outright FDI. In other words, we can hold that it is particularly difficult for productive systems based on SMEs to go for their productive outsourcing by directly acquiring productive capacity abroad. Nevertheless, such productive outsourcing to low-labour-cost countries (largely to Eastern European economies) is vital for these firms to safeguard their competitive hedge in their traditional goods of specialization (the so called goods of the "made in Italy" spectrum) implying a considerable use of unskilled labour.

And, indeed, Italian SMEs have largely outsourced their productive processes especially to Eastern Europe, where geographic vicinity adds to high human capital endowments and still very low labour costs. Outsourcing often involved specific phases, regarding particularly those stages that could be more easily standardized and with higher unskilled labour content, leaving instead in Italy the higher skill-based stages before production (e.g. design and definition of new products) and after production (e.g. finishing and commercialization). In this sense, outsourcing gave rise to large flows of temporary exports (the so-called outward processing trade, OPT), followed then by the related large flow of imports. Analysing OPT by destination highlights the fundamental role played by Eastern Europe, as the main partner for productive restructuring at Italian SMEs: for example, above 46% of the OPT originating from manufacturing firms in Veneto goes to Eastern Europe (Gisolo and Iodice, 2002).

Given its highly fragmented nature, manufacturing internationalization in Italy might benefit more than in other countries of synergies with national banks' internationalization. It is, in fact, difficult to think that the coordination mechanisms typical of the industrial districts can easily work their way through developing a financial setup adequate to support manufacturing firms' internationalization. Accordingly, should their banking partners accompany them, it might be much easier for these firms to go international.

However, up until very recently, Italy's banks were little internationalized (De Bonis, et al., 2000). Their significant M&A activity in Eastern Europe in recent years was their first real internationalization on a retail basis (at least referring to the recent decades). It is then a truly crucial question to establish whether the productive outsourcing in Eastern Europe by Italy's SME-based industrial districts and the concurrent internationalization to Eastern Europe of Italy's leading banks were two related phenomena or whether they were independent from each other.

MAPPING INTERNATIONALIZATION TO EASTERN EUROPE FOR ITALY'S BANKS AND INDUSTRIAL DISTRICTS

Methodology

In principle, the most appropriate method to answer the research question we just raised would be to study directly on the field at banks and/or firms whether and to what extent the two forms of internationalization to Eastern Europe have been related or independent. Nevertheless, lacking such detailed information, we may still try to infer something in this respect via an indirect methodology. The approach we selected here hinges on evaluating whether the penetration in the local credit markets of the industrial districts that have significantly outsourced their production to Eastern Europe has recently increased for those Italian banking groups which in recent years have acquired a retail network in Eastern Europe. To be sure, even if we were to find supportive evidence to that, this would provide neither a necessary nor a sufficient condition to ensure that the two types of internationalization were indeed related to each other. The finding would not make a necessary condition because those bank groups might have assisted Italy's SMEs in their outsourcing to Eastern Europe even without expanding their market share in traditional credit business back home. Nor would the finding be a sufficient condition in that even an increasing loan market share by such banks in the industrial districts significantly outsourcing to Eastern Europe might not mechanically imply that those banks effectively assisted national SMEs in their internationalization in Eastern Europe. Nonetheless, it is quite clear that the finding of supportive evidence would lead us to presume that Italy's bank and SME internationalization to Eastern Europe have to some extent been related.

From an operational point of view, our analysis consists of three logical steps. In the first step we identify and assess the degree of productive outsourcing to Eastern Europe by the various Italian industrial districts. This allows us to draw a detailed map of such productive outsourcing distinguishing which specific Eastern European country has become involved into that[3]. Our second step identifies, instead, the detailed map of the presence in each one of the

Eastern European countries by each of the Italian banking groups that have moved to the area with subsidiaries and/or branches. The third step of our analysis employs econometric instruments to test whether and to what extent the correspondence between the two maps delivers higher penetration in industrial districts for banks that have moved to Eastern Europe. At this point, however, we need to give more details on how we have structured the three steps we just described.

Our first problem is how to identify the degree to which and the destination where productive outsourcing has occurred. In principle, we should consider both the intensity/destination of FDI and of outward processing trade (OPT). However, this was impossible because: (i) adequate data on FDI for Italian manufacturing firms are lacking[4], and (ii) information on OPT published by Istat does not offer adequate territorial breakdown[5].

The only way we could think of to reach a more detailed territorial breakdown is to use external trade data, which are published detailing exports by province of origin (in Italy) and by individual country of destination, thus allowing us to identify trade vis-à-vis each country in Eastern Europe. Nevertheless, even these data can be useful to us only after we make an additional hypothesis, namely after we assume that large flows of exports to Eastern European countries in those productive sectors typical of industrial districts specialized in the goods in the "made in Italy" rank actually identify OPT and not sales of final goods. In other words, exports to those mid-low income countries in industrial districts' goods – typically directed to high-price segments of the market – conceal, in reality, either OPT or export flows provoked by productive fragmentation between industrial district SMEs and their Eastern Europe subsidiaries, acquired through FDI in the area[6].

After accepting to use data on exports, we may start from the classification of the various industrial districts according to their main productive specialization. However, we must also face the additional constraint that the highest detail for export data is the individual province and not the individual Local Labour System (LLS)[7]. To overcome such constraint, we develop an index of "industrial district intensity" for province *i*, constructed as follows[8]:

$$x_i = \frac{\text{Num.of industrial employees in the district LLS of province } i}{\text{Num.of tot.industrial employees in province } i}$$

where obviously the "industrial district intensity" x_i varies between 0 and 1[9].

Table 9.1 reports the values of the index of "industrial district intensity" calculated according to the above. Classifying as high "industrial district intensity" those provinces having a value of the index above the mean, we select 37 provinces (in decreasing order of "industrial district intensity"): Prato, Ascoli Piceno, Lecco, Padua, Pistoia, Treviso, Reggio Emilia, Modena, Como, Cremona, Biella, Pesaro, Vicenza, Teramo, Brescia, Parma, Bergamo, Macerata, Lucca, Lodi, Varese, Udine, Mantova, Arezzo, Ravenna, Forlì, Ancona, Rovigo, Novara, Siena, Perugia, Verbania, Verona, Sondrio, Viterbo, Piacenza, Pisa.

Table 9.1 Industrial district intensity in Italian provinces

Provinces	District	Provinces	District intensity
Prato	1.000	Bolzano	0.030
Ascoli Piceno	1.000	Rieti	0.030
Lecco	1.000	Terni	0.020
Padova	0.990	Genova	0.010
Pistoia	0.990	Savona	0.010
Treviso	0.980	L'Aquila	0.010
Reggio Emilia	0.980	Aosta	0.000
Modena	0.960	Imperia	0.000
Como	0.950	La Spezia	0.000
Cremona	0.950	Gorizia	0.000
Biella	0.940	Trieste	0.000
Pesaro	0.940	Grosseto	0.000
Vicenza	0.930	Livorno	0.000
Teramo	0.930	Massa	0.000
Brescia	0.870	Latina	0.000
Parma	0.860	Roma	0.000
Bergamo	0.820	Pescara	0.000
Macerata	0.770	Campobasso	0.000
Lucca	0.750	Isernia	0.000

Lodi	0.740	Caserta	0.000
Varese	0.730	Napoli	0.000
Udine	0.730	Salerno	0.000
Mantova	0.710	Brindisi	0.000
Arezzo	0.700	Lecce	0.000
Ravenna	0.620	Matera	0.000
Forlì	0.590	Potenza	0.000
Ancona	0.590	Catanzaro	0.000
Rovigo	0.540	Reggio Calabr.	0.000
Novara	0.530	Crotone	0.000
Siena	0.470	Agrigento	0.000
Perugia	0.410	Caltanissetta	0.000
Verbania	0.400	Catania	0.000
Verona	0.370	Enna	0.000
Sondrio	0.350	Messina	0.000
Viterbo	0.340	Palermo	0.000
Piacenza	0.330	Ragusa	0.000
Pisa	0.320	Siracusa	0.000
Pavia	0.290	Trapani	0.000
Ferrara	0.290	Cagliari	0.000
Milano	0.280	Nuoro	0.000
Trento	0.280	Sassari	0.000
Asti	0.270	Oristano	0.000
Belluno	0.260		
Firenze	0.250	*Average*	*0.299*
Avellino	0.200	*Median*	*0.106*
Pordenone	0.150		
Bari	0.150		
Taranto	0.120		
Cuneo	0.110		
Bologna	0.110		
Rimini	0.110		
Frosinone	0.110		
Vercelli	0.100		
Alessandria	0.080		
Chieti	0.080		
Foggia	0.070		
Vibo Valentia	0.070		
Venezia	0.060		
Benevento	0.060		
Torino	0.050		

As reported in Table 9.2, for each of the 37 provinces we count from a minimum of 1 to a maximum of five of the nine identified industrial district specializations (food and beverages; textiles an clothing; leather and shoes; furniture; metals; mechanics; petro-chemicals; paper and publishing; gold and musical products, etc.). The few provinces with a single industrial district specialization are: Biella, Parma, Pisa, Prato, Rovigo, Verbania and Viterbo. Those with five specializations are: Como and Cremona.

We may reasonably hold that productive outsourcing to Eastern Europe by industrial districts in province *i* can be measured by the exports to Eastern European countries from province *i* if these exports belong to the productive specialization of the industrial districts identified in province *i*[10]. In practice, we define an index of the "degree of outsourcing" by each industrial district specialization *h* of the industrial district province *i* towards Eastern European country *j*:

$$x_{hij} = \frac{\exp_{hij}}{\exp_{hi}} \tag{9.1}$$

where $\exp_{hi}$ identifies the total exports in industrial district specialization *h* from province *i*, while $\exp_{hij}$ indicates the part (in absolute value) of $\exp_{hi}$ directed to Eastern European country *j*. Obviously, x_{hij} varies between 0 and 1. Values of x_{hij} significantly above 0 identify active loci where industrial district outsourcing took place. This completes our first logical step.

Next, we establish a double threshold to identify effective industrial district outsourcing. First, we consider as outsourced those specialization sectors of industrial district provinces for which the share of exports to Eastern European countries in total world exports is above 10%, much higher than the 7% circa of Italy's overall exports going to the sum of Central Eastern European countries and South Eastern European countries[11]. By so doing, and using data referred to exports for 2001, we obtain effective industrial district outsourcing for only 21 of the 37 provinces with high industrial district intensity and, more precisely, for 30 (those marked in Table 9.2 of the 64 industrial district/province productive specializations relating to the 21 provinces[12]. Furthermore, in order to identify to which one(s) of the ten countries such outsourcing was directed, we computed the share for each of the ten countries and considered only those countries with an index above 12.5%.

Table 9.2 Specialization in the 37 provinces with high industrial district intensity

	Specializations				
Provinces	1	2	3	4	5
Novara	Mechanics	Textiles & Cloth.			
Biella [c]	Textiles & Cloth.				
Verbania [c]	Mechanics				
Lecco [c]	Mechanics	Food & Beverages	Textiles & Cloth.		
Lodi [c]	Mechanics	Petro-Chemicals			
Bergamo[a]	Petro-Chemicals	Mechanics	Textiles & Cloth. [b]		
Brescia[a]	Textiles & Cloth. [b]	Mechanics	Metals	Petro-Chemical	
Como	Textiles & Cloth.	Furniture	Mechanics	Petro-Chemical	Food & Beverag
Cremona[a]	Food & Beverages	Mechanics	Textiles & Cloth. [b]	Furniture	Metals
Mantova[a]	Textiles & Cloth. [b]	Food & Beverages	Furniture	Mechanics	
Sondrio[a]	Food & Beverages	Textiles & Cloth. [b]			
Varese	Textiles & Cloth.	Petro-Chemicals			
Padova[a]	Mechanics	Textiles & Cloth. [b]	Furniture [b]		
Rovigo[a]	Textiles & Cloth. [b]				
Treviso[a]	Leather & Shoes [b]	Textiles & Cloth. [b]	Furniture	Mechanics	
Verona[a]	Furniture	Textiles & Cloth. [b]	Mechanics [b]	Leather & Shoes [b]	
Vicenza[a]	Textiles & Cloth. [b]	Gold & Mus.	Leather & Shoes	Furniture	
Udine	Furniture	Mechanics			
Forlì[a]	Furniture	Textiles & Cloth. [b]	Paper & Publish. [b]	Leather & Shoes	
Modena	Mechanics	Textiles & Cloth.	Furniture		
Parma	Food & Beverages				

Piacenza	Mechanics	Food & Beverages		
Ravenna	Food & Beverages			
Reggio Emilia[a]	Mechanics	Furniture	Textiles & Cloth.[b]	
Arezzo[a]	Textiles & Cloth.[b]	Gold & Mus. Prod.	Furniture	Paper & Publish.[b]
Lucca	Leather & Shoes	Paper & Publish.	Furniture	
Pisa	Leather & Shoes			
Pistoia[a]	Textiles & Cloth.[b]	Leather & Shoes	Mechanics	
Siena	Furniture	Food & Beverages	Leather & Shoes	
Prato[c]	Textiles & Cloth.			
Perugia[a]	Textiles & Cloth.[b]	Paper & Publish.	Furniture	
Ancona[a]	Leather & Shoes	Textiles & Cloth.[b]	Gold & Mus. Prod.	Food & Beverage
Ascoli Piceno[a]	Textiles & Cloth.[b]	Leather & Shoes[b]		
Macerata[a]	Textiles & Cloth.	Furniture	Leather & Shoes[b]	Gold & Mus. Prod.
Pesaro[a]	Textiles & Cloth.[b]	Furniture		
Viterbo[a]	Furniture[b]			
Teramo[a]	Textiles & Cloth.	Furniture[b]		

Notes: [a] The provinces with productive outsourcing to Eastern Europe.
[b] The specific industrial district specialization(s) for which outsourcing occurred.
[c] New provinces created during the 1990s.

Descriptive Evidence

We identify 63 outsourcing nodes in Eastern Europe for industrial district/province productive specializations (Table 9.3). More than half (35 nodes) pertain to textiles and clothing; the following ranks are for, in the order, leather and shoes (9 nodes), furniture (6 nodes), paper & publishing (6 nodes), petro-chemicals (4 nodes) and mechanics (3 nodes). The country receiving the largest number of outsourcing nodes is Romania, counting 25 of them, while Poland counts 13 nodes, Hungary counts 9 nodes, Bulgaria, the Czech

Republic and Ukraine count 4 nodes each, Croatia counts 3 nodes and Slovenia counts only 1 node. The provinces with the largest outsourcing nodes are Verona (6 nodes), Arezzo, Brescia and Macerata (5 nodes), with the other provinces following with fewer nodes.

Figure 9.1 reports the geographical distribution of outsourcing to Eastern Europe for the 21 provinces with high industrial district intensity and by specific country of destination, where this time the share is not over the number of nodes but over the amount of exports to those nodes[13].

Table 9.3. Destination countries for districts' outsourcing by specialization

Sector/ Province	Country of productive outsourcing								
(data for 2001)	Bulgaria	Croatia	Poland	Czech	Slovenia	Ukraine	Hungary	Romania	N° Countries
Textiles-Clothing									
Bergamo			1					1	2
Brescia								1	1
Cremona							1	1	2
Mantova			1				1		2
Sondrio			1						1
Padova	1							1	2
Rovigo								1	1
Treviso		1					1	1	3
Verona		1						1	2
Vicenza				1				1	2
Forlì								1	1
Reggio Emilia	1		1				1	1	4
Arezzo	1							1	2
Pistoia			1					1	2
Perugia			1					1	2
Ancona						1		1	2
Ascoli Piceno								1	1

Macerata						1		1	2
Pesaro								1	1
Sub-Total	*3*	*2*	*6*	*1*	*0*	*2*	*4*	*17*	*35*
Leather-Shoes									
Treviso							1	1	2
Verona								1	1
Ascoli Piceno	1		1					1	3
Macerata			1			1		1	3
Sub-Total	*1*	*0*	*2*	*0*	*0*	*1*	*1*	*4*	*9*
Furniture									
Padova			1	1					2
Viterbo						1			1
Teramo		1	1					1	3
Sub-Total	*0*	*1*	*2*	*1*	*0*	*1*	*0*	*1*	*6*
Mechanics									
Verona			1				1	1	3
Petro-Chemicals									
Brescia			1	1			1	1	4
Paper-Publishing									
Forlì				1			1	1	3
Arezzo			1		1		1		3
Sub-Total	0	0	1	1	1	0	2	1	6
Total	*4*	*3*	*13*	*4*	*1*	*4*	*9*	*25*	*63*

We notice again the prominent position of Romania, receiving 59.5% of the exports to outsourcing nodes in Eastern Europe, with the other countries following at a considerable distance: Hungary (14.6%), Poland (10.5%), Croatia (7.2%), the Czech Republic (3.0%), Bulgaria (2.8%), Ukraine (2.4%), Slovenia (0.03%), with nil for both Macedonia and Slovak Republic.

Figure 9.2 presents the geographical distribution of the above outsourcing from Italy to Eastern Europe distinguishing among the different economic areas of the country where industrial districts belong (i.e. North-West, North-East and Centre, as there was no industrial district in the South-Islands according to the 1991 Istat classification to which we refer). We detect the selection of Romania as the destination for outsourcing is more pervasive in the North-East and the Centre than in the North-West, which outsources comparatively more to Poland and Hungary. A further noteworthy feature is that only the Centre outsources to Ukraine and Slovenia.

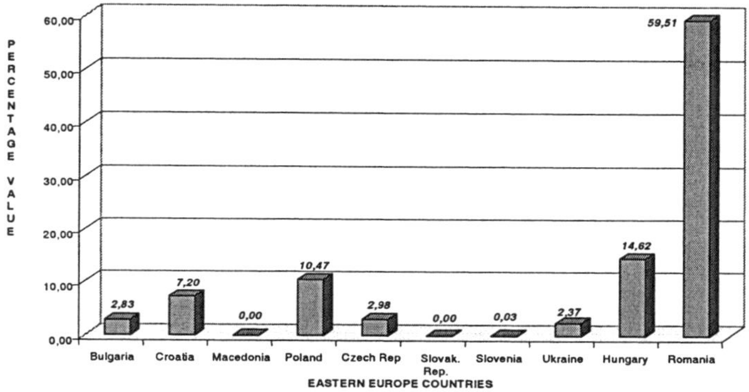

Figure 9.1 Distribution by country of industrial districts' outsourcing to Eastern Europe

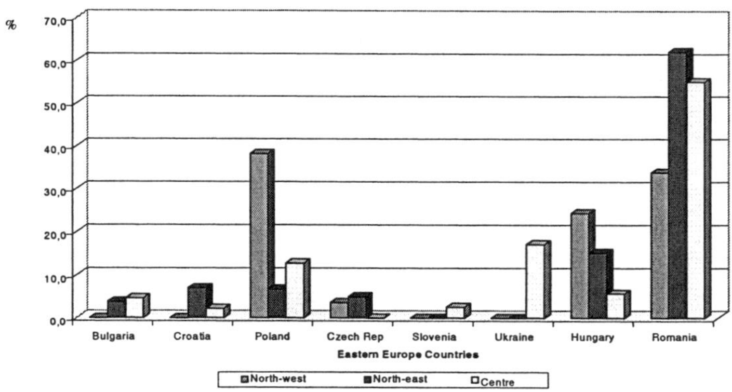

Figure 9.2 Distribution by country and Italy's areas of industrial districts' outsourcing to Eastern Europe

The intensity of productive outsourcing across the nine sectors of industrial district specialization is highest for textiles and clothing, and is also above average for leather and shoes; paper and publishing (Figure 9.3). On the contrary, outsourcing is below average in petrochemicals; furniture; mechanics. No outsourcing is detected for food and beverages; metals; gold and musical products, etc..

Finally, industrial district outsourcing to Romania is intense for all productive segments, even though smaller for furniture; paper and publishing. Specifically, Romania is the only target for the segment leather and shoes and covers half of productive outsourcing in the sector textiles and clothing (Figure 9.4). Productive outsourcing in the segment furniture goes to a large extent to Poland, Croatia and Ukraine while that in the segment paper and publishing largely goes to Hungary, Slovenia, Poland and the Czech Republic; mechanics goes to Romania, Poland and Hungary.

The next step consists in drawing the map of the presence of Italy's banks in the same ten Eastern European countries, distinguishing for each one of the six banking groups present in the area. In practice, for each banking group k, we define a dummy b_{kj} taking value 1 in each Eastern European country where such banking group is present and value 0 in the other countries.

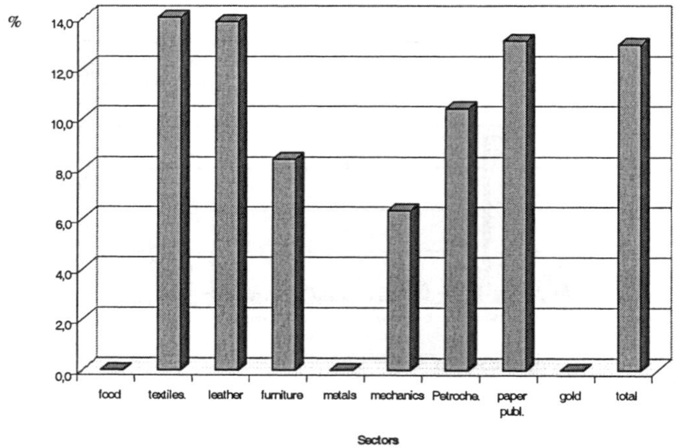

Figure 9.3 Index of outsourcing to Eastern Europe by industrial district specialization

Values differing from 0 for b_{kj} identify active nodes of the presence of banking group *k*. This map is represented in Table 9.4. We can count six banking groups having a presence in at least one of the ten Eastern European countries we consider[14]. In terms of the number of countries, group B is present in seven countries (lacking only Macedonia, Slovenia and Hungary), group A is present in five countries, while each one of the other four is present in only one of the ten countries.

The acquisition of a branch network in Eastern Europe on the part of Italy's banking groups is a recent phenomenon (Figure 9.5). By end 1996 only group C was present in one of the ten countries. Group D shows up with one presence (in Romania) in 1997 and also group A counts a presence since 1998. The intensity of banking group presence grows starting with 2000, when the two largest players, groups A and B upgrade their presence, respectively, from one to three countries, and up to six of the ten countries. The prominent role played by Romania in the trade and productive links with the Italian economy is also confirmed from observing that five out of the six banking groups are present in Romania, while their presence in each one of the other countries is lower.

The final step in our methodology consists in verifying whether when Eastern European nodes match the presence of banking group *k* and the productive outsourcing by industrial district specialization/province *hi* then the loan market share of banking group *k* in industrial district specialization/province *hi* increases. Since both banking and productive outsourcing nodes have become active only relatively recently, we try to detect any impact on market shares over the period 1998-2002.

Specifically, we refer to the market share in loans – granted to industrial districts that have significantly outsourced production to Eastern Europe – over the years 1998-99 (on average) for the banking groups that have acquired a presence in Eastern Europe. Referring to the four most important countries of productive outsourcing, Figure 9.6 contrasts such market shares with those recorded (on average) over the years 2000-02, the period in which the presence in Eastern Europe of Italian banks has intensified[15].

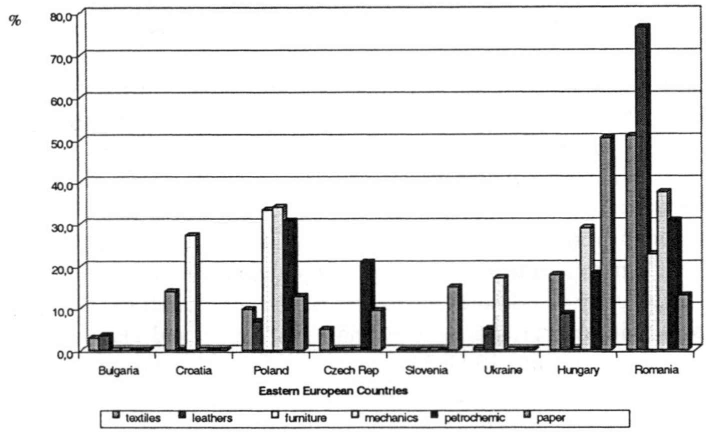

Figure 9.4 Outsourcing to Eastern Europe by country and industrial district specialization

Prima facie, Figure 9.6 does not identify a decisive impact promoting market shares: while for Croatia and Romania we detect a slight increase, for Poland and Hungary we notice a reduction, more marked in the latter case. Even if, instead of considering it by country, we evaluate the overall market share for the six banking groups over the industrial district nodes with significant productive outsourcing to Eastern Europe, it decreases from 27.9 to 27.4% across the two periods. Nevertheless, the decrease in market shares for the six banking groups in outsourcing industrial districts must be evaluated also against the evolution of the overall market share (in the whole of Italy) for the six banking groups which, over the two periods, decreases by more than two percentage points (Figure 9.7). This comparison leads us to conclude that the loss in the loan market share for the six banking groups with a presence in Eastern Europe was smaller in the industrial districts significantly outsourcing production to Eastern Europe than in the rest of Italy. In addition, Figure 9.7 reports market shares in the industrial districts with lower outsourcing (the first quartile of the outsourcing index) and in those with higher outsourcing (the fourth quartile). The first group shows a decreasing market share (from 28.9% to 27.2%), while the second reports an increase (from 37.7% to 39.0%).

Table 9.4 Presence of Italian banking groups in Eastern Europe by end 2002 (*)

	Group A	Group B	Group C	Group D	Group E	Group F	Total
Bulgaria	0	1	0	0	0	0	1
Croatia	1	1	0	0	0	0	2
Czech Rep.	0	1	0	0	0	0	1
Hungary	1	0	0	0	0	0	1
Macedonia	1	0	0	0	0	0	1
Poland	0	1	0	0	0	0	1
Romania	0	1	1	1	1	1	5
Slovak Rep.	1	1	0	0	0	0	2
Slovenia	1	0	0	0	0	0	1
Ukraine	0	1	0	0	0	0	1
Total	5	7	1	1	1	1	

Notes: (*) The value 1 (0) indicates that the banking group is (is not) present in the country. The total by column counts the number of Eastern European countries where the banking group is present. The total by row counts the number of Italian banking groups present in each Eastern European country.

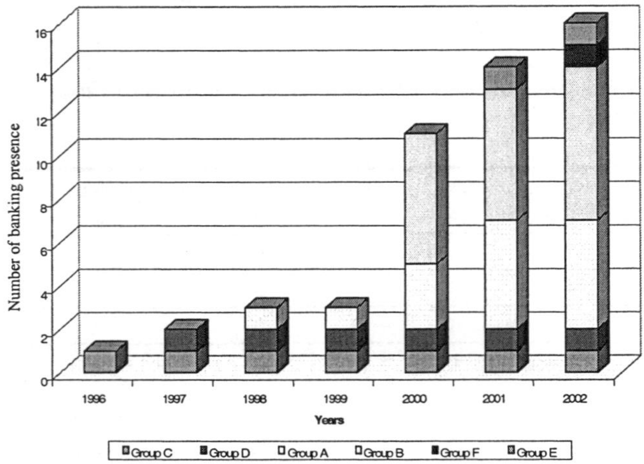

Figure 9.5 The recent increase in the presence of Italian banks in Eastern Europe

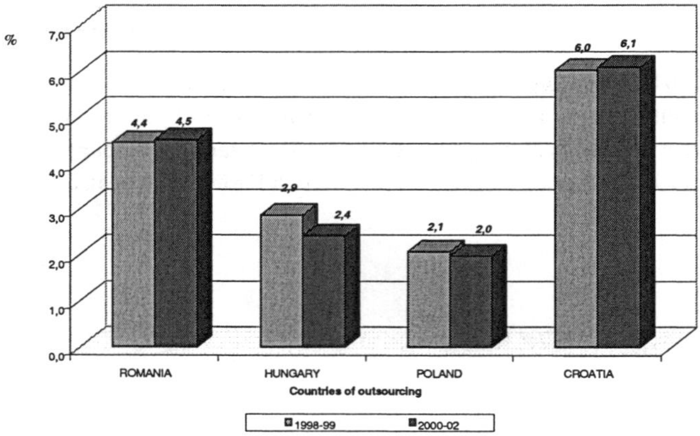

Figure 9.6 Market shares of the banks with a presence in Eastern Europe in the industrial districts heavily outsourcing to Eastern Europe

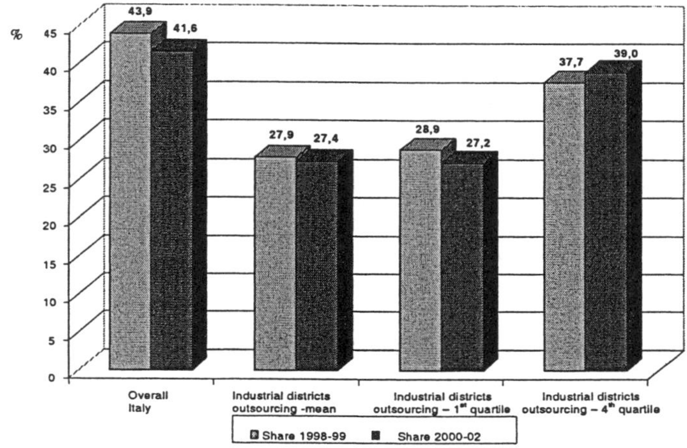

Figure 9.7 Loan market shares of the banks with a presence in Eastern Europe in the industrial districts outsourcing to Eastern Europe and overall in Italy

Some Econometric Results

Before settling on the previous inconclusive descriptive evidence, we try to test our hypothesis via more rigorous regression analysis. Specifically, we estimate the possible links between the change in the market share in loans to each one of the industrial districts that have significantly outsourced production to Eastern Europe, focusing our attention on the most important sector in terms of outsourcing (namely textiles and clothing) and introducing a control sample made up of industrial districts with no outsourcing to Eastern Europe. Our hypothesis will receive support if loan market shares by our six banks in those industrial districts that have significantly outsourced is significant while there are no effects in the other industrial districts.

We define a dummy for outsourced districts *OUTSD* (which takes value 1 if the district *j* is outsoursed and 0 otherwise) and two variables relating to the size and the seniority of each bank's presence in Eastern Europe ($EETA_i$ is the weight of group *i*'s total assets in Eastern Europe taken as a ratio to group *i*'s total assets in Italy and OLD_i a dummy index taking value 1 for those banking groups already present in Eastern Europe by 2000). Furthermore, we introduce two interaction variables: the first one is $EETAOUTSD_{ij}$ (given by $EETA_i*OUTSD_j$); the second one is $OLDOUTSD_{ij}$ (given by $OLD_i*OUTSD_j$). The null hypothesis is no positive effect on market shares for the six banking groups in the industrial districts that have significantly outsourced (positive effect when $OUTSD_j$=1) and/or a positive effect for the banking groups with a longer (positive effect of $OLDOUTSD_{ij}$) and a stronger (positive effect of $EETAOUTSD_{ij}$) presence in Eastern Europe countries.

The estimated equation runs as follows:

$$\begin{aligned} MSH02_{ij} = {} & \alpha+\beta_1 MSH01_{ij}+\beta_2 \Delta MSHB_i+\beta_3 LOTA_i+\beta_4 LTA_i+ \\ & +\beta_5 EETAOUTSD_{ij}+\beta_6 EETAOUTSD^2_{ij}+ \\ & +\beta_7 OLDOUTSD_{ij}+\beta_8 DCOU_j\ \varepsilon_{ij} \end{aligned} \qquad (9.2)$$

where $MSH02_{ij}$ is the market share for each one of the six banking groups in the local market at the end of 2002, $MSH01_{ij}$ is the same variable measured at the end of 2001, $\Delta MSHB_i$ is the change in the market share of loans of the of banking group i between 2001 and 2002, $LOTA_i$ is the ratio between loans and total assets for banking group i, LTA_i is the logarithm of the total assets of banking group i. We also add the variable $EETAOUTSD^2_{ij}$ (the square of $EETAOUTSD_{ij}$) in order to capture likely non linearity with the dependent variable; in addition we introduce a control variable for each country of outsourcing, since this variable is significant.

Results – presented in Table 9.5 – show no impact of the variable *OUTSD* but confirm a significant effect for the banking groups with a longer and stronger presence in Eastern Europe and this effect is only in the industrial districts that have significantly outsourced. In particular, in the latter the market share is higher 0.9 % for the banks with longer presence in Eastern Europe and about 2% for banks with a value of *EETAOUTSD* at the 75th percentile.

Table 9.5. OLS Regression on market share of individual bank groups moving to eastern europe: textiles and clothing districts with and without outsourcing.

Dep. Var.:	First specification		Preferred specifications			
MSH02 [a]	Coefficient	t-stat	Coefficient	t-stat	Coefficient	t-stat
MSH01	0.8991	22.29***	0.9082	25.36***	0.9124	24.94***
ΔMSHB	-0.1537	-1.07	-	-	-	-
LOTA	0.0837	1.51	0.1320	2.71***	0.0696	1.61
LTA	0.0101	2.27**	0.0111	2.41**	0.0068	2.16**
CZECH REP.	-545.6092	-6.94***	-555.9867	-8.87***	-555.9867	-7.09***
OUTSD	-61.5438	-1.66	-	-	-	-
OLDOUTSD	79.9619	1.66	90.3737	2.00**	-	-
EETAOUTSD	0.7976	1.07	-	-	1.1216	1.80*
EETAOUTSD2	-0.0009	-1.03	-	-	-0.0012	-1.64
CONSTANT	-839.3033	-2.07**	-1139.3440	-3.14***	-640.8965	-2.38***
N° observ.	112		112		112	
F	(8,102) 203.50***		(4,106) 375.06***		(5,105) 254.11***	
R2	0.940		0.938		0.938	

Notes: [a] We estimate an equation in the following form:

$$MSH02_{ij} = \alpha + \beta_1 MSH01_{ij} + \beta_2 \Delta MSHB_i + \beta_3 LOTA_i + \beta_4 LTA_i + \beta_5 EETAOUTSD_{ij} + \beta_6 EETAOUTSD^2_{ij} + \beta_7 OLDOUTSD_{ij} + \beta_8 DCOU_j \, \varepsilon_{ij}$$

The dependent variable ($MSH02_{ij}$) is the market share of banking group (BG) *i* in local market *j* where an industrial district was present and it significantly outsourced production to Eastern Europe (e.g., considering the case of textile-clothing in the province of Bergamo, where an industrial district significantly outsources production to Romania, we take the ratio of the loans by each of the five BG present in Romania granted to the textile-clothing sector in that industrial district and the total loans by the entire banking system to textile-clothing in that industrial district) by end 2002 (data source: Banca d'Italia).

$MSH01_{ij}$ is the same variable at end 2001. $\Delta MSHB_i$ is the change in the market share of total loans (taken as a ratio to the total for the 6 BG) of BG *i* between end 2001 and end 2002 (data source: Banca d'Italia). $LOTA_i$ is the ratio loans/total assets for BG *i* at end 2002 (data source: Banca d'Italia). $EETAOUTSD_{ij}$ is the ratio, for each BG, between total assets in Eastern Europe and total assets in Italy (evaluated in its 2000-01 average; data source: Banca d'Italia) multiplied by the dummy OUTSD (which takes value 1 when the district is outsourced and 0 otherwise). $EETAOUTSD^2_{ij}$ is the square of $EETAOUTSD_{ij}$. $OLDOUTSD_{ij}$ is a dummy variable taking value 1 for BGs (A, B, C, D) that established their presence in Eastern Europe earlier on multiplied by OUTSD. LTA_i is the logarithm of total assets for BG *i* (evaluated at end 2001; data source: Banca d'Italia). $DCOU_j$ (Bulgaria, Croatia, Czech Rep., Hungary, Poland, Slovenia, Ukraine and Romania) are *dummies* whose value is 1 if the industrial district outsources to that country and is 0 otherwise. Reported t-statistics are obtained via the OLS method and are heteroschedastic consistent according to the Huber-White correction. ***, ** and * indicate, respectively, that the hypothesis of the coefficient being zero may be rejected at the 1%, 5% and 10% confidence level.

CONCLUDING REMARKS

The last decade has seen the occurrence of two important phenomena of internationalization from Italy to Eastern Europe. First, many SME-based industrial district systems, already enjoying strong export performance for final goods (Bagella et al. 1998), have considerably outsourced to Eastern Europe (relevant phases of) their productive process, attracted there by vicinity, by relatively high human capital endowments and, above all, by very low labour costs. It is also thanks to this change in the organization of their production that industrial district SMEs have been able to limit their declining competitiveness on international markets, where they were increasingly challenged by exports from low-cost-of-production emerging economies. Second, even though Italy's banking system was traditionally hesitating to go international, some Italian banks strategically entered retail banking markets in Eastern Europe.

The research question we tackled in this chapter is whether the two phenomena were independent from each other, or, rather, they were somewhat related. As we lacked direct information on the support given (or not given) by those Italian banking groups with a presence in Eastern Europe to Italy's industrial district SMEs in their productive internationalization to Eastern Europe, we devised an alternative strategy. Specifically, we argued that we could presume that the two phenomena were related to each other if we were to find that the banking groups that have gone international to Eastern Europe increased their market shares precisely in those industrial districts which more heavily outsourced production to Eastern Europe.

After overcoming – hopefully convincingly – a series of obstacles toward identifying in detail the geographical distribution of industrial districts' outsourcing to Eastern Europe, we could draw a map of such outsourcing. At the same time, we also drew the map of the presence in Eastern Europe of Italy's banking groups: we found 6 of them. The final step consisted in verifying whether the correspondence between a bank's internationalization nodes to a specific Eastern European country and productive outsourcing nodes to the same country from a specific industrial district has an impact on the market share of that bank in that industrial district. The first result was that the overall market share of the six banking groups – summing them up – declined between 1998-99 and 2000-02, however such decline was smaller in those industrial districts that have considerably outsourced production to Eastern Europe: hence, their presence in Eastern Europe seems to have provided these banks with a competitive hedge in those local markets in Italy. Secondly, referring to each of the six individual bank's market shares between 2001 and 2002, we found that these increased for the banking groups already present from a longer time in Eastern Europe and for those with a more quantitatively significant presence in Eastern Europe over 2000-01; we would like to stress that this outcome is valid for the textile and clothing industrial districts which have outsourced production (indeed the bulk of industrial districts' outsourcing) while it is not observable for the districts which have not outsourced. Accordingly, our empirical results support the hypothesis that the internationalization of Italian banks and that of Italian industrial district SMEs (both to Eastern Europe) were somewhat related.

This result does not amount to saying that Italian banks are doing all they could to help the productive internationalization of Italian industrial district SMEs, but at least we may rule out that the two forms of internationalization are independent of each other. Since productive outsourcing from industrial districts to Eastern Europe is so vital to safeguard manufacturing competitiveness, our results suggest that also Italian banks are playing a role in this respect. Obviously, the above is based more on some suggesting evidence and a reasonable argument than on absolute certainty. But, if our presumption were to be confirmed, then we could somehow play down the usual complaint that Italy's different institution and economic actors are unable to "play as a team".

The results we proposed bear implications also for Italy's banking structure. It is well known, in fact, that local banks (often cooperative ones) played a primary role providing financial support to industrial district SMEs. However, will this hold for the future? If we look at the internationalization of Eastern Europe, up to now the main banking players have been some large banks, not the local banks. Since the internationalization of their productive processes is going to be key for industrial district SMEs also in the near future, we may envisage that large national banks might defeat local banks in their traditional market niches, unless the latter banks too acquire a capacity to support SME's internationalization.

NOTES

1. Fabio Farabullini: Research Department, Banca d'Italia – Via Nazionale, 91 – 00184 Rome, Italy - email: fabio.farabullini@bancaditalia.it.
Giovanni Ferri: Professor of Economics – Department of Economics – University of Bari – Via C. Rosalba, 53 – 70124 Bari, Italy – email: g.ferri@dse.uniba.it – fax: +39-080-5049149. The authors would like to thank Giorgio Di Giorgio, Dario Focarelli, Alberto F. Pozzolo, Luigi Federico Signorini and Roberto Tedeschi for very useful suggestions and discussion. This research was conceived as part of the project "Local Economies, agglomeration models and international opening", new research by the Banca d'Italia on territorial development. The views expressed here are those of the authors alone and should not be attributed to the Banca d'Italia.
2. Some authors, on the contrary, hold the opposite view: e.g. Weller (2000) remarks that foreign banks, rather than providing more liquidity, may abandon the country when the negative shock occurs since they have no commitment to stay in the country.

3. The Eastern European countries we consider are the ten where by end 2001 at least one Italian bank was present with at least a subsidiary, that is: Bulgaria, Croatia, the Czech Republic, Hungary, Macedonia, Poland, Slovak Republic, Romania, Slovenia, Ukraine.
4. See, e.g., Cominotti, et al. (1999).
5. Such data have a satisfactory breakdown by sector, but have inadequate territorial detail both across originating province (data are only published with a regional breakdown, which is inappropriate to capture the dynamics at the level of the industrial districts) and across destination countries (all Eastern European countries are bunched in a single group).
6. A propos the relation between productive fragmentation and the internationalization of Italy's productive system, see, e.g., Ferragina and Quintieri (2002).
7. Each LLS aggregates two or more municipalities belonging to the same economic gravity area. LLS provide a full partition of Italy. Approximately only one out of eight LLS is an industrial district.
8. This procedure is not entirely new. For instance, see Bronzini (2000) and Iuzzolino (2000).
9. It is worth highlighting that when an individual LLS belongs to two (or more) provinces, all its employees are computed as district employees in each of the two (or more) provinces. To check that this did not introduce biases in our data, we alternatively measured the industrial district intensity of the province attributing the employees of the district only to the "prevailing" province: results did not change significantly. In addition, we should point out that the data on employees refer to the 1996 Census. Finally, we use the map of industrial districts published by Istat built on 1991 Census data.
10. Let us give an example. If the province of Ascoli Piceno – where leather-shoes industrial districts are present – records large exports of shoes to Romania, this identifies industrial district productive outsourcing from Ascoli Piceno to Romania. If, instead, we come across exports of furniture from Ascoli Piceno to Romania – since in the province of Ascoli Piceno there is no industrial district specialising in furniture – this does not identify industrial district productive outsourcing from Ascoli Piceno to Romania.
11. Still referring to 2001, the share of exports going to the sum of the ten Eastern European countries we consider is 8.4% for the 37 industrial district provinces.

12. The share to the ten countries over total exports from the 21 provinces with industrial district specializations outsourced to Eastern Europe rises up to 9.8%.
13. This index is constructed summing the absolute value of exports going to outsourcing nodes in Eastern Europe (measured as described above) and computing its distribution across the 10 countries. In practice, summing the shares for the ten countries adds up to 100.
14. In order not to disclose private information (since we are using also reserved data), we will label the banking groups A, B, C, D, E, F. In order to preserve the comparability of data, the structure of each banking group is the same over the entire period observed.
15. For each Eastern European country market shares refer to the banking groups – that have acquired an operational presence in that country – in those industrial districts which have heavily outsourced to that Eastern European country. For instance, in the case of Romania market shares refer to loans granted by banking groups B, C, D, E and F (group A is not present) in those industrial districts that outsource production to Romania, only for the sectors that are effectively outsourced (i.e., textiles and clothing for the industrial districts belonging to the province of Bergamo, textiles and clothing and also petro-chemicals for the industrial districts belonging to the province of Brescia, and so on).

REFERENCES

Arndt, S. and H. Kierzkowski (2001 eds), *Fragmentation. New Production Patterns in the World Economy*, Oxford University Press.

Bagella, M., L. Becchetti and S. Sacchi (1998), "The Positive Link between Geographical Agglomeration and Export Intensity: the Engine of Italian Endogenous Growth?", *Economic Notes*, 27, No. 1: 1-34.

Baldone, S., F. Sdogati and L. Tajoli (2001), "Patterns and Determinants of International Fragmentation of Production. Evidence from Outward Processing Trade between the EU and the Countries of Central-Eastern Europe", *Welwirtschaftliches Archiv*.

Bronzini, R. (2000), "Sistemi Produttivi Locali e Commercio Estero: un'Analisi Territoriale delle Esportazioni Italiane", in Signorini (eds) Lo Sviluppo Industriale. Un'indagine della Banca d'Italia sui Distretti Industriali, Donzelli, Rome.

Claessens, S., A. Demirgüç-Kunt and H. Huizinga (1998), "How Does Foreign Entry Affect The Domestic Banking Market?", World Bank, *Policy Research working paper*, No. 1918, June.

Cominotti, R., S. Mariotti and M. Mutinelli (1999), *Italia Multinazionale 1998. VII Rapporto Biennale predisposto per il CNEL da R&P*, Roma, CNEL.

Dages, B.G., L. Goldberg and D. Kinney (2000), "Foreign and Domestic Bank Participation in Emerging Markets: Lessons from Mexico and Argentina", *Federal Reserve Bank of New York Economic Policy Review*, 6, No. 3.

De Bonis, R., F. Farabullini and M. Piazza (2000), "L'Attività Internazionale delle Banche Italiane: una Sintesi degli Ultimi Dieci Anni", *Moneta e Credito*, 212.

Ferragina, A.M. and B. Quintieri (2002), "I Processi di Frammentazione Produttiva dell'Italia verso l'Area Mediterranea e l'Est Europeo", in G.P. Galli and L. Paganetto (eds), *Rapporto sulla competitività dell'Italia: le imprese*, Il Sole 24 Ore Edizioni, Milan.

Focarelli, D. and A.F. Pozzolo (2000), "The Determinants of Cross-Border Bank Shareholdings: an Analysis with Bank-level Data from OECD Countries", Bank of Italy, Research Department.

Gisolo, E. and P. Iodice (2002), "I Processi di Internazionalizzazione delle Imprese Venete", Banca d'Italia, mimeo.

Iuzzolino, G. (2000), "I Distretti Industriali nel Censimento Intermedio del 1996", in Signorini (eds) Lo Sviluppo Industriale. Un'indagine della Banca d'Italia sui Distretti Industriali, Donzelli, Rome.

Kaminsky, G.L. and C. Reinhart (1999), "The Twin Crises: The Causes of Banking and Balance-of-Payments Problems", *American Economic Review*, Vol.89, No.4, pp. 473-500.

Papi, L. and D. Revoltella (1999), *Foreign Direct Investment in the Banking Sector: A Transitional Economy Perspective*, Bocconi University, Development Studies Working Papers, n. 133, November.

Reynoso, A. (2002), "Can Subsidiaries of Foreign Banks Contribute to the Stability of the Forex Market in Emerging Economies? A Look at Some Evidence from the Mexican Financial System", *NBER Working Paper* No. W8864.

Signorini, L.F. (eds), *Lo Sviluppo Locale. Un'indagine della Banca d'Italia sui Distretti Industriali*, Donzelli, Rome.

Weller, C.E. (2000), "Financial Liberalization, Multinational Banks and Credit Supply: the Case of Poland", *International Review of Applied Economics*, 14, No. 2.

PART III

Regulation, Supervision and Monetary Policy

10. Financial Regulation in the New Europe

Martin Summer and Michael Würz

INTRODUCTION

We give a comparative analysis of banking regulation and supervision in the EU and in the Central and Eastern European Accession countries (CEEC). Drawing on public data sources and on sources from OeNB we try to get a structural picture on the state of regulatory and supervisory convergence between the CEEC and the EU.

There is a fairly broad consensus among financial economists that a smoothly functioning banking system is dependent on a functioning regulatory and supervisory infrastructure. The banking system is an important pillar in the financial system because it fulfills certain functions that cannot easily be substituted by other institutions. Modern banking theory has argued that banks can help solve market failures and play a compensating role for the limitations of financial markets (see Allen and Gale, 2000; Freixas and Rochet, 1997). These limitations result from frictions such as market incompleteness, transaction costs, externalities and informational asymmetries.

How the regulatory and supervisory infrastructure *exactly* supports the functioning of the banking system is however still imperfectly understood. Historically regulatory regimes around the globe have been quite different. For instance the banking system in the US was the most heavily regulated in the early 1970s. Much of the US regulation was implemented after the Great Depression. The United Kingdom at that time was for instance formally completely unregulated. Other places like Germany and Switzerland had formal regulation in place since the 1930s but it was more liberal than in the United States. Only recently there has been some convergence towards a consensus view on a set of best practice principles laid down in the Core Principles of the Basel Committee. This institution has played an important coordinating role for regulators around the globe. Also the empirical literature on the effectiveness of supervisory regimes is scarce. The papers by Barth et al. (2001) are pioneering contributions but have not yet led to definite conclusions.

In our analysis we therefore restrict ourselves to the task of getting a descriptive structural picture about the relative position of regulation and supervision of the CEEC countries as compared to the EU based on empirical indices suggested by Barth et al. (2001) drawing on data publicly available from the World Bank, the IMF and the European Bankers Federation. We complement this analysis by summarizing for the CEEC group as a whole the assessments that have been reached during the first two rounds of the Peer Review Process of the European Union. Proceeding in this way we hope to get a broad and relatively comprehensive picture about the current state of regulation and supervision in both groups.

The chapter is organized as follows. The first section gives a structural overview about the banking systems in the EU and the CEEC. The next section compares both groups by using the World Bank Data collected by Barth et al. Finally we make an attempt to draw an overall conclusion from what we have learned from the Peer Review Process drawing on data from OeNB. The final section concludes.

THE BANKING SYSTEM IN THE EU AND IN THE CENTRAL AND EASTERN EUROPEAN ACCESSION COUNTRIES: AN OVERVIEW

At the beginning of the new millennium and on the eve of EU accession the countries of Central and Eastern Europe that will take part in the first round of EU enlargement are looking back at a fairly turbulent first decade of transition, in which they managed to successfully build a new financial system basically from scratch. There was no possibility of building on the old banking system. Under socialism the financial system was barely more than a bookkeeping mechanism for recording the allocation decisions of the authorities. Resources were assigned according to centralized investment plans and at administered interest rates. There was no institutional separation between the central bank and commercial banks and a bankruptcy law as well as creditor rights were non-existent. Also capital markets did not exist.

A little more than ten years after the fall of the old regimes these countries all have built a modern banking system and functioning capital markets that are internationally strongly integrated. Also the legal and supervisory infrastructure that is indispensable for a smoothly working financial system has been developed and implemented at an impressive speed. A fairly detailed description of this process for the Czech Republic, Poland and Hungary can be found in Reininger, Schardax and Summer (2002). The developments for the larger group of countries are for instance reported in some detail in Caviglia et al. (2002) or in the Transition Reports published annually by the EBRD.

The transition did however not take place entirely smoothly. All countries in the accession group went through severe recessions in the early phase of transition with contractions in output from 10 up to 50% (see Cavaglia et al. 2002). Severe banking crises, expensive recapitalization programs and a huge stock of bad loans was the typical situation for the countries in the accession group in the early stages of transition. Now after the first decade, the financial systems including the banking systems have been successfully established and stabilized. Recent studies on banking reform are however concerned that bank intermediation still functions relatively poorly and point out the need to identify the obstacles to development in the banking sector (see for instance Fries and Taci, 2002). Caviglia et al. (2002) conclude that three key features of financial sector development in the accession group are "a relatively low level of financial intermediation, strong dominance of the commercial banking sector over capital markets and a high and widespread degree of foreign involvement in the financial sector."

Before we start our comparative description and analysis of supervision in the EU and in the CEEC first round enlargement group, we want to give an overview of some structural features of the banking system in the first round accession group compared to the EU to gauge our comparative analysis of banking regulation and supervision, which is the focus of our study.

Size of the Banking Sector

A rough measure of comparative size is the banking sector's total assets as a percentage of GDP. We give this description in Figure 10.1.

Figure 10.1 shows the ratio of banking assets to GDP both as a box and whiskers plot which graphically summarizes the distribution of this indicator. The lower graph displays the information for the EU group - Austria (AU), Belgium (BE), Denmark (DE), Finland (FI), France (FR), Germany (GE), Greece (GR), Ireland (IR), Italy (IT), Luxembourg (LU), Netherlands (NL), Portugal (PT), Spain (SP), Sweden (SE) and the United Kingdom (UK) - the upper graph for the CEEC consisting of the Czech Republic (CZ), Estonia (ES), Hungary (HU), Latvia (LA), Lithuania (LI), Poland (PO), the Slovak Republic (SK) and Slovenia (SL). The boxes are plotted around the lower and the upper quartile of the indicator distribution. The median is shown as a vertical bar through the boxes. Observations outside the quartiles are connected with the sides of the box by lines. As additional information the individual values of the indicator for each country in the group is shown graphically where countries are described by their international country abbreviation. Both graphs are vertically aligned and have the same tick units at the x-axis so the values can be visually easily compared. We will use this form of visualizing the data throughout the chapter.

What we see is that the size of the banking sector measured as the ratio of total assets to GDP differs considerably between the groups. The median size within the EU group is more than three and a half times larger than in the CEEC group. The largest banking sectors in the CEEC group are the sectors in the Czech and Slovak Republics. From the graph we see that the banking sectors within the EU group are not only larger on average but basically they are uniformly bigger in size.

A comparison of the ratio of domestic credit in percent of GDP, shown in Figure 10.2, yields a similar picture. It shows the relative difference in size between the EU and the banking sector of the accession countries. This figure closely resembles the basic message of the previous picture. The median ratio of domestic credit to GDP is roughly three times higher in the EU group than in the comparison group of the CEEC. The overall picture shows that as with the ratio of total assets to GDP the EU group has a uniformly larger banking sector.

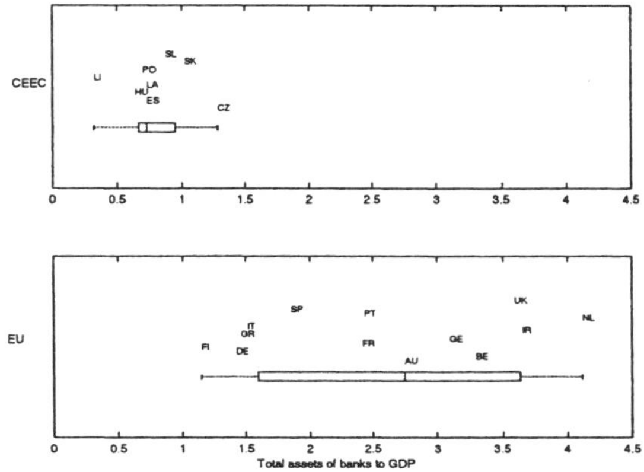

Source: IMF Financial Statistics, European Banking Federation.

Figure 10.1 Total assets of banks to GDP 2001

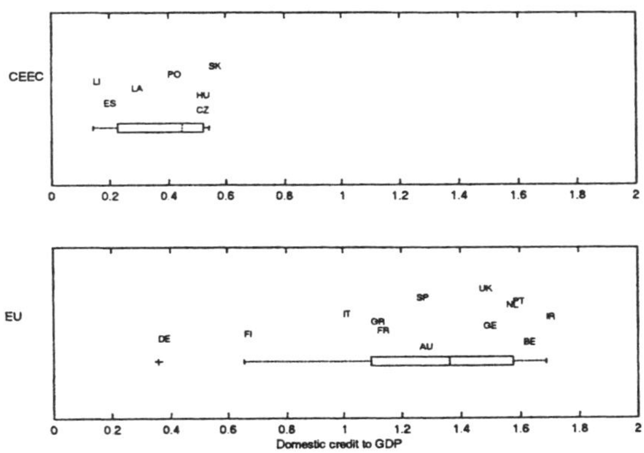

Source: IMF international financial statistics.

Figure 10.2 Domestic credit to GDP 2001

The Relative Size of Core Intermediation Business to Overall Banking Activities

The traditional banking business consists of granting loans that are predominantly financed by deposits. For instance Freixas and Rochet (1997) give the definition: “A bank is an institution whose current operations consist in granting loans and receiving deposits from the public”. These are the core intermediation activities and we can take a comparative look at banks in both groups also from this perspective. We can describe what is the role of loans on the asset side of the bank’s business and to what extent these activities are refinanced by deposits on the liability side.

In order to do so, we compare the ratio of loans and deposits to total assets. Since the loan figure comprises all loans and advances to resident and non-resident non-bank customers an additional useful piece of information is to look at the ratio of domestic credit to the private sector to total domestic credit, which gives a rough picture about the extent to which loans provide external finance to the domestic enterprise sector.

Beginning with the ratio of loans to total assets, shown in Figure 10.3, we see that both groups are not particularly different. The median of the ratio is about the same in both groups and loans constitute 40-60% of total assets in both groups.

On the liability side of the bank balance sheet we look at the ratio of deposits to GDP, which is displayed in Figure 10.4. The figure shows that the refinancing of banks by deposits plays a predominantly larger role in the CEEC group than in the EU group. The median in the CEEC group is about a factor of 1.5 higher than in the EU group. However the EU group does not show a clear pattern and we see considerable dispersion. This indicates that banks in the EU group seem to have access to a larger variety or refinancing opportunities besides of the traditional deposit business. After accession is completed this pattern might change fairly quickly. The overall picture shows that deposits have a share of 60-70% of total assets in the CEEC group whereas the EU group is characterized by a predominant share of deposits to total assets of roughly 35-55%.

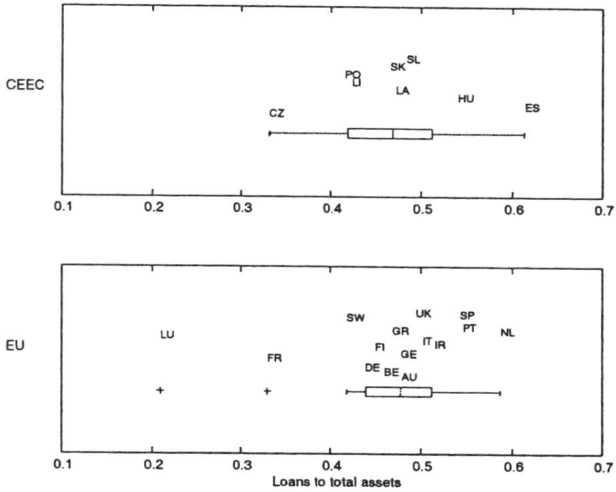

Sources: IMF Financial Statistics, European Banking Federation.

Figure 10.3 Loans to total assets

Some observers of financial transition have been concerned that intermediation is still stunted even in the most advanced group of accession countries, which is the group of countries analyzed in this chapter (see Fries and Taci, 2002). To get a rough figure to assess these concerns, let us have a closer look at the ratio of private domestic credit to total domestic credit, which is displayed in Figure 10.5. What we see in the picture is that both groups of countries look similar with respect to the median ratio of private domestic credit to total domestic credit. However a look at the whole distribution shows that there is more dispersion within the CEEC group.

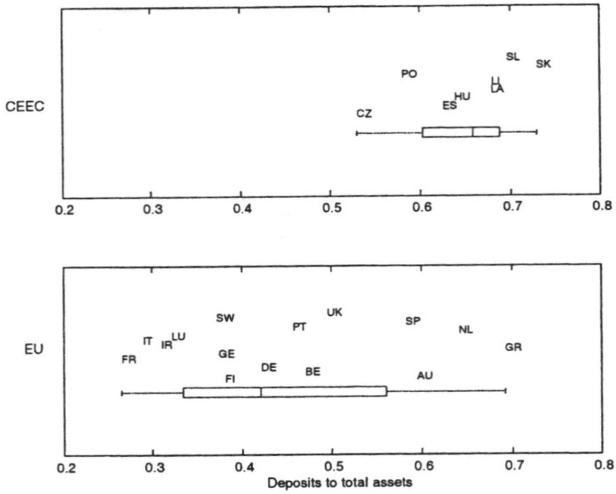

Sources: IMF Financial Statistics, European Banking Federation.

Figure 10.4 Deposits to total assets

Market Structure and Competition

Going to the issues of market structure and competition we first look at the margins banks can earn in their traditional intermediation business. The Figure 10.6 reported below shows the spreads between the lending and deposit rate for both groups. The median spread in the CEEC group is roughly one and a half times higher than in the EU group as a whole. However the variation is relatively huge within the EU group. The EU countries with the highest spread are close to the median of the CEEC group, while the two countries in the CEEC group with the lowest margins are almost at or below the EU group median. Measured by the lending-deposit rate spread the EU group is more competitive than the CEEC group.

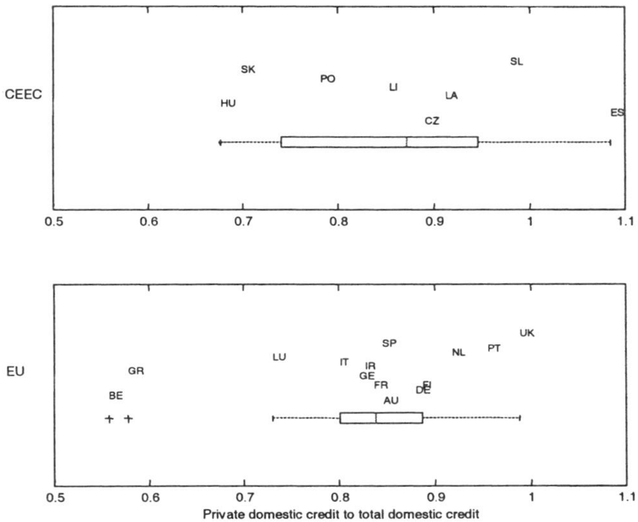

Sources: IMF Financial Statistics, European Banking Federation.

Figure 10.5 Private domestic credit to total domestic credit 2001

Complementing the picture by a measure of concentration, we display in Figure 10.7 the so-called five bank concentration ratio, which is reported in the World Bank Data. This ratio measures the share of total assets of the five largest banks. By looking at this ratio we can check whether the differences in spreads are reflected in differences in market power. The median concentration ratio is slightly higher in the CEEC group. The EU group shows however considerably more variation and has some countries with very low concentration ratio. In the CEEC group we find no country with a five bank concentration ratio of lower than 57%.

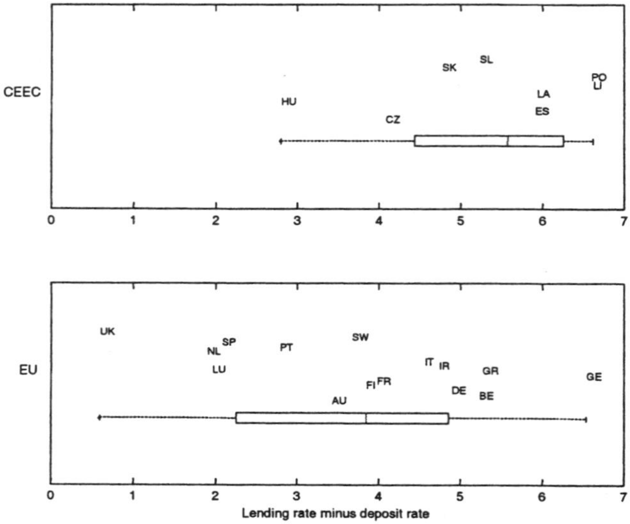

Source: IMF International Financial Statistics.

Figure 10.6 Difference between lending rate and deposit rate 2001

A considerable difference occurs when we look at foreign ownership in the banking sector. Data collected by the World Bank (Barth, et al. 2001) confirm observations that have been made in the literature, for instance by Caviglia, et al. 2002. Foreign ownership of banks plays a predominantly larger role in the CEEC group than in the EU group which is to the largest extent domestically owned. In Figure 10.8 we can see that the median of foreign ownership in banking assets is by a factor of ten higher in the CEEC group than in the EU accession group. Whereas the median of banks that are more than 50% foreign owned is 5% in the EU group, it is 48% in the CEEC accession group.

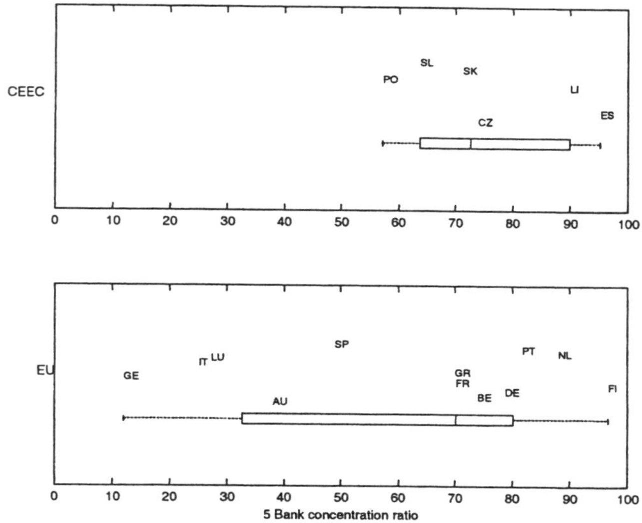

Source: World Bank.

Figure 10.7 Bank concentration ratio 2001

Finally we look at data about the extent to which banks are restricted in their activities to engage in securities underwriting, insurance and real estate investment and development suggested by Barth et al. (2001). Based on the answer to these questions a restrictiveness index is constructed ranging from unrestricted to fully restricted (Figure 10.9). The index gives a rough picture whether banks can act as classical universal banks or whether they have to confine themselves to particular lines of business.

The picture shows that the banking systems in both groups are pretty much identical. The median of the restrictiveness index is the same and the picture shows that banking systems in both groups may fairly be described as based on a model of universal banking.

To summarize our descriptive comparison of banking systems in the EU and the CEEC accession group we can say that the banking sector in the accession group is still comparatively small. Both groups are fairly close with respect to the share of loans in total assets. A comparison of the share in domestic private credit to total credit shows that the major part of loans goes to the private domestic sector. However some countries in the CEEC group seem to have a fairly large part of the loan business in government lending. On the liability side the banks in the CEEC group depend more strongly on deposits in their refinancing activities.

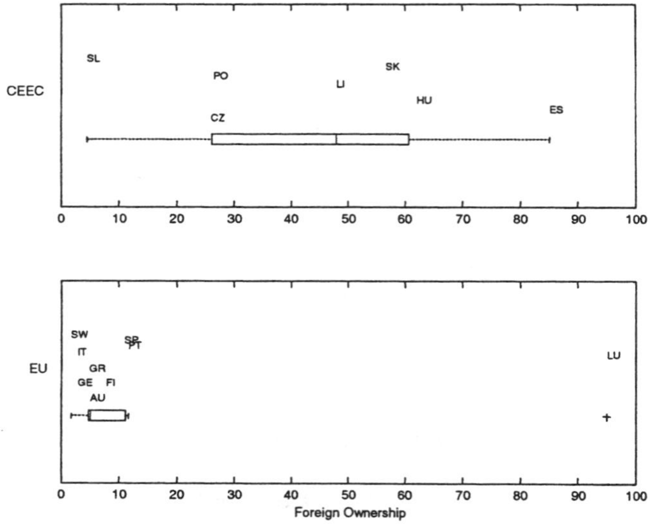

Source: World Bank.

Figure 10.8 Percentage of banking system's assets in banks that are 50% or more foreign owned

As measured by lending and deposit rate spreads the banking sector in the CEEC group is less competitive and has a slightly higher five bank concentration ratio than in the EU. The CEEC group has a fairly large share of foreign ownership in the assets of the banking system which is by a factor of ten higher than in the EU group where banking assets are predominantly domestically owned. Both systems are universal banking systems with comparatively few restrictions with respect to business they might undertake.

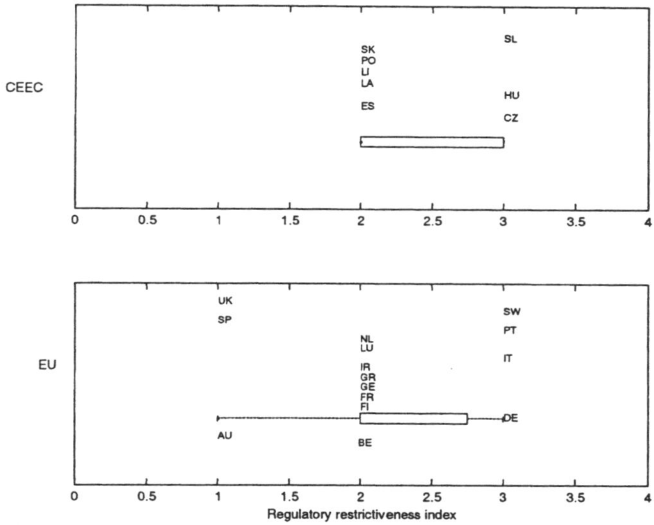

Source: World Bank.
Notes: Index ranges from 1 to 4 a higher index indicating higher restrictiveness. The detailed description of the index is in Barth et al. (2001).

Figure 10.9 Regulatory restrictiveness index

BANKING SUPERVISION IN THE EU AND THE CEEC

In this section we give a descriptive comparative account of banking supervision in both the EU and the CEEC countries. Our analysis is based on two independent sources. In the first instance we draw on the database on banking supervision around the globe, which has been collected by Barth, et al. (2001) at the World Bank. In the second instance we make an attempt to draw conclusions from the Peer Review Process in which we have been involved as experts for some of the countries.

Banking Regulation during the past two decades has moved successively towards establishing regimes of capital adequacy, risk management and supervisory standards and has moved away from regulations that restrict competition, business activities and entry into domestic banking markets. This focus is also reflected in the work of the Basel Committee on Banking Supervision. While the regulatory framework of the Bretton Woods area was mainly characterized by a regulatory regime that protected the domestic banking sector against competition, the process of financial globalization made such regulatory regimes successively more and more costly and most governments had to abandon these policies. What we have seen as a reaction to this process is the attempt to protect domestic depositors from the consequences of financial fragility and crises by an improved regime of prudential regulatory policies (for an analysis of this process see Rosenbluth and Schaap 2000). This is reflected in our approach to the comparative analysis of banking supervision in the EU and the CEEC. We will be concerned mainly with capital regulation, deposit insurance and the supervisory regime.

The World Bank Data

Capital regulation

Capital adequacy has been the focus of the regulatory debate during the past decade. The work of the Basel Committee on Banking Supervision has been mainly concerned in developing guidelines for a risk adequate capital regime for banks. Bank capital is supposed to reduce risk taking incentives and to play an important buffer role against shocks.

It is difficult to measure the stringency of capital regulation. Drawing on the work of Barth et al. (2001) we compare three alternative indicators. The first index, called the overall capital stringency index, measures the extent of regulatory requirements regarding the amount of capital banks have to hold relative to specific guidelines. A second index focuses on the funds that can be counted as regulatory capital and on the enforcement of the capital adequacy rules. Finally a third index aggregates the previous two into an overall capital regulatory index. We should perhaps point out that the theoretical rationale for capital adequacy regulation is still controversial as is the empirical evidence on its effectiveness. So what the description given below yields is just the relative position of the

EU and the CEEC group with respect to capital regulation as measured by the three indices of the World Bank.

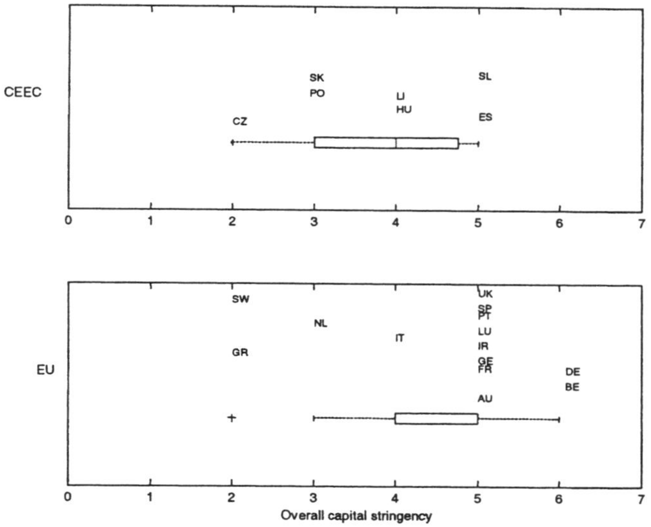

Source: World Bank.
Notes: The index tries to capture whether there are explicit regulatory requirements regarding the amount of capital that a bank must have relative to various guidelines. The index ranges from 0 to 6, a higher index indicating higher overall capital stringency. A detailed description can be found in Barth et al. (2001).

Figure 10.10 Overall capital stringency index

Beginning with the overall capital stringency index, shown in Figure 10.10, we see that the median in the EU group is about one rank above the CEEC group. Thus with respect to the amount of capital that has to be held according to various guidelines the EU group appears to be more stringent. In both groups we see however a considerable variation across different countries.

Turning to the sources of funds that can be counted as regulatory capital we compare the initial capital stringency index for both groups.

This index is shown in Figure 10.11. Here we also see that on average the EU appears to be more restrictive. However there seems to be considerable variation with three country clusters.

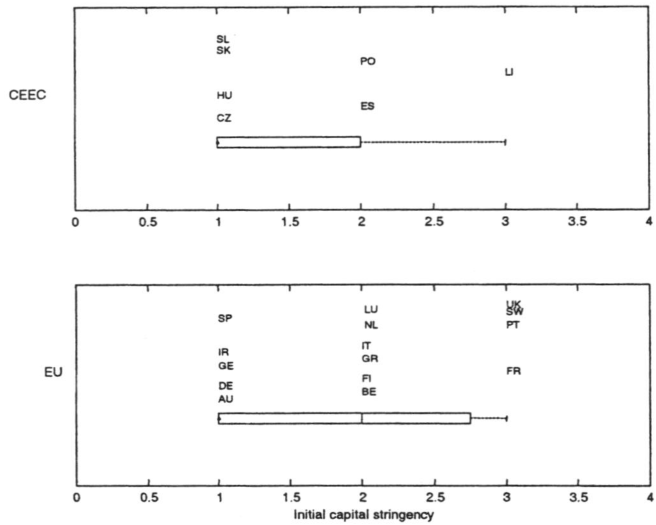

Source: World Bank.
Notes: Index tries to capture whether the source of finds counted as regulatory capital can include assets other than cash of government securities and borrowers as well as whether the sources are verified by the regulatory or supervisory authorities. For details see Barth et al. (2001).

Figure 10.11 Initial Capital Stringency.

Aggregation of both indices gives us an overall index for both groups shown in Figure 10.12. The aggregate index mirrors the results shown in the two subcomponents. The EU group median is higher than in the CEEC group but the variation in both groups is considerable.

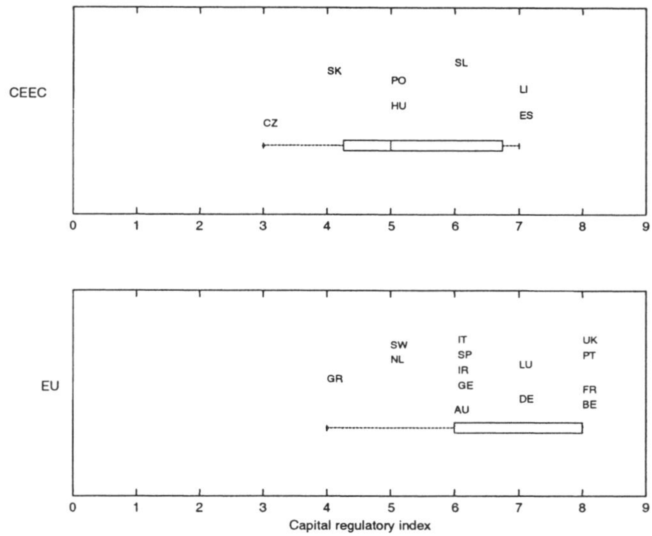

Source: World Bank.
Notes: Sum of previous initial capital stringency index and overall capital stringency index: Ranges from 0 to 9, a higher index indicating higher stringency. For details see Barth et al. (2001).

Figure 10.12 Capital Regulatory Index

Deposit insurance

Deposit insurance has become a standard element of bank regulatory regimes. Deposit insurance is an instrument of consumer protection against the adverse effects of financial fragility and crises that hit the banking system. From a theoretical point of view there is however also a stabilizing role of deposit insurance. This has been frequently emphasized in various papers following the classical work by Diamond and Dybvig (1983). Deposit insurance has a stabilizing role because it can prevent bank runs due to coordination failures by depositors that lead to a socially wasteful liquidation of assets.

Though deposit insurance has also been criticized on moral hazard grounds, since it might weaken the monitoring incentives of depositors, most developed countries have some form of deposit insurance regime in place. In the following we compare various indicators relating to the deposit insurance system between the two country groups.

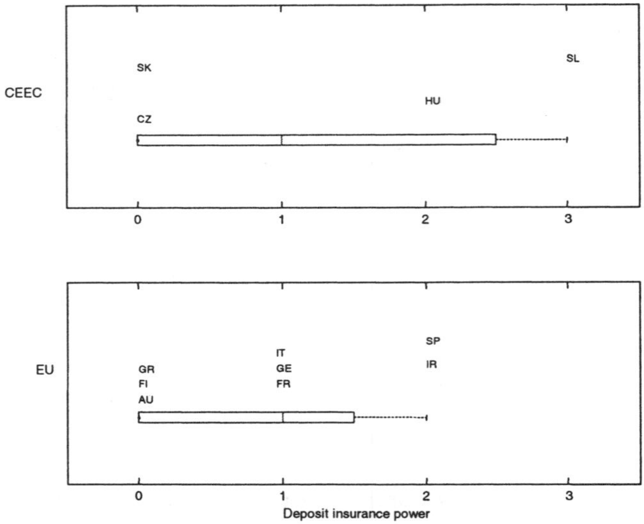

Source: World Bank.
Notes: Index ranges from 0 to 3 a higher index indicating higher deposit insurance power. For details see Barth et al. (2001).

Figure 10.13 Deposit insurance power

The first indicator compares the formal power of the deposit insurance agency to take disciplinary measures before a direct insurance case occurs. It is displayed in Figure 10.13. On average both groups do not differ in the disciplinary power assigned to the deposit insurance. Both groups show a fair amount of variation.The indicator "Insurance payout delay", which we see in Figure 10.14 shows the average time in months that it takes to pay depositors of a failed bank in full. Both groups rank equally in the median. But if we look at the variation in the index we see that the CEEC countries seem to have a quicker procedure. If we look at the size of the deposit insurance fund relative to total assets we see a fairly homogenous picture. The median relative size of the deposit insurance fund, as can be seen in Figure 10.15, is about the same size and both groups look quite homogenous, if we discard the two outliers in the EU group.

In conclusion the two country groups look relatively similar with respect to the deposit insurance variables. With respect to the average payout delay the CEEC group seems to outperform the EU group.

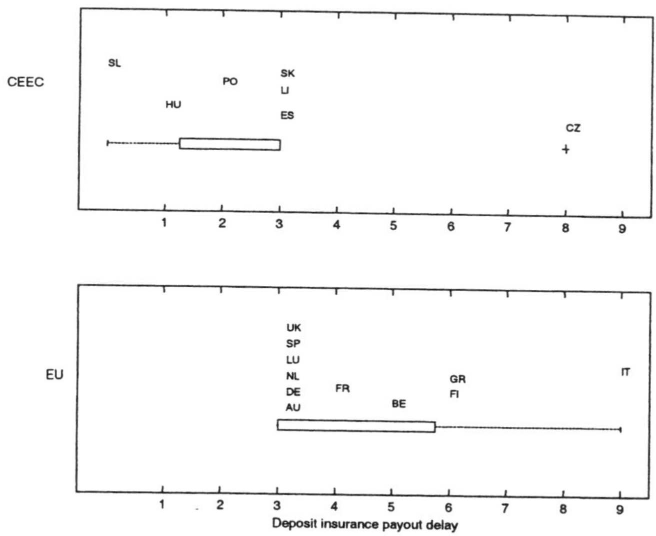

Source: World Bank.

Figure 10.14 Deposit insurance payout delay (in month)

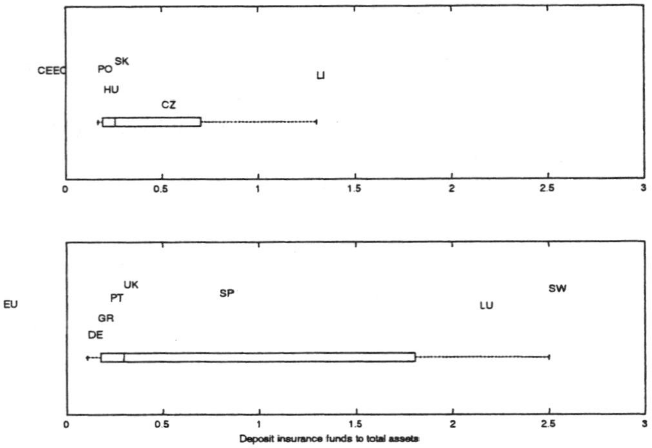

Source: World Bank.

Figure 10.15 Deposit insurance funds to total assets

Supervisory power and resources

Supervision is an important part in any system of prudential regulation. Usually there are two aspects to the official power. On the one hand we can look at the formal side of supervision, the legal rights given to supervisory authorities. On the other hand we can look at supervisory resources. Finally most countries are looking for a balance between official supervisory discipline and market discipline. In the following section we give an account of all three aspects of supervision.

The official supervisory power index suggested by Barth et al. (2001) measures the supervisory authority's ability to take specific actions and to correct problems. Details about the questions according to which the index is constructed are given in the Appendix.

The index shown in Figure 10.16 we see that the median of the official supervisory power index is about four ranks higher in the CEEC than in the EU. The individual values of the index suggest that in the CEEC group the legal scope for supervisory action seems to be higher. This might perhaps reflect that supervisory legislation was newly designed during the 1990s with the help of international advisors from various institutions who brought the experiences of recent international financial crises into the advisory process.

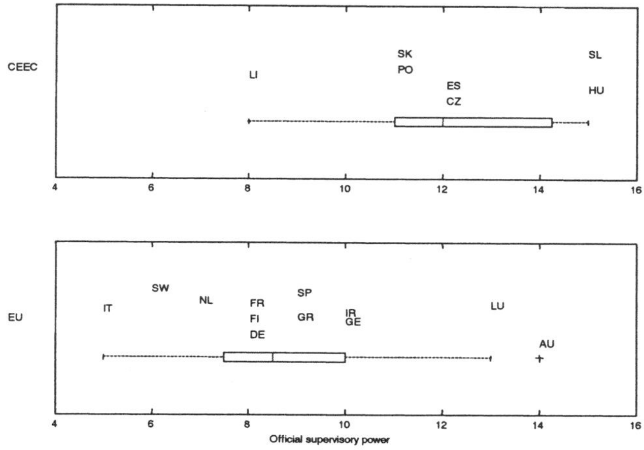

Source: World Bank.

Figure 10.16 Index ranges from 0 to 16 a higher index indicating greater official supervisory power

The official supervisory power index is basically composed of three subcomponents that measure the legal opportunities for prompt corrective action in case of solvency deterioration, of restructuring power by the supervisory authorities and the power to declare insolvency. The legal opportunities of supervisors have to be contrasted with the actual enforcement of supervisory rules and with the supervisory resources. As far as enforcement is concerned, Barth, et al. (2001) suggest an index of supervisory forbearance discretion. This index measures to what extent authorities may engage in forbearance when confronted with violations of laws or regulations or with other imprudent behavior on the part of banks. The index is shown in Figure 10.17.

Here both groups look similar in the median with a rank of three. The EU group in contrast to the CEEC has a relatively large number of countries with a low forbearance discretion index whereas the CEEC group has a relatively large group with a high index.

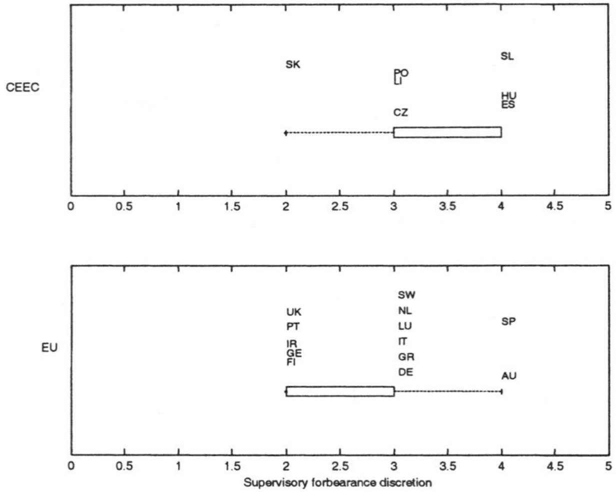

Source: World Bank.
Notes: Index ranges from 0 to 4 a higher index indicating higher supervisory forbearance discretion. For details see Barth et al. (2001).

Figure 10.17 Supervisory forbearance discretion

Going next to supervisory resources as measured by the number of professional bank supervisors per institution, shown in Figure 10.18, we see that both groups look fairly similar. The CEEC group has a slightly higher median than the EU group.

Finally we compare both groups with respect to the possibilities for private monitoring by looking at the private monitoring index suggested by Barth et al. (2001), shown in Figure 10.19. What we see from the data is that the EU group ranks higher in the median compared to the CEEC countries. The scope for private monitoring and discipline as compared to official supervisory discipline appears to be higher in the EU group.

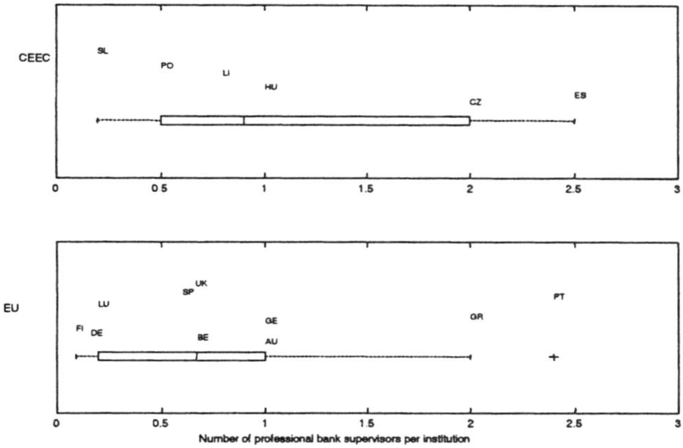

Source: World Bank.

Figure 10.18 Number of professional bank supervisors per institution

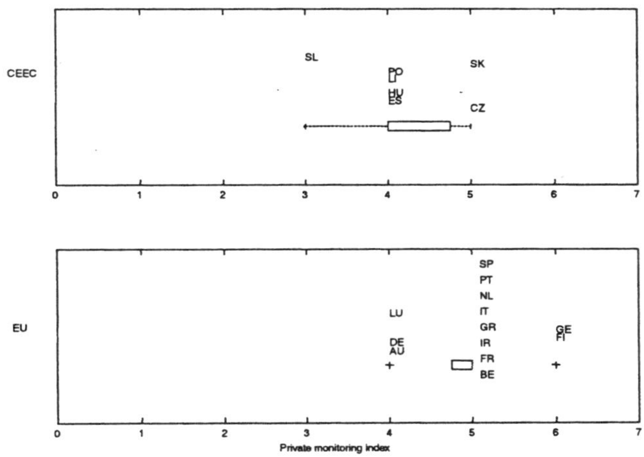

Source: World Bank.

Figure 10.19 Private Monitoring Index

Results from the Peer Review Process

During 2000 and 2002 the financial systems of accession countries were scrutinized by the European Commission by a so-called Peer Review Process. The idea of the Peer Review is that independent experts from EU supervisory authorities assess current practice in supervision of banking, insurance and securities markets.

The evaluation is based on meetings with experts in the countries, the analysis of information materials made available by the countries to the expert team. The expert teams give an assessment and usually also give recommendations for further necessary measures. In particular the Peer Review checks the progress that has been made with respect to compliance with the so-called Core Principles for Effective Banking Supervision made available by the Basel Committee. The Core principles were released in 1997 and have been endorsed by the G-10 central bank governors.

The core principles consist of 25 basic principles that relate to preconditions of effective banking supervision, licensing and structure, prudential regulations and requirements, methods of ongoing banking supervision, information requirements, the formal powers of supervisors and cross-border banking. In the following we give a general summary of the experience that has been gained in the Peer Review Process based on our own experience or on the experience of colleagues at other institutions that have been involved as experts. Since the documents of the Peer Review are confidential we can only give overall accounts of the findings and cannot discuss the individual countries. We think however that this summary information might be useful to complement the findings reached in the analysis of the World Bank data.

The general account of the Peer Review Process for the accession countries was that there has been uniformly substantial progress towards a regulatory framework that is in line with EU legislation and that regulatory standards to a huge extent are already in line with generally agreed principles of best practice.

For most countries shortcomings were identified mainly with respect to consolidated supervision and in the development of professional skills in supervision. In many countries in the CEEC group the assessments saw room for improving the coordination between supervisory bodies and with external auditors. Sometimes recommendations were issued to improve enforcement of regulatory and supervisory rules. The overall assessment however has been predominantly positive with the general view that convergence towards an agreed set of best practice principles in banking supervision has been largely achieved.

To conclude the lesson from the peer review we present statistics for an index measuring compliance with the Basel Core Principles. Drawing on the results of the Peer Review and also on results from the IMF FSAP we construct the Core Principles Compliance Index as follows.

For each principle there is an assessment whether the country is non-compliant, largely compliant or fully compliant. We assign for each assessment a numerical value of 0, 1 or 2 depending on the answer. The aggregate value gives the numerical value of the Core Principles Compliance Index with a range from 0 to 60. Figure 10.20 shows a box plot summarizing the distribution of the index for different assessments that took place between 2000 and 2002. Since the individual country reports are confidential we do not display individual country values.

The median of the compliance index is at a value of 39, which confirms the overall assessment reached in the Peer Review. There has been substantial progress towards large of full compliance with the Basel principles although the picture shows that there is a fair amount of variation between individual countries.

If we look at the distribution of the percentage of Core Principles that were assessed as non-compliant, shown in Figure 10.21, we see that in the group as a whole the median percentage is relatively low at 10 percent whereas there are individual countries which were still at a relatively high share of non compliance at the date of the assessment.

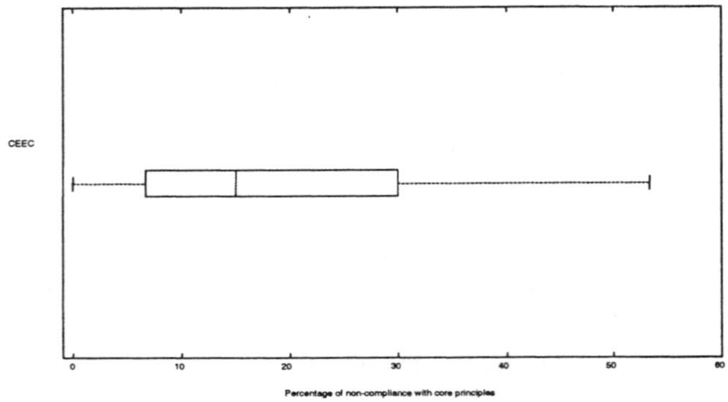

Source: OeNB.
Notes: Index ranges from 0 to 60 a higher index indicating higher compliance with core principles. For each principle a value of 0 is assigned if the country is not compliant, a value of one is assigned if the country is largely compliant and a value of 2 is assigned if the country is fully compliant.

Figure 10.20 Percentage of non compliance with core principles

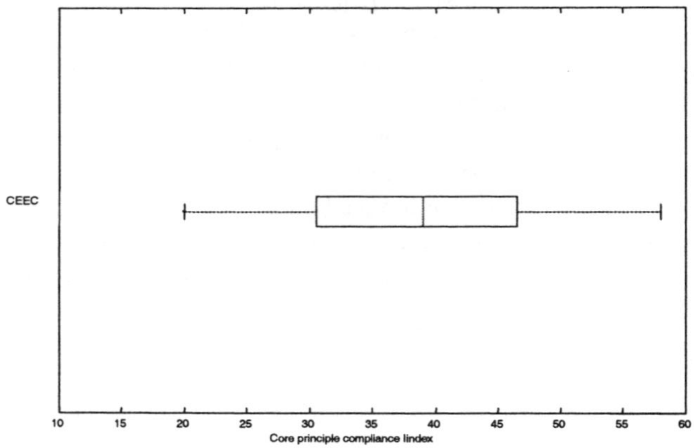

Source: OeNB

Figure 10.21 Percentage of non-compliance with Basel core principles

CONCLUSIONS

The comparative analysis of banking supervision and regulation in the CEEC and the EU reveals a high level of convergence. While both banking systems differ structurally mainly by size and the degree of foreign ownership such a clear pattern cannot be found with respect to supervision and regulation. The regulatory legislation that has been put in place shows a fairly high congruence with the Basel Core Principles and gives a high degree of official supervisory power to the authorities. With respect to most of the indices suggested by Barth et al. (2001), both groups look fairly similar on average with quite high intragroup variation.

REFERENCES

Allen, Franklin and Gale, Douglas (2000), *Comparing Financial Systems*, Cambridge Mass., MIT Press.

Barth, J., Caprio, G.and Levine, R. (2001) 'The Regulation and Supervision of Banking Systems Around the Globe: A New Database', Working Paper, World Bank.

Caviglia, G., Kruase, G. and Thimann, C. (2002), 'Key Features of the Financial Sectors in EU accession countries', in Thimann, C., (ed.), *Financial Sectors on EU Accession Countries*, European Central Bank, pp. 15-31.

Diamond, D. and Dybvig, P. (1983), 'Bank Runs, Deposit Insurance and Liquidity', *Journal of Political Economy*, **91**, 401–419.

Freixas, Xavier, Rochet, Jean Charles and Gale, Douglas (1997), *The Microeconomics of Banking*, Cambridge Mass., MIT Press.

Fries, S. and Taci, A. (2002), 'Banking Reform and Development in Transition Economies, Working Paper Nr. 71, EBRD.

Reininger, T., Schardax, F. and Summer, M. (2002), 'Financial System Transition in Central and Eastern Europe: The first Decade', *SUERF Studies*, 16.

Rosenbluth, F. and Schaap, R. (2000), 'The Domestic Policies of Financial Globalization', mimeo.

11. Single Authority in Financial Markets Supervision: Lessons for EU Enlargement[1]

Donato Masciandaro and Angelo Porta

INTRODUCTION

In this chapter we will present an analysis of recent trends in the architectures of financial supervision, focused on the Single Authority Model. This work can be useful for evaluating the European situation, from the perspective of the upcoming enlargement process.

The financial blurring process poses at least three questions in the debate on financial supervisory structure[2]: 1) sectoral (institutional) approach versus functional approach; 2) single supervisory model versus multi-authorities model, and 3) in the European Union, centralized setting versus decentralized setting.

It is a fact that, in the perspective of increasing financial integration, the relevance of the first question has been rapidly declining. Theoretically, the institutional approach is based on the possibility of separating the banking, securities and insurance markets. The progressive erosion of market separation is likely to cause the "default" of the institutional approach[3]. Institutionally, the above hypothesis that the financial blurring trend favors the alternative functional supervisory approach is confirmed by the fact that various models ("pure" or "mixed") of such an approach have been adopted recently or are currently under discussion in several countries.

From the other standpoint, in the European context[4], the centralized versus decentralized question seems to be 1) a second-order problem, given that alternative solutions are likely to be strictly dependent on the various European national answers or positions on the optimal design of the financial supervisory framework, and 2) closely linked to the answer to the single supervisory approach versus multi-authorities approach dilemma.

Today, therefore, given the dominance of the functional approach and the "deferred" nature of the centralized-decentralized questions, the alternative between the single financial authority (SFA) model and the multi-financial authorities (MFA) model seems to be the more relevant one, when the success of the SFA model seems to be growing, particularly in the European area. Among the 15 members of the European Union, Austria, Denmark, Germany, Sweden, and the UK have in fact chosen to delegate financial supervision to a single authority, different from the central bank. The single supervisor has been adopted also in four accession countries – Estonia, Hungary, Latvia, Malta – and in Norway and Iceland too. The chapter is organized as follows. Section two reviews the debate on the financial supervisory architecture, focusing on the single authority versus multi-authority dilemma. In section three a comparative analysis is performed, using institutional indicators of the degree of consolidation in the supervisory powers and of the level of the involvement of the central bank in the supervisory structure. After a general review of the possible determinants of the consolidation process, section four sheds light on the current trends in the EU area, with particular attention to the countries involved in the enlargement process. Section four puts forward some conclusions as well as perspectives for further research.

THE DIVISION OF POWER AMONG THE FINANCIAL SECTOR AUTHORITIES: REVIEW OF ALTERNATIVE MODELS

The intense evolution undergone by the financial system in recent years has gradually leveled many of the barriers between the component sectors of financial intermediation. The clear distinction among the three traditional sectors of activity (banks, securities markets and insurance) has become blurred as part of a process tending to unify the financial markets, caused by the gradual attenuation of functional specialization within the intermediaries operating in those markets.

This lowering of the traditional barriers separating the various sectors of activity has required a drastic rethinking of the procedures by which the powers supervision are exercised over the financial system. In particular, the problem of dividing the powers among the various financial sector authorities has become an increasingly critical issue. When the distinctions among the various sectors of financial activity were rather rigid, it was normal to attribute the control powers to a number of authorities, each specialized in a particular sector. In the current context, one wonders whether other forms of power division are possible other than those by sector, or whether it might not be better to assign all the powers to a single authority to oversee the entire financial system.

These aspects have been intensely debated in recent years, and we shall rapidly review the debate in this section. First, we shall examine the chief alternative models of division of tasks and present a simplified scheme that will assist us in understanding the problems caused by the leveling of the barriers separating the various compartments of the financial structure. The focus will then shift to the structure in which there is a single control authority with a discussion of the principal costs and benefits associated with that structure. The picture is completed by some remarks on the changes in the distribution of control power that have been introduced in the principal industrialized countries in recent years.

The Alternative Models

The problem of assigning power to the financial sector authorities is linked first to the differences just mentioned among the three principal *sectors* of financial activity (*banking systems, securities markets and insurance).* The sectors in question differ in many respects, and precisely because of their diversity the solution of assigning control over each sector to a different authority has long been viewed as the natural one within many legal systems. This solution continues to be practiced in many countries in spite of the leveling of sector barriers.

The problem is complicated by a second circumstance, i.e. the fact that the action of the control authorities is intended to serve a number of *objectives*. The purposes that can be assigned to financial supervision are numerous and do not lend themselves to schematic representation like that of the sectors.

With some simplification[5], however, we can discern at least four distinct objectives to which all the regimes attribute particular importance. The first purpose is *macroeconomic stability*, achieved by wielding the instruments of *monetary policy,* to pursue such objectives as supporting economic activity and controlling inflation. A second important purpose is to maintain *microeconomic stability:* the goal here is to ensure the solidity of the financial institutions and avoid crisis situations. A third purpose relates to market *transparency*, which is accomplished by ensuring adequate availability of information to the users of financial services. A final purpose concerns the pursuit of *efficiency* in the financial system.

The foregoing objectives are vastly different in nature, and achieving them may require procedures so different as to justify the assignment of each of the purposes to a different control authority.

The problem of the division of powers among the control authorities emerges in all its complexity when we jointly consider the aspects just examined. An intermingling is created, in fact, between the division of powers by sector and by objective that can result in highly differentiated schemes for the allocation of tasks among the authorities

To point up certain crucial aspects of this complex intermingling, we should start by analyzing a simplified case in which we consider only two sectors and two objectives ("2 x 2 scheme"). For the sectors, we shall omit insurance and concentrate on banking and the securities markets. For the objectives, we shall consider only microeconomic stability and transparency, leaving aside macroeconomic stability and efficiency.

The "2 x 2 scheme", in all its simplicity, lets us focus on the aspects that have received the greatest attention, both in the theoretical literature and in the debate of recent decades regarding the allocation of power to control authorities[6].

Within this scheme we can first identify a simple model that refers to the situation in which banking and securities activity are completely separate (*segmented structure*) and then move on to consider the problems that arise when an *integrated structure* is created, in which the barriers between banking and securities activities are lowered.

The segmented structure

When totally separate institutions conduct banking and securities activities, one can imagine a supervisory scheme in which the two institutions are subject to different types of control and where the controls are exercised by two separate authorities.

Underlying this structure (which we shall call *segmented*) is the conviction that banks present specific features with respect to institutions that operate in the securities markets. The particular nature of banks requires a more stringent oversight, accomplished by making it subject to a broad system of controls (limits on permitted activities, reserve obligations, balance sheet ratios, etc.) designed to ensure their *stability*. The diverse natures of banking and securities activities can also be illustrated by referring to the distinction between informed and uninformed saving. This distinction is based on the assumption that there is less awareness and information regarding the functioning and performance of the markets, as well as less propensity to risk by the persons who allocate their funds to bank deposits (*uninformed saving*) than those who utilize more sophisticated forms of saving, such and debt or equity securities (*informed saving*). For this latter type of saving, no particular form of protection is necessary, given the characteristics of the parties who utilize it: it is sufficient to ensure the availability of adequate information (*transparency*).

In the segmented structure there are two distinct control authorities with clearly specified powers (upper part of Table 11.1). The purpose of the authority responsible in overseeing the banking system (authority B) is to maintain its *stability*. The authority responsible for supervising the securities markets (authority S) is assigned the task of ensuring the transparency of those markets.

The integrated structure

The distribution of tasks among the control authorities is much more complicated when the separation between banking and the securities markets we have considered thus far disappears.

The barriers between the two sectors are eliminated, on the one hand, through the extension of bank operations into the field of securities and, on the other, by the expansion of the range of services offered to customers by non-banking financial institutions (which in some cases have extended their offering to instruments similar to bank deposits). To simplify the presentation, we shall limit our consideration in Table 11.1 to the case where the banking system extends its sphere of activity by adding "securities activity" to its normal "banking activity". This creates a *gray area* consisting of the securities activity conducted by the banking system, on which various divisions of tasks between the two control authorities are possible.

The lower part of Table 11.1 indicates the numerous options available, even in this simplified scheme, related to the division of powers between the authorities.

In particular, the table shows how complex the division of tasks can become if one assumes that *specialized authorities* continue to exist in this context of financial integration.

The tasks can be divided by *sector*, establishing that authority B will oversee all the activities in the banking system (including those in securities) and that authority S will supervise the securities markets (from the standpoints of both stability and transparency). This division of tasks presents the problem that it is based on an institutional distinction that is losing significance due to current developments in the financial markets. Another problem presented by this division is that it requires the authorities forced to deal with issues for which they lack specific expertise.

Another way to divide the tasks is based on the type of activity conducted, regardless of the sector to which the institution belongs (division by *function)*. In this case authority B's control responsibilities are limited to banking activities other than those related to securities, while authority S is responsible for controlling the securities-related activities of both banks and securities intermediaries (for purposes of stability and transparency).

Then there is the possibility of dividing supervision by *objective.* One might imagine that one authority (authority B, for example) is empowered for controls related to stability for all intermediaries (including securities intermediaries) and that the other authority is responsible for controls linked to *transparency*.

These last two modes of allocating the powers reflect the integration among the various segments of the financial markets and offer positive aspects, since they exploit the institutional expertise of the two control agencies (especially in the case of division by *objective)*. The two structures in question may also involve high costs of implementation. Particularly in the case of allocation by objective, both the control authorities must extend their activities outside the financial market segment to which their attention was traditionally reserved. From the standpoint of the parties controlled, the presence of two different supervisors may generate rather onerous control systems.

Table 11.1 The division of powers among control authorities in the "2 x 2 scheme"

A. Segmented structure

	Banking system	Securities markets
Stability	B	
Transparency		S

B. Integrated structure

a) Independent specialized supervisor

a.1) Division of power by sector

	Banking system		Securities markets
	Banking activity	Securities activity	
Stability	B	B	S
Trasparency	B	B	S

a.2) Division of power by function

	Banking system		Securities markets
	Banking activity	Securities activity	
Stability	B	S	S
Transparency		S	S

a.3) Division of power by objective

	Banking system		Securities markets
	Banking activity	Securities activity	
Stability	B	B	B
Transparency		S	S

b) Single Supervisor

	Banking system		Securities markets
	Banking activity	Securities activity	
Stability	U	U	U
Transparency		U	U

Notes: B = authority specialized in the banking system; S = authorities specialized in the securities markets; U = single authorities for all sectors.

These problems of task allocation disappear is we assume the existence of a *single authority* (U) empowered to control all the sectors and pursue all the purposes.

The Single Financial Authority: Costs and Benefits

The principal advantage of a single authority lies precisely in the fact that it avoids the complex issues associated with the allocation of tasks. In a more detailed analysis, the benefits that the use of a single authority brings can be better identified in the aspects indicated below[7].

The use of a single authority may result in economies of scale and scope, especially where various operating divisions can be created. The economies of scale and scope may derive from the fact that the single authority can benefit from a centralized operating unit, with benefits from the standpoint of human resources, information systems, etc. Furthermore, it avoids the useless multiplication of costs associated with the existence of multiple supervisory authorities. The presence of a single authority may also lead to a reduction in costs of information coordination and sharing of information, because cooperation and interchange can be better ensured among the various supervisory sectors. The costs associated with supervision can generally be reduced.

There can be significant benefit (in terms of efficiency) for the supervised parties, who need deal with only a single interlocutor, especially regarding authorization procedures. Also for the supervised parties, avoiding the multiplication of costs and obligations toward a number of authorities may result in benefits in terms of efficiency and reduction of supervision-associated costs. All ambiguities regarding tasks – who exercises supervision and is responsible for each procedure – are eliminated.

Another advantage of the single authority is that it may reduce the risks of arbitrage in supervision and the risks of competition among the various sectors of the financial system, ensuring greater neutrality of regulation through the harmonization (or even unification) of the sector regulations.

The single authority model also presents problems and potential risks. According to some authors[8], the cost advantages associated with a single authority are not necessarily true, since the single authority compromises specialized divisions that may themselves be affected by problems of coordination, information interchange, etc. It seems unlikely, however, that the costs of information coordination and sharing sustained by the various divisions of a centrally managed authority could exceed the costs associated with cooperation between different authorities[9].

One possible argument against the single authority is its potentially higher profile. This model of supervision could be associated with the idea, not necessarily true, of a totally secure financial system, an idea that would reduce the incentives for the supervised parties to have operating systems based on prudence and would relax the caution of consumers–investors toward the financial services offered[10].

A further argument against the single authority refers to the fact that the "institutional failure" of such an authority, since it is active in several sectors, would generate broader negative effects.

THE DEGREE OF CONCENTRATION OF POWER IN FINANCIAL SUPERVISION

The preceding section made it manifestly evident that the quest for an optimal degree of concentration of powers in financial supervision cannot be pursued through a simple analysis of the costs and benefits expected from the possible alternative structures.

If, in fact, one proposes to compare the two alternative models – a single authority versus a system with multiple agencies – one realizes that each of them offers expected benefits, but also expected risks. So a theoretical analysis of the *potential effects* of alternative supervisory structures does not take us very far.

The first natural response to this problem would therefore be to estimate the *real* effects the two alternative supervisory models have on key economic variables. But this immediately fosters at least three orders of difficulty.

Firstly, as evidenced in the preceding section, the emergence of a single authority is only the most striking aspect of a more general and gradual phenomenon: diversification, from country to country, in the degree of centralization of financial supervisory power. What has occurred is that, compared to the traditional model of control by sectors, some countries have confirmed that model, others have radically changed it by adopting a single authority, while others have taken or confirmed intermediate choices. This raises the problem of measuring the degree of concentration of powers, country by country, in order to attempt the quantitative description of a qualitative phenomenon. Hence the first objective of the research agenda is to improve the *descriptive* analysis.

Secondly, the issue of the optimal degree of concentration of financial supervisory powers has emerged only recently[11], with the reforms adopted in various countries, so considering the type of supervisory regime as an explicative or *exogenous* (though not unique) variable of any other economic phenomenon means undertaking an analysis of extremely short historical series, with all the related problems of interpretation.

Thirdly, completely and satisfactorily identifying what the key economic variables are, and the most possible object of an estimate, on which a supervisory structure makes it effect felt, is not a simple problem. As already underscored in the preceding section, alternative supervisory structures may, for example, affect the level of efficiency of the public resources invested in monitoring the financial markets. Indicators can be found for the efficiency phenomenon, and empirical analysis can therefore proceed.

The point is that alternative structures may also (perhaps especially) affect other variables that are important but less easily expressed in concise indicators. Examples are reputation risk, or the risk that the authority will be captured by the policymakers or by the controlled intermediaries.

Thus a quantitative search for the effects of alternative supervisory structures is probably premature[12]. It might be interesting, rather, to ask: are there any common determinants in the decision each country makes to maintain or reform its control structure? Finding a response would help us not only to interpret what has happened in the past but also to project scenarios of change for the future, with a particular focus on prospects within the European Union.

Thus the second objective of the research agenda – that we pursue in this chapter – is to attempt to concentrate on an analysis of the *causes* that have helped bring about a given supervisory structure in the countries involved in the EU enlargement process.

Our analysis will is consistent with a political delegation approach to the supervisory design[13]. The approach we intend to follow here – extending the indication that the new political economy[14] has formulated in analysing the definition of public policies – is to consider the supervisory structure with one or more authorities as a dependent variable, determined in turn by the dynamics of other structural variables, economic and institutional, that can summarize and explain the *political* process that leads a country to maintain or reform its supervisory structure.

A country confirms or reforms its supervisory structure when its policymakers decide it is advisable to do so. While we do not believe that policymakers are always and ever benevolent dictators, nor do we wish to exclude this *a priori*, we can assume that these decisions are generally determined, in turn, by structural factors of a financial, economic and institutional nature. The search for these factors is a task for economic analysis.

The Measurement of the Degree of Financial Supervision Concentration

If, therefore, we wish to consider the financial supervision regime as a dependent variable, the first problem is to construct this variable. The question is: how to "measure" the degree of concentration of financial powers[15]?

To this end we use a Financial Authorities Concentration Index (FAC Index)[16]. The creation of the index is based on an analysis of which and how many authorities in 69 countries are empowered to supervise the three traditional sectors of financial activity: banking, securities markets, insurance. To transform the qualitative information into quantitative indications, to gauge the degree of consolidation of each specific regime of national supervision, it has been assigned a numerical value to each type of authorities design, according to the following scale:

- 7 = Single authority for all three sectors (total number of supervisors = 1);
- 5 = Single authority for the banking sector and securities markets (total number of supervisors = 2);
- 3 = Single authority for the insurance sector and the securities markets, or for the insurance sector and the banking sector (total number of supervisors=2);

- 1 = Independent specialized authority for each sector (total number of supervisors = 3).

The rationale with which the values have been assigned considers the concept of concentration of supervisory powers: the greater the concentration, the higher the index value.

It has been elected to assign a value of 5 to the single supervisor for the banking sector and securities markets because of the predominant importance of banking intermediation and securities markets over insurance in every national financial industry. It is also interesting to note that, in the group of integrated supervisory agencies' countries, there seems to be a higher degree of integration between banking and securities supervision than between banking and insurance supervision[17]; therefore, the degree of concentration of powers is, ceteris paribus, greater[18].

These observations do not, however, weigh another qualitative characteristic: different countries are characterized by the fact that one sector is supervised by more than one authority.

It is likely that, other conditions being equal, when two control authorities exist in a given sector, one of which has other powers in a second sector, the degree of concentration of power is greater. When, on the other hand, there are two control authorities in a given sector, neither of which has other powers in a second sector, the degree of concentration is diminished, because the total number of supervisors increases.

It would therefore seem advisable to include these aspects in evaluating the various national supervisory structures by modifying the index as follows:

- adding 1 if in the country there is at least one sector with two authorities assigned to supervision, and one of these authorities is also responsible for at least one other sector;
- subtracting 1 if in the country there is at least one sector with two authorities assigned to supervision, but none of these authorities has responsibility for another sector;
- 0 elsewhere.

Lastly, there are three qualitative characteristics of supervision regimes that we have decided not to consider in constructing the index.

Firstly, the nature of the authorities involved in the financial supervision setting has not been considered. In particular, in several countries it is the central bank – i.e. the authority responsible for monetary policy – that is responsible for at least one of the three sectors considered, typically the supervision of the banking industry. The attribution of supervisory power to the central bank has been at the centre of an intense theoretical and institutional debate over the past decade[19], which in analogy with the problem discussed here has come to no general conclusions, perhaps for the same methodological reasons illustrated earlier.

Furthermore, we have not considered the legal nature – public or private – of the supervisory agencies, nor their relationships with the political system (degree of independence, level of accountability, etc.)

Therefore the index captures the degree of concentration of financial supervisory power regardless of the nature of the institutions involved in this process, i.e. stressing just the importance of the number of supervisors involved. The role of the nature of the authorities is considered later on, when we shall deal with the role of the central bank in the overall architecture of financial controls[20].

Secondly, at least in each industrial country, there is an authority to protect competition and the market, with duties that impinge on the financial sectors. But, since it is a factor common to all the structures, we have decided not to take the antitrust powers into account in constructing the index[21].

The FAC Index for the 69 countries is shown in Table 11.2. The analysis of Table 11.2 lends itself to some comments. Let us first consider the current member states of the Union[22]: we note that six countries out of 15 (Austria, Denmark, Germany, Ireland, Sweden and the UK), equal to 40% of the total sample, reach the maximum level of FAC Index, while the average level of this index is 4.4. The level of the consolidation process is more or less the same in the European Union sample and in the European industrialized countries sample, given that the composition of the two samples is quite similar.

Secondly, let us analyze the countries involved in the 2004 enlargement process. We note that four countries out of 10[23] (Estonia, Latvia, Malta and Hungary), equal to 40% of the total sample, reach the maximum level of FAC Index, while the average level is 3.5. As a consequence, comparing the current EU member states with those aspiring to join, the latter show on average a lower level of concentration but an equal number of single financial authorities.

Lastly, if we consider also the three countries involved in the 2007 enlargement process[24], in the sample of the 13 accession countries we find that the countries at the maximum level of the FAC Index represent 30% of the total, while the average level is 2.9. Thus, compared to the current EU situation, we would have a lower degree of concentration of powers.

The Measurement of the Degree of Central Bank Involvement

At this point, we should also consider the nature of the institutions involved in the supervision responsibilities. Any supervisory regime has to provide a link between the supervision and the central bank, given the potential relationships between monetary stability and financial stability[25]. It has been correctly pointed out[26] that, irrespective of what role, if any, assigned to the central bank with respect to the prudential supervision, it is universally the case that the central bank must be the authority for the stability of the payment system, liquidity assistance to markets and solvent institutions, and systemic stability. The debate of the optimal characteristics of this link is particular important in the European Union, where monetary policy is separated from financial supervision[27].

Therefore we must ask what role the central bank plays in the various national institutional structures[28]. Focusing on the degree of involvement the central bank has in financial supervision as a whole can be immediately explained with the specific nature of that institution with respect to the others, since in every country it is the authority responsible for monetary policy and for the stability of the payment system.

So, to highlight that role, we use an index of the central bank's involvement in financial supervision: the Central Bank as Financial Authority Index (CBFA Index)[29]. For each country, and given again the three main possible financial sectors (banking, securities and insurance) the index is[30]:

- 1= the central bank has no responsibility in any sector[31];

- 2 = the central bank has responsibility in one sector;
- 3 = the central bank has responsibility in two sectors;
- 4 = the central bank has responsibility in all three sectors.

Therefore, each national supervisory regime can be identified with at least two characteristics: the degree of concentration of powers (FAC Index) and the degree of involvement of the central bank in that distribution of powers (CBFA Index) (Table 11.2).

Also regarding the central bank involvement the analysis of Table 11.2 lends itself to some comments[32]. Let us first consider the current member states of the Union: the level of the central bank involvement is higher in the European Union sample (1.93) than the European industrialized countries sample (1.69).

Secondly, let us analyze the countries involved in the 2004 enlargement process: the average CBFA Index is 1.50. If we consider also the three countries involved in the 2007 enlargement process, in the sample of the 13 accession countries we find that the average level of the index is 1.53. Therefore comparing the current EU member states with those aspiring to join, the latter show on average a lower level of central bank involvement. In general the differences in the degree of central bank involvement (20%) seems to be lower than the differences in the degree of financial supervision consolidation (34%).

Table 11.2 CBFA INDEX & FAC INDEX in 69 countries (year 2002)

	Countries	CBFA Index	FAC Index
1	Albania	2	1
2	Argentina	2	1
3	Australia	1	6
4	Austria	1	7
5	Belarus	2	1
6	Belgium	1	5
7	Bosnia	2	0
8	Brazil	3	2
9	Bulgaria	2	1
10	Canada	1	3
11	Chile	1	3

12	Colombia	1	3
13	Croatia	2	1
14	Cyprus	2	1
15	Czech Republic	2	1
16	Denmark	1	7
17	Ecuador	1	3
18	Egypt	2	1
19	Estonia	1	7
20	Finland	1	5
21	France	3	1
22	Georgia	2	1
23	Germany	1	7
24	Greece	2	1
25	Hong Kong	2	1
26	Hungary	1	7
27	Iceland	1	7
28	India	2	0
29	Ireland	4	7
30	Israel	2	2
31	Italy	3	2
32	Jamaica	2	3
33	Japan	1	7
34	Jordan	2	1
35	Latria	1	7
36	Lithuania	2	1
37	Luxembourg	1	5
38	Macedonia	2	1
39	Malaysia	3	3
40	Malta	1	7
41	Mauritius	2	3
42	Mexico	1	5
43	Moldova	2	1
44	Netherlands	3	2
45	New Zealand	2	1
46	Norway	1	7
47	Pakistan	3	4

48	Peru	1	3
49	Philippines	3	2
50	Poland	1	1
51	Portugal	3	2
52	Romania	2	1
53	Russia	2	1
54	Singapore	4	7
55	Slovak Republic	2	2
56	Slovenia	2	1
57	South Africa	2	3
58	South Korea	1	7
59	Spain	3	1
60	Sri Lanka	2	1
61	Sweden	1	7
62	Switzerland	1	5
63	Thailand	2	1
64	Trinidad and Tobago	2	1
65	Tunisia	2	1
66	Turkey	1	1
67	UK	1	7
69	Ukraine	2	1
69	USA	2	0

The Determinants of the Financial Supervision Concentration

The descriptive analysis conducted in the preceding pages claims that each country has its index of concentration of powers of financial supervision, which reaches its maximum level in cases where there is a single authority and the minimum when there are more than three supervisors.

Now we are spontaneously prompted to ask: can common determinants be found in the decisions the policymakers in each country have made in recent years to maintain or reform their supervisory structures?

Our response is precisely to regard the supervisory structure with single or multiple authorities as a dependent variable, determined in turn by the dynamics of other structural, economic and institutional variables, which can summarize and explain the *political* process that leads the policymakers in one country to decide to maintain or reform its supervisory regime.

What are the structural variables that can explain the decisions of national policymakers? Policymakers can decide the architecture of controls on the basis of *institutional* characteristics and of the *economic* and *financial* characteristics of their country. In particular, we can assume that the physiognomy of the institutional system, and that of the banking and financial system, are relevant in each country. And having identified in the above section a possible relevance of the role the central bank plays in the supervisory regime, it may be interesting to consider this aspect as well.

To assess the relationship between the policymakers' decisions to determine the financial architecture, and given country economic and institutional characteristics, we can estimate a model of the probability of different regime decisions as a function of these structural variables.

In fact the supervisory regimes can be viewed as resulting from a continuous, unobserved variable: the *optimal degree of financial supervisors' concentration*. Each regime corresponds to a specific range of the optimal financial supervisors' concentration, with higher discrete FAC values corresponding to a higher range of financial concentration values. Since the FAC Index is a qualitative ordinal variable, the estimation of a model for such a dependent variable necessitates the use of a specific technique.

Our qualitative dependent variable can be classified into more than two categories, given that the FAC Index is a polychotomous variable. But the FAC Index is also an ordinal variable, given that it reflects a ranking. Then the ordered multinomial model can be use for estimation in a context of an ordinal polychotomous variable[33].

Let assume the unobserved continuous variable, the optimal degree of financial supervisors' concentration, y^*, is a linear function of a set of explanatory variables x, with parameter vector β, and an error term ε:

$$y^* = \beta' x + \varepsilon$$

As usual, y^* is unobserved. What is observed is the choice of every policymaker to maintain or to reform the financial supervisory architecture: this choice is summarized in the value of the FAC Index. Given that the FAC Index ranges from 0 to 7:

$$y = 0 \ \text{if}\ y^* \leq \mu 1$$

$$y = 1 \ \text{if}\ \mu 1 \leq y^* \leq \mu 2$$

$$\dots \ \dots$$

$$y = 7 \ \text{if}\ \mu 7 \leq y^*$$

The μs are unknown partition boundaries (or cut points) that define the ranges of the FAC Index; these parameters must be estimated in conjunction with the β vector. Estimation proceeds by maximum likelihood, assuming that ε is normally distributed across countries' observations, and the mean and variance of ε are normalized to 0 and 1. This model can be estimated with an ordered Probit model or with a ordered Logit model[34].

We have produced an econometric analysis of the Probit and Logit types: the dependant variable is the FAC Index, while the independent regressors proved are a broad set of economic, financial and political variables, based both on our own assessment of variables that could play a significant role in explaining the financial regime, and on data availability. The selected sample is the broader one, represented by 68 countries[35].

As has been claimed above, no theory exists on the relationships between politics and financial supervisory architecture. Therefore we try to test the more general hypotheses.

Firstly, the policymaker choices made with a view to maintaining or to reforming the financial supervisory architecture could be depended on the structure of the financial systems itself. In the modern debate on financial structure, it is usual to confront the equity dominance model (or *market based regime*) with the bank dominance model (or *bank based regime*). Furthermore, recent literature points out the close relationship, in every country, between the financial structure model and corporate governance model, with particular attention to the relative political determinants[36]. Therefore, the first relevant question is: does the financial structure model (i.e. the private governance model), the *private governance factor*, matter in defining the policy- maker choices on the level of concentration in the supervisory structure?

The expected sign of the relationship between the degree of supervision consolidation and the private governance factor is undermined. In section two we stressed the importance of the blurring process for the banking and the financial market worldwide. The blurring process means potential changes in the nature and in the dimensions of intermediaries (the *financial conglomerates effect*). In a bank based regime, if we think that the policymakers' choices depend on the features of their own regime, we can suppose a positive relationship between the kind of regime and the degree of financial supervision consolidation, in the face of the financial conglomerates effect. At the same time, however, the blurring effects mean potential changes in the nature and in the dimensions of the financial markets (the *securitization effects)*. Therefore, also in a market based regime, we can expect a positive relationship between the kind of regime nature and the degree of financial supervision consolidation, in the face of the securitization effect.

Secondly, the institutional environment (i.e. the public governance climate) determines the ability of the policymakers to implement their choices. Then the second relevant question is: does the quality of the public governance (*public governance factor*) matter in defining the policymaker choices on the level of concentration in the supervisory structure?

Also, the expected sign of the relationship between the degree of supervision consolidation and the public governance factor is undermined. In section two we note that a policymaker, whatever is the financial regime of his country, can choose a higher degree of consolidation in order to improve the capacity to face the challenges proposed by the blurring process. Then we can suppose a positive relationship between good governance indicators and financial supervision consolidation. But, at the same time, a policymaker can prefer a single financial agency in order to increase his probability of capturing the supervisory structure. Therefore we could also expect a positive relationship between bad governance indicators and the financial supervision consolidation.

Finally, given the above descriptive analyzes, we conclude our search for the explanatory variables by using the CBFA Index. The political choice of the optimal level of financial supervisors' concentration could be dependent on the role of the central bank in the financial architecture. The third relevant question is: does the degree of central bank presence (*central bank factor*) in the financial supervision matter in defining the level of concentration in the supervisory structure? Given the descriptive analysis developed above and the two possible explanations – the *blurring hazard effect* and the *monopolistic bureau effect*[37] – the expected sign of the relationship between central bank involvement and financial supervision consolidation is negative.

We obtained the Equation (11.1) as best specification:

$$\begin{aligned}(FAC)_i = \beta_1 + \beta_2(CBFA)_i + \beta_3(MvBdum)_i + \beta_5(mcap)_i + \\ + \beta_6(goodgov)_i + \varepsilon_t \\ \text{with country } \; i = 1, \ldots, 68 \qquad (11.1)\end{aligned}$$

where the independent variables are the following:

1. CBFA Index is the indicator of involvement of the bank in supervision, defined in the above section;
2. MvBdum Index (Market vs. Bank Index): is a structural indicator (dummy) that expresses the financial system model of a given country, market based versus bank based, constructed on the basis of the indices created by Demigüç-Kunt and Levine[38].
3. mcap = Market capitalization/GDP[39] shows a measure of the securities market size, relative to the GDP.
4. goodgov = Good Governance, which shows the structural capacity of the government to formulate and implement sound policies. The index is build using all the indicators proposed by Kaufmann et al. (2003)[40]. They define (public) governance as the exercise of authority through formal and informal traditions and institutions for the common good, thus encompassing: 1) the process of selecting, monitoring and replacing governments; 2) the capacity to formulate and implement sound policies and deliver public services, and 3) the respect of citizens and the state for the institutions that govern economic and social interactions among them. Furthermore, for measurement and analysis purposes, these three dimensions of governance can be further unpacked to comprise two measurable concepts for each of the dimensions

above for a total of six components: 1) voice and external accountability; 2) political stability and lack of violence; 3) government effectiveness; 4) lack of regulatory burden; 5) rule of law, and 6) control of corruption. The authors present a set of estimates of these six dimensions of governance for four time periods: 1996, 1998, 2000, 2002. For every country, therefore, we calculate first the mean of the four time values for each dimension of governance; then we build up an index of global good governance in the period 1996-2002, calculating the mean of the six different dimensions.

The estimation results of Equation (11.1) are reported in the first column, Table 11.3. The second column of Table 11.3 reports the estimation results of the same Equation (11.1) using an ordered Logit model. Note that the impact of a change in an explanatory variables on the estimated probabilities of the highest and lowest of the order classifications – in our case the Single Authority model and the "pure" Multi Supervisory model – is unequivocal: if βj is positive, for example, an increase in the value of xj increases the probability of having the Single Authority model, while decreasing the probability of having the "pure" Multi Supervisory model.

These first econometric results seem interesting. The probability that a country will move toward a Single Authority model is higher: 1) the lower the involvement of the central bank in these powers; 2) the smaller the financial system[41]; 3) the more equity-dominated the private governance model, and 4) the more the public governance is good. Now, how should the empirical results be interpreted?

The empirical analysis, firstly, seems to suggest that the choices of the policymaker in terms of "whom" to delegate the supervisory policy to are closely linked to those regarding "how many" institutions to delegate, according to an inverse relationship. In particular, the more the central bank is involved in financial supervisory powers, the lower the degree of unification of those powers is likely to be[42]. The first econometric analysis confirms the descriptive trade off between supervision consolidation and central bank involvement, that can be explained by the existence of a blurring hazard effect, and/or a monopolistic bureau effect.

Table 11.3 Ordered probit and logit estimates

Variables	Probit	Logit
Dependent variable	FAC	FAC
CBFA		
Coefficient β_2	-0.65	-1.32
Std. Error	(0.19)	(0.39)
P>z	0.00***	0.00***
MvBdum		
Coefficient β_3	0.73	1.48
Std. Error	(0.37)	0.67
P>z	0.04*	0.02*
mcap		
Coefficient β_5	-0.59	-1.00
Std. Error	(0.26)	(0.45)
P>z	0.02**	0.02**
goodgov		
Coefficient β_6	0.85	1.38
Std. Error	(0.21)	(0.39)
P>z	0.00***	0.00***
No. of observations	68	68
LR chi2(5)	34.40	36.98
Prob>chi2	0.00	0.00
Pseudo R2	0.15	0.16
Log likelihood	-94.73	-93.44

Note: *** indicates statistical significance at 1%; ** indicates statistical significance at 3%; * indicates statistical significance at 5%.

Secondly, the choice of the degree of unification of supervisory powers seems to be influenced especially by the characteristics of the financial markets: more specifically, the smaller these markets, the more likely it seems that the probability of unification will increase, perhaps confirming the hypothesis of policymakers conditioned by the "small country" situation illustrated earlier.

Furthermore, a positive relationship between the market based regime and the degree of supervision consolidation seems to hold[43]. This fact could be explained by the focus of policymakers on the role of financial conglomerates, if there were evidence of a positive relationship between the degree of financial deepening and development of cross-sector intermediaries. The policymakers, in face of the possible effects of the growing presence of the financial conglomerates, prefer to increase the degree of consolidation in the supervision structure. Alternatively, the policymakers might be sensitive to the preferences of a highly concentrated banking and financial industry that appreciates a single supervisor (*captive hypothesis*).

Thirdly, the choice of policymakers to establish a unification of supervisory powers seems to be facilitated by an institutional environment characterized by good governance[44]. The relationship between good governance and supervision unification process can be explained if we assume that a policymaker who cares about soundness and efficiency may prefer the single financial authority as the optimal one faced with the blurring challenges.

THE DEGREE OF CONCENTRATION OF POWER IN FINANCIAL SUPERVISION: THE EU ACCESSION COUNTRIES

What happens now if we use these results to analyze a different sample, composed of the 28 potential member states of an enlarged European Union? In this case, the regression analysis cannot take us far, given the limited nature of the sample. The results, however, can at least give us some empirical feelings for investigation, if we carefully consider the structural characteristics of the ten countries aspiring to become members of the European Union.

Four of them (Estonia, Latvia, Malta and Hungary) have already adopted the model with a Single Financial Authority, and at the same time they register the less involvement of the central bank in the powers of financial supervision. However, only two countries (Cyprus and Malta) have a financial system that, based on our indicators, can be regarded as relatively developed; and again, only two countries (Malta and Hungary) have a market-based model of intermediation.

The foregoing qualitative evidence is confirmed and strengthened if we look at the numerical values of the various indicators in the countries currently members of the EU, compared to those in the aspiring members (Table 11.4).

The average index of financial concentration in the aspiring member states is lower than that in the current members, but not by much (difference between the two averages: 32%), and the degree of central bank involvement in the two groups of countries is essentially similar (difference between the two averages: 18%). The two groups are quite different, however, from the standpoint of their financial structures: the current member states have rather well developed banking systems and securities markets (for bank development, the difference between the two averages is 203%, while for securities market development the difference between the two averages is 182%). The attitude of the governments toward market-oriented regulatory policies is also stronger in the current group of member states (the difference between the two averages for the two groups is 57%). The only figure that goes – just a little bit - against the trend regards the concentration of the intermediaries, where the average for the EU-aspiring countries is slightly greater than that for the current member states (the difference between the averages of the two groups is 3%).

Lastly, regarding the reform of the regulatory structure toward a greater degree of concentration, a reform mechanism seems to have manifested itself in the group of countries involved in the EU enlargement process that, following the interpretative model used thus far, seems to be consistent with a strategy of "anticipation", given a “small country” situation (except Hungary), even though market development and the adoption of a market-oriented model have not yet been achieved or consolidated.

CONCLUSIONS

The objective of this chapter was to determine whether there is a current tendency toward the concentration of powers of financial supervision into a single authority, with particular attention to the European situation.

Table 11.4 The countries of an enlarged EU: economic and institutional indicators

	Countrie	Financial Authorities Concentration Index	Central Bank Financ. Auth Index	Financial Development		Mkt vs Bank Index	Bank Conc Index	Governance Quality
				Bank Develop Index	Market Develop Index			
EU Members	1 Austria	7	1	0.40	-0.29	-0.88	0.72	1.19
	2 Belgiu	5	1	0.14	-0.11	-0.27	0.65	0.58
	3 Denmar	7	1	-0.28	0.00	0.40	0.74	1.09
	4 Finland	5	1	-0.11	0.51	2.34	0.88	1.42
	5 France	1	3	0.20	0.19	0.34	0.41	0.59
	6 German	7	1	0.55	0.29	0.06	0.45	1.08
	7 Greece	1	2	-0.17	-0.11	0.80	0.77	0.71
	8 Ireland	7	4	0.26	0.19	-0.01	0.74	1.33
	9 Italy	2	3	-0.04	0.11	0.41	0.36	0.59
	10 Luxembour	5	1	0.99	1.03	0.68	0.76	1.49
	11 Netherland	2	3	0.44	0.84	1.28	0.74	1.50
	12 Portugal	2	3	0.36	0.01	-0.25	0.46	0.81
	13 Spain	1	3	0.25	0.49	0.64	0.47	1.08
	14 Sweden	7	1	0.43	0.65	1.04	0.88	1.08
	15 UK	7	1	0.60	0.61	129	0.56	1.32
	Average	4.46	1.93	0.27	0.29	0.52	0.64	1.06
	Variance	5.57	0.78	0.11	0.15	0.61	0.03	0.11
Potenzial EU	16 Bulgaria	1	2	-0.49	-0.31	-0.64	0.71	0.16
	17 Cyprus	1	2	0.06	-0.33	-0.89	0.88	0.83
	18 Estonia	7	1	-0.32	-0.30	-0.46	0.99	1.09
	19 Latvia	7	1	-0.47	-0.35	-0.86	0.68	0.30
	20 Lithuani	1	2	-0.50	-0.33	-0.53	0.94	0.30
	21 Malta	7	1	0.32	0.30	0.38	0.82	0.33
	22 Poland	1	1	-0.40	-0.28	-0.39	0.59	0.41
	23 CzeclRep	1	2	-0.06	-0.27	-0.58	0.84	0.54
	24 Romani	1	2	-0.55	-0.34	-0.79	0.78	-0.28
	25 Slovakia	2	2	-0.26	-0.33	-0.83	0.74	0.27
	26 Slovenia	1	2	-0.27	-0.31	-0.77	0.70	0.52
	27 Hungary	7	1	-0.38	-0.05	0.69	0.61	0.88
	Average	3.00	1.58	-0.28	-0.24	-0.47	0.77	0.45
	Variance	8.33	0.27	0.07	0.04	0.25	0.02	0.13

Firstly, the phenomenon does exist; the comparative analysis of 69 countries, based on institutional indicators (FAC Index and CBFA Index), confirmed the qualitative impression that an increase in the degree of concentration of powers was evident in the developed countries, particularly in the European Union, considering both the current 15 member states and the prospective enlargement to 25 members.

Secondly, to empirically gauge the possible structural determinants of the degree of concentration of powers, we use the results of an econometric analysis of the Probit and Logit types, using the FAC

Index as an endogenous variable and a broad set of institutional and economic variables as possible regressors.

The results – that have to be theoretically and empirically developed in future researches[45] – seem interesting. From an economic point of view, the empirical analysis, firstly, seems to suggest that the choices of the policymaker in terms of "whom" to delegate the supervisory policy to are closely linked to those regarding "how many" institutions to delegate, according to an inverse relationship.

In particular, the more the central bank is involved in financial supervisory powers, the lower the degree of concentration of those powers is likely to be.

Secondly, the choice of the degree of concentration of supervisory powers seems to be influenced especially by the characteristics of the financial markets: more specifically, the smaller these markets, the more likely it seems that the degree of concentration will increase, perhaps confirming the hypothesis of policymakers conditioned by the "small country" situation. The degree of concentration of intermediaries also seems to be a relevant factor. This fact could be explained by the focus of policymakers on the role of financial conglomerates, if there were evidence of a positive relationship between degree of concentration and development of cross-border intermediaries. In other words, policymakers might be sensitive to the preferences of a highly concentrated banking and financial industry that appreciates a single supervisor.

Thirdly, the choice of policymakers to increase the degree of concentration of supervisory powers seems to be facilitated by good governance environment.

Finally, we closely examined the structural characteristics of the ten countries that aspire to become member states of the European Union. Four of them (Estonia, Latvia, Malta and Hungary) have already adopted the model with a single financial authority, and at the same time they register minimal involvement of the central bank in the powers of financial regulation and supervision. However, only two countries (Cyprus and Malta) have a financial system that can be regarded as relative developed, based on the indicators, and only two countries (Malta and Hungary) have a market based model of intermediation.

These initial empirical indications are confirmed by a numerical analysis of the indicators. The average index of financial concentration is lower in the aspiring member states than in the current member states but not by much, while the degree of involvement of the Central Bank is basically the same for the two groups of countries. The two groups are quite different, however, from the standpoint of financial structure: both the banking system and securities markets are much better developed in the current member states. The affinity of governments for market oriented regulatory policies is also stronger in the current member states. The only figure slightly contrary to this trend relates to the concentration of the intermediaries, where the average for the aspiring countries is slightly higher than that for the current member states.

Therefore, looking at the group of countries involved in the Union enlargement process, that established a single supervisor, the reform mechanism, staying with the model followed thus far, can be interpreted as consistent : 1) with the trade-off between the Single Financial Authority Regime and the Central Bank Dominated Multiple Regulators Regime (the central bank factor); 2) with the "small country hypothesis", (excluding the Hungarian case), that claims the importance of the expected efficiency gains of the single supervisory model for countries characterized by small dimensions and/or shortage of supervisory resources[46], and 3) on the contrary, the "public governance factor" does not seem to be relevant in these specific samples of countries.

In conclusion, a couple of comments on the perspective of the European supervision can be made. In the 1990s the definition of the European monetary system was facilitated by the existence of a dominant model: the independent central bank. Now it is evident that actually a dominant supervisory model does not exist. The polarization phenomena are quite evident in the European Union case. For the actual EU members, we have, on the one hand, countries with a high concentration of powers with low central bank involvement (Single Financial Authority Regime), with eight countries; on the other, countries with a low concentration of powers with high central bank involvement (Central Bank Dominated Multiple Supervisors Regime), with six countries. Ireland is the exception, with a regime characterized by both a high degree of consolidation and a high level of central bank involvement. If we consider the hypothetical European

Union of 27 member states, again we see a huge polarization of the supervisory models: on the one hand the Single Financial Authorities Regime (12 countries), on the other the Central Bank Dominated Multiple Supervisors Regime (11 countries); excluding Ireland, the three remaining countries are characterized by both a low degree of consolidation and a low level of central bank involvement.

Furthermore, the analysis stressed the importance of the trade off between the unification of supervisory powers and the role of the central bank. From a European perspective, this result could produce the following prediction: the more the European Central Bank is involved in the financial supervision architecture, the less likely the establishment of a European Single Financial Authority will be.

NOTES

1. Paper prepared for the Conference "Financial Intermediation in the New Europe: Economics, Policies and Institutions", organized by the Paolo Baffi Centre for Monetary and Financial Economics at Bocconi University on 22 September, 2003. A precedent draft of the paper was presented at the 24th SUERF Colloquium, Tallin, Estonia. The authors wish to thank, without implicating, Alessandro Malinverno and Margherita Saraceno for excellent research assistance. The authors are indebted for helpful comments and suggestions to Franco Bruni, Jacob de Haan, Giorgio Di Giorgio, Darren Hannah, Iman van Lelyveld, David Llewellyn, Dirk Schoenmaker, Martin Schuler. All remaining errors are the authors' responsibility. The authors gratefully acknowledge financial support from the Italian Consiglio Nazionale delle Ricerche (grants 00.00452.ST74-115.20074 and 000.00445.ST74-115.35905)
2. See Di Giorgio and Di Noia (2003).
3. See Di Giorgio and Di Noia (2003).
4. On the European supervision debate see Padoa Schioppa (1999), Vives (1999), European Commission (2000), European Central Bank (2002), OECD (2001) and (2002), Di Giorgio and Di Noia (2003).
5. A very detailed analysis and classification of different financial regulatory policies and of their objectives can be found in Bruni (2001).
6. The two objectives not considered in the "2 x 2 scheme" have been the subject of more specific literature. A subject intensively debated are the relations and conflicts between monetary policy (designed to achieve macro economic stability) and prudential policies (designed to achieve

microeconomic stability). A basic reference in this field of literature is Goodhart and Schoenmaker (1992).

7. For more details see Lannoo (2000) and Briault (1999).
8. Goodhart et al. (1998).
9. Lannoo (2000).
10. Lannoo (2000).
11. In Europe the trend toward the concentration of supervisory powers has been rather strong in recent years: in addition to Norway – the first country to establish a single supervisor in 1986 – and the Iceland (1988), five other countries, members of the European Union (Austria, Denmark (1988), Germany (2002), Sweden (1991) and United Kingdom (1997)) have assigned the task of supervising the entire financial system to a single authority different and independent from the central bank. Also four countries involved in the EU enlargement process (Estonia (1999), Latvia (1998), Malta (2002) and Hungary (2000)) have reformed their structures, concentrating all the powers in a single authority, while out of Europe the unified agency was established in Korea (1997).
12. Barth et al. (2001) empirically analyze the relationship between specific regulatory measures (capital ratios, deposit insurance, inspection rules, etc.) and some bank performance indicators (asset growth, intermediation margin, costs, loan losses) and institutional indicators (corruption). The difference from the analysis performed here is evident: the object of analysis is the general design of the controls, not the individual rules of supervision. Above all, however, this work does not resolve the difficulties pointed out here: even individual supervisory measures have changed in various countries in recent years, so saying that all the data already fully reflect the effects of reforms is a rather bold statement; secondly, a complete judgment on the effects produced is not possible, since the set of performance indicators used is obviously partial.
13. The approach is described in Masciandaro (2004).
14. For the new political economy approach see Persson and Tabellini (2000).
15. The consolidation process of the financial supervision powers cannot be described using a discrete variable (Single Authority or not). De Luna Martinez and Rose (2001) correctly claim that also in the group of integrated supervisory agencies is not homogeneous as it seems.
16. See Masciandaro (2003).
17. De Luna Martinez and Rose (2001).
18. Alternatively, an index has been proposed (FAC Two) according to the following scale: 5 = Single Authority for all three sectors (total number

of supervisors = 1); 3 = Single Authority for two sectors (total number of supervisors = 2); 1 = Independent Specialized Authority for each sector (total number of supervisors = 3). As Masciandaro (2004) demonstrated, the econometric performances of the two indices (FAC and FAC Two) are quite similar.

19. See Goodhart and Schoenmaker (1992), Masciandaro (1993) and (1995), Tuya and Zamalloa (1994), Di Giorgio and Di Noia (1999), Bruni (2001). More recently, Garcia Herrero and del Rio (2003) analyzed the relationship between financial stability and monetary policy design, finding that focusing the central bank objectives on price stability reduces the likelihood of instability, and that the same is true locating regulatory and supervisory responsibilities at the central bank.
20. Barth et al. (2002) claim that the key issues for banking supervision are 1) whether there should be one or multiple supervisory authorities, and 2) whether the central bank should be involved in bank supervision. Here we use the same intuition to build up the two indices of financial authorities consolidation.
21. The relationship between competition policies and stability are examined in Carletti and Hartmann (2002).
22. Austria, Belgium, Denmark, Finland, France, Germany, Greece, Ireland, Italy, Luxembourg, Netherlands, Portugal, Spain, Sweden, UK.
23. Cyprus, Czech Republic, Estonia, Hungary, Latvia, Lituania, Malta, Poland, Slovak Republic, Slovenia.
24. Bulgaria, Romania and Turkey.
25. See Garcia Herrero and Del Rio (2003). On the role of the central bank in banking supervision see Goodhart and Schoenmaker (1995), Haubrich (1996), Peek at al. (1999), Abrams and Taylor (2001).
26. Llewellyn (2001).
27. See Schoenmaker (2003), Padoa Schioppa (2003), Goodhart and Schoenmaker (1995), Eijffinger (2001), Vives (2001), Goodhart et al. (2002).
28. See Oosterloo and de Haan (2003).
29. See Masciandaro (2003).
30. Alternatively, the different levels of central bank involvement can be measured using the identical scale of the FAC Index (labelled CBFA Two Index): 1 = the central bank has responsibility in no sector; 3 = the central bank has responsibility in one sector; 5 = the central bank has responsibility in two sectors; 7 = the central bank has responsibility in

all three sectors. Obviously – see Masciandaro 2004 – the econometric performances of the two indices (CBFA and CBFA Two) are equal.

31. It has been considered 'without supervision responsibility' each central bank involved in the payment system and liquidity management only (and consequently in the crisis procedures).
32. Obviously, a difference of 0.1 between two values of the FAC Index, that range from 0 to 7, means a 1% gap, while the same difference between two values of the CBFA Index, that range from 0 to 4, means a 2% gap.
33. For further details on the ordinal polychotomous variable estimation see Wooldridge (2002).
34. The maximum likelihood estimations were carried out by a packaged ordered Probit and ordered Logit commands in STATA.
35. Initially we drop the peculiar case of the Monetary Authority of Singapore (MAS), that only on 1 October 2002, after the merger with the Board of the Commissioners of the Currency, became a central bank. The nature of exception of Singapore is stressed in De Luna Martinez and Rose (2003). We have to note also that in Ireland in May 2003 the Department of Enterprise, Trade and Employment (DETE) responsibilities for the insurance sector were attributed to the Irish Central Bank. In any case in Masciandaro (2004) we performed the econometric analyzes considering also these cases (see above).
36. Pagano and Volpin (2000), Perotti and Von Thadden (2003).
37. It has been argued – Llewellyn (2001) – that the reason of the trade off between the supervision consolidation and the central bank involvement is because of a fear that the safety net – central bank function of lender of last resort – might be spread to a wider set of institutions than just banks if the central bank is also involved in supervising insurance and securities trading firms (*blurring hazard effect*). Furthermore, a political economy explanation – Masciandaro (2004) – could be added to this economic interpretation: in the country in which the central bank is deeply involved in supervision, the policymakers might fear the creation of a too much powerful bureaucratic agency, and therefore they prefer to have more supervision agencies, and consequently a less consolidated supervisory regime (*monopolistic bureau effect*). For more details see Masciandaro (2004).
38. Demigüç-Kunt and Levine (1999).
39. World Bank, 2001, *World Development Indicators*, Stock Markets 5.3.
40. Kaufmann et al. (1999, 2000, 2002, 2003).

41. If we think to the sample of the countries (14) with a Single Supervisor only, the UK seems to be the exception in the inverse relationship between the degree of financial supervision consolidation and the financial market dimension. In fact, if the same regressions are performed without the UK, all the results are confirmed, with a bit of improvement. If we include Singapore, using the post 2003 Reform indexes of FAC and CBFA, the results on the role of central bank involvement and of the governance are confirmed, while the other relationships become weaker. The same if we consider Ireland using the post 2003 Reform indexes of FAC and CBFA.
42. At the same time, the variables that could explain the degree of central bank involvement in the financial supervision does not coincide with those that we use to analyze the degree of consolidation; in fact if you perform Probit and Logit regressions – see Masciandaro 2004 – using CBFA as dependent variable and the same vector of financial and institutional variables, the results are not significant at all.
43. Note that the correlation index between the financial regime variable (MvBdum) and the market capitalization variable (mcap) is high, but they influence the dependent variable with the opposite sign.
44. All the three main results are confirmed if the FAC Two Index is used instead of the FAC Index, as indicator of supervision consolidation. See Masciandaro (2004).
45. How robust are the results obtained thus far? To answer this question, Masciandaro (2004) inserted control variables into the estimates. Firstly, based on the descriptive analyzes, the question was asked whether the choices made by the policymakers to increase the degree of concentration of supervisory powers would depend on the level of development in their respective countries. The geographical factor might also be important, in terms of membership, actual or potential, in the European Union. Secondly, the relationship between the degree of concentration and the characteristics of the banking and financial markets might "obscure" the importance of other institutional variables, themselves determinants in explaining the characteristics of the banking and financial markets. Recently, the structure of the financial markets was explained with three different approaches: the law and finance view, in the static and dynamic versions; the politics and finance view, and the endowment view. In this chapter, we have inserted control variables related to the law and finance view and the endowment view, while the politics and finance view was already represented by the indicator of governance. Furthermore, the same institutional variables can explain the significant role of the good

governance variable in Equation (11.1). The results of the estimates, with the control variables inserted, show an improvement in their fitness and the robustness of at least two results. First, the probability of a single financial authority is still inversely and significantly related to the involvement of the central bank. Second, the concentration of powers also seems to be linked to the institutional framework, especially to the Germanic and Scandinavian roots of the legal institutions. These results are confirmed with different samples too.

46. Abrams and Taylor (2001) and Goodhart (2002) claim that the economies of scale argument is most applicable in small countries or those with small financial systems. Abrams and Taylor (2001) argue that the shortage of supervisory resources is a serious problem particularly in emerging market economies.

REFERENCES

Abrams, R.K. and Taylor, M.W., 2001, "Assessing the Case for Unified Sector Supervision", Risk Management and Insurance International Conference, mimeo.

Barth, J.R., Caprio, G. Jr. and Levine, R., 2001, "The Regulation and Supervision of Bank Around the World: A New Database", in R.E.,Litan and R., Herring (eds), *Integrating Emerging Market Countries into the Global Financial System*, Brookings-Wharton Papers on Financial Services, Brookings Institution Press.

Barth, J.R., Nolle, D.E., Phumiwasana, T. and Yago G., 2002, "A Cross-Country Analysis of the Bank Supervisory Framework and Bank Performance", mimeo.

Briault, C., 1999, "The Rationale for a Single National Financial Services Regulator", FSA Occasional Paper.

Bruni, F., 2001, "Financial Stability, Regulation, Supervision and Modern Central Banking", in Santomero, A., Viotti, S. and Vredin, A. (eds), *Challenges for Central Banking,* Kluwer Academic Publishers, Dordrecht.

Carletti, E. and Hartmann, P., 2002, "Competition and Stability: What's Special about Banking?", European Central Bank, Working Paper Series, n.146.

De Luna Martinez, J. and Rose, T.A., 2003, "International Survey of Integrated Financial Sector Supervision", mimeo.

Demigüç-Kunt, A. and R. Levine, 1999, "Bank Based and Market Based Financial Systems: Cross Countries Comparisons", Development Research Group, Finance Department, World Bank.

Di Giorgio, G. and Di Noia, C., 2003, "Financial Market Regulation and Supervision: How Many Peaks for the Euro Area?", *Brooklyn Journal of International Law*, n.28, pp.463-493.

Di Giorgio, G. and Di Noia, C., 1999, "Should Banking Supervision and Monetary Policy Tasks be given to Different Agencies?", *International Finance*, n. 3.

Eijffinger, S.C.W., 2001, "Should the European Central Bank Be Entrusted with Banking Supervision in Europe", Briefing Paper on *The Conduct of Monetary Policy and an Evaluation of the Economic Situation in Europe,* Brussels, European Parliament.

European Central Bank, 2002, "The Role of Central Banks in Prudential Supervision", www.ech.int.

European Commission, 2000, *Institutional Arrangements for the Regulation and Supervision of the Financial Sector.*

Garcia Herrero, A. and del Rio, P., 2003, "Implication of the Design of Monetary Policy for Financial Stability", 24th SUERF Colloquium, Tallin, Estonia.

Goodhart, C., 2002, "The Organizational Structure of Banking Supervision", Financial Market Group, LSE, mimeo.

Goodhart, C., Shoenmaker, D., and Dasgupta, P., 2002, "The Skill Profile of Central Bank and Supervisors", *European Finance Review*, n.6, 539-560.

Goodhart, C., Hartmann, P., Llewellyn, D., Rojas-Suarez, L. and Weisbroad, S., 1998, *Financial Regulation. Why, how and where now?*, Routledge, London and New York.

Goodhart, C. and Shoenmaker, D, 1995, "Should the Functions of Monetary Policy and Banking Supervision be Separated?", *Oxford Economic Papers*, n.47, 539-560.

Goodhart, C., and Shoenmaker, D., 1992, "Institutional Separation between Supervisory and Monetary Agencies", *Giornale degli Economisti e Annali di Economia*, 9-12.

Haubrich J.G., 1996, "Combining Bank Supervision and Monetary Policy", *Economic Commentary*, Federal Reserve Bank of Cleveland, November.

Jonk, A., Kremers, J.E. and Schoenmaker, D., 2001, "A Cross Sector Model for Financial Supervision", Working Paper.

Kaufmann, D., Kraay, A. and Zoido-Lobaton, P., 1999, "Aggregating Governance Indicators", World Bank Policy Research Department Working Paper, No. 2195.

Kaufmann, D., Kraay, A. and Zoido-Lobaton, P., 2000, "Governance Matters", World Bank Policy Research Department Working Paper, No. 2196.

Kaufmann, D., Kraay, A. and Zoido-Lobaton, P., 2002, "Governance Matters II: Updated Indicators for 2000/01", World Bank Policy Research Department Working Paper.

Kaufmann, D., Kraay, A. and Mastruzzi, M., 2003, "Governance Matters III: Governance Indicators 1996-2002", World Bank Policy Research Department Working Paper.

Lannoo, K., 2000, *Challanges to the Structure of Financial Supervision in the EU*, 22nd SUERF Colloquium, Wien.

Llewellyn, D., 2001, "Unified Financial Supervision: Some Key Issues and Perspectives", mimeo.

Masciandaro, D., 2004, "Central Banks or Single Financial Authorities? A Political Delegation Approach", in D. Masciandaro (ed.), *Central Banks and Single Financial Authorities in Europe,* Edward Elgar, Cheltenham (forth.).

Masciandaro, D., 2003, "Unification in Financial Sector Supervision: the Trade Off between Central Bank and Single Authority", *Journal of Financial Regulation and Compliance* (forth.).

Masciandaro, D., 1995, "Designing a Central Bank: Social Player, Monetary Agent or Banking Agent?", *Open Economies Review*, n. 6, 399-410.

Masciandaro, D., 1993, "Central Bank Independence, Banking Supervision and Inflation", IGIER Working Paper, n.53.

OECD, 2002, *Supervision of Financial Services in the OECD area*, April.

OECD, 2001, *Consolidated Supervision in Theory and Practice*, Committee on Financial Markets, Technical Paper, March.

Oosterloo, S. and De Haan, J., 2003, "An Institutional Framework for Financial Stability", mimeo.

Padoa Schioppa, T., 2003, "Financial Supervision: Inside or Outside Central Banks", in J. Kremers, D. Shoenmaker and P. Wierts (eds), *Financial Supervision in Europe*, Edward Elgar, Cheltenham.

Padoa Schioppa, T., 1999, "EMU and Banking Supervision", *International Finance*, n.2.

Pagano, M. and Volpin, P., 2000, "The Political Economy of Corporate Governance", CSEF Working Paper, University of Salerno.

Peek, J., Rosengren, E.S. and Tootle, G.M.B., 1999, "Is Bank Supervision Central to Central Banking?", *Quarterly Journal of Economics*, n.64, 629-653.

Perotti, E. and von Thadden, E.L., 2003, "The Political Economy of Bank and Equity Dominance", CEPR Discussion Paper, n.3914.

Persson, T. and Tabellini, G., 2000, *Political Economy: Explaining Economic Policy*, MIT University Press, Cambridge MA MIT Press.

Quintyn, M., and Taylor, M., 2002, "Regulatory and Supervisory Independence and Financial Stability", IMF Working Paper.

Schoenmaker, D., 2003, "Financial Supervision: from National to European?", *Financial & Monetar Studies* (forth.).

Tuya, J. and Zamalloa, L., 1994, "Issues on Placing Banking Supervision in the Central Bank", in T. Balino and C. Cottarelli (eds.), *Frameworks for Monetary Stability: Policy Issues and Country Experiences*, International Monetary Fund, Washington.

Vives, X., 2001, "Restructuring Financial Regulation in the European Monetary Union", *Journal of Financial Services Research*, n.19, 57-82.

Vives, X., 1999, "Banking Supervision in the European Monetary Union", mimeo.

Wooldridge, J.M., 2002, "Econometric Analysis of Cross Section and Panel Data", MIT Press, Cambridge, MA.

12. Deposit Insurance in the New Europe

Giorgio Di Giorgio[1]

INTRODUCTION

In May 2004, the EU will become a 25-country area. Some of the new member countries will apply for joining the European monetary union and adopt the single currency in the near future, provided that they show compliance with the Maastricht criteria of nominal and fiscal convergence.

In spite of the relevant recent progresses made by most countries in terms of liberalizing and privatizing their domestic economies, a considerable amount of different features still characterize both the banking and financial systems as well as the productive and consumer sectors of these accessing countries.

In this chapter, we focus on one such different feature, namely the protection given to bank depositors through an explicit scheme of Deposit insurance. An explicit scheme of Deposit insurance may be defined as the instrument through which the banking system guarantees that funds deposited by the public in a bank are independent of the solvency and liquidity conditions of the bank itself, so that depositors may be sure of being reimbursed at any time. Recently, much attention has been given in the literature to the role of legal, political and regulatory institutions as important determinants of the evolution in both the financial structure and efficiency as well as the macroeconomic performances of one country. And in the aftermath of the many banking and financial crises that have shaken the world in the last two decades, many institutional reforms of the financial system have indeed relied on the introduction of explicit deposit protection.

The Central-Eastern European countries that are about to enter the EU are not an exception in this picture. Most of them have introduced explicit deposit insurance in the 1993-98 period, during the highly difficult and pervasive phase of restructuring, consolidation and privatization of the domestic banking systems. This was indeed a fundamental period in the evolution of the national governments from their previous status of satellite economies to a new era of political and economic independence.

At the start of such transition, more than ten years ago, the road to the European Monetary Union still appeared uncertain and difficult. After the signature of the Maastricht Treaty, in 1992, the European Monetary System experienced a profound crisis that led to the practical dismissal of the Exchange Rate Mechanism in the summer of 1993. It was only in late 1995 that the decision to move on to the third phase of the Delors plan was confirmed, and January 1999 established as the date for the future ECB to take responsibility for managing monetary policy in what we now call the Euro area.

Hence, it is no wonder that the EU 1994 Directive on Deposit insurance could only be marginally taken into account in the different institutional programmes of reforming the financial system of the Central and Eastern European Economies. These programmes were shaped by the standard dominant approach proposed by international organizations such as the IMF and adopted by the newly born EBRD. However, today the accessing countries face the challenge of meeting the higher requirements established in the EU law regarding this regulatory instrument. On the one hand, this motivates our interest in assessing the distance of each accessing country from the standards established in the EU Directive. On the other hand, this occasion could prove useful to allow for a reconsideration of the contents of the Directive itself, trying to assess whether and in what direction it should be modified.

The plan of the chapter is the following. We start by discussing the role of explicit deposit insurance in the financial safety net as well as the peculiar features of different deposit insurance schemes across countries. Than, we review the current state of accessing countries' regulatory arrangements in the field of deposit protection and highlight what differences emerge with respect to internationally recognized best practices and with respect to the 1994 EU Directive. Finally, we provide some reflections on the need to modify such a Directive.

THE RATIONALE FOR EXPLICIT DEPOSIT PROTECTION

Two main targets are usually associated with an explicit scheme of deposit protection: contributing to systemic stability and protecting individual depositors. Another objective that is sometimes mentioned is linked to its effect in enhancing competition in the banking sector. Here, the story is that in absence of deposit protection, small banks would be disadvantaged as investors would recognize the implicit protection provided by the monetary authorities to big banks that, because of their size cannot be left to fail ('too big to fail' doctrine). Under explicit deposit protection, small banks would become more or less equally attractive for individual depositors.

Deposit insurance clearly introduces a different treatment of (some) bank deposits with respect to all other financial activities where saving can be allocated. It has the consequence of putting other financial intermediaries in a situation of comparative disadvantage with respect to banks, and, inside the banking sector, it favours deposit collection vis-à-vis other bank liabilities.

It has been underlined (Benston and Kaufman, 1998, Dale, 2000) that deposit protection involves a typical problem of moral hazard, providing more incentives for bank managers to undertake risks. Moreover, a moral hazard problem affects also depositors' behaviour: by relying on the full reimbursement of their deposits' nominal value, they have no interest in choosing a specific bank, nor are they interested in monitoring banks[2]. This moral hazard problem increases when the insured quota of bank deposits is higher and is one of the main theoretical arguments put forward by the opponents of explicit systems of deposit insurance.

Indeed, the first theoretical papers on deposit insurance were kind of optimistic. Diamond and Dybvig (1983) were the first authors to explicitly model bank runs as liquidity crises. In their model deposit insurance could prove useful in eliminating the sunspot equilibrium inducing a bank run. However, bank assets were totally riskless in their analysis and runs driven only by exogenous expectations, with the consequence that the role of deposit insurance is not clearly different from the one of lending of last resort. On the other side, Goodhart (1999) underlines that pure liquidity crises do not exist in the modern world, but only mask solvency crises. If this view is accepted, then the role of deposit insurance and lending of last resort may be better defined. As a matter of fact, it is the lending of last resort function that has to deal with the possible threats to systemic stability posed by the working of the payment system, the interbank market and the use of derivatives. Systemic stability is not so much threatened by retail deposits, to which deposit protection is normally limited.

This view is shared by Di Giorgio and Di Noia (2002) who, in order to rationalize whether and how deposits should be given protection, start by analyzing the role of the two main targets usually assigned to explicit deposit insurance (i.e. protection of depositors and systemic stability). These authors observe that no consensus has been reached on which target is more relevant, the reason being also that such targets seem mutually inconsistent. On one side, the objective of depositors' protection excludes interbank deposits from coverage if the target is to provide insurance mainly to small and naïve investors who are not able to monitor banks. On the other side, systemic stability is at risk mostly because of the strong interbank links in the payment system and in monetary policy operations. This ambiguity may be dangerous: the practical managing of deposit protection schemes tries to simultaneously protect the system from the threat of financial contagion after a banking crisis and, at the same time, tries to avoid subsidizing bank risk because that encourage imprudent choices and banking practices. The clear objective of deposit protection should be what is exactly and explicitly stated in its name, providing depositors with a safe way to transfer resources over time while keeping their immediate liquidity[3]. The objective of macroeconomic financial stability can be pursued with a full set of other tools, including fiscal policy, reserve and capital requirements, lending of last resort; the objective of microeconomic stability, that is avoiding bank failures, maybe, is simply wrong.

But why do deposits or depositors have to be protected? Sight deposits have been considered "special" as they combine certainty of nominal value with immediate liquidity (shares of money market mutual funds are also very liquid, but they are market priced although their price volatility is low). This justifies lower or even zero return in terms of interest earned. But, are these features not compatible with risk? It is quite difficult to sustain such a thesis. The other traditional reason to consider deposits as a "special" asset is linked to their important role in funding bank loans. If bank loans are a "special" source of finance, because of their informational content and because sometimes they are the only source of funding for bank dependent firms, then deposits should also be viewed as particularly relevant in the economy. However, bank loans can be equally (and actually are) funded via other bank liabilities, such as bonds or Certificates of Deposits. Moreover, bank loans are also always less "special", since they can be reorganized and more or less easily liquidated through securitization. If one agrees with such arguments, then the only rationale to protect private sight deposits is to assume that their special feature of combining immediate liquidity with nominal value certainty makes them a natural target also for naïve and unsophisticated investors. And such investors would deserve strengthened protection with respect to the general level of protection given to all kinds of savings.

Private holders of sight deposits should then be given protection essentially because it would be probably impossible, or extremely costly, to prove in court who is a sophisticated investor and who is not (hence becoming eligible for reimbursement). Hence, Di Giorgio and Di Noia (2002) arrived at a practical motivation for deposit protection, which is linked to the right objective of protecting uninformed and naïve savers. But they also underline that no solid theoretical reason exists to justify this practical solution[5]. In addition, one may also notice that this argument was surely more valid at times in which the financial system was less developed and financial culture and information much more limited. It is less applicable today, as banks are always less special as collectors of savings and investors always more sophisticated, as is witnessed by the boom in mutual and pension funds, life insurance and direct equity trading that characterize OECD countries[4].

Recently, quite a relevant empirical literature has been developed focusing on the effect of deposit insurance on banking and financial systems. This literature has been spurred on by the projects undertaken at the IMF and the World Bank and directed at constructing international databases that could prove useful for this area of research. A survey of the first results obtained is presented in Demirgüç-Kunt and Kane (2002).

Maybe, the most important empirical work in the field is the one by Demirgüç-Kunt and Detragiache (2002), who show that moral hazard matters. Indeed, these authors use data from 61 countries in the 1980-1997 period and find that the presence of an explicit deposit insurance scheme increases the likelihood that a country will experience a banking crisis. They estimate a model in which the dependent variable is the probability of a country experiencing a banking crisis and include in the regressors a set of controlling variables and a dummy variable relative to the presence of deposit insurance. The coefficient of this variable is generally positive (although not always significant at the standard 95% confidence level). Moreover, when they introduce among the regressors some proxies for the quality of institutions, they find that the positive contribution of deposit insurance to bank fragility is strong and determinant only in countries where the institutional setting is very poor. The result does not hold in countries with stronger institutional and regulatory environments.

A negative effect of explicit deposit protection on the development and efficiency of the financial system (also when coupled with poor institutions) is found in the work of Cull et al. (2002), in Laeven (2002) and Demirgüç-Kunt and Huizinga (2001). In particular, the first paper finds that the establishment of a scheme for deposit protection retards the development of financial markets and of financial depth in general, while the other two papers show that it reduces market discipline in the sense of lowering banks' interest rate expense and making it less sensitive to bank risk and liquidity. Carapella and Di Giorgio (2003) address the question of how deposit insurance affect international bank interest rates. One would expect that deposit protection should raise the lending deposit spread by mainly affecting the deposit rate (negatively). An explicit deposit insurance scheme should in fact reduce deposit rates because it makes deposits safer. They find a positive effect of deposit insurance on the spread, controlling for structural and institutional variables. However, when they move to study the reaction of the spread components, they find that the main effect seems to arise from an increase in the lending rate, and interpret this result as coherent with the large theoretical literature that underlines the presence of relevant moral hazard problems related to this instrument. They also find that higher quality of institutions lowers lending deposit spreads, thus contributing to eroding sources of market power in the banking sector. Higher quality of institutions reduces both lending and deposit rates, although the impact is stronger on the former.

DEPOSIT PROTECTION AROUND THE WORLD: SUMMARY OF THE BEST PRACTICES

In spite of the relevant problems linked to deposit protection and discussed above, most advanced countries have adopted an explicit scheme of bank deposit insurance. Recent surveys conducted by the IMF and the World Bank show that Deposit protection is currently and explicitly a crucial component in the financial safety net of 72 countries around the world (Garcia, 2000). The financial crises experienced in the 1980s and the 1990s have surely contributed to the diffusion of explicit systems of deposit insurance in recent times: for example, 30 of the 72 countries mentioned in the study cited above have introduced explicit deposit protection in the 1990s (49 in the last two decades) and 33 countries have reformed their schemes in the same period.

As noted, explicit deposit protection may be designed to achieve different policy targets. However, the two main objectives are consumer protection and macroeconomic stability. It is argued that small depositors have to be (preferably partially) insured against losses, as they lack the ability to monitor the banks where they place their money. Furthermore, they have to be provided with a mechanism to quickly recover the funds they are supposed to use for transactions. In addition, given the strong links among banks due to the working of the payment system and the management of monetary policy, it is necessary to avoid or at least minimize the risk that a bank failure spreads out fears of financial contagion in the system, inducing depositors to withdraw their funds even from safe and solid banks (bank runs). Deposit protection is hence viewed as an essential component in the financial safety net, together with the lending of last resort provided by the central bank, standard banking regulation and supervisory controls.

Deposit protection is not offered homogeneously to depositors across countries, as underlined by the investigations performed at the IMF and the World Bank[6]. The currently adopted schemes differ widely with respect to many dimensions. Deposit insurance is surely a function of public interest. But its provision can be assigned either to a public or to a private (or mixed) agency. Participation in the system can be mandatory or voluntary, and financial resources devoted to payouts can be collected via ex-ante contributions or by raising funds only when needed (ex-post). The Deposit insurer can be given only the task of reimbursing depositors or can be assigned a broader mandate and participate with information collection, crises management and supervisory activities in the banking sector. Only some categories of deposits can be insured - or all types, and each deposit account or each depositor can be eligible for partial or full payout.

Obviously, the nature and backing (public/private/mixed) of the scheme shapes the kind of mandate and powers that are given to the protection scheme. In advanced countries[7], supervisory powers are usually not assigned to deposit insurers, the most relevant exception being the FDIC in the United States. In the same countries, participation to a system of deposit protection is normally compulsory. This avoids serious adverse selection problems linked to voluntary participation. In some countries more than just one scheme is active, but it is not always the case that banks are free to choose their insurer simply as a result of competition: actually, in most countries the market is segmented ex-ante, with certain types of institutions (cooperative or local banks) being obliged to use a system and other types adopting a different scheme.

A protection system is sounder where the number of insured institutions is higher and where the banking sector is less concentrated, as the payouts for a failed bank can be spread on a considerable number of institutions of adequate size. In countries where a few banks have high shares of the market, the failure of a large player can instead put too heavy a weight on the shoulders of other participating members. At the end of 2000, Japan was the only country where deposit protection was complete, that is no limit was established for reimbursment to depositors. This was done as an emergency measure, and remained in place until April 2002. Partial insurance was provided by all other countries, with Mexico, the US and Italy offering particularly generous protection to depositors (100,000 US dollars or more).

A major difference (and highly discussed item) among deposit protection schemes related to the contribution system. This can be based on ex-post payouts or through raising a fund which is established and managed before crises arise. In this case, ex-post contributions are only asked for in order to re-establish the desired level of the fund after interventions, or in case payouts exceed the available funds. Clearly, the existence of a fund makes it quicker and easier to reimburse depositors. It also contributes to increasing confidence in the protection scheme and in the banking industry. The appropriate dimension of the fund level is clearly a function of the insured deposits.

Obviously, all countries where a fund has been raised face the important problem of managing it in such a way as to balance the trade off between the objective to minimize ex-post reintegration following future payouts (that is, maximizing its expected return) and the objective to count on a safe, quick and easy to use amount of funds for immediate needs. In practice, most countries seem to rely heavily on the bond market (more than on either cash or stocks), where the previously quoted trade off may be optimized[8].

If the practical rationale for deposit protection highlighted in section 2 is accepted, what kind of features should a modern insurance scheme have in advanced industrial countries? The main objective has to deal with the moral hazard problems mentioned above and underlined by Benston and Kaufman (1998), among others. The following broad guidelines can be suggested.

First, the costs of deposit protection should be at least partially borne by the industry, and the scheme should then be either privately managed or "mixed"[9]. This provides the correct incentives for bankers to maintain soundness and avoid participants having to pay the costs of bank failures (not the case when the burden is entirely put on taxpayers' shoulders). However, a mixed scheme is to be preferred as a totally private one is less credible in the case of financial contagion, as it may lack the resources to back the obligations of a large number of banks. Some form of government guarantee or a special credit line open with the central bank is hence desirable.

Second, blanket coverage is clearly not an efficient solution under normal circumstances, as it increases the moral hazard problems already linked to deposit insurance. In theory, explicit limited coverage is to be preferred to full insurance as it provides incentives to monitor bank behaviour. The same task could be pursued via a mechanism of coinsurance, where each depositor is reimbursed only up to a certain percentage of his credit. In any case, the amount of coverage should not be too high if the main object of protection is the small and naïve investor. Insurance should be excluded for selected types of deposit accounts, such as inter-bank deposits, government deposits, illegal deposits or deposits that are given higher rates of return.

Summing up, an ideal protection scheme should provide limited but extensive coverage. That is, most depositors should be protected, but the level of individual protection should not be excessive[10] in order to induce wealthier depositors (who are supposed to be more sophisticated and informed) to monitor banks, thereby actively participating in supervision and reinforcing market discipline.

Third, protection should be given according to a proper mechanism of ex-ante contribution by banks, where the insurance premiums should explicitly be risk-weighted[11]. It is essential that the premia be paid for each additional deposit, although the required premia may be lowered once the level of the fund has reached a certain dimension with respect to the amount of insured deposits. Such a dimension might be established according to the best practice of OECD countries in the last two decades; this leads to a coverage ratio that should be around 1 or 2%. In order to correctly measure risks, it would be desirable to adopt methods at least broadly coherent with those envisaged by the New Basel Framework for Capital Adequacy. Risk classes should hence be a function of both the solvency ratio and other indicators of bank liquidity and deposits' volatility [12].

Fourth, it is essential to have the general public aware of the existence and the extension of deposit protection. This might call for a campaign of advertising jointly conducted by the banking supervisory agency and the banking industry.

Finally, it is important to establish appropriate institutional relationships between a deposit guarantee scheme and other banking supervisory agencies and political bodies. The deposit protection agency should have absolute political independence. Economic independence will be provided by ex-ante contributions. It should have limited supervisory powers, and should participate in the decisional process about intervention, working in close collaboration with the banking supervisory agency. It would be interesting to evaluate whether merging the banking supervisory agency with the deposit protection agency would be desirable. The deposit protection agency should be accountable to the banking supervisory agency, to the industry and to the agencies responsible for customer protection.

The board of the agency should include “independent” administrators, with the explicit task of safeguarding the interest of private depositors.

WHERE DO ACCESSING COUNTRIES STAND?

With the exception of Malta and Slovenia, all other accessing countries had established an explicit system of Deposit Protection by the end of the past millennium. Table 12.1 provides information about the date in which the system was established.

Table 12.1 Year in which system was established

Bulgaria	1998
Croatia	1997
Czech Republic	1994
Estonia	1998
Hungary	1993
Latvia	1998
Lithuania	1996
Poland	1995
Romania	1996
Slovak Republic	1996

In all these recently established schemes, the system does rely on private funding by member banks. Official backing is guaranteed by either the government (as in Bulgaria, Estonia and Lithuania), the central bank (Croatia, Latvia and the Slovak Republic) or both (Czech Republic, Hungary, Poland and Romania).

All the schemes therefore, satisfy the first requirement mentioned in the previous section. Moreover, in Croatia, the Czech Republic, Hungary, Latvia, Lithuania and Poland, depositors and the deposit insurance agency have explicit legal priority over other stakeholders (as in Austria and Italy).

The main difference in the currently active schemes with respect to most EU15 countries lies in the amount of protection guaranteed to each depositor. As a matter of fact, as reported in Figure 12.1 (2000-01 data) the minimum level of 20.000 Euro is a target to reach in order to enter the EU, but not a current feature, for all the insurance schemes[13].

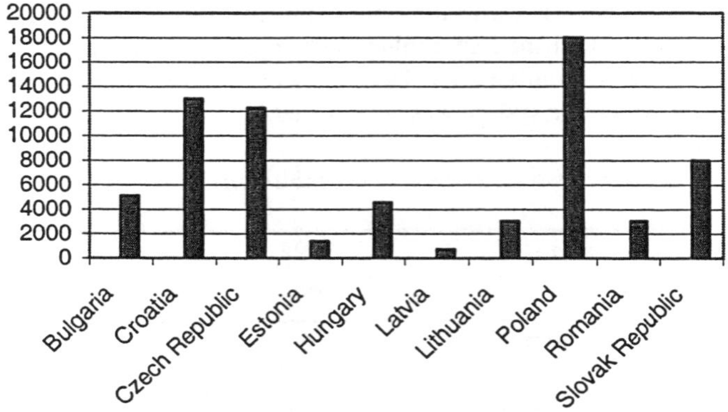

Figure 12.1 Limit of deposit protection

Most of the countries have declared their intention to gradually raise deposit protection up to the EU threshold. However, it is fair to recognize that considerably high differences still exist in the GDP per capita of EU15 and accessing countries (see Table 12.2)[14], so that the lower level of protection given today in most accessing countries can be regarded as overall appropriate with maybe the exception of Latvia and Estonia (in the latter country, as well as in Bulgaria, the Czech Republic, Lithuania and Poland a Coinsurance system is also in place)[15].

Such an assessment is also based on the previously mentioned recent literature devoted to investigating the effects of deposit insurance on the banking and financial system. This literature, in fact, shows that generous deposit protection might retard financial development, increase market power in banking and raise the likelihood of banking crises, in particular when such protection is associated with poor institutional quality and weak governments[16].

Table 12.2 GDP per capita in EU15 and accessing countries (in US dollars, average of 1996-2001)

Austria	25708,91	Cyprus	11882,290
Belgium	24371,37	Bulgaria	1512,607
Finland	24401,15	Croatia	4471,283
France	24334,53	Czech Rep.	5380,410
Germany	25657,89	Estonia	3408,545
Greece	11275,66	Hungary	4719,026
Ireland	23476,82	Latvia	2609,344
Italy	19934,44	Lithuania	2780,156
Luxembourg	43149,97	Malta	9000,128
Netherlands	24908,20	Poland	3938,342
Portugal	10738,17	Romania	1668,692
Spain	14972,18	Slovak. Rep.	3796,248
Denmark	32281,38	Slovenia	9515,709
Sweden	26713,20		
UK	22871,03		
EU15	23506,14	Average	4662,535

Table 12.3 lists different measures of institutional and governance quality in accessing countries and compares these measures with the average value in the EU15. The institutional quality indicators are the Rule of Law index and the Hall and Jones index. The former is taken from Kaufmann et al. (2002), and summarizes "in broad terms the respect of citizens and the state for the institutions which govern their interactions". They include "several indicators which measure the extent to which agents have confidence in and abide by the rules of society. These include perceptions of the incidence of both violent and non-violent crime, the effectiveness and predictability of the judiciary, and the enforceability of contracts. Together, these indicators measure the success of a society in developing an environment in which fair

and predictable rules form the basis for economic and social interactions. The Rule of Law index is measured on a [-2.5, +2.5] scale.

Table 12.3 Institutional quality

	Hall and Jones	Rule of law	Governance quality
EU15	0.913	1.332	1.06
Cyprus	0.723	0.927	0.83
Bulgaria	0.706	-0.149	0.16
Czech Republic	0.763	0.543	0.54
Estonia	Na	Na	1.09
Hungary	0.788	0.705	0.88
Latria	Na	Na	0.30
Lithuania	Na	Na	0.30
Malta	0.622	0.863	0.33
Poland	0.694	0.537	0.54
Romania	0.516	-0.087	0.28
Slovak Republic	Na	Na	0.27
Slovenia	Na	Na	0.52
Average	0.687	0.477	0.45

The Hall and Jones (1999) index is a measure of social infrastructure across countries. It can be considered a proxy for "the wedge between the private return to productive activities and the social return to such activities". It combines an index of government anti-diversion policies[17] with an index of the openness of a country to trade with other countries[18], which are equally weighted so that the index is measured on a [0,1] scale. Since data for five of 12 countries are missing, we also add the Governance quality index, an enlarged and updated version of the Rule of Law[19].

From Table 12.3, it is evident that all measures indicate a relevant gap for accessing countries in terms of institutional quality and government. Thereby, the banking system should not provide excessive generous protection to depositors, as this would harm the incentives of the public to monitor banks' behaviour. One should also observe that, although the lending deposit spread and a measure of concentration in the banking sector do not show huge diversities between EU15 and accessing countries (see Table 12.5 in the Appendix), the message is quite different if one breaks the interest spread in its two components, a mark up of the loan rate on government bond yield and a mark down of the deposit rate with respect to the same variable. This exercise shows that the mark up is more than the double in accessing countries with respect to EU15, while the mark down is less than half on average. Although the data show high volatility, with the exception of Estonia and Lithuania, loan rates are so high with respect to government yields in accessing countries that this induces some scepticism about screening and monitoring activities performed by the banking sector.

Another dangerous feature is that deposit protection schemes are based on risk weighted premia only in Croatia, Hungary, Poland and Romania. Quite a strong debate has been raised concerning the principle of contribution. i.e. if it has to be proportional to insured deposits or to the risk of the bank. From a theoretical point of view, risk adjusted contribution allows to avoid incentive problems and prevents discrimination and penalizing costs for sound institutions. However, the implementation of such a strategy appears problematic when supervision authorities do not have clear and objective instruments to evaluate the stability of single banks (i.e. scoring systems at the supervisory level like CAMEL in the USA). This may be still the case for most accessing countries.

IS THE EU DIRECTIVE STILL USEFUL?

After a first Recommendation approved in 1986 and stating some general principles on the need and opportunity for member states to establish a compulsory deposit protection scheme, in 1994 the European Commission issued a Directive (n.19/1994) establishing a minimum amount of protection at the level of 20,000 Euro and foreseeing a review of this limit every five years, the next round being in 2005. Apart from establishing a platform of minimum harmonization, the Directive did not aim at unifying deposit protection in the EU, an objective that was indeed too ambitious in the early 1990s. Today, within a single currency area, it looks much more natural to think about the possibility of going further and establishing a common system of deposit protection in the Euro area, where banking and financial integration is constantly increasing.

In the second section, we argued that (partial) deposit insurance can be practically justified because of the special need to protect naïve and unsophisticated investors. In this direction, such an institute still allows us to look at banks as somehow "different" or "special" financial institutions. However, the limited protection given to depositors cannot be considered an element relevant enough to defend a set of rules and controls for banks totally different from those applicable to other financial intermediaries. According to many other points of view, products and services offered by banking, insurance and security markets are becoming undistinguishable (Allen and Santomero, 1998 and 1999). In modern industrial countries, the financial regulatory architecture should hence move from an "institutional" model based on different financial authorities, each competent for a given segment of the financial system and a certain class of intermediaries, to regulatory models that ensure equal treatment to all financial actors in the entire financial system[20].

Such a regulatory model can be the one "by objectives", which postulates that all intermediaries and markets be subjected to the control of more than one authority, each single authority being responsible for one objective of regulation regardless of both the legal form of the intermediaries and of the functions or activities they perform. According to this scheme, an authority, eventually different from the central bank which is in charge for monetary policy and macro-stability, is to watch over prudential regulation and micro-stability of both markets and all intermediaries, whether in banking, finance or insurance; another authority will be responsible for the transparency of financial markets and will control the behaviour of banks, financial intermediaries and insurance companies toward customers; a third authority will guarantee and safeguard competition over the entire financial market and among intermediaries. The advantage of this four-peak model (the 4th peak being the central bank) lies in the fact that it is particularly effective in a highly integrated market context and in the presence of poli-functional operators, conglomerates and groups operating in a variety of different business sectors. Moreover, it provides uniform regulation for the different entities engaged in the same activities.

Another supervisory model which emphasizes similarities more than differences in the financial market is the single-regulator model, which is based on just one control authority, separated from the central bank, and with responsibility over all markets and intermediaries regardless of whether in the banking, financial or insurance sector. This authority would be concerned with all the objectives of regulation (stability, transparency and investor protection, maybe competition). The advantages of this approach lie in the economies of scale that it produces. Fixed costs and logistical expenses, the costs of administrative personnel and the compensation for the top management are all considerably reduced. By the same token, the costs of supervision charged to the subjects regulated and/or to the taxpayer decrease. However, the presence of a sole regulator might render collusive relations more immediate and direct ("regulatory capture"). It might also exacerbate problems of self-contradiction in the event that the authority should find itself forced to pursue conflicting supervisory objectives. Given that the most likely conflict is concerned with the objectives of stability and the one of efficiency, a better practical solution would be to explicitly handle this problem by keeping a separated agency responsible for antitrust and competition. Therefore, we could view the single regulator model as a particular case of the model by objectives, where two objectives, microeconomic stability and investor protection, are assigned to the same agency.

In this financial architecture, the task of managing an explicit system of deposit insurance could easily be assigned to the agency in charge of both microstability and investor protection. Cooperation between supervisory authorities would be therefore enhanced and prompt actions guaranteed in the interest of depositors. The deposit insurance agency would be involved in the closure of troubled banks (as happens in the US) and would allow the implementation of menu-like regulatory policies with premium schedules linked to capital ratios. Obviously the application of such a model to the Euro area is not easy.

This area, although increasingly integrated, is still characterized by important differences in fiscal, corporate and bankruptcy laws, just to name a few. Di Giorgio and Di Noia (2003) suggested following the successful example of the ESCB, and establishing a federal system with central agencies regulating the main items and domestic branches responsible for the implementation and specification of general principles into operative rules and the supervision of markets and intermediaries.

In such a picture, deposit protection would be completely harmonized in the Euro area, but not necessarily in the EU. This arrangement would be justified by considering the different features in banking, finance and monetary policy transmission of both some of the new accessing countries as well as of countries like the United Kingdom, Denmark and Sweden. As a consequence, accessing countries will be left more time to accomplish their transition before qualifying to eventually enter the Euro area, and adopt a more stringent regulation in terms of deposit insurance.

NOTES

1. The author gratefully acknowledges financial support received by MIUR (Cofin 2001).
2. Even Deposit Protection Agencies may pose moral hazard problems, especially in the case of a public system. Managers, in order to maintain their position, could be more interested in implementing forbearance policies than in a prompt solution of the crisis, as their target would simply be to avoid bank failures during their term of tenure.
3. For an opposite view, see Santomero (2001), who argues that the main target should be that of macroeconomic stability.
4. Kocherlakota (2000) has a model in which deposit insurance is efficient in providing insurance against realizations of adverse aggregate shocks to the value of collateral required in debt contracts. The result however is not fully generalizable.
5. We could also go further and sustain an even more provocative argument. Often, the existing Deposit Protection Schemes do not even really provide "insurance" to depositors in the sense that they reimburse the funds after a bank crisis. And this happens because the intervention of the Protection scheme is often intended to solve the crisis in a way different from the simple failure and closing of a bank, thus pursuing the wrong target of microeconomic stability (at least, this seems to emerge from some answers to the FITD Survey mentioned above).
6. See Garcia (2000) and Demirgüç-Kunt and Sobaci (2001).

7. See also the recent study of the Italian Interbank Deposit Fund (FITD, 2001).
8. See FITD, 2001.
9. Another interesting topic, that we leave to future research, is the choice between multiple or single Deposit Protection Schemes. In some countries deposit protection is assigned to a unique agency while in other countries a bigger scheme is active. Is it better to have one scheme or even in this particular field may competition be beneficial? Does the different nature or legal status of a bank (financial institution) support the choice of "specialized" funds, each one dedicated to a "class" of institutions or to a market segment? Or, is it better to have one big fund, including investor compensation schemes and eventually insurance schemes of insurance companies?
10. The recent FDIC proposal to raise individual protection up to 200,000 dollars in the USA goes, in our view, in the wrong direction.
11. It is interesting to note that in a very recent contribution, Boyd et al. (2002) develop a general equilibrium analysis of deposit insurance programmes and obtain results that are not fully consistent with some of the above suggested guidelines. For example, in their paper, actuarially fair pricing of deposit insurance is not always desirable, while some bank subsidization is. Also, large losses of the deposit insurance agency are not necessarily bad in terms of welfare, nor are risk-based deposit insurance premia always good for reducing moral hazard.
12. Subordinated debt may be an additional effective method of ensuring a certain degree of market discipline. The evaluation of risks by subordinated debt owners may be reflected in the structure of subordinated interest rates. The guarantee scheme might consider such rates as a useful indicator for pricing insurance premia, as well as an indicator of the bank's solvency.
13. In most schemes, protection is not offered to deposits held in foreign bank branches.
14. In the Appendix we provide some additional macroeconomic and banking sector data on these countries and compare them with the EU15 average.
15. In the Slovak Republic, for example, Deposit Protection covers about the double of per capita GDP.
16. See Cull et al. (2003), Carapella and Di Giorgio (2003), Demirgüç-Kunt, A., and Detragiache (2002).
17. It is focused on the government's role in protecting against private diversion and the government's possible role as a diverter. So it includes a

measure of law and order, of bureaucratic quality, of corruption, risk of expropriation and government repudiation of contracts.

18. It is the Sachs and Warner index that measures "the fraction of years during the period 1950 to 1994 that the economy has been open", according to the satisfaction of specific criteria: nontariff barriers cover less than 40% of trade, average tariff rates are less than 40%, any black market premium was less than 20% during the 1970s and 1980s, the country is not classified as socialist, and the government does not monopolize major exports.
19. See Masciandaro and Porta (2003). The source is Kaufmann at al. (2002).
20. See Di Giorgio and Di Noia (2003).

REFERENCES

Allen, F. and Santomero, A. (1998) 'The Theory of Financial Intermediation', *Journal of Banking and Finance*, 21: 1461-85.

Allen, F. and Santomero, A. (1999), 'What Do Financial Intermediaries Do?', *Wharton Financial Institutions Center Working Paper No. 30.*

Barth, R. James, Caprio Jr., G., and Levine, R. (2000), 'Guide to Database on Bank Regulation and Supervision', *Worldbank database.*

Beck, T., Demirgüç-Kunt, A.and Levine, R. (1999), 'A New Database on Financial Development and Structure', *World Bank database.*

Benston, G.J. and Kaufman G.G. (1998), 'Regulating bank safety and performance', in Haraf, W.S. and Kushmeider R.M. (eds). *Restructuring Banking and Financial Services in America.* American Enterprise Institute, Washington D.C.

Boyd, J., Chang, C. and Smith, B. (2002), 'Deposit Insurance: a Reconsideration', *Journal of Monetary Economics*, 49.

Bryant, J. (1980), 'A Model of Reserves, Bank Runs and Deposit Insurance', *Journal of Banking and Finance*, 4: 335-344.

Carapella, F. and Di Giorgio, G. (2003), 'Deposit Insurance, Institutions and Bank Interest Rates', Columbia University, Dept. of Economics, Discussion Paper 06.

Cull, R., Senbet, L. and Sorge, M. (2002), 'The Effect of Deposit Insurance on Financial Depth: a Cross Country Analysis', *Quarterly Review of Economics and Finance*, 42.

Dale, R.S. (2000), 'Deposit Insurance in Theory and Practice', *SUERF papers*, February.
Demirgüç-Kunt, A., and Detragiache, E. (2002), 'Does Deposit Insurance Increase Banking System Stability? An Empirical Investigation', *Journal of Monetary Economics*, 49, 1373-406.
Demirgüç-Kunt, A. and Kane, E. (2002), 'Deposit Insurance Around the Globe: Where Does it Work?', *Journal of Economic Perspectives*, 2.
Demirgüç-Kunt, A. and Huizinga, H. (2001), 'Market Discipline and Financial Safety Net Design', mimeo World Bank.
Demirgüç-Kunt, A. and Sobaci, T. (2001), 'Deposit Insurance Around the World: a Database', *World Bank Economic Review*, 15.
Dewatripont, M. and Tirole, J. (1994), 'The Prudential Regulation of Banks', MIT Press, Cambridge.
Diamond, D.W. and Dybvig, P.H. (1983), 'Bank Runs, Deposit Insurance and Liquidity', *Journal of Political Economy* 91: 401-419.
Di Giorgio, G. and Di Noia, C. (2002), 'Which Deposit Insurance in the E-banking World?', *Revue Bancaire et Financière*, 2.
Di Giorgio, G. and Di Noia, C. (2003), 'Financial Market Regulation and Supervision: How Many Peaks for the Euro Area?', *Brooklyn Journal of International Law*, 2.
FITD (2001), 'Deposit Insurance Practices around the World/Results from a Questionnaire and Issues for Future Discussion', presented at the FITD Confernce *The Role of Deposit Insurance Within the Financila Safety Net*', 2 July, Rome.
Garcia, G.H. (2000), 'Deposit Insurance: Actual and Good Practices', *IMF Occasional Paper No. 197.*
Goodhart, C. (1999), 'Myths About the Lender of Last Resort', FMG Special Papers sp120, Financial Markets Group.
Hall, Robert E. and Jones Charles, I. (1999), 'Why do Some Countries Produce so Much More Output Per Worker than Others?', *Quarterly Journal of Economics*, 83-116.
Kaufmann, Daniel Aart Kraay and Zoido-Lobaton, Pablo (2002), 'Governance Matters II: Updated Indicators for 2000/2001', *World Bank working paper.*
Kaufmann, D., Kraay, A. and Mastruzzi, M., 2003, "Governance Matters III: Governance Indicators 1996-2002", World Bank Policy Research Department Working Paper.

Kocherlakota, N.R. (2000), 'Risky Collateral and Deposit Insurance', *Federal Reserve Bank of Minneapolis, Research Department Staff Report No. 274.*

Laeven, L. (2002), 'International Evidence on he Value of Deposit Insurance', *Quarterly Review of Economics and Finance*, 42.

Levine, Ross (2002), 'Bank-Based or Market-Based Financial Systems: Which is Better?', *Journal of Financial Intermediation 11*, 398-428

Masciandaro, D. and Porta, A. (2003), 'Single Authority in Financial Markets Supervision: Lessons for the EU Enlargement', forthcoming in Masciandaro, D. (ed.), *Financial Intermediation in the New Europe*, Edward Elgar.

Santomero, A. (2001), 'Deposit Insurance in the United States', Paper presented at the FITD Conference *The Role of Deposit Insurance Within The Financial Safety Net*, Rome (Italy), 2 July 2001.

APPENDIX: MACROECONOMIC AND BANKING SECTOR DATA IN ACCESSING COUNTRIES

Table 12.4 Average real growth and inflation (1996-2001)

	Real growth	Inflation
EU15	0.035	0.022
Cyprus	0.037	0.027
Bulgaria	-0.084	0.601
Croatia	0.037	0.046
Czech Rep.	0.009	0,062
Estonia	0.051	0.085
Hungary	0.147	0.131
Latvia	0.052	0.060
Lithuania	0.038	0.064
Malta	0.034	0.025
Poland	0.051	0.108
Romania	-0.001	0.462
Slovak Rep.	0.039	0.077
Slovenia	0.041	0.086
Average	0.034	0.141

Source: IFS.

Table 12.5 Concentration and intermediation (1996-2001)

	Concentration	Spread	Mark down	Mark up
EU15	0,4208333	4.133	2.364	1.769
Cyprus	0,6083333	2.195	-0.122	2.318
Bulgaria	0,5555556	20.785	-7.436	28.222
Croatia	0,4534722	11.317	8.535	2.781
Estonia	0,5305556	6.567	6.364	0,140277778
Hungary	0,4055556	3.835	2.182	1.652

Source: IFS, Barth et al. (2000).

13. Interest Rate Pass-Through in EU Acceding Countries: The Case of the Czech Republic, Hungary and Poland

Jesús Crespo Cuaresma[1], Balázs Égert[2] and Thomas Reininger[3]

INTRODUCTION

The transmission of monetary policy actions to macroeconomic variables, such as real GDP and its components, unemployment and inflation, is usually separated into various channels. A rough classification of the main channels differentiates them by means of the variables through which the monetary policy action is propagated to the real economy. The traditional models, in particular those dealing with the interest rate, the exchange rate, and the asset price channel, focus on macroeconomic variables. The more recently developed microfoundation of the transmission mechanism focuses on the credit channel, with the bank lending channel and the balance sheet channel as important sub-channels.

During most of the first decade after systemic transformation, most transition countries have relied on exchange rate policies that took the exchange rate as a nominal anchor for the economy, as the exchange rate channel was considered the strongest and most effective channel of monetary policy in transition economies. This was based also on the observation that the monetization of the economy, as measured, for instance, by the level of money stock to GDP or domestic credit to GDP, was relatively low, which implied that the interest rate channel and the credit channel were not considered particularly effective. In recent years, however, monetary policy in Central European EU Acceding Countries shifted towards floating exchange rate regimes by substantially widening or completely abandoning currency bands. At the same time, direct inflation targeting (DIT) was introduced in some of these countries. This monetary policy shift increased the reliance on the interest rate and the credit channel, while not necessarily completely ignoring the exchange rate channel. This is exactly the case of the three EU acceding countries that will be included in this study, i.e. the Czech Republic, Hungary and Poland. By now, they all follow a (managed) floating exchange rate regime (within wide currency bands) and combine this with an inflation targeting strategy.

There are several good reasons to study the monetary transmission mechanism in these EU acceding countries. First, a genuine and precise understanding of how fast and to what extent a change in the central bank's interest instrument modifies inflation lies at the heart of inflation targeting. Second, with joining the European Monetary Union on the horizon, it is important to find out more about whether the euro area would grow more inhomogeneous with respect to monetary transmission mechanism. Third, financial sector institutions may be able to improve their various decision-making processes if they can acquire a better understanding of the interrelations between the various kinds of interest rates.

This chapter contributes to the comprehensive topic of monetary transmission mechanism in EU acceding countries by focusing on the interest rate pass-through as the first stage of both the interest rate and the credit channel. More precisely, this paper investigates the transmission of monetary policy actions to various components of the interest rate structure. Nominal or real changes in interest rate policy will be considered as monetary policy action. The impact of these monetary policy actions on interbank money market rates, on interest rates for nonbank deposits and loans, denominated in local currency, as well as on interest rates for government securities will be empirically analysed. The characteristics of the interest rate pass-through are investigated for the period stretching from the mid-1990s up to the end of 2002.

THEORETICAL BACKGROUND: THE INTEREST RATE TERM STRUCTURE AND THE EXPECTATION CHANNEL

Monetary policy has long been a Mecca of economic research as many economists have put pen to paper in an attempt to scrutinisze its effect on the real economy. Popular wisdom asserts that although ineffective in the longer run, monetary policy is a powerful tool in influencing economic activity at shorter horizons. According to the stylized fact given in Christiano et al. (1996), in the US, monetary policy actions impact on the real sector with an average delay of four months and their effect can last up to two years. This finding is also borne out in Romer and Romer (1989). Another salient feature of monetary policy, put forth in Barth and Ramey (2000), is that small changes in short-term interest rates could result in large changes in output (amplification effect). These findings are, however, rather suggestive than conclusive as the lag of the pass-through to the real economy appears to change over time and across countries.

Nonetheless, Bernanke and Gertler (1995) deem the mechanism through which monetary policy actions are transmitted to the real economy as a black box. The interest in resolving this conundrum has given rise to a large body of theoretical literature and to a plethora of empirical papers that take pains in matching theory with real data. The most traditional explanation is the interest rate channel developed in textbook IS-LM models. However, the early observation that the interest rate channel cannot neatly explain output fluctuations entailed by monetary policy actions has given birth to the credit channel literature. Asset prices are also believed to constitute a bridge between nominal and real variables, and importantly, monetary policy can also exert its effect through changes in exchange rates.

However, the focus of this paper is only the very first step in the monetary transmission mechanism: the interest rate pass-through from short-term interest rates towards long-term rates[4]. The connection between short- and long-term nominal interest rates is provided by the term structure. The slope and the dynamics of the term structure can be explained by a combination of theories. First, the longer is the horizon of an investment, the less liquid it is, and thus the higher is the interest rate required by investors. Second, short-term and long-term interest rates could be determined independently on segmented markets. But most importantly, it is a widely held view that the expectation conjecture is at the heart of the shape of the yield curve. According to this position, long-term interest rates are obtained as an average of expected future short-term interest rates. So, expectations as to whether, say, an interest rate hike is high enough to curb down inflation will by large dominate the yield curve. This is often referred to as the *expectations channel*, which also plays an important role in the asset price and exchange rate channels.

Another facet of the transmission is how interest rate changes on the money and capital markets influence bank deposit and loan interest rates. The reaction of deposit rates on time deposits hinges on the extent to which other financial assets such as government bills and bonds are substitutes for bank deposits. The speed of the transmission eventually depends on the maturity structure of the stock of deposits and the proportion of fixed and variable interest rates. As deposits represent part of banking resources, loan rates are often expected to follow changes in deposit rates, provided volatility of the credit risk premium imbedded in loan rates is stable over time.

AN OVERVIEW OF THE EMPIRICAL LITERATURE

Before going into further detail regarding empirical studies on CEE countries, it seems useful to overview the available empirical results for industrialized countries. This would provide a good background for our empirical investigation aimed at establishing the interest rate transmission in the Czech Republic, Hungary and Poland. Mizen and Hofmann (2002) seek to uncover how the official base rate affects deposit and mortgage rates of commercial banks and building societies in the UK. Using monthly data for 1986-1999, the estimations indicate that there is complete pass-through from base rates to deposit rates. By contrast, changes in the base rate feeds into mortgages rates only in an incomplete manner. Results also reveal the existence of asymmetries in the adjustment process towards the estimated long-term relationship, which connects the base rate and the retail rates.

The full pass-through found by Mizen and Hofmann (2002) is in strong contrast with other studies, which usually give evidence concerning the incompleteness of the pass-through with which base rates are transmitted to bank deposit or lending rates. For instance, Bredin et al. (2001) take a look at the case of Ireland using monthly data. By estimating the long-term cointegration relationship between the one-month wholesale money market rate and a series of retail lending rates such as mortgage rate, consumer lending rate and corporate lending rate for SME, the pass-through is found to vary between 0.54 for the consumer lending rate and 0.94 for the prime rate of banks over the period 1980 to 2001. Similarly, whereas the effect of a change in the policy rate is transmitted into prime rates in two months, consumer rate reacts only sluggishly, i.e. with a lag of ten months. Furthermore, Bredin et al. (2001) not only reveal structural changes in the long-term relationship but also find structural breaks in the adjustment mechanism towards long-term equilibrium.

Mojon (2000) considers six euro zone countries, namely Belgium, France, Germany, Italy, the Netherlands and Spain. The transmission from the money market rate to retail rates is analysed by means of a VAR model. A score of different rates is used for the retail deposit and lending rates during the period 1979 to 1998. The pass-through turns out to be incomplete and seems rather sluggish, especially for rates of higher maturity. Several sub-periods are studied given the presence of two interest rate cycles, the first one spanning from 1979 to 1988 and the second starting in 1988 and ending in 1998. With the exception of Belgium, it appears that increasing money market interest rates during the first half of the interest rate cycles feeds into lending rates faster and to a greater extent compared with the second stage of the cycles, that is characterized by a decrease in money market rates. The opposite happens to the deposit rates: the pass-through is lower when money market rates are on the rise and it becomes higher with a decline in the money market rates. This phenomenon is termed by Mojon (2000) as the interest rate cycle asymmetry. Furthermore, and more importantly, some light is also shed on the heterogeneity among countries. The pass-through is found to be the strongest in the Netherlands followed by Germany, France and Italy, whilst in Spain and Belgium, changes in the money market rates are transmitted only partly into deposit and lending rates.

Similarly to Mojon (2000), Donnay and Degryse (2001) also make use of the VAR technique and set out to estimate the pass-through between the money market rate on the one hand and several bank lending rates for households and firms and government bond rates, on the other, for a set of 12 EU countries from 1980 to 2000. The estimation carried out using monthly data indicates an incomplete pass-through except for short-term bank lending rates. Government bonds and long-term rates for households react fairly smoothly. On average, the pass-through seems the most important for Spain, Italy, Greece and the Netherlands, while only half of the changes in money market rates are reflected in deposit and lending rates in Ireland, Belgium, Portugal, Austria and the UK. Results for France, Germany and Finland are somehow in between these extremes. Especially for Spain, these results are in disagreement with what is found in Mojon (2000), and for the UK they also conflict with outcomes by Mizen and Hofmann (2002).

We now turn to reviewing those contributions aimed at studying the interest rate pass-through in countries of Central and Eastern Europe. Hanousek and Kocenda (1997) seek to determine the causal relationship structure of the Czech money market by running Granger causality tests on daily data for one-day, one and two-week, one, two, three, six and nine-month and one-year Prague Interbank Offer and Bid Rates (PRIBOR and PRIBID). The period studied covers 1993 to 1997, and the causality tests are conducted on a year-by-year basis. That is, results for each year can be recapitulated in two separate 9 × 9 matrices for PRIBOR and PRIBID. For the first four years, the causal structure of PRIBOR and PRIBID rates of different maturity shows an incomplete and time-varying pass-through from short-term rates towards longer-term rates. Strikingly, almost every maturity appears to Granger cause the one-day rate, both in the case of the offer and the bid rates. By contrast, in 1997, a stronger and more complete picture emerges as shorter-term rates systematically Granger cause longer-term rates. But the causality is bilateral because rates of longer maturity also cause short-term rates. In addition to this, causality tests are also performed between the aforementioned money market rates and the German mark and the dollar exchange rates. In 1997, at all maturities, interest rates bear a unilateral causal relationship to the German mark, except for the one and two-week and the one-month rates where the relationship is bilateral. For the dollar, relationships seem bilateral for maturities under two-month whilst for and above three-month rates, the relationship runs from interest rates to the dollar exchange rate.

Árvai (1998) studies the pass-through from T-bill rates to bank lending rates for the private sector in Hungary. Following a descriptive analysis of interest rate developments from 1992 to 1998, cointegration analysis is conducted between bank loan rates and T-bill rates over the short and the long run, respectively. In the former case, the three-month T-bill is used whereas in the latter the 12-month maturity is considered. Because an obvious structural break occurred in 1995, monthly data are used for the period 1995-1998. The author reports several specifications in which cointegration relationships could be found, but argues that the results are very fragile because of the short time span and the number of specification errors.

A CLOSER LOOK AT THE INTEREST RATE PASS-THROUGH IN THREE EU ACCEDING COUNTRIES

The Empirics of the Interest Rate Pass-Through in Acceding Countries

On the basis of the *term structure of interest rate*, the interest rate pass-through has to be examined along the lines "key rate – interbank money market rate – treasury bill rate – government bond rate", "key rate – interbank money market rate – short-term loan rate – long-term loan rate" and "key rate – interbank money market rate – short-term deposit rate – long-term deposit rate". One may expect an increase in the size of the long-run elasticity of various market rates, and in particular of the interbank money market rate, with respect to the key policy rate in all three EU acceding countries over time, on the basis of the argument that the structural changes within the banking sector should enhance interbank competition. Alternatively, one may argue that the continuing strong impact of other factors affecting the interbank rates, like, in particular, the sizeable capital inflow related to (privatization-linked) FDI, hinders the smooth working of the interest rate channel between key rates and interbank rates (despite having floating exchange rate regimes in place).

The three empirical issues concerning the interest rate pass-through in the Czech Republic, Hungary and Poland that we will tackle in this piece of research are the following:

- Is there evidence of complete pass-through from policy rates to various market rates, like the deposit and loan rates to non-banks? That is, do retail rates react one-to-one to changes in key policy rates in the long-run? If so, does this long run relationship act as an attractor to the dynamics of retail interest rates?
- How do the estimates of the long-run reaction to the key policy rate behave dynamically? Is there evidence of convergence/divergence across interest rates and/or across acceding countries over time. Can these developments be tracked down to competition issues in the banking sector?

- Is there evidence of asymmetric adjustments to the equilibrium depending upon the direction of change in the policy rate?

Data Description

The data used are monthly time series of per annum interest rates in percentage points. The source of the data is Reuters, Datastream, Bloomberg, national central banks and ministries of finance of the respective acceding countries. Special care was taken to make the time series homogeneous and comparable across countries. The starting date of the empirical investigation is determined by the starting dates of the involved time series, but not earlier than January 1994. All series contain data ranging at least up to December 2002, and in some cases interest rates up to mid 2003 were available.

The following interest rates were used for each country. For the case of the Czech Republic, the *key policy rate* used is the two-week repo rate, with monthly data existing only from December 1995 onwards. Data on the *interbank money market rate* and the *five-year T-bonds rate* were collected starting from January 1994 and February 1997, respectively. Different long- and short-term deposit and loan rates to non banks have been used:

- *Non-bank Deposit Rate (>O/N, average):* weighted average of all maturities above overnight.
- *Non-bank Deposit Rate (>O/N, =12 months):* weighted average of maturities above overnight up to one year.
- *Non-bank Deposit Rate (>12 months, =4 years):* weighted average of maturities above one year up to four years.
- *Non-bank Loan Rate (=12 months):* weighted average of all maturities below and including one year.
- *Non-bank Loan Rate (>12 months, =4 years):* weighted average of maturities above one year up to four years.

Deposit and loan rates are on stock of deposits and loans to all non-banks, respectively, and refer to the average rate weighted by volumes, end of month values. The data for the Czech Republic is plotted in Figure 13.1.

In the case of Hungary, data on the *key policy rate* refers to the active overnight repo rate until December 1995, the passive one month repo rate from January 1996 to February 1999 and the two week deposit rate thereafter. Data on the *interbank money market rate,* the *12 month and five year T-bonds rate* are available from January 1994, September 1995 and March 1997, respectively. The long and short term deposit and loan rates to households and firms that have been used in the analysis are:

- *Household Deposit Rate (O/N):* rates on sight deposits.
- *Household Deposit Rate (>O/N, average):* weighted average of all maturities above overnight.
- *Household Deposit Rate (12 months):* rate on fixed deposits for one year.
- *Household Deposit Rate (>12 months, average):* weighted average of all maturities above one year.
- *Enterprise Loan Rate (=12 months, average):* weighted average of all maturities below and including one year.
- *Enterprise Loan Rate (>12 months, average):* weighted average of all maturities above one year.

All deposit rates refer to rates to households, and are on new deposits. All loan rates are to enterprises and refer to new loans. The weighting scheme is based on volumes, and the values are measured at the end of the month. The data for Hungary is plotted in Figure 13.2.

For Poland, the *key policy rate* refers to the yield on short-term NBP bills ("intervention rate"). Data on the *interbank money market rate,* the *12-month and five year T-bonds rate* are available from January 1994 (February 1994 for the five year bond). The long- and short-term deposit and loan rates to households and firms that have been used in the analysis for Poland are:

- *Household Deposit Rate (O/N):* rates on checking accounts.
- *Household Deposit Rate (>O/N, average):* weighted average of all maturities above overnight.
- *Household Deposit Rate (12 months):* rate on deposits for one year.
- *Household Deposit Rate (>12 months):* rate on deposits for three years.
- *Enterprise Loan Rate (12 months):* rate on loans, one year.
- *Enterprise Loan Rate (three years):* rate on loans, three year.

All deposit rates refer to rates to households, and are on the stock of deposits. All loan rates are to enterprises and refer to rates on the stock of loans. The weighting scheme is based on volumes, and the values are measured at the end of the month. The data for Poland is plotted in Figure 13.3.

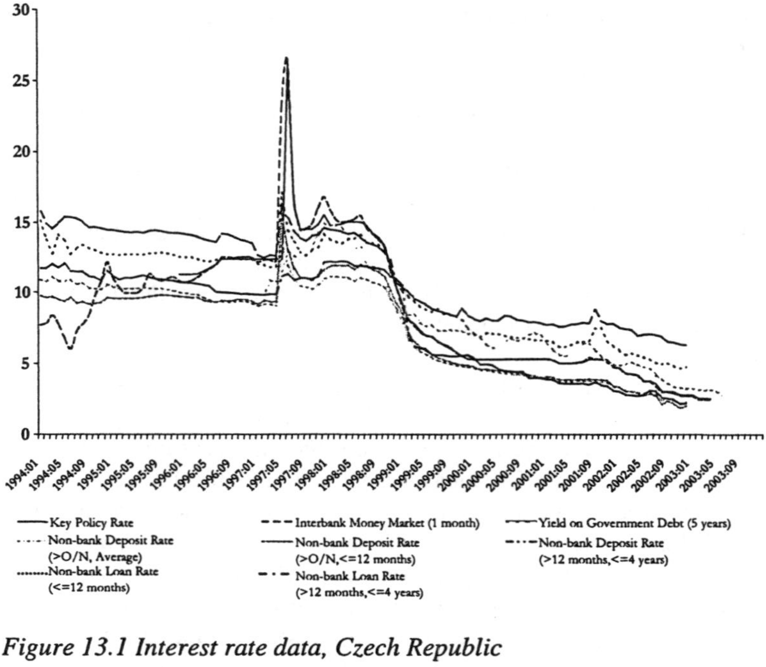

Figure 13.1 Interest rate data, Czech Republic

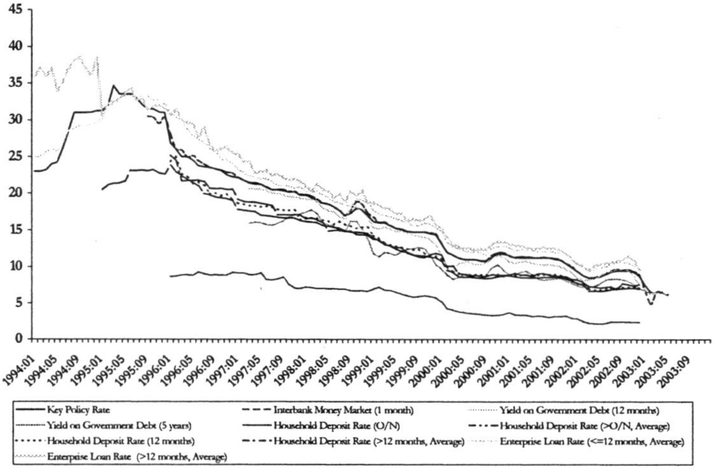

Figure 13.2 Interest rate data, Hungary

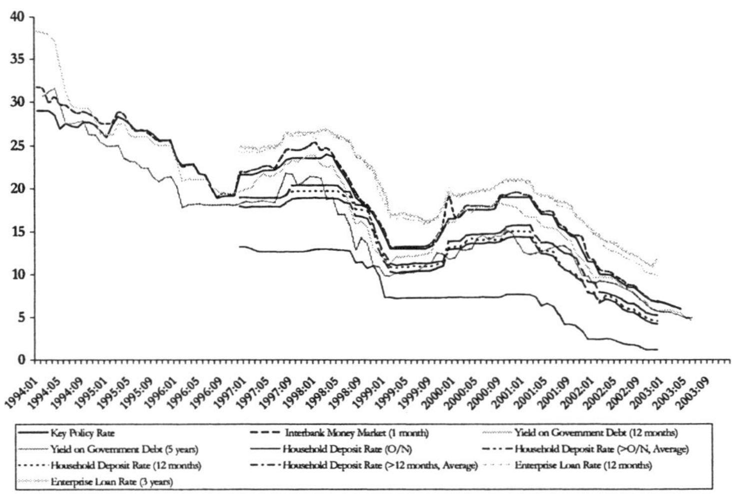

Figure 13.3 Interest rate data, Poland

Methodological Approach: Econometric Framework

Throughout our study, we will assume that the relationship between the policy interest rate and a given market interest rate can be specified as an autoregressive distributed lag (ARDL) relationship such as

$$i_t^m = \alpha_0 + \sum_{j=1}^{p} \alpha_j i_{t-j}^m + \sum_{k=0}^{q} \beta_k i_{t-k}^p + \varepsilon_t \tag{13.1}$$

where i_t^m is the market interest rate, i_t^p is the policy rate and ε_t is a white noise disturbance with constant variance σ_ε. Equation (13.1) can be rewritten using the lag operator as

$$A(L)i_t^m = \alpha_0 + B(L)i_t^p + \varepsilon_t \tag{13.2}$$

where $A(L) = 1 - \sum_{j=1}^{p} \alpha_j L^j$ and $B(L) = \beta_0 + \sum_{k=1}^{q} \beta_k L^k$.

Notice that the long-run relationship implied by this parametrization is given by

$$i^m = \frac{\alpha_0}{A(1)} + \frac{B(1)}{A(1)} i^p \tag{13.3}$$

The error correction (EC) representation of (13.1) can be written as

$$\Delta i_t^m = \delta_0 + \sum_{j=1}^{p-1} \mu_j \Delta i_{t-j}^m + \sum_{k=0}^{q} k_k \Delta i_{t-k}^p + \gamma\left(i_{t-1}^m - \lambda i_{t-1}^p\right) + \varepsilon_t \tag{13.4}$$

where there is a one-to-one mapping between the parameters in (13.4) and in (13.1). Notice that the term in brackets acts as an attractor, and represents the long-run equilibrium (i.e. $\lambda = B(1)/A(1)$). Given that the existence of a unit root in the autoregressive representation of all the series included in the analysis cannot be rejected at the usual significance levels using the augmented Dickey-Fuller test, γ can be interpreted as the speed of adjustment to the cointegration relationship given by (13.3)[5]. Several methods have been proposed in the literature to estimate the parameters in (13.4), starting with the seminal contributions by Engel and Granger (1987) and Johansen (1988, 1995). We will follow the approach suggested by Wickens and Breusch (1988), which implies obtaining estimates for the parameters in (13.4) directly from the OLS estimates of (13.1)[6]. Numerically similar results are obtained if the Bewley (1979) transformation of (13.1) is used to retrieve the long-run responses of the market interest rates to the policy rate.

Empirical Results: The Interest Rate Pass-through in the Czech Republic, Hungary and Poland

Tables 13.1, 13.2 and 13.3 present the estimates of λ and γ (the long-run multiplier and the speed of adjustment, respectively) for different market rates, using the open market rate as policy instrument. The lag length of the ARDL models was chosen as the pair that jointly minimizes the Schwarz information criterion, setting a maximum of 12 lags for each variable. All the results are based on models including only one market rate and the open market rate. For Hungary and Poland the full range of data was used to obtain the estimates, while estimations for the Czech Republic were done for data starting in July 1997 in order to avoid distortions in the estimates caused by the 1997 crisis[7]. For each chosen specification, full interest rate pass-through, corresponding to the restriction λ=1 in (13.4), was tested. The results of the test are indicated in the tables.

The first feature of the results worth discussing is that the cross-country differences in the long-run adjustment are very significant. While the null of complete pass-through cannot be rejected for any interest rate in Poland, there is evidence of incomplete pass-through in Hungary for the deposit rates (both short- and long-term) and the yield on the five-year government bond. The point estimates of the long-run elasticities range in Hungary between 0.49 for overnight deposit rates and 1.02 for the interbank money market rate. The overshooting effect observed in the interbank money market rate is however quantitatively tiny and only marginally significant.

The results for the Czech Republic give evidence of incomplete pass-through for all rates except for the interbank money market rate. All other estimates of the long-run elasticity of market rates to the key policy rate are significantly below one, and range between 0.64 for the long-term loan rate and 0.85 for the long-term deposit rate (between one and four years). In all estimations the estimates of γ are negative and significant, indicating that the equilibrium relationship actually acts as an attractor in the (i_t^p, i_t^m) plane. The point estimate for the adjustment rate in the interbank money market rate in Hungary and Poland is the highest among all other interest rates in each one of these countries, while in the Czech Republic the estimate of the correction to equilibrium for the interbank money market rate is significantly lower than that associated with long-term loan rates.

Table 13.1 Czech Republic: long-run responses and adjustment estimates

	λ	σ_λ	γ	σ_γ	(p,q)
Interbank money market (1 month)	0.895 [a]	0.054	-0.213	0.035	(8,8)
Yield on government debt (5 years)	0.768	0.066	-0.151	0.074	(2,1)
Non-bank Deposit Rate (>O/N, Average)	0.747	0.021	-0.252	0.044	(1,4)
Non-bank deposit rate (>O/N, =12 months)	0.838	0.023	-0.239	0.038	(1,4)
Non-bank deposit rate (>12 months, =4 years)	0.851	0.039	-0.303	0.047	(1,1)
Non-bank loan rate (=12 months)	0.763	0.033	-0.249	0.057	(1,3)
Non-bank loan rate (>12 months, =4 yeas)	0.636	0.010	-0.687	0.144	(1,1)

Note: [a] indicates that complete pass-through ($\lambda = 1$) cannot be rejected at a 5% significance level.

The cross-country differences are especially interesting, as the error correction parameter estimates for Poland, the only country with evidence of complete pass-through for all interest rates, tend to be smaller in magnitude than those of Hungary and the Czech Republic, although the equilibrium to which interest rates converge need not be that of complete pass-through.

Table13.2 Hungary: long-run responses and adjustment estimates

	λ	σ_λ	γ	σ_γ	(p,q)
Interbank money market (1 month)	1.020	0.006	-0.760	0.141	(5,3)
Yield on government debt (12 months)	0.980 [a]	0.035	-0.229	0.106	(3,1)
Yield on government Debt (5 years)	0.837	0.047	-0.222	0.067	(6,3)
Household deposit rate (O/N)	0.491	0.033	-0.159	0.038	(1,1)
Household deposit rate (>O/N, average)	0.887	0.008	-0.520	0.042	(12,1)
Household deposit rate (12 months)	0.922	0.018	-0.354	0.087	(1,3)
Household deposit rate (>12 months, average)	0.908	0.023	-0.354	0.070	(3,1)
Enterprise loan rate (=12 months, average)	1.014 [a]	0.026	-0.197	0.031	(1,1)
Enterprise loan rate (>12 months, average)	1.021 [a]	0.012	-0.694	0.064	(3,12)

Note:[a] indicates that complete pass-through (λ =1) cannot be rejected at a 5% significance level.

In order to complement the results presented in Tables 13.1, 13.2 and 13.3, we performed an exercise so as to assess both the robustness of the long-run elasticity estimates and the dynamic behaviour of the long-run relationship between the key policy rate and the different market rates.

Equation (13.4) was estimated for the sample ranging up to January 2000 and then recursively re-estimated adding new observations until reaching the end of the available sample.

Figures 13.4 to 13.6 present the estimates of λ for these different estimation ranges. For the sake of readability, only the point estimates, without confidence intervals, are plotted. There is, however, small variability in the estimates of the standard errors of λ.

Table 13.3 Poland: long-run responses and speed of adjustment estimates

	λ	σ_λ	γ	σ_γ	(p,q)
Interbank money market (1 month)	1.002[a]	0.019	-0.322	0.070	(2,5)
Yield on government debt (12 months)	0.954[a]	0.049	-0.201	0.032	(4,2)
Yield on Government debt (5 years)	0.800[a]	0.158	-0.086	0.034	(1,1)
Household deposit rate (O/N)	0.770[a]	0.201	-0.048	0.030	(1,1)
Household deposit rate (>O/N, average)	0.941[a]	0.062	-0.139	0.050	(1,1)
Household deposit rate (12 months)	0.979[a]	0.075	-0.126	0.048	(1,1)
Household deposit rate (>12 months)	0.960[a]	0.040	-0.241	0.063	(1,1)
Enterprise loan rate (12 months)	1.023[a]	0.047	-0.229	0.059	(1,1)
Enterprise loan rate (3 years)	0.979[a]	0.055	-0.172	0.052	(1,1)

Notes: [a] indicates that complete pass-through (λ =1) cannot be rejected at a 5% significance level.

This exercise also reveals significant cross-country differences in the dynamic behaviour of the long-run elasticities. In the case of the Czech Republic, three clusters of estimates can be found. The interbank money market rate and the deposit rate (short- and long-term) present higher estimates (although the range is always significantly below one) and a clear trend towards higher completeness of the pass-through, while the estimates of the long-run elasticity long-term loan rate do not show clear signs of convergence and are clearly below the rest of the estimates for the whole range of the exercise. In Hungary, only the recursive estimates of the long-run elasticity for the overnight deposit rate stay outside the (0.9,1.1) range for the whole period. The results for Poland present a higher degree of variability, with an divergent behaviour of the elasticity point estimate for the household deposit rate from mid-2002. The significant reduction in the variability across estimates for the rest of the rates which is observable for the whole period paints a picture of convergence across pass-through estimates.

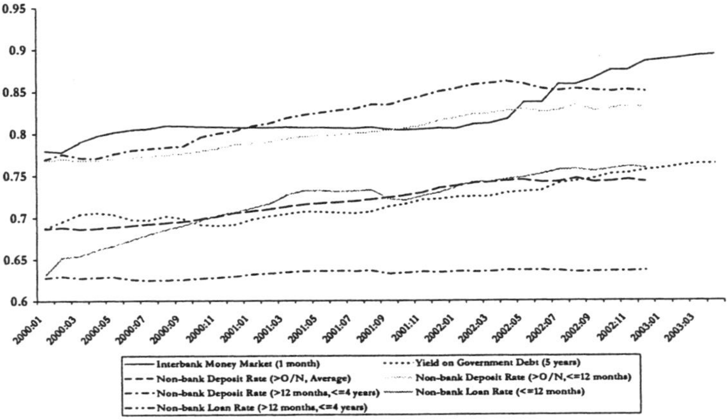

Figure 13.4 Czech Republic: recursive estimates, long run elasticity

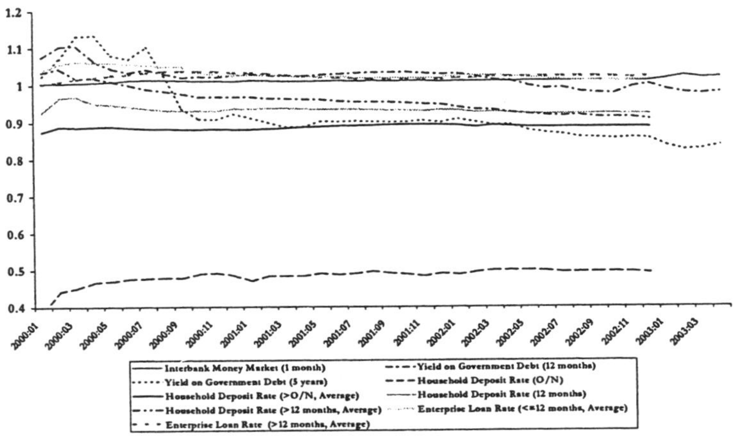

Figure 13.5 Hungary: recursive estimates, long run elasticity

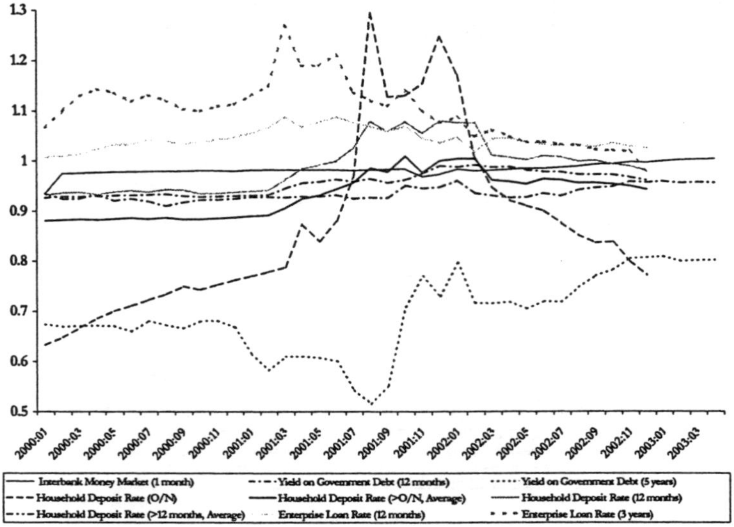

Figure 13.6 Poland: recursive estimates, long run elasticity

Recently, some contributions to the empirics of the monetary transmission mechanism have tended to stress the potential asymmetry of the interest rate pass-through. Reactions to changes in the key policy rate may depend upon the size and direction of these changes, thus leading to asymmetric responses in retail interest rates (see e.g. Mojon, 2000, or Mizen and Hofmann, 2002). A generalization of our EC specification, allowing for an asymmetric behaviour of the speed of adjustment can be given by the following expression,

$$\Delta i_t^m = \delta_0 + \sum_{j=1}^{p-1} \mu_j \Delta i_{t-j}^m + \sum_{k=0}^{q} \kappa_k \Delta i_{t-k}^p + I\left(\Delta i_{t-1}^p < 0\right)\gamma_1\left(i_{t-1}^m - \lambda i_{t-1}^p\right) +$$

$$+\left[1 - I(\Delta_{t-1}^i < 0)\right]\gamma_2\left(i_{t-1}^m - \lambda i_{t-1}^p\right) + \varepsilon_t \qquad (13.5)$$

where $I(\bullet)$ is a Heavyside function taking value one if the argument is true and zero otherwise. Specification (13.5) allows for two speeds of adjustment to the long-run relationship (corresponding to γ_1 and γ_2) depending on whether the adjustment follows a negative or positive change in the key policy rate[8]. A simple test for symmetry is then given by the F-test for equality of γ_1 and γ_2. A rejection of the null would indicate that the speed of adjustment to the long-run equilibrium is significantly different for increases and decreases of the policy rate. The F-test statistics are shown in Tables 13.4, 13.5 and 13.6 for all rates in the three countries of interest, together with the p-value for the test $\gamma_1 = \gamma_2$.

Table 13.4 Czech Republic: tests for asymmetric adjustment

	Test statistic $\gamma_1 = \gamma_2$	p-value
Interbank money market (1 month)	0.215	0.645
Yield on government debt (5 years)	0.521	0.473
Non-bank deposit rate (>O/N, average)	0.084	0.773
Non-bank deposit rate (>O/N, =12 months)	0.241	0.625
Non-bank deposit rate (>12 months, =4 years)	0.055	0.815
Non-bank loan rate (=12 months)	0.428	0.515
Non-bank loan rate (>12 months, =4 years)	1.902	0.173

There is overall evidence of symmetry in the adjustment for the interest rate pass-through. None of the rates can reject equality of adjustment speed for increases and decreases on the policy rate in the Czech Republic and Poland. For the case of Hungary, only the short-term enterprise loan rate rejects the null (p-value 0.02). In this case, the estimate of γ_1 is –0.26 (standard error 0.04) and that of γ_2 is –0.13 (standard error 0.04). The speed of adjustment to the long-run equilibrium for decreases in the policy rate is thus approximately twice as high as for increases.

Table 13.5 Hungary: tests for asymmetric adjustment

	Test statistic $\gamma_1=\gamma_2$	p-value
Interbank money market (1 month)	0.156	0.694
Yield on government debt (12 months)	0.111	0.740
Yield on government debt (5 years)	0.274	0.602
Household deposit rate (O/N)	0.002	0.960
Household deposit rate (>O/N, average)	0.247	0.621
Household deposit rate (12 months)	0.089	0.767
Household deposit rate (>12 months, average)	0.121	0.729
Enterprise loan rate (=12 months, average)	5.484	0.021
Enterprise loan rate (>12 months, average)	0.005	0.944

Table 13.6 Poland: Tests for asymmetric adjustment

	$\gamma_1 = \gamma_2$	p-value
Interbank money market (1 month)	0.029	0.866
Yield on government debt (12 months)	2.366	0.127
Yield on government debt (5 years)	0.114	0.736
Household deposit rate (O/N)	2.193	0.142
Household deposit rate (>O/N, avera ge)	0.072	0.789
Household deposit rate (12 months)	0.006	0.941
Household deposit rate (>12 months, average)	0.157	0.693
Enterprise loan rate (12 months)	0.223	0.638
Enterprise loan rate (3 years)	0.672	0.415

CONCLUSION

Making use of autoregressive distributed lags (ARDL) models, we studied the characteristics of the interest rate pass-through in the Czech Republic, Hungary and Poland.

Concerning the completeness of the pass-through of policy rate changes, as measured by long-run elasticities of market interest rates to changes in the key policy rate, significant differences could be found across countries as well as across market interest rates. While the pass-through seems to be complete in Poland for all market interest rates under study, it is complete only for some market interest rates in Hungary and rather incomplete in the Czech Republic, with the exception of interbank rates. By type of market rate, the pass-through tends to be rather complete for (one-month) interbank rates, (short- and long-term) bank lending rates to non-banks and yields on 12-month government securities.

For (short- and long-term) bank deposit rates to non-banks and yields on five-year government securities, the pass-through tends to be rather incomplete. It follows that it is a rather difficult strategy to stimulate savings by rate hikes.

Generally, the long-run elasticity of five-year T-bond yields is relatively high, though clearly below 1 and smaller than the elasticities of interbank rates and 12-month T-bill yields. This result seems to reflect both the downward shift of the yield curve amidst a strong disinflation process and the simultaneous twist of the yield curve from inverse to flat or normal, i.e. positively sloped.

Concerning the dynamic behaviour of the pass-through of policy rate changes, as measured by changes in the size of the long-run elasticities of market interest rates to changes in the key policy rate, significant differences could be found across countries again. In Hungary, the long-run elasticities were very stable from January 2000 to December 2002 (or June 2003), despite the widening of the exchange rate band against the euro in spring 2001 from +/-2.25% to +/-15.00%. In contrast, in the Czech Republic, there was a general upward trend of long-run elasticities of most market rates during that period, albeit from a relatively lower level.

This phenomenon may be explained by an increased competition within the banking sector, in particular after foreign take-overs of major commercial banks have taken place via privatization. Another possible explanation considers the size of the interest rate pass-through as being endogenous to the monetary policy framework. It follows that the pass-through should strengthen with the direct inflation targeting (DIT) being longer in place and gaining credibility, as disinflation or price stability persists. In case of the Czech one-month interbank rate, the long-run elasticity does not increases until mid-2002, contrary to most other market interest rates. This may reflect the strengthening of the capital inflow management in spring 2002 via the active use of the special foreign-currency denominated government account with the CNB to deposit privatization-linked FDI inflows. In Poland, a general convergence of long-run elasticities to unity could be found across market rates. Moreover, the change of the long-run elasticity is particularly remarkable in the case of the loan rates and the T-bond yields. The loan rates showed a significant overshooting during the period of sizeable rate hikes in the year 2000. Probably, this overshooting phenomenon exacerbated the restrictive effect of the very strong monetary policy tightening, thus contributing to the sharp decline of real gross fixed capital investment. The T-bond yield's long-run elasticity witnessed a turning year in 2001. Initially, strong market expectations of sizeable rate cuts, which had triggered a fall in yields, were disappointed by the NBP's reluctance. Its slow small-step policy even led to an upward correction of yields. Then, in view of the sharp economic slowdown and the strong disinflation, a bond rally started in parallel to further small cuts, increasing the long-run elasticity sharply.

Concerning the possible asymmetry of the pass-through of policy rate changes, no significant deviation from symmetry in the speed of adjustment to equilibrium is found in the data, except for the case of the short-term loan rate for enterprises in Hungary.

NOTES

1. Department of Economics, University of Vienna, Brünnerstrasse 72, A-1210 Vienna (Austria). E-mail: jesus.crespo-cuaresma@univie.ac.at.
2. Foreign Research Division, Oesterreichische Nationalbank (OeNB), Otto-Wagner-Platz 3, POB 61, A-1011 Vienna (Austria). E-mail: balazs.egert@oenb.at, Research fellow at MODEM, University of Paris X-Nanterre and at the William Davidson Institute.
3. Foreign Research Division, Oesterreichische Nationalbank (OeNB), Otto-Wagner-Platz 3, POB 61, A-1011 Vienna (Austria). E-mail: thomas.reininger@oenb.at. The views expressed in this paper are those of the authors and do not necessarily represent the position of the Oesterreichische Nationalbank. The authors are indebted to the participants in the conference "Financial intermediation in the new Europe: Economics, policies and institutions", held at Bocconi University in September 2003 for helpful comments.
4. For a macroeconomic model comprising a more general monetary transmission mechanism for the same economies studied here, see Golinelli and Rovelli (2003).
5. Detailed results on the results of the augmented Dickey Fuller tests are not reported but can be obtained from the authors upon request.
6. Gerrard and Godfrey (1998) give evidence that diagnostic tests for EC models are relatively sensitive to the estimation method used and recommend the Wickens-Breusch method based on Monte Carlo simulations.
7. Estimates for the Czech Republic using the full sample are available from the authors upon request.

8. In principle, extra asymmetries can be built upon (5) in a straightforward manner by allowing also the short-run dynamics (materialized in the μ_j and κ_k parameters) to depend upon the nature of the change in the key policy rate. Given that the results concerning evidence of asymmetry did not change, we present only the estimations based on (5).

REFERENCES

Árvai, Z. (1998), 'A Piaci és Kereskedelmi Banki Kamatok Közötti Transmisszió 1992 és 1998 Között' (The Transmission between Market and Retail Banking Interest Rates from 1992 to 1998), *National Bank of Hungary Working Paper* No. 10, November.

Barth, M. J. and V. A. Ramey (2000), 'The Cost Channel of Monetary Policy', *NBER Working Paper* No. 2000, April.

Bernanke, B. S. and M. Gertler (1995), 'Inside the Black Box: The Credit Channel of Monetary Policy', *Journal of Economic Perspectives*, **9**(4), 27-48.

Bewley, R. (1979), 'The Direct Estimation of the Equilibrium Response in a Linear Dynamic Model', *Economics Letters*, **3**, 357-361.

Bredin, D., T. Fitzpatrick and G. O'Reilly (2001), 'Retail Interest Rate Pass-Through: The Irish Experience', *Central Bank of Ireland Technical Paper* No. 6, November.

Christiano, L. J., M. Eichenbaum and C. Evans (1996), 'Identification and the Effects of Monetary Policy Shocks', in Blejer M., Z. Eckstein, Z. Hercowitz and L. Leiderman (eds), *Financial Factors in Economic Stabilization and Growth*, Cambridge University Press.

Donnay, M. and H. Degryse (2001), 'Bank Lending Rate Pass-Through and Differences in the Transmission of a Single EMU Monetary Policy', *KU Leuven Working Paper* No. 16.

Engel, R. F. and C. W. J. Granger (1987), 'Co-integration and Error Correction: Representation, Estimation and Testing', *Econometrica*, **55**, 251-276.

Gerrard, W.J. and L.G. Godfrey (1998), 'Diagnostic Checks for Single-Equation Error-Correction and Autoregressive Distributed Lag Models', *The Manchester School*, **66**, 222-237.

Golinelli, R. and R. Rovelli (2003), 'Monetary Policy Transmission, Interest Rate Rules and Inflation Targeting in Three Transition Countries', *Journal of Banking and Finance*, forthcoming.

Hanousek, J. and E. Kocenda (1997), 'Czech Money Market: Emerging Links Among Interest Rates', *William Davidson Institute Working Paper* No. 95, November.

Johansen, S. (1988), 'Statistical Analysis of Cointegrating Vectors' *Journal of Economic Dynamics and Control,* **12**, 231-254.

Johansen, S. (1995), 'Likelihood-Based Inference in Cointegrated Vector Autoregressive Models', Oxford: Oxford University Press.

Mizen, P. and B. Hofmann (2002), 'Base Rate Pass-Through: Evidence from Banks' and Building Societies' Retail Rates', *Bank of England Working Paper* No. 170, December.

Mojon, B. (2000), 'Financial Structure and the Interest Rate Channel of ECB Monetary Policy', *ECB Working Paper* No. 40, November.

Romer, C. and D. Romer (1989), 'Does Monetary Policy Matter? A New Test in the Spirit of Friedman and Schwartz', *NBER Macroeconomic Annual*, **4**, 121-170.

Wickens, M.R. and T.S. Breusch (1988), 'Dynamic Specification, the Long Run and the Estimation of Transformed Regression Models' *Economic Journal,* **98**, 189-205.

Index

UNIVERSITY OF WARWICK LIBRARY

UW 0519753 8